Contemporary History is NOT
that what has been happening around
– It is the statement of facts about what
the people considered significant in that given time

Grosvenor House
Publishing Limited

THE LIVING HISTORY OF PAKISTAN
[13th Book]

RISE & FALL OF IMRAN KHAN [2018-22]

by

INAM R SEHRI

REAL FACTS ABOUT
PROMISES & PERFORMANCE

Grosvenor House
Publishing Limited

All rights reserved
Copyright © Inam R Sehri, 2024

(However, scholars & students are permitted
to use material of this book by quoting the exact reference)

The right of Inam R Sehri to be identified as the author of this
work has been asserted in accordance with Section 78
of the Copyright, Designs and Patents Act 1988

The book cover is copyright to Inam R Sehri

This book is published by
Grosvenor House Publishing Ltd
Link House
140 The Broadway, Tolworth, Surrey, KT6 7HT.
www.grosvenorhousepublishing.co.uk

A CIP record for this book
is available from the British Library

Paperback ISBN 978-1-83615-024-4
Hardback ISBN 978-1-83615-025-1
eBook ISBN 978-1-83615-026-8

Material Sourced From

OBSERVATIONS/REPORTS

OF

THE LOCAL & FOREIGN MEDIA

Other Books from
INAM R SEHRI

KHUDKUSHI
(on Suicide) [in Urdu] (1983)
{Details of historical perspective of 'Suicide' in various societies; & investigation techniques differentiating in Murder & Suicides}

WARDI KAY ANDAR AADMI
(Man in uniform) [in Urdu] (1984)
{Collection of short stories keeping a sensitive policeman in focus}

AURAT JARAIM KI DALDAL MEIN
(on Female Criminality) [in Urdu] (1985)
{Describing various theories and cultural taboos concerning Female Criminal Behaviour}

POLICE AWAM RABTAY
(on Police Public relationship) [in Urdu] (1986)
{Essays describing importance of mutual relationships}

DEHSHAT GARDI
(on Terrorism) [in Urdu] (1987)
{Various theories and essays differentiating between Freedom Fighting & Terrorism in Middle Eastern perspective}

QATL
(on Murder) [in Urdu] (1988)
{The first book written for Police students & Lawyers to explain techniques of investigation of (difficult) Murder cases}

SERVICE POLICING IN PAKISTAN
[in English] (1990)
{A dissertation type book on which basis the PM Benazir Bhutto, in 1990, had okayed the Commissionerate System of Policing in Pakistan. Taking Karachi as the pilot project, later, it was levied for all major cities and still going on as such}

SHADI
(on Marriages) [in Urdu] (1998)
{A detailed exposition of Marriage explained in various religions, cultures, countries and special groups; much applauded & commented upon on PTV in 1998-99}

All the above URDU books were published by Pakistan's one of the top publishers

SANG E MEEL PUBLICATIONS, 25 - The Lower Mall LAHORE, Pakistan

And are normally available with them in latest re-prints.

Judges & Generals in Pakistan VOL-I
[in English] (2012)

Judges & Generals in Pakistan VOL-II
[in English] (2012)

Judges & Generals in Pakistan VOL-III
[in English] (2013)

Judges & Generals in Pakistan VOL-IV
[in English] (2013)

The Living History of Pakistan Vol-I
[in English] (2015)

The Living History of Pakistan Vol-II
[in English] (2016)

The Living History of Pakistan Vol-III
[in English] (2017)

The Living History of Pakistan Vol-IV
[in English] (2017)

The Living History of Pakistan Vol-V
[in English] (2017)

The Living History of Pakistan Vol-VI
[in English] (2018)

Inam R Sehri

The Living History of Pakistan Vol-VII
[in English] (2018)

History of A Disgraceful Surrender [2021]
[in English] (2022)

SAFAR E AQSA (A journey into OLD JERUSALEM with 245 Pics)
(in Urdu) (2022)

{The **FOUR** volumes of *'Judges & Generals in Pakistan'* are not the stories or facts about only the honourable judges or respectable military Generals of Pakistan but also an authentic record of contemporary history linked or associated with them.

Living History of Pakistan Vol-1 to 7 are the continuation of the same series with only a change in name of the same product. It is just for the change of taste otherwise the SCENARIOS and the PAGE NUMBERS are in the same continuity. All the above books deal with Pakistan's chequered history of massive financial & intellectual corruption, abortive rule by two political parties in succession with higher judiciary's gimmicks during 1971 onwards; Constitutional Amendments which made political parties as family businesses & apex court's nexus making the politicians more corrupt.}

History of A Disgraceful Surrender [2021]: It's all about America's quit from Afghanistan in August 2021 after staying there for two decades. These are real facts in detail which are considered responsible for the US defeat after Korea and Vietnam. The content of this book is mainly sourced from America's own official documents and the Western Media.

SAFAR E AQSA, a hard-bound, pictorial and coffee-table book, is printed in ISLAMABAD whereas the other mentioned 4+8 volumes in English, 4615 pages in continuity, are published by

Grosvenor House Publishing Ltd
**LINK HOUSE, 140 THE BROADWAY, TOLWORTH
SURREY UK   KT6 7HT**

It's me; my Friends!

Inam R Sehri

- Born in Lyallpur (Pakistan) in April 1948
- First Degree from Government College Lyallpur (1969)
- Studied at Government College Lahore & got first Master's Degree from Punjab University Lahore (1971);
- Attachment with AJK Education Service (1973-1976)
- Central Superior Services (CSS) Exam passed (batch 1975)
- Civil Service Academy Lahore (joined 1976)
- National Police Academy Islamabad (joined 1977)
- LLB from BUZ University Multan (1981)
- Master's Degree from Exeter University of UK (1990)
- Regular Police Service: District Admin, Police College, National Police Academy, the Intelligence Bureau (IB), Federal Investigation Agency (FIA) [1977-1998] then migrated to the UK permanently.

A part-script copied from the earlier volumes:

Just spent a normal routine life; with hundreds of mentionable memoirs allegedly of bravery & glamour as every uniformed officer keeps, some times to smile at and next moment to repent upon but taking it just normal except one or two spills.

During my tenure at IB HQ Islamabad I got chance to peep into the elite civil and military leadership of Pakistan then existing in governmental dossiers and database.

During my stay at FIA I was assigned to conduct special enquiries & investigations into some acutely sensitive matters like Motorway Scandal, sudden expansion and build-up of Sharif family's industrial empire, Sharif's accounts in foreign countries; Alleged Financial

Corruptions in Pakistan's Embassies in Far-Eastern Countries; Shahnawaz Bhutto's murder in Cannes (France); Land Scandals of CDA's Estate Directorate; Ittefaq Foundry's 'custom duty on scrap' scam, Hudaibya Engineering & Hudaibya Paper Mills enquiries, Bhindara's Murree Brewery and tens more cases like that.

> [*Through these words I want to keep it on record that during the course of the above mentioned, (and also which cannot be mentioned due to space limits) investigations or enquiries, the then Prime Minister Benazir Bhutto, or [late] Gen Naseerullah Babar the then Federal Interior Minister, or G Asghar Malik the then DG FIA, had never ever issued direct instructions or implicit directions or wished me to distort facts or to go malafide for orchestrating a political edge or other intangible gains. Hats off to all of them!*]

I should feel proud that veracity and truthfulness of none of my enquiry or investigation could be challenged or proved false in NAB or Special Courts; yes, most of them were used to avail political compromises by Gen Musharraf's government.

That's enough, my dear readers.

Contents

THE 13ᵀᴴ SUBMISSION

- IMRAN KHAN: SIGN OF CHANGE (*Tabdeeli*)
- NAYA PAKISTAN OF THE PTI
- PTI vs PDM - THROUGH STATISTICS

Scenario 242
GENERAL ELECTIONS IN PAKISTAN [2018]   4642
- EARLIER, PMLN HAD LOST SARAIKI SUPPORT
- ELECTION DAY & RESULTS
- PTI DECLARED VICTORIOUS
- KHAN's VICTORY SPEECH (2018)
- RIGGING ALLEGATIONS
- MOST OLD HORSES BEATEN
- PAWNS OF ESTABLISHMENT (?)

Scenario 243
TOUGH AGENDA AHEAD FOR PTI   4667
- PTI ON THE LITMUS TEST 2018
- 100 DAYS AGENDA ANNOUNCED
- INAUGURAL ADDRESS OF PM KHAN
- CABINETS & POLICIES ANNOUNCED
- …ABOUT MORE REFORMS & INITIATIVES

Scenario 244
ECONOMY DURING KHAN's REGIME   4687
- FACTS ABOUT COMPARATIVE PUBLIC DEBT
- IK NOT DESTROYED PAK-ECONOMY – FACTS
- IMF – 'KASHKOL' REVIVED
- FY20 REMITTANCES UP - RECORD $23bn
- PAK-ECONOMY UP BEYOND EXPECTATIONS (?)
- PTI's MANIFESTO – ECONOMIC BETRAYAL (?)

Scenario 245
COVID-19 PANDEMIC IN PAKISTAN 4706
- EFFECTS OF GLOBAL DETERIORATION
- DECISIONS IN WAKE OF COVID-19
- STATE-WRIT FLOUTED BY THE CLERGY
- COVID-19: PAKISTAN's ECONOMY
- WORLD-OPINION ABOUT COVID-19 IN PAKISTAN

Scenario 246
FAIZABAD 'DHARNA' CASE VERDICT (2019) 4728
- BACKGROUND OF 2017's DHARNA CASE
- TOTAL ADMINISTRATIVE FAILURE
- SC JUDGMENT ON SIT-IN CASE
- MOVE TO REMOVE J FAEZ ISA
- DHARNA POLITICS IN PAKISTAN
- RE-SURGENCE OF FAIZABAD CASE
- COURT COMMISSION's REPORT

Scenario 247
QAZI FAEZ ISA's.......... 4759

[CENSORED]

Scenario 248
FOREIGN POLICY IN PM KHAN's TIME 4761
- PRE-ELECTION (2018) LANDSCAPE
- KHAN CONFRONTED THE US
- US's 'DO MORE' MANTRA – NO MORE
- RELATIONS WITH SAUDI ARABIA TENSE
- MOST SIGNIFICANT CHINA GOT ANGRY
- KHAN's FOREIGN POLICY: PAKISTAN ISOLATED
- KASHMIR ISSUE IN PM KHAN's TIME
- MOSCOW VISIT OF IMRAN KHAN
- SHAH M QURESHI's LAST ADDRESS AS F M

Scenario 249
SHARIFs IN FOCUS DURING PM KHAN's TIME   4783
- THE VIDEO SCANDAL
- ACCOUNTABILITY JUDGE SENT HOME
- SHAHBAZ SHARIF AT MAIL-ON-SUNDAY
- DFID REPORT ON ERRA PERFORMANCE
- LEGAL NOTICES TO DAILY MAIL ETC
- JOURNALIST DAVID ROSE RESPONDED
- DAILY 'THE MAIL' IN COURT AT LONDON
- SHAHBAZ SHARIF IN HOT WATERS [*via* NAB]
- SHAHZAD AKBAR: ADVISOR TO PM KHAN
- NAWAZ SHARIF's PLATELETS PROBLEM

Scenario 250
MADINA MODEL – NAYA PAKISTAN OF PM KHAN   4808
- MADINA- CONCEPT OF MR KHAN
- MADINA MODEL PROJECTED IN UN
- 'NAYA PAKISTAN' OF IMRAN KHAN
- MADINA MODEL AFTER 3 YEARS
- SOCIAL MEDIA CRITICS ON MADINA MODEL
- NAYA PAKISTAN HOUSING PROGRAM FAILED

Scenario 251
CPEC DURING KHAN's PREMIERSHIP – FACTS   4833
- CPEC – YEARS AFTER 2015
- POLITICAL MESS AND CORRUPTION
- CPEC – THE GAME CHANGER
- US + INDIA BLOCKED THE CPEC, IN FACT
- CPEC AUTHORITY – A WHITE ELEPHANT (?)
- PMLN / PDM GOVT OPPOSED CPEC-A
- PROPAGANDA: CPEC SLOWED DOWN IN KHAN's ERA

Scenario 252
PAKISTAN IS DRYING UP: WATER CRISIS   4853
- TARBELA-5 INSTALLED BY PM KHAN
- UNDER CONSTRUCTION DAMS IN PAKISTAN
- MOHMAND DAM & DIAMER-BHASHA DAM
- DASU DAM

- CHINIOT DAM
- CHAHAN DAM PROJECT
- HINGOL DAM

Scenario 253
DIAMER-BHASHA DAM DURING KHAN's TENURE — 4867
- THE ORIGINAL CONCEPT
- PM KHAN BOOSTED THE PROJECT's WORK
- PROJECT's BORDER DISPUTE RESOLVED
- A CRITICAL NOTE ON DIAMER-BHASHA DAM

Scenario 254
JUDICIARY's HI-VERDICTS (2018-22) — 4881
- J SHAUKAT SIDDIQUI – A JUDGE ON TRIAL
- GEN MUSHARRAF SENTENCED
- BBC's NOTE ON JUSTICE SETH
- IHC RELEASED CONVICTED PRISONERS
- ATIF ZAREEF CASE OF 2021
- SCP BANS EXECUTIONS OF MENTALLY-DISABLED PRISONERS
- NCM - DETALED JUDGMENT OF 7th APRIL 2022

Scenario 255
100 DAYS OF PM IMRAN KHAN-I — 4905
- ANALYSIS OF PM KHAN's 51 PROMISES
- PROMISES LEFT IN PIPELINES
- CONCLUSION

Scenario 256
100 DAYS OF PM IMRAN KHAN-II — 4919
- ON WOMEN EMPOWERMENT IN PTI ERA
- PTI PROMISES ON EDUCATION
- REVAMPING OF MADRASSAHS
- PTI ON TECHNICAL EDUCATION
- PTI PROMISES ON HUMAN DEVELOPMENT
- LITERACY CENTRES IN MOSQUES
- TELE-SCHOOL — A DEDICATED TV CHANNEL
- PTI ON HEALTH & HOSPITALS

Scenario 257
100 DAYS OF PM IMRAN KHAN-III 4944
- MASS-TRANSIT SYSTEM (MAS) IN KARACHI
- KARACHI CIRCULAR RAILWAY
- WATER FOR KARACHI…
- FOCUS ON OVERSEAS PAKISTANIS
- 10bn TREE TSUNAMI – CLIMATE CHANGE
- EHSAAS — WELFARE PROGRAM
- UNDP REPORT 2021

Scenario 258
IMRAN KHAN: CAUSES OF DOWNFALL 4963
- EMPTY SLOGANS OF NAYA PAKISTAN
- PAKISTAN's DEPRIVED ECONOMY
- DIRECT ALLEGATION ON 'NEUTRALS'
- CRITICAL ANALYSIS OF FAILURES
- KHAN's AUTHORITARIAN POLITICS
- IMRAN KHAN's TEAM ISSUES
- STANCES OF KHAN's ODD-BEHAVIOUR
- …. MISTAKES ADMITTED AT LAST

Scenario 259
PM's DOWNFALL – 'OTHER' KEY FACTORS 4994
- CM USMAN BUZDAR FACTOR
- CM BUZDAR – WHY SO DESPARATELY NEEDED?
- SARAIKI SUBA (PROVINCE)
- SARAIKI SUBA: PROGRESS IN PTI ERA
- SARAIKI SUBA: FINALLY IN OFFING?
- IK DITCHED HIS (INVESTOR) FRIENDS

Scenario 260
PM KHAN – ARMY RELATIONSHIP 5020
- PRO-ARMY STALWARTS LOST IN ELECTION-2018
- Mr KHAN - GEN BAJWA - TLP
- GEN BAJWA's EXTENSION CASE IN SCP
- ON THE SAME PAGE *MANTRA*
- ANTI-WEST FOREIGN POLICY

- KHAN & MILITARY – HOW FELL APART
- 3 OPTIONS FROM THE '*UPPERS*' (?)
- PETITION FILED IN HIGH COURT

Scenario 261
NO-CONFIDENCE MOVE [NCM] (2022)   5040
- SUMMARY
- NO-CONFIDENCE MOVE [NCM] DEPOSITED
- PDM's POWER SHARING FORMULA
- DISSIDENT PTI MNAs AT SINDH HOUSE
- MR KHAN's 'CYPHER-RALLY' & AFTER
- NATIONAL ASSEMBLY DISSOLVED ON IK'S ORDERS
- THE SCP DISCARDED DY SPEAKER'S RULING
- IMRAN KHAN's TERM FINISHED
- PTI's MASS RESIGNATIONS FROM PARLIAMENT
- PTI's LAST SESSION IN PARLIAMENT
- PINCHING & CONCLUSIVE ANALYSIS

NAME – Islamic Republic of Pakistan.
System of governance is Islamic Democracy
but in practice it's neither Islamic nor Democratic.
In 2021 and still, most populace is illiterate
[Pakistan ranks **113** in a total of **120** countries surveyed – UNESCO];
Thus, being fooled by successive rulers, civil & military both.......
Who would seriously find reasons behind this catastrophe?

THE 13TH SUBMISSION

Since its inception in 1947, the story of Pakistan in the contemporary realities went different from what Mr Jinnah had missioned and expected - a story in which deception and contradictions acquired more significance than some good deeds. Pakistan never became an ideal modern-nation state nor a complete Islamic nation – rather exists in the middle of a tight balance between the two extremes. See a script from media pages:

> *"(The fact persisted) that Pakistan itself never remained in peace due to its corrupt leadership, administrative inefficiencies, communal and ethnic complexities along with sub-regional nationalism. Minor issues like localized languages, cultures and sectarian radicalism became giants which raised Pakistan as an uncertain state.*
>
> *An unholy Alliance between civil bureaucrats and the military during years 1951 to 1971, profoundly led to the legitimization of the Pak Army's involvement in civil issues due to which some top Generals became the sole power-keepers in the country – AND the same scheme of governance is still continuing today."*

With the above hard notes of history, Imran Khan's political party, *Pakistan Tahreek-e-Insaaf* (PTI) entered into the murky waters of Pakistani politics in 1996. Some considered Imran Khan as the last ray of hope for progress and positive changes in Pakistan. While others, mostly his political opponents, considered him as an opportunist seeking the approval of those in the establishment for grabbing power. The Gen Musharraf era (1999-2008), the next regimes of PPP (2008-13) and PMLN (2013-18) again and again failed to secure stability and progress for Pakistan on sustainable basis.

Through 2018 general elections, with around twenty years' political struggle, Imran Khan finally succeeded in making himself atop and his party a power to be reckoned with and a qualified alternative to fill power vacuum created by the two main political parties — the PPP and the PMLN. It was in that situation that the people of Pakistan saw Imran Khan and his party as the last ray of hope for recovery of a hopeless & condemned country.

In the words of Atika Reman of PROSPECT magazine [Ref: April 2023]: At his peak, Imran Khan was a star cricketer, philanthropist and the face of major brands at home and abroad. In a cricket-obsessed nation, the Oxford-educated sportsman appealed to the military establishment's vision of *'new Pakistan'* where corrupt, feudal politicians would be shunned—or jailed. Having won the World Cup in 1992 and later funding a state-of-the-art hospital in Lahore and an expansive university in his hometown (Mianwali), Khan was seen as a man who could deliver.

Imran Khan's nationalistic vision and Islamic populism found support among men in uniform. Speaking passionately in both Urdu and English, he dared the electorate to dream that Pakistan could become a country where rich and poor would be treated equally and a country that would not be a *'slave to western masters'*. He vowed to fight for Pakistan's sovereignty and challenged the US on the war on terror. He pledged to make Pakistan so robust economically that *'people from outside would come to seek jobs in Pakistan'*. Besides, Imran Khan was also considered as someone who was not greedy for money and his life was almost free from stains of alleged corrupt practices.

Imran Khan needed to do something tangible for the socioeconomic betterment of the Pakistani people. He needed to work in the areas such as eradication of corruption in real terms, achieving maximum literacy rate (could be 100%), assurance of rule of law and equality, reform and restructuring of existing state institutions to make them actually functional for and accountable before the people.

Since the Pakistan into being, the general atmosphere of law & order and administration of justice remained such that people wait decades for redressing of their grievances. For running large and populous states like Pakistan, institutions could have been established on modern lines – by picking up any developed country's model.

- Instead of putting up 51 promises before the nation, Imran Khan could have done ONLY ONE to start with: *Political & institutional reforms AND total re-casting of PPC, CrPC & Evidence Act with establishing Summary Courts in all districts* – REAL & SPEEDY JUSTICE could be made available to the populace without any regard to their social status – recalling famous sayings of Mr Churchill during 2nd WW & Hazrat Ali (RA)'s words that '... *society cannot go alive without JUSTICE*'.

- In fact, all 51 promises, economy, welfare of the poor & disabled, employment, <u>Riyasat-e-Madina</u> Ideology, laying down NRAA institution etc could take start automatically.

The Pakistanis needed genuine leadership to show their performance to make national institutions functional and purposeful for the people through modern administrative and procedural infusions. The people wanted and expected Imran Khan to deliver. Allegedly, the socio-political and economic problems of the country remained ignored as had been in previous eras. Preferential governance style, perks and privileges for the powerful (*especially for higher Judiciary, Civil & Military bureaucracy, Cabinets & members of the Legislatures*), lack of rule of law and massive corruption in high power corridors remained as such.

Why and How – the book in hand has ample references for that...

IMRAN KHAN: SIGN OF CHANGE (*Tabdeeli*)

How Imran Khan, the face of promised *tabdeeli*, changed the political game in Pakistan – see through the prism of his political journey. See how Imran Khan, defined his premature exit from PM office on 10th April 2022. To define his premature exit on his own terms, Khan kicked up a constitutional crisis and attracted blame. For some Imran Khan, as per events of early 2022, left behind nothing more than the debris of a ruthless battle. A battle fought by him against already beaten and defeated enemies, only to ensure that they were unable to rise again.

Yet, that disgruntled lot came back with plans carrying revenge & retaliation and were able to force him out of power, of course with the help of the establishment (again). In fact, all three pillars of state — the legislature, the judiciary and the executive — were diminished when he departed. Worse than that, he was leaving behind multiple crises that his successors were to grapple with for many months to come.

During Mr Khan's tenure, Pakistan experienced *tabdeeli* (change) in the name of **NAYA PAKISTAN** but not in the way it was promised or hoped. Though, Pakistan's gross domestic product (GDP) was $378 billion in 2022 as compared to $315 billion in 2018 BUT the people were expecting it becoming Norway or Denmark, as was promised by Mr Khan.

The realization of most of his promises hinged on transparent governance. But, unfortunately, Pakistan's ranking on Transparency International's Corruption Perceptions Index fell constantly during his government. In year 2022 alone, Pakistan's rank fell 16 places to 140 from 124, out of 180 countries chosen for the poverty catalogues.

While peeping into Khan's mid-life events; the future historians would begin at the most glorious and eventful year of his life that, according to his own account, defined his life's work – world cup in 1992. By retiring from cricket in that year, he opened a new chapter in life that took him to the pinnacle of power in Pakistan. Khan used his World Cup victory to fulfil his other dreams — the construction of a cancer hospital AND the politics. Khan married Jemima Goldsmith, the 22-year-old daughter of a British billionaire, in May 1995; next year, he founded the Pakistan *Tehreek-i-Insaf* (PTI), finally becoming a listed politician.

See a media comment on his life:

> "*Having retired from cricket, Khan also started showing signs of changes often associated with a midlife crisis. After decades of a lifestyle that had earned him a playboy image, he became a born-again Muslim. Fired up with the zeal of a new convert, he wanted everyone— the whole country in fact—to embrace the new change;*"
>
> Zaigham Khan's write up Published in **daily DAWN** dated 10th April 2022 is referred.

On 25th April 1996, he launched his Pakistan *Tehreek e Insaaf* (PTI) as political party. Monthly '**the** *Herald*', a magazine of the *Dawn* Media

Group was given a chance to interview Mr Khan and his two comrades at that time — Gen Hamid Gul and Mohammad Ali Durrani.

> [*Gen Gul, a former head of the ISI, retired in 1992 and represented the 'ideology' of the then establishment. Durrani, on the other hand, headed Pasban, a youth wing of the Jamaat-i-Islami (JI) that he had run away with after staging a rebellion. Later, Pasban was an independent youth group. Both Gul and Durrani enjoyed strong mutual bonds because of their association with the 'Afghan Jihad'.*]

At that stage, Khan was captivated of Gen Gul and his ideas. He once said: *"I developed a great liking for him... he played a great role in Afghanistan — I called him a mujahid."* Thus, all three appeared to have immense hatred against the ruling elite — and by the ruling elite they meant only politicians. They wanted the middle class to get politicized and take charge of the nation's affairs. The group, however, did not materialize.

Later, Khan realized the cost of the political alliance with Gen Gul. He once told the Herald in another interview: *'After forming a link with Hamid Gul, everyone thinks that I am some sort of puppet ... being led by a string, and I am doing what Hamid Gul asks me to do.'*

Only a year after formation of the party, the PTI entered the electoral arena with much fanfare. Expectations for the success of the new party were so high that the Pakistan Muslim League-Nawaz *(PMLN) offered to support PTI candidates in 30 constituencies,* in exchange for forming an electoral alliance. <u>Khan rejected the offer – but PTI could not win even a single seat; it barely trapped 1.7 percent votes, compared to 46 percent votes for the PMLN and 22 percent for the Pakistan Peoples Party</u> (PPP).

In September 1999, Khan joined the Pakistan Awami Ittehad, an alliance of 19 opposition parties, including the PPP, headed by Allama Tahirul Qadri. But soon after Gen Musharraf's coup, Qadri received a *basharat* — a sacred tiding in a dream — that he would soon be the prime minister of Pakistan and he left the alliance to support Gen Musharraf and his referendum. <u>Khan also left the alliance and supported the referendum;</u> perhaps Khan also wanted the prime ministerial slot in that military government.

Gen Musharraf's government held elections in 2002. The arena was now empty of the two politicians who had dominated the nation's politics for two decades, as <u>both Benazir Bhutto and Nawaz Sharif had been forced into exile</u>. Like other military strongmen, Gen Musharraf was trying to prop up reconcilable politicians through a king's party. He had claimed in interviews that <u>Khan negotiated with him, but the deal could not materialize because Khan's assessment of his own strength was out of touch with reality</u>.

> [Gen Musharraf's intelligence apparatus had estimated that PTI would win no more than 10 seats in that 2002-elections; General still offered him 30, but Khan wanted to be given almost 100 seats in the National Assembly. Gen Musharraf's estimation of the PTI's chances was again optimistic. <u>This time the PTI performed even worse; with 0.7 percent votes, it stood at 10th position</u>, while the Pakistan Muslim League-Quaid (PMLQ) and the PPP bagged 25.7 and 25.8 percent votes respectively; the PMLN could get 9.4 percent votes only.]

Imran Khan could win only one seat for himself in the National Assembly from his ancestral city, Mianwali – that mainly due to his personal appeal and clan affiliations. The newly formed king's party, the PMLQ, was able to form a government with NO SUPPORT from Gen Musharraf's accountability apparatus (NAB).

NAYA PAKISTAN OF THE PTI:

Referring to **Monthly Herald**'s write up by *Zaigham Khan*, also available on other media pages, dated 10th April 2022; things started changing for Imran Khan's *Pakistan Tehreek e Insaf* (PTI) after the 2008 elections were boycotted by him. The PPP was able to form a government at the centre with 30.7 percent votes while the PMLN, which was seen as dead and buried after 1999's overthrow, made a comeback securing 19.6 percent votes and formed a coalition government in Punjab. BUT then polls after polls started hinting at proportional drop in the popularity of the PPP. It was the time when people were sizzling with anger due to conspiracy theories and the judiciary, headed by CJ Iftikhar M Chaudhry, which were trying to make the government dysfunctional by keeping the PPP in the dock.

With Benazir Bhutto's assassination, the PPP had lost a charismatic leader. It still appeared enigmatic that loyal PPP voters would join a new party, whose leader (Mr Khan) was often labelled a Taliban supporter. This created an impression in the bleeding province of KP that the PTI could guarantee peace through reconciliation with the Taliban.

Additionally, there was the demographic shift in Punjab and KP that tilted scales in favour of the PTI. Thus, in 2013 elections, the number of registered voters and turn-out increased significantly; indicating that PTI was fully recognized in Khyber PK.

> [Not only were there more than five million new voters, but the voter turnout also increased from 44 percent in 2008 to 55 percent in 2013; the PTI's real success was seen in mobilizing the middle class, mostly youth and women, which had remained uninterested in country's politics till then, and winning over new classes of voters.]

While the PPP had its roots in socialism, the PTI was born in the lap of new liberal capitalism. The growth in the economy had created new wealth and widened the base of the well-off urban middle class. These sections of society wanted to assert themselves in the power arena and wanted a better deal for themselves. Meanwhile, the PTI also became the most powerful front for the inter-elite struggle; a progressive start it was.

Pakistan's power salaried lot, mostly belonging to the middle class till they retire, also tilted towards PTI gradually. Many of Khan's colleagues were children of government servants who, through their hard work, dedication and ambition, made it possible for their children to become businessmen and politicians. That growth in the middle class had made it possible to finally challenge the traditional political elite and electables in most poll-competitions.

The fact remains that Khan's charisma, based on his sports achievements, played a pivotal role in the PTI's rise in politics. Interestingly, the generation that hailed Khan as a cricketing hero did not vote for him; it was the generation that was born after his World Cup win which followed him. Political parties everywhere are formed by charismatic individuals; the PTI was no exception; like the PPP under Z A Bhutto, the PTI relied on the charisma of Imran Khan.

For his young followers, Khan is an unfailing and dependable deity who alone can deliver for Pakistan. After doing necessary political mobilization, Khan gave up attempts to bring internal democracy into the party. The PTI admitted that the first intra-party elections held in 2013 were astonishingly flawed. The most serious allegations, orchestrated by the then-PTI member Justice Wajihuddin Ahmed, were related to the use of money to influence those elections.

Not sure why the traditional politicians and friendly capitalists started joining the PTI in large numbers in 2011. Mr Khan justified it by saying that the said capitalists made huge investments in the party, while traditional politicians, aka the *'electables'*, were also needed to ensure seats in the assemblies. The PTI, as a result, allegedly arrived at a new definition of the corrupt political elite. Later, **only those politicians were considered part of the 'corrupt elite' who had not joined the PTI, or its political opposition.**

Then the day came when Imran Khan was given enough seats in Elections-2018 to make out a coalition government with the help of the same ELECTABLES and CORRUPT ELITE. He formed the government with that odd stuff which didn't help him to steer smoothly through the rough waters of acceptable governance. Economic field remained particularly unresponsive with often causing black shades over the neat & clean administration; most of the times looking towards IMF and other donor-states for relief.

From the first day's speech, Imran Khan started playing an old-beaten card of **'Politico-religiosity'** – as had been played by President Gen Zia (1977-88) when he ruled Pakistan on *KHILAFAT* lines under guidance of the then Amir of *Jama't-e Islami* (JI), Ch Tufail. Imran Khan had all the best wishes to turn Pakistan into **Riyasat e Madina** without keeping in mind that he was going to rule a country of manifested pretenders, opportunists and *Mir-Jaffers – and NOT kafirs* (atheists) *or munafiqs* (hypocrites). Khan wanted to candle the pitched darkness BUT..... – see the world opinion about Pakistani population:

- Over 9m *TikTok* videos removed in Pakistan in last quarter, <u>second highest in the world – 9,851,404</u> – taken down for violating community guidelines; daily **DAWN** dated <u>14th October 2021</u> is referred.

- A fair indication that it's a nation of liars; nothing to do except fabricating lies FOR or AGAINST someone all the times.

For the aforesaid noble cause, Khan also launched **National Rehmatul-lil-Alameen Authority** (NRAA) but it couldn't prosper due to various similar reasons.

PM Khan had, inter-alia, announced that NRAA would oversee and supervise the national curriculum and syllabi of schools - what a damp squib it was! No school textbook in Pakistan — even science ones — was (and still is) exempt from rigorous religious censorship. For the news media, multiple monitoring organisations were already existing.... **NRAA's purpose was plainly political, not religious.** '<u>Making a mishmash of religion and politics won't turn Pakistan into a welfare state</u>'; the political scientists kept the opinion.

Some, who had attended NRAA's inaugural speech narrated: that at first Khan spoke passionately like religious *IMAMs* - but quickly switched to politics. After ridiculing and humiliating his predecessors and decrying electoral fraud, he made a pitch for electronic voting machines (EVMs). The talk on the then ongoing Gen Bajwa-PTI tussle on the DG ISI's appointment suggested some implicit messaging here: **'I'm the boss and Generals better obey me'.** Even if Khan was right here, using a religious occasion for a political purpose was mistaken.

Countless power-hungry politicians in history have exploited religion, promising people the moon but delivering exactly nothing. Promises of *Riasat-e-Madina* also brought nothing — except promises followed by still more promises. To paraphrase <u>Karl Marx</u>: **'when you can't feed the masses, try opium – and religion is the best kind of it'.**

The <u>2021's UNDP report</u> detailed:

> "... <u>how in Pakistan, wealth disparities have massively multiplied. Elite groups have captured the state and become richer.</u> A staggering $17.4bn was given in the form of subsidies to the military, corporate sector, feudal landlords, and the political class. Among others, the Fauji Foundation (running 19 industrial units) and Army Welfare Trust (running all HOUSING PROJECTS) are tax exempt.
>
> *The poorest and richest Pakistanis effectively live in completely different countries, with literacy levels, health outcomes, and living standards that are poles apart - that those doling out privileges receive the same.*"

Imran Khan had raised a slogan before elections of 2018 that his government would NEVER BEG from IMF as the previous governments have been doing to (falsely) boost country's economy. <u>However, just during the first year of the term, his financial team advised him to approach IMF for loan – to keep the country's economy in order</u>. First, they arranged friendly loans from Saudi Arabia, United Arab Emirates (UAE) and China to avoid tough IMF conditions. In 2019, when economic conditions worsened, they had to knock at IMF's doors for a loan of US$1 billion. IMF gave that tiny loan but attached humiliating conditions with it; such as hike in energy tariffs, removal of energy subsidy, increase in taxation, privatization of public entities and revisiting fiscal policies to the budget.

During ending 2021, Imran Khan's govt placed before the Pakistan's parliament a series of austerity measures in an effort to resume a stalled $6bn IMF loan program. A finance bill was introduced to the lower house *to cut development spending, end subsidies for electricity & gas and remove sales tax concessions on some raw materials and pharmaceuticals.* The measures were designed to raise Rs:600bn ($3.4bn then) in the financial year ending June 2022. The IMF restarted payments of financial support package that was agreed in 2019; the measures were necessary to secure the next instalment of $1bn as the loan program was stalled. To tackle inflation, the State Bank of Pakistan responded by raising the benchmark interest rate twice to 9.75 pc.

> "The bill got through parliament but the unpopularity of the austerity measures had added to the mounting political challenges for PM Khan; opposition parties planned to hold street protests against the PTI government.....Yet concerns about a spiralling balance of payments crisis forced him to accept the fund's unpopular terms – though GROWTH in Pakistan was going relatively robust";
>
> The Financial Times
dated 29th December 2021 is referred.

Mr Khan had grand ambitions, and sincerely too, but to reach the position, he needed experienced team which he couldn't identify, manage and engage; *his PTI couldn't break through the thick wall of status quo.* More generally, Imran had the best intentions but couldn't turn them into reality. He posed but NOT skilled at everything; his mostly ineffective cabinet didn't know how to build strong teams with them, nor could they prioritize public policies; perhaps that single 5-year term was not enough to address the plethora of issues Khan had inherited.

Imran Khan didn't follow the viable option to target one or two of the most fundamental problems, and to first work out a practical plan for solution – it was governance and management which Imran had never done before. In his speech to the nation, right after being sworn in, he listed over 50 separate subjects and challenges his government was going to take on. Mostly he meant what he said but the historians and intelligentsia knew he was going to fail. Unfortunately for Pakistan, the unseen forces and political intrigues didn't allow Khan to navigate the treacherous tides of the nation's true needs, where the strongest party was the military establishment perpetually in power – and since decades.

PTI vs PDM - THROUGH STATISTICS:

When Imran Khan and the establishment started falling apart in October 2021, the opposition parties BLAMED KHAN FOR BAD ECONOMY and launched planned campaigns against the PTI government taking kick-start from Punjab, the weakest point of the PTI due to zero-performance of CM Buzdar there. Raising voices on PRICE-HIKES of general commodities was the PDM's first attack. They planned street agitations in big cities of Punjab in the name of RISING INFLATION; an old tested tactic to be used again in the name of poor population and poverty.

Some media gurus and paid anchors on private TV channels were engaged to discuss about the economic disasters in Pakistan during PTI government then so that a tempo of CHANGE could be developed amongst general public – and finally to charge-sheet the PTI government for their weak performance. No doubt, the after-effects of Covid-19 had started showing face in all the countries, but the poor & developing ones like Pakistan suffered more.

BUT, even then, the PTI govt's performance was not BAD at all; even the Financial Times like media giants (*referred to a script in earlier paragraphs*) had written that the situation was much better and exemplary GROWTH was there in Pakistan in 2021. See the actual situation in PTI's rule compared with Shahbaz Sharif's performance immediately after the PTI-period through the prism of STATISTICS BUREAU OF PAKISTAN here:

Ser No	Product	PTI (2021)	PDM (2022-23)
a.	GDP Growth	6.2	0.3
b.	GDP in Billions	$ 378	$ 378.48
c.	Foreign Exch Reserves	$9.6bn	$3bn
d.	Remittances	$26.1 bn	$22.7 bn
e.	Revenue to GDP ratio	12	11.4
f.	Current Acc't Deficit	6.1	4.6
g.	The debt servicing cost	3.18 trn	5.83 trn
h.	Interest Rate	13.75%	21%
i.	Inflation	13.4%	36.4%
j.	Poverty Rate	37.2%	35.7%
k.	Unemployment	6.3%	8.5%

***Source**: Govt of Pakistan Bureau of Statistics

The tenures of Shehbaz Sharif and Imran Khan were marred by the allegations of political victimization and dwindling economic situation. Both sides had been accusing each other of putting the country on the brink of default. Both, PTI's Khan and PMLN's Shahbaz Sharif had been projecting success of their policies while claiming that they had put Pakistan on the right track economically and in foreign policy domains; the readers would decide who were correct:

PRICES OF BASIC COMMODITIES:

Ser No	Product	PTI (2021)	PDM (2022-23)
a.	Wheat Per KG	58	110
b.	Cooking Oil	490	630
c.	Meat (Chicken)	450	700
d.	Sugar per kg	86	160
e.	Milk	182	220
f.	Pulse Moong	167	272
g.	Rice Basmati	103	450
h.	Onion	62	61
i.	Tomato	154	121
j.	Eggs	130	230

*Source: Govt of Pakistan Bureau of Statistic

Even a cursory view of the above OFFICIAL STATISTICS of Pakistan government (2024) show about the performance of the PTI and its Chief Imran Khan was much better.

However, what happened then – should not have been happened; Khan was dethroned un-ceremonially in April 2022. Months before, the things had started taking shape with dissociation of the Establishment, especially the then Army Chief Gen Bajwa. Every ruler is bound to do mistakes – even Mr Bhutto had done more serious errors. **Bhutto was not forgiven for his slip-ups – so, Imran Khan also suffered for his faulty mode of governance.** The following pages are, in fact, analysis of his policies and deliverance being the custodian of power and authority vested in him and his PTI.

Keeping all the above facts and analysis in mind, the picture crops up that the Pakistani populace missed another train for prosperity and true democracy, a humiliating datum for all – and thus, Imran Khan and its PTI too.

Inam R Sehri
Manchester UK

Scenario 242

GENERAL ELECTIONS IN PAKISTAN [2018]

On 25th July 2018; general elections in Pakistan were held after another term of Pakistan Muslim League – Nawaz [PMLN] was completed. The party had stayed in power for full term of five years and then, for three months, had handed over the reins to their own chosen team of interim administrators as per constitutional provisions. Seeing through the campaigning period of various contesting parties gave an interesting study.

Let us start from little earlier days.....

EARLIER, PMLN HAD LOST SARAIKI SUPPORT:

The Punjab game, in fact, had slipped out of PMLN's hand **on 21st April 2018** when *Junoobi Punjab Sooba Mahaz* [JPSM] president Makhdoom Khusro Bakhtayar had urged all the political parties to support their demand of SEPARATE PROVINCE and added that it would only be possible with consensus of all the political parties.

Terming the JPSM a voice of 35+m people of south Punjab, Mr Bakhtiar said:

> "If someone cannot contribute to resolve their problems, they should not create hurdles – ours is a one-point agenda of the creation of south Punjab province for the political and financial well-being of the people of the region. In the past all political parties made commitments to us - but were never fulfilled.
>
> It is regretted that the budget for the Orange Line Metro Train Lahore was over Rs:240bn [then] whereas the budget for the whole south Punjab region stood at Rs:206bn."

On 8th May 2018; the negotiations between *Pakistan Tehreek-i-Insaf* [PTI] and JPSM concluded. The JPSM group, which comprised of more than 21 sitting and former elected representatives of the PMLN, made its merger official after meeting PTI Chairman Imran Khan there and then.

In fact, the PMLN had not fulfilled its promise of declaring the Southern Punjab a province during its full tenure of five years – thus the reaction was evident. Mr Bakhtiar highlighted it categorically that the PMLN had been ruling Punjab for the last 30-35 years keeping south Punjab with itself not for the sake of federation but just to keep on ruling. Next day, during the joint media conference, Mr Bakhtiar explained his agenda that '…..*new provincial demarcations are the need of the time. The demarcation of new provinces will ensure that funds allocated for Rajanpur are not given to Multan.*'

Later, the said estranged PMLN lawmakers making JPSM officially merged into the PTI to contest the 2018 general elections under the PTI banner. PTI's Imran Khan had assured the JPSM leaders that agreeing to the formation of a new province was not a political decision but [his] conviction.

> [Hard luck for the PMLN; on the last day of scrutiny of nomination papers, their seven candidates from Southern Punjab returned their tickets leaving no option for PMLN to field alternate candidates, depriving them an opportunity to win those seats.]

During the interim government period, JPSM were ready for dialogue with any party. But the PTI had backed the JPSM's demand for a separate province - not for linguistic reasons but on administrative grounds to mitigate the miseries being faced by some 35 million people living in Bahawalpur, Multan and Dera Ghazi Khan Divisions.

As per their written and signed contract, the PTI had agreed to include the formation of southern Punjab province in the PTI's agenda for the first 100 days – if they came in power. Contrarily, PMLN's Federal Minister Maryam Aurangzeb had claimed that 'those lawmakers' had already been planning to quit the party, and termed them a 'bunch of opportunists'.

On another front, news & reports of collusion between the judiciary and military for PTI were triggered. Justice Shaukat Aziz Siddiqui, Islamabad High Court [IHC]'s senior justice, released a statement on 22nd July 2018 alleging that judges were pressured by the ISI not to release Nawaz Sharif before the election. *However, he provided no evidence and was at that time facing corruption charges pending at the Supreme Judicial Council, leading to rumours about the timing of his statement.*

Pakistan's Chief Justice Saqib Nisar said he felt '*saddened at J Siddiqui's comments*', and whilst criticising them, stated that "*as the head of judiciary, I assure you that we are not under any sort of pressure"* - Staff Report of **Daily 'DAWN'** dated 22nd July 2018 is referred.

> [Referring to **Reuters** dated 11th May 2018; media polls had suggested PMLN's lead had narrowed in the run up to the elections, that the party had suffered *'blow after blow'* in setbacks to re-election; most importantly the ruling PMLN facing a number of desertion and corruption charges.]

Opinion polling prior to campaigning had shown leads for the PMLN over the PTI. However, from an 11-point lead, the PMLN's lead began to diminish in the final weeks of the campaign, with some polls close to the election showing PTI with a lead. In the election day's poll assessment, the PTI made a net gain with 31.82% of the vote, whilst the PMLN made a net loss with 24.35%; **BBC report** dated 4th July 2018 is referred.

ELECTION DAY & RESULTS:

For General Elections to be held on 25th July 2018:

- As many as 105.96 million registered voters of the country were given a right to franchise in that 2018's general elections which included 55.9% male voters while 44.1% female voters.

- 272 seats of the National Assemblies were there to be grabbed by contesting parties. 60 seats reserved for women and 10 for minorities were to be allocated later by the ECP on the basis of proportionate performance of the parties on the Election Day.

- More than 30 political parties and 12,570 candidates were competing for their seats in the national and four provincial assemblies.

- Electioneering officially came to a close on 23rd July mid-night, with all the major parties making one final push to convince voters.

- PTI's Mr Khan held a series of rallies in the eastern city of Lahore, PMLN's political heartland.

- PMLN President Shahbaz Sharif also addressed a rally in the central town of Dera Ghazi Khan, Punjab, urging the nation to *'give respect to the vote'* (**vote ko izzat do**), PMLN's cry that referred to their allegation that the military and judiciary were interfering in the political process.

- Polls were held for the national and four provincial assemblies on the same day of 25th July 2018.

- This was the third civilian transfer of power in Pakistan's 70-year history.

- Polls were closed in time in Pakistan but the Election Commission said voters who were still inside polling booths at the close at 6pm [14:00 GMT] could complete the voting process.

- Election material including ballot boxes, seals, polling booths, ink, ballot papers and other necessary items were delivered to polling stations countrywide a day before under tight security arrangements.

- Up to 800,000 police and 371,000 military-men were deployed in about 85,000 polling stations throughout the country in a bid to ensure the vote proceeds peacefully.

- The *Muttahida Majlis-e-Amal* [MMA], an alliance of religious political parties, secured 12 National Assembly seats in the said elections of 2018.

- While Mr Khan maintained a commanding lead in that day's polls, his party was not be able to form a majority government; 137 seats were needed to form a government.

- At least 203 people were killed in the weeks leading up to 25th July's vote, with a series of suicide attacks targeting election rallies throughout the country.

- Millions of Pakistanis flocked to polling stations to vote amidst violence, including a suicide attack in the western city of Quetta that claimed at least 31 lives.

> [SUICIDAL ATTACK IN QUETTA: *At least 31 people were killed, including two policemen, in a bomb blast near a polling station in the Quetta city. More than 40 others were wounded in the blast on the election-day. The blast, which appeared to target a police convoy, had taken place just hours after polls opened in all over Pakistan. The Islamic State of Iraq and the Levant [also known as ISIS] group claimed responsibility for the attack.*
>
> *The attack was carried out by a suicide bomber operating on motorcycle. Most victims included voters so the atmosphere was*

tense but the voter turnout was high with people coming out in large numbers throughout the capital; **daily ALJAZEERA**'s report dated 26th July 2018 is referred.

Earlier, on 13th July 2018, 154 people were killed in an attack on a political rally in the city of Mastung in Balochistan, the second deadliest attack ever on Pakistani soil.]

As per the Election Commission of Pakistan [ECP]'s official notification about results of the general elections 2018, *Pakistan Tehreek e Insaf* [PTI] stood victorious after bagging 116 National Assembly seats with a total of 16.85 million of the popular vote out of a total of 52.8 million votes cast. The Pakistan Muslim League-Nawaz [PMLN], which came second with 64 seats, got 12.89 million votes while the Pakistan People Party [PPP], ranking third with 43 seats, grabbed 6.89 million votes of the total votes cast.

In the provincial break-up, PTI was the most popular party in two out of the four provinces, Punjab and Khyber PK. In Punjab alone, PTI got 11.1 million votes, while in KPK it got 2.1 million votes. PTI was the third and fourth largest party in Sindh and Baluchistan respectively. The PMLN lost its throne in Punjab and came in second, grabbing 10.5 million votes, while PPP was the most popular party in Sindh with 3.8 million votes.

The most popular party of Baluchistan was Baluchistan Awami Party [BAP] with 0.43 million votes, while the *Muttahida Majlis-e-Amal* [MMA] was the second biggest party there. The later bagged the fourth highest number of votes nationally with 2.5 million votes, and the newly formed *Tehreek-e-Labbaik Pakistan* [TLP] got 2.1 million votes nationally, becoming the fifth largest party.

[**On 24th July 2018,** *only a day before general elections, unknown attackers killed four military troops escorting an election convoy in the volatile district of Turbat Baluchistan. The assailants first fired rocket-propelled grenades as the convoy passed through the Niwano area, then shot at troops with automatic weapons. Three army soldiers and a member of the paramilitary force were killed. Thirteen people - eight soldiers, a member of the paramilitary force, and four civilians - were also wounded in this ambush.*]

During the general elections of 25th July 2018, the statistics appeared that 4.67 million votes were cast in favour of members of religious parties who contested for National Assembly seats across the country. Candidates of religious parties received the highest number of votes from Punjab where they bagged a total of 1.86 million votes from NA-55 to NA-195 constituencies.

The second highest votes in favour of candidates of religious parties were cast in Khyber PK; 1.35 million votes were cast for them in NA-1 to NA-51. Meanwhile, in Sindh - 1.124 million votes; and in Baluchistan 0.3 million votes were cast in favour of religious parties from NA seats of NA-196 to NA-256 and NA-257 to NA-272 respectively. Further, religious parties got a total 39,804 votes from three Islamabad constituencies — NA-52 to 54.

The new picture appeared on Pakistan's canvas was that all political parties of Pakistan contested the 2018 elections on solo flight except the MMA. The PTI got majority seats in the National Assembly. The second largest political party was PMLN while the PPP got the third position. The PTI also got victory in KPK, formed its own government there without any partner; it formed coalition governments in Baluchistan and Punjab with other political Parties. The PPP got majority seats in Sindh and formed its own government.

The most important development in elections was the MMA's poor performance in KPK and other parts of the country setting new trends of 'humiliating defeat' in the country. On the other hand, the *Tehreek e Labbaik* [TLP] got the fifth largest votes in the country was much surprising for all.

The victory of PTI was also a new development in the political arena of Pakistan. PLMN performed well and in a very narrow margin lost the provincial government in Punjab. It was the first time in the history of Pakistan that political process continued for the third term with the encouraging trends to believe in democracy. Two democratic governments had completed their five year terms each despite the fact that they lost two prime ministers during this period. The youth and women participation were the most important developments giving emergence to new trends in Pakistani politics.

For the first time in Pakistan's history, **three minority candidates were elected on general seats in the National Assembly and the Sindh Assembly;** thus the people of Sindh rejected the politics of hate, and electables regardless of their religion. Interestingly, all three candidates were contesting on PPP tickets. Notably, majority of the Hindu voters reside in Sindh, of which c 40% live in two districts; Umerkot and Tharparkar.

PPP leader Mahesh Kumar Malani clinched victory in the NA-222 constituency of Tharparkar after securing 106,630 votes. PPP's Hari Ram was proven to be victorious in PS-147 Mirpurkhas-1 constituency after securing 33,201 votes. Giyanoo Mal of the same party secured victory in PS-81 constituency of Jamshoro after getting a total of 34,927.

The ECP announced holding re-election on two constituencies of the National Assembly, *NA-10 and NA-48, where the turnout of women voters was recorded below 10 percent;* as per Elections Act 2017 women voters' turnout should not be below 10% in any parliamentary constituency.

However, elections of 2018 saw upsets for major political bigwigs who lost to novice candidates in 25th July polls. Among women politicians up to grab National Assembly seats, prominent candidates who lost the race were Dr Firdous Ashiq Awan, Saira Afzal Tarar and Ayesha Gulalai. **Eight women made it to the National Assembly through direct vote.** Amongst the victorious women were:

- ***Mehnaz Aziz;*** *of the PMLN secured victory from NA-77 Narowal-I constituency after securing 106,366 votes.* ***Ghulam Bibi Bharwana*** *of the PTI emerged victorious from NA-115 Jhang–II constituency after securing 91,434 votes.* ***Zartaj Gul*** *of PTI claimed victory in NA-191 Dera Ghazi Khan-III constituency after securing 79,817 votes against former PMLN minister Sardar Awais A Leghari.*

- ***Nafisa Shah*** *of PPP clinched victory in NA-208 Khairpur constituency after securing 107,847 votes.* ***Shazia Marri*** *of PPP was elected from the NA-216 Sanghar-II constituency after securing 80,752 votes.* ***Fahmida Mirza*** *of the Grand Democratic Alliance (GDA) stood triumphant from NA-230 Badin-II constituency in a closely contested competition against PPP's Haji Rasool Bux Chandio.*

- ***Shamsun Nisa*** *of PPP won in the NA-232 constituency of Thatta after securing 152,691 votes.* ***Zubaida Jalal*** *of Balochistan Awami Party [BAP] created history after she was elected as the only women candidate for National Assembly from Baluchistan.*

PTI DECLARED VICTORIOUS:

Before elections, some major story lines in media were:

- Would PTI successfully replace the dominant PMLN party from its political heartland of Punjab? If it does, it would go a long way towards securing the government.

- Pakistan's north-western tribal areas were going to vote for the first time as part of directly-governed Pakistan, after being merged with Khyber PK province earlier that year. Which way would the tribal areas - where a widespread rights movement had challenged the status quo - vote?

- In Karachi, would the sprawling metropolis of more than 20 million still vote for MQM, or could other parties finally gain a foothold there for the first time in 30 years?

The unofficial results of 259 constituencies out of 270 of the National Assembly showed that *Pakistan Tehreek-e-Insaf* (PTI) had won 114 seats followed by Pakistan Muslim League-Nawaz (PMLN) and Pakistan Peoples Party (PPP) with 62 and 42 seats respectively.

PTI Chairman Imran Khan made history by winning from all the five constituencies in the general election as he became the first politician to clinch this number. In 1970 election, Zulfikar Ali Bhutto had contested from four National Assembly seats and could win three of them.

The ECP postponed elections on two National Assembly seats, NA-60 and NA-103, due to conviction of a candidate from court and suicide of one of the candidates respectively. The PTI needed support of independents and other parties to form a coalition government in the centre. The unofficial results showed that independents and *Muttahida Majlis-e-Amal* (MMA) each had won 11 NA seats, Pakistan Muslim League (PML), *Muttahida Qaumi Movement-Pakistan* and Baluchistan National Party each won four seats, and Baluchistan Awami Party won 2 seats.

The Grand Democratic Alliance (GDA) that was contesting against the PPP candidates in interior Sindh could bag only two seats. *Awami National Party* and *Awami Muslim League* had won one seat each.

Punjab Assembly had a total of 297 general seats and results of 294 of them were received till then to the ECP. The PMN had won 130 seats of the provincial assembly followed by PTI with 120 seats, PPP with 6, independents, 29, PML - 7, MMA and *Awami Raj Party* each won one seat.

In Sindh, out of 130 seats, the results of 120 seats were received till then. These results showed that PPP won 77 seats followed by PTI with 20 seats, GDA with 10, MQM-P, 9, and two seats each were won by MMA and Tehreek Labbaik Pakistan. The PPP was comfortable to form its government in the province.

In Khyber PK province, results of 96 seats out of 99 had been received till that day. These results showed the PTI had secured two-third majority in the province by clinching 66 seats followed by MMA with 10 seats, ANP - 6, five seats each by PMLN and independents, and four seats were won by PPP.

Baluchistan Assembly had a total of 51 seats and results of 43 seats were received. BAP won 11 seats followed by MMA 9; independents 5; BNP 6; PTI 4; ANP 3; and one each by PkMAP, Jamhoori Watan Party and BNP-Awami.

Earlier, speaking to media persons, ECP Secretary had admitted that Result Transmission System (RTS) could not perform in a manner it was expected to perform. He said that polling agents at every polling station were given copies of Form 45. Also, that there were complaints about the slowness of the 8300-information service which was powered by the ECP.

Next day, the **'Washington Post'** dated 26th July 2018 opined:

> "Pakistan just held a national election Wednesday, but it ended in a major controversy. ….
>
> The election was essentially between Pakistan's two largest political parties, the Pakistan Muslim League-Nawaz (PMLN) and the PTI.
>
> Pre-election polls suggested the two parties were locked in a tight contest. The unofficial results showed PTI won about 110 out of 272 seats in Pakistan's National Assembly. PMLN has won about 64. Trailing behind the two is the PPP, with close to 40 seats. PMLN has rejected the results, claiming the election was rigged."

Pakistan's Election Commission [ECP] announced the full results of general election paving the way for the winner, Imran Khan, to begin searching for coalition partners. Although Mr Khan appeared to fall short of the 137 seats needed for a majority in the National Assembly, his better-than-expected results had no apparent problems forming a government with a handful of small coalition partners.

Jailed former Prime Minister Nawaz Sharif's PMLN had bagged 63 seats. The PPP leader Bilawal Zardari, the son of assassinated two-time Prime Minister Benazir Bhutto could get through only one seat from Larkana; he was miserably defeated at two other seats from where he contested.

- PMLN leader Shahbaz Sharif met his brother, Nawaz Sharif, in jail. The meeting was held at Rawalpindi's Adiala jail which lasted for 30 minutes; they discussed the future course of action to go ahead.

- The key question was that how the political opposition was going to react to PTI's governing policies.

- Was this going to lead to more political instability or could the politicians reconcile with the fact that they had suffered a major defeat; whereas the traditional parties were booted out and a new party, which was promising accountability and change, was voted in by a vast majority of the Pakistani populace.

- This was, in fact, the result of 22 years of conviction, relentless efforts, determination and not giving up by Imran Khan and its PTI.

Soon PTI's main rival PMLN announced that it would sit on the opposition benches; Imran Khan in his well-articulated *'victory speech'* next day pledged to safeguard the interests of ordinary citizens while **promising not to resort to retaliatory measures against his political rivals.** According to preliminary and unofficial results, PTI had managed to grab 119 general seats in the National Assembly, enough for it to form a government at the Centre with suitable allies.

Imran Khan knew that as the PTI had taken lead in Pakistan's general election by knocking down the traditional stalwarts of the PPP and PMLN, it was likely to face multiple challenges as a new ruling party. The first and foremost was to chalk out a strategy to calm down the major political parties which had declared the whole election rigged; though it has been a routine fashion in Pakistan that after each election, whether national, local or bi-election, the looser persons and invariably all parties never accept their defeat – elections of 2013, 2008, 1997 and others stand witness to this fact.

Imran Khan's 22-year-old dream to change the fate of Pakistan finally came true. PTI was in a comfortable position to form governments in the Centre and two provinces. The entire nation hoped that Imran Khan would talk for a *'Naya Pakistan'* despite giving up his ideology of not relying on *'electables'* to come into power. Several key issues ranging from a crippled economy, electricity outrages, a worsening water crisis, and corruption mafias all around were there to test his determination, luck and muscles.

KHAN's VICTORY SPEECH (2018):

On 26th July 2018; while addressing the nation on TV, Imran Khan offered an olive branch to the opposition and said he was happy for them to have any constituency investigated where they thought there were irregularities. *He pledged there would be no political victimisation and all state institutions would be strengthened.*

However, the opposition didn't respond with positive tone. Imran Khan announced to set a personal example of austerity and offered himself for accountability so that a corruption-free society could be realised. He vowed to drag the nation out of the poverty trap; and also, that he would strive to have harmonious relations with all neighbouring countries including India.

Here is the full text of Imran Khan's VICTORY SPEECH after winning the general elections:

- *"Briefly, I want to describe the kind of Pakistan I want to see … look, my inspiration is the Prophet Muhammad (PBUH), the city of Medina that he founded, how it was based on humanity. For the first time, that state was formed based on humanitarianism.*

- *That is my inspiration, that Pakistan should have that kind of humanitarian state, where we take responsibility for our weaker classes.*

- *The weak are dying of hunger. I will try my best – all of my policies will be made to raise our weaker classes, for our labourers … for our poor farmers, who work all year and get no money … 45 percent of* children have stunted growth, they don't reach the right height, or their brains don't develop.

- There are countries with less than 25 million people, and we have that many children out of school. My effort will be that we try our best to raise these people up, that all of our policies be focused on human development. I want the whole country to think like this. No country can prosper when there is a small island of rich people, and a sea of poor.

- I want all of Pakistan to unite. I want to make it clear that anyone who was against us, who voted against us, I think the kind of personal attacks that I have seen, no one has seen those, but I have forgotten all of those, they are behind me. ... my cause is far bigger than me. **We will not do any kind of political victimizing.** We will establish supremacy of the law ... whoever violates the law, we will act against them.

- Our state institutions will be so strong that they will stop corruption. Accountability will start with me, then my ministers, and then it will go from there. We will set an example of how the law is the same for everyone. If the West is ahead of us today, it is because their laws are not discriminatory .... this will be our guiding principle.

- The biggest challenge we are facing is the economic crisis ... we have never had such a huge fiscal deficit. All of this is since our economy is going down because of dysfunctional institutions. We need to make an atmosphere for doing business.

- I think our greatest asset is our overseas Pakistanis ... we will fix our governance and invite them to invest here.

- Our second problem is unemployment. We have the second youngest population in the world ... they need jobs.

- Where Pakistan is standing right now, **I am telling you that we will run Pakistan like it has never been run before** ... and we will start with ourselves. All rulers who have come so far, they spend money on themselves .... the way our ruling elite spends money, how will anyone pay tax?

- People don't pay taxes, because they see how our ruling elite spends that money [on themselves]. I promise that I will protect the people's tax money. We will cut all of our expenses. I am telling you here that the PM House, this huge mansion ... in a country where there are so many poor people, I would be embarrassed to live there.

- We will use it (the PM House) as an educational institute ... all governor houses will be used for the public. We might convert some of them into hotels, as we did in Nathia Gali.

- My point is that what we have seen in Pakistan so far, the way the ruling elite has lived off the country's taxes, I will end this. We have to escape this economic crisis. No one is coming to save us. We will strengthen the anti-corruption institutions ...

- Hopefully, our farmers, the whole government will work to make sure the farmers make money somehow. We will help small businesses. We will bring in new things to bring in employment for young people.

- The next thing I want to talk about is that we face a very big foreign policy challenge; if any country needs peace right now, it's Pakistan.

- Our economic crisis is such that we want to have good relations with all our neighbours ... China gives us a huge opportunity through CPEC, to use it and drive investment into Pakistan. We want to learn from China how they brought 700 million people out of poverty ... The other thing we can learn from China is ... the measures they have taken against corruption, how they have arrested more than 400 ministers there.

- Then there is Afghanistan, a country that has suffered the most in the war on terror. Afghanistan's people need peace. We want peace there. If there is peace in Afghanistan, there will be peace in Pakistan. We will make every effort to achieve peace there. We want to have open borders with Afghanistan one day.

- With the US, we want to have a mutually beneficial relationship ... up until now, that has been one way, the US thinks it gives us aid to fight their war ... we want both countries to benefit, we want a balanced relationship.

- We want to improve ties with Iran. Saudi Arabia is a friend who has always stood by us in difficult times. Our aim will be that whatever we can do for conciliation in the Middle East, we want to play that role. Those tensions, that fight, between neighbours, we will try to bring them together.

- **On India:** I was saddened in the last few days, how the media in India portrayed me as a Bollywood film villain. It seemed like India feared everything bad would happen if Imran Khan came into power. I am the Pakistani who has the most familiarity with India, I have been all over that country. I think it will be very good for all of us if we have good relations with India. We need to have trade ties, and the more we will trade, both countries will benefit.

- The unfortunate truth is that Kashmir is a core issue, and the situation in Kashmir, and what the people of Kashmir have seen in the last 30 years .... they have really suffered. Pakistan and India's leadership should sit at a table and try to fix this problem.

- We are at square one right now [with India]. If India's leadership is ready, we are ready to improve ties with India. If you step forward one step, we will take two steps forward. I say this with conviction, this will be the most important thing for the subcontinent, for both countries to have friendship.

- To end, I pledge to my Pakistani nation that I will prove that we can fix our governance system in this country, we can also bring a governance system that can make the people's lives easier.

- I pledge this to you today, it will be my foremost aim to remain as simple as possible ... in this poor country, these huge symbols, these mansions and protocols, on public's money, I pledge that there will be a different kind of governance in Pakistan.

- I am saying to you today, that for the first time, Pakistan's policies won't be for the few rich people, it will be for the poor, for our women, for our minorities, whose rights are not respected. My whole aim will be to protect our lower classes and to bring them up.

- Finally, on rigging. Today political parties claim there was rigging. The first thing I will say is that this election commission was formed by the two main political parties, the PPP and PMLN. This was not PTI's election commission. I say to you today, if you say there was rigging in any one constituency, we will stand with you and aid in its investigation. This is the cleanest election in Pakistan's history."

RIGGING ALLEGATIONS:

On Elections-Day, the media observed people turning up early in Islamabad. It was indeed a tough-fought election. There was a lot at stake. All three mainstream political parties were saying that they were going to get a high number of votes and seats. But after the results:

- Shahbaz Sharif, the PMLN chief, announced his party would reject the vote count in the general election due to alleged rigging; saying that: *"We completely reject this result, completely. Today what has happened, we are taking Pakistan 30 years into the past; the peoples' mandate has been disrespected and dishonoured."*

- Pakistan Peoples Party leader Bilawal Zardari questioned the delay in announcing the first set of official results.

Next day, Babar Yaqoob, Secretary of the ECP told media that:

"There's no conspiracy, nor any pressure in delay of the results. The delay is being caused because the result transmission system has collapsed. The delay in announcing the official results was due to a technical issue with the Results Transmission System (RTS).

We were supposed to get 85,000 forms through the RTS but only 25,000 managed to come through. The forms bearing results from the polling stations would be transported by road to the Returning Officers. We haven't received a single result yet."

However, the fact remains that though marred by the allegations of *'pre-poll engineering and post-poll manipulation'*, the ECP eventually succeeded in holding *'free, fair and transparent'* general elections in the country on 25th July 2018. In these polls, the pro-change PTI just outperformed its primary political competitor PMLN, a party which had ruled Pakistan thrice.

The **Free and Fair Election Network** [Fafen] expressed satisfaction over the 25th July election process. Similarly, terming the overall election results **"credible"**, the **European Union Election Observation Mission** [EU EOM] generally praised the ECP's role in the conduct of those elections in Pakistan. However, EU EOM also said that *"although there were several legal provisions aimed at ensuring a level playing field, there was a lack of equality of opportunity provided to contesting parties"*.

The fact remains that the results of every general election in the country have been quite controversial; it is Pakistan's history. There was a massive protest by PTI against the alleged electoral rigging in the country following the 2013's general elections; the party had openly and actively disputed the credibility and fairness of those elections. Once, the ECP issued a notice to PTI chairman Imran Khan saying his vote could be disqualified after he cast his ballot in front of television cameras, violating *'the secrecy of the ballot paper'* – it was the joke of that day.

Shiraz Khan Paracha, Director of Abdul Wali Khan University Mardan, told **AL JAZEERA** in an interview from Islamabad:

> *"....the 'horrific suicide attack' in Quetta, which killed at least 31 people, has not deterred people from voting. What we are observing is that despite the very serious incident, people are still coming to the polling stations, there are long queues all across Pakistan and the expectation is that this time the turnout could be even higher than the previous elections."*

Since 2013 till that elections day of 2018, more than 509 Shia Muslims - mainly ethnic Hazaras - were killed in a campaign of targeted shootings and bombings in Baluchistan province, according to the government data. Maulana Ramzan Mengal of Sunni Tehreek said *'....his party has no connection to the violence, but police have arrested him several times in recent years during investigations into the attacks.'*

However, the media reports claimed that *'....he has often been seen leading crowds of hundreds in chants of "**Kaafir, kaafir, Shia kaafir!**".*

Important points to note were:

- The outgoing PMLN and other parties that underperformed, unsurprisingly, said it was not fair, but the ECP was standing by the results, saying any complaint should be filed with accompanying evidence. The opposition's complaints seem to centre on the vote counting process, with at least six political parties alleging their representatives were not allowed to witness the counting process, as mandated by law, and that the final counts were not documented as it should have been under the given regulations.

- FAFEN, an independent Pakistani election observer network, noted in at least 35 constituencies, **the winning margin was less than** *the number of votes rejected by electoral officials, often a red flag for possible manipulation;* BUT the number was similar in 2013 elections.

- The EU's Observers Mission in Pakistan said while there were positive changes to Pakistan's legal framework for elections, the polls were *"overshadowed by restrictions on freedom of expression and unequal campaign opportunities"*. However, PTI's chief Mr Khan - who himself alleged widespread rigging in 2013 - said his party would fully cooperate with any investigation into all charges whatsoever.

- According to former Indian Chief Election Commissioner SY Quraishi, a member of the international observers group in Pakistan, the election system was transparent, free and fair, and the minor technical glitches which showed up later in the day were due to inexperience.

Most charges stemmed from delays in announcement of the election results by the Election Commission of Pakistan [ECP] which had promised most of the results would be out within eight hours from the end-time of the vote. Allegedly the ECP's Result Transmission Service [RTS] crashed on Election Day and official results were delayed. However, PTI's senior leadership immediately discarded the allegations – as per previous routine in Pakistan.

Indeed, Imran Khan was ready to bear a heavy burden after being new prime minister. First and foremost, he had *to ensure that he would re-establish good relations with the military which was gravely disrespected and dishonoured during the past two regimes of the PPP and PMLN*. Simultaneously, he also had to safeguard his own credibility by not appearing as the junior partner of the Pak-Army.

The controversies regarding 2018's general elections in Pakistan largely revolved around the instant collapse of the Results Transmission System [RTS] besides a large number of rejected votes in some constituencies. The much-hyped RTS introduced by ECP that year eventually proved to be a damp squib. There were many constituencies where these invalid votes just surpassed the winning margin thus many losing parties drew intended inferences from that apparent correlation between the invalid votes and the winning margin – recounting could have done in those polling stations.

During the 2018's elections, there were many complaints about the insufficient election material, especially the Form-45, a prescribed printed paper used to prepare, compile and declare election results at a specific polling station by presiding officers. Thus the PMLN formally demanded the formation of a judicial commission to probe into rigging allegations after terming the said elections as the most controversial polls.

The losing candidates also levelled an objection that 90% of Forms-45 were not signed by any polling agent, which was a violation of the Election Act 2017. However, an ECP spokesperson clarified that there was no designated space on the Form-45 to obtain the signatures of polling agents. The signatures were instead done on tamper-evident bags that were used to transport the results to the given destinations.

The entire elections process remained peaceful throughout the day in Karachi as no violent incident or report of polls rigging were reported from any part of the metropolis except one in Lyari area. The voters turn out also remained very low till noon as major political parties like MMA, PPP, PTI, PSP and MQM-P did not field their polling agents – in fact showing confidence in Pak-Army and Rangers who were there outside the polling premises for security.

Although the ECP rejected rigging allegations but initially a recount was ordered in 14 constituencies because of procedural errors; which later led to a recount on 70 constituencies. Imran Khan's PTI was officially declared the winner in Federal elections. The margin for the Punjab election was narrow between Khan's PTI and PMLN, but independents and PMLQ factions endorsed federal winners PTI, which led to Khan's party forming government in Punjab also. Thus PMLN lost the elections both at the provincial and the federal level becoming the opposition, nominating Shehbaz Sharif to be leader of the opposition at the federal level and his son Hamza Shahbaz as opposition leader in Punjab.

In his 1st address to the nation **on 26th July 2018**, Imran Khan, the PTI chief dismissed allegations of rigging made by some political parties; however, promised his cooperation to investigate such allegations. He said:

> *"Speaking about rigging, I would like to say that neither was the election commission from PTI nor was the caretaker government made without the acceptance of any party. All of you opposed me when I asked only for four constituencies to make open [referring to general elections of*

2013]. However, we will help you. We will open the constituencies you want for scrutiny."

On 27th July 2018; applications for recounting of votes made by several candidates were accepted by the returning officers [ROs] of the respective constituencies; Pakistan PTI's Abdul Aleem Khan filed it for NA-129 and PMLN's Saad Rafique and Abid Sher Ali filed their applications for NA-131 and NA-108 respectively. PPP leaders Abdul Qadir Gilani in NA-154 Multan-I and Ali Musa Gilani in NA-157 Multan-IV filed their petitions with the ROs concerned which were also approved.

Shahbaz Sharif's application was rejected in NA-249 Karachi by the RO; here he had lost against PTI's Faisal Vawda who had won the constituency with a narrow margin of about 700 votes. Aleem Khan lost to PMLN's Ayaz Sadiq by around 8,000 votes; Saad Rafique and Abid Sher Ali lost to Imran Khan and PTI's Farrukh Habib respectively with very thin margins - under 1,500. More applications for recounting of votes were expected as it has been the Pakistani culture since decades.

Imran Khan declared victory with a large lead in the nearly complete vote count that day. The party of *jailed ex-PM Nawaz Sharif said elements of the powerful military suppressed its campaign* and made accusations of rigging during the counting process after polls day.

See Jemima Goldsmith on tweet -

@Jemima_Khan at 7:42 AM - Jul 26, 2018

> "22 years later, after humiliations, hurdles and sacrifices, my sons' father is Pakistan's next PM. It's an incredible lesson in tenacity, belief & refusal to accept defeat. The challenge now is to remember why he entered politics in the 1st place. Congratulations @ImranKhanPTI"

MOST OLD HORSES BEATEN:

PMLN's Shahbaz Sharif, the brother and aspiring successor of deposed Prime Minister Nawaz Sharif reacted to the result, saying: "......we reject this result." PPP's chairman Bilawal Zardari joined the chorus of those complaining of serious irregularities on polling day alleging that their polling agents were kicked out of the final count sessions. The irony was that everyone hinted at but did not name who they thought was responsible: the ECP or the respective interim government which they had chosen themselves.

> [*The biggest upset of the 2018 general election was the defeat of **Bilawal Zardari** from Lyari, NA-246 Karachi South-1, a long-time stronghold of the PPP. Lyari did the unthinkable when it rejected Bilawal in favour of the Imran Khan-led PTI. What's even more shocking was the PPP chairman's failure to be the runner-up even. Bilawal could manage to win from Larkana, the Bhutto Dynasty, but also lost to the PTI in NA-8 Malakand.*]

PTI was set to form a government for the second time in Khyber PK [KPK] where it secured 65 seats out of 99, vindicating the party's claim of carrying out development in the province during its previous tenure. Soon after the election results started pouring in, almost all the major political parties including PMLN and PPP levelled allegations of rigging *'behind closed doors'* and rejected the results. However, PMLN President Shahbaz Sharif immediately announced to sit in the opposition. In NUT-SHELL:

- The PTI's victory was based on two major wins. First, it was able to wrest much of southern and northern Punjab from the outgoing PMLN, breaking the party's vote bank in its political heartland.

- Second, it was able to hold on to most of its seats in Khyber PK, which had historically always voted out its incumbent party. The PTI won the most seats in KPK in 2013, but holding on to them represented an historic act of phenomenal change.

- For the last 35 years, the MQM, an ethnic *Muhajir* party, ruled Pakistan's largest city Karachi, with an iron fist. Since late 2013, however, a paramilitary operation targeted the party's alleged criminal enterprises, jailing dozens of workers and leaders. The operation finally led to the fractionalisation of the party, with Chief Altaf Hussain, living in exile in London since decades, unable to manage this time.

- As a result, 2018 saw an open fight over Karachi city for the first time in decades, and the results were clear: the PTI swept 14 of the city's 21 seats, beating major MQM leaders along the way. It even managed to beat PPP chief Bilawal Zardari in his party's historical stronghold of Lyari - 246.

- This election was a mixed bag for Pakistan's far-right parties, with the newly emerged *Tehreek e Labbaik Pakistan* [TLP] firmly establishing itself as the dominant **hard-line Barelvi Sunni Muslim party**, but others failing to make an impact. The TLP won two provincial assembly seats in Sindh province but, crucially, emerged as the third-placed party in a number of national constituencies across the country, regularly registering more than 10,000 votes, and going as high as 42,000 in some urban constituencies.

    - *{Interestingly, the Ahle Sunnat Wal Jammat [ASWJ], an alleged political front for the Lashkar-e-Jhangvi [LeJ] armed group, and the Milli Muslim League [MML], the alleged political front for the Lashkar-e-Taiba [LeT] armed group, both fared badly at both the provincial and national levels.}*

- Pakistan's military deployed more than 371,000 soldiers for the 2018 election; more than it has ever done before, and ensured fair poling where positioned. Each of the country's 85,000 polling stations was secured by army personnel, with civilian law enforcement and, in some cases, electoral officials, relegated to a supporting role.

- Entry to the polling stations was strictly controlled, and in several instances, media workers reported being disallowed from entering into the polling stations by military personnel - despite having proper accreditation. The army played *'no direct role'* in the polling process; and it only ensured security.

- Depending on how you look at it, the PPP - a party that had ruled Pakistan on four occasions since the party's inception in the 1970s - either failed miserably - thus relegated to third-party status in Pakistan. OR it over-performed expectations by holding on to its base in Sindh and picking up a few seats in southern Punjab province.

- The MQM's loss of its political base in Karachi was a major blow to the party, and the failure of even the breakaway *Pak Sarzameen Party* [PSP] to win a single national seat also suggested political atmosphere had changed in Pakistan's largest city.

- The Awami National Party [ANP], a Pashtun nationalist party in north-western KP province, only managed to win one single seat, cementing its decline since ruling the province from 2008-13.

- Miserably failed was the religious right, represented by the *Jamiat Ulema Islam-Fazal* [JUI-F], *Jamaat e Islami* [JI], and others largely failed at the polls, winning just 13 seats nationwide. Ironically, the JUI-F called for widespread protests against the results; the PMLN formulated a way forward and the PPP straightaway accepted the results though hesitantly.

PTI contacted smaller parties and independents to form a government. MQM won six seats, PMLQ won four, *Baluchistan Awami Party* [BAP] had four, Grand Democratic Alliance [GDA] in Sindh had two, and thirteen independent candidates were invited to join the PTI-led government. Additionally, *Awami Muslim League* [AML] led by Sheikh Rashid, the party's only MNA, had already vowed its support to PTI before the elections. PMLQ pledged its support to PTI's candidates for possible nomination as Chief Minister of Punjab, making it unlikely to oppose PTI in the National Assembly; BAP also announced its support for a PTI led federal government.

ALLEGED PAWNS OF ESTABLISHMENT:

Allegations of rigging by the opposition parties were generally raised as per routine with fingers pointed in all directions, including the security forces. However, the results of elections 2018 suggested that major politicians who were known as the *'pawns of the establishment'* suffered a defeat while the so-called army critics won their seats. The results surprisingly suggested that two major politicians linked to the *Pashtun Tahafuz Movement* [PTM], Ali Wazir and Mohsin Dawar, won elections from NA-50 South Waziristan and NA-48 North Waziristan, respectively.

Two of the biggest critics of the army within the PMLN, former defence minister Khawaja Asif and Rana Sanaullah, won elections from NA-73 Sialkot and NA-106 Faisalabad respectively. On the other hand, elections 2018 proved to be a nightmare for most of the politicians who had moderate views about the military openly or covertly.

Almost all candidates of *Pak-Sarzameen Party* PSP, allegedly planted by the establishment to dislodge *Muttahida Qaumi Movement-Pakistan* [MQM-P] from urban Sindh, lost their seats. Chairman of PSP Mustafa Kamal also lost the elections from both his National Assembly seats in Karachi. PSP leader Raza Haroon saw the same fate.

PMLN's ex-interior minister Ch Nisar Ali Khan, a political bigwig hailing from a mighty military family, suffered defeat at the hands of PTI's Ghulam Sarwar Khan from both NA-59 and NA-63 Rawalpindi. Also, chief of *Baluchistan Awami Party* [BAP] faced defeat in NA-272 in 2018 elections. Another political asset Lt Gen [R] Qadir Baloch lost in NA-268 Chaghai; he was a federal minister in PMLN government since 2013.

Another stalwart politician Amir Muqam from KPK lost to PTI's little-known politicians from two National Assembly constituencies – NA-2 Swat and NA-29 Peshawar. Ijazul Haq, son of Gen Ziaul Haq, suffered defeat in Bahawalnagar though he had been winning from here since three decades.

The Election Commission of Pakistan (ECP), on 22nd May 2018, published the final electoral rolls ahead of General Elections 2018. According to the rolls, 105.96 million voters were able to cast their vote in the upcoming elections. Of these, 59.22m are male and 46.73m are females, with the gender gap between male and female rising to around 12.5m. Accordingly, 55.9pc of the registered voters were males while 44.1pc were females.

The numbers were approximately 23 per cent higher than the figures for the 2013 elections when the total number of voters stood at 86.19m.

In Punjab, total voters were 60.67m (23pc increase from 2013), of which 33.68m were male and 26.99m were female. A total of 22.39m voters (18pc increase over 2013) were registered in Sindh, according to the figures provided by the ECP, of which 12.44m were male and 9.95m were female.

Khyber PK, the third largest province of the country, was home to 15.32m registered voters (25pc higher than 2013) including 8.71m male and 6.61m female voters. Baluchistan had a total of 4.3m registered voters — 29pc more than 2013 — including 2.49m male and 1.81m female voters.

On polling day, amidst strict security measures, with personnel of both the police and military deployed, polling began at 8 am and, without any break, concluded at 6 pm across 17,758 polling stations of the Sindh province, out of which 2,716 had been declared highly sensitive whereas 10,864 were declared as sensitive.

Referring to daily **'Pakistan Today'** dated 26th July 2018:

> "…..results are pouring in from various constituencies after successful and peaceful holding of general elections 2018 in the country, the dwellers of Karachi have largely disappointed 'bigwigs' of the major political parties by defeating Pakistan People's Party (PPP) Chairman Bilawal Zardari and Mutthida Qaumi Movement-Pakistan's (MQM-P) Dr Farooq Sattar."

The PPP had ruled Sindh over the past ten years [till then] but could not save its own Chairman Bilawal Zardari in NA-246 Lyari, once the stronghold of PPP while MQM-P's Dr Farooq Sattar was in the run for NA-245 and NA-247 of Karachi South and East but lost at both his parental constituencies. Interestingly, Dr Farooq Sattar lost NA-245 constituency while securing only 35,247 votes against his competitor Dr Aamir Liaquat of PTI who got 56,615 votes.

PPP's Shehla Raza and MQM-P's Ali Raza Abidi lost NA-243 constituency against PTI Chairman Imran Khan who got 91,358 votes. Moreover, MQM-H's leader Afaq Ahmed who was contesting elections for NA-240 and PSP's Asif Hasnain also lost against MQM-P's Iqbal Muhammad Ali Khan. PSP leader and former mayor Mustafa Kamal was contesting elections on various constituencies including NA-253, PS-124 and PS-127, but could not win on either of those seats.

Muttahida Majlis Amal [MMA]'s Asadullah Bhutto and PMLN's former federal finance minister Miftah Ismail lost NA-244 against PTI's Ali Haider Zaidi. Most interestingly, Irfanullah Marwat of Grand Democratic Alliance [GDA] also lost PS-104 against PPP's Saeed Ghani.

In short, PTI surprisingly emerged as a major political party in Karachi; it was ahead on 12 National Assembly [NA] seats out of 21. 2018's general elections produced surprise results in the metropolis for the first time in almost 30 years as Karachi's most popular party MQM-P could get six NA seats only. The Karachiites turned down the election boycott call of MQM's London based Altaf Hussain made **on 23rd July 2018** via video message. However, the peaceful citizens of the metropolis city rejected his call and voted for change.

With Nawaz Sharif and his daughter Maryam in prison and the PMLN headed by Shahbaz Sharif, and with several legal cases hanging over the heads of the PPP's leadership most notably Bilawal Zardari's father and aunt, street agitation was neither likely nor anticipated. But even if complete calm were to prevail at home, the PTI government was expected to face challenges in the foreign policy field. It was clear that Pakistan's turbulent politics was not likely to set sail for smooth waters.

On **27th July 2018**; while making a demand for transparent re-election, a multi-party conference was held in Islamabad which announced that a joint protest movement would be launched against the rigging and massive irregularities in elections. All of the parties, except PMLN, agreed that their successful candidates wouldn't take oath for the membership of the newly-formed assemblies. *Ironically, most of those political leaders, who were then favouring boycotting assemblies, had already lost their personal seats in those polls.*

On **1st August 2018**; MQM was told by the PPP that it had to choose between sitting in a coalition with them in Sindh or sitting in a coalition with PTI in the centre. On the same day, MQM-P convener Khalid Maqbool Siddiqui announced the party's six MNAs would lend their support to the PTI in the National Assembly. Next day, PMLN, PPP, MMA and ANP announced to form a **Grand Opposition Alliance** whereby the Speaker, Prime Minister and other key posts were jointly nominated and elected.

On **16th August 2018**; after the elections for speaker, PPP decided to withdraw their support for Shahbaz Sharif for the post of Prime Minister, owing to previous statements made by the individual about the party's co-chairman and ex-President of Pakistan Asif Zardari. Other parties pledged their support towards the PTI nominees for speaker & deputy speaker. Those parties included Baluchistan National Party [Mengal], Grand Democratic Alliance [GDA] and *Jamhoori Watan Party* [JWP]. In addition to that, nine independents also joined the PTI.

Scenario 243

TOUGH AGENDA AHEAD FOR PTI

As the 1st priority, the new PTI government was required to ensure China stay committed to its planned $62bn investment in the China-Pakistan Economic Corridor [CPEC] which was expected to develop direly needed infrastructure for the 220-million-strong country.

Highlighting Pakistan's **FOREIGN POLICY** in his first address of 26th July 2018, Imran Khan said that:

> "Afghanistan is a country that has seen the most of the war on terror. The people there have endured the highest levels of pain. Additionally, peace in Afghanistan means peace in Pakistan."

> "Since the United States [US] is involved in Afghanistan, we would want to have a mutually beneficial, balanced relationship with it."

> "Saudi Arabia is a friend that stands with Pakistan in the hour of need every time. We hope to maintain that."

> "The Indian media portrayed me in a way that I seemed like a bollywood villain ready to destroy their country. On the contrary, I am the Pakistani who thinks that if our relationship with each other is healthy and trade is expanded, it would benefit the entire subcontinent and especially the poverty problem we face.
>
> I say this with conviction that it is in the interest of the subcontinent that India and Pakistan get along. Take one step towards us, we will take two steps towards you. We need to have a dialogue to settle our issues.
>
> I am hopeful that we can sit at the table and get done with the issue of Kashmir once and for all."

> "We will strengthen and improve our relations with China. We want to work towards success of CPEC. We also want to send teams to learn poverty alleviation and how they curbed corruption".

Imran Khan was going to face some **MAJOR CHALLENGES** including the **DEBT CRISIS** being at the top. His immediate priority was to correct imbalances in the country's economics. Last year's current-account deficit of 5.7% of GDP was very difficult to handle as there was no guarantee that an 18% drop in the rupee value would fill the gap. *From December 2017 till the Election Day, the rupee was devalued in four rounds by the State Bank of Pakistan by around 21% to stimulate exports,* which could only grow by 14% to $23.228 billion during fiscal year 2017-18.

The Pak-rupee's nearly 21% slump had put it among the 11 worst-performing currencies of the world that year. *Foreign exchange reserves had plunged to a four-year low and as of 13th July 2018, State Bank reserves were recorded at $9,063.6 million only. More devastating fact was that the imports skyrocketed to a record high of $60.898 billion,* growing 15.1% and contributing to the trade deficit reaching $37.670 billion in FY2017-18 ending on 30th June 2018.

The economic mismanagement of the previous PMLN government, rising external and domestic debt, the balance of payments problem challenges was there to create severe headache for PTI. Although, the economy grew at 5.8% during FY2017-18, the highest in a decade but *Fitch* in its advisory earlier that month had warned that after general elections, the next government would have limited time to address its debt problems which were bound to accelerate in 2019. An economist opined that:

> *"The previous govt's window dressing has left the real economy in shambles while the informal economy has flourished due to lack of checks and balances. Shifting resources from informal to formal channels will be a painful process and many toes will be stepped on.*
>
> *On the economy front, besides the moon-shot of some significant angel financing from friendly countries, we likely have no choice but to go to the IMF and one can expect them to turn the screws tight this time given the lax compliance from the previous bailout."*

Thus, as the PTI was going to take hold, it was **severely restricted on the FINANCIAL** front, an immediate request to the IMF for bailout was the only option left and the global trend of rising interest rates and increasing oil prices were two more obstructions. On **WATER & POWER** Front Pakistan was on the verge of an ecological disaster due to looming water shortages. As well as combating **extremism** and managing delicate civil-military relations, Pakistan's new govt was in need to re-define its parameters.

There is virtually no public education on water conservation in Pakistan. Shortage of dams has been depriving the country of low-cost electricity and a viable alternative to coal-based power production. Despite being on cards, *the construction of dams had been pushed down to the bottom due to political machinations in and out of the parliament; apparently amidst intellectual and financial corruption.*

Pakistan's primary & principal problem is the **POPULATION GROWTH**; means the conservative Pakistan since decades. With its limited family planning, the country has the highest birth rates in Asia at around three children per woman; the World Bank and state statistics are referred. Pakistan has had a fivefold increase in population since 1960; the figure was touching 207 million; 2017's draft results from census are there to ponder upon. Discussing contraception in public is a serious taboo in Pakistan. The fact remains that all development plans are negated and hard-won economic and social progress go paralysed with such growth rate of population.

Like other rulers, Imran Khan also inherited that problem in 2018. Analysts say unless more is done to slow growth, the country's natural resources — particularly drinking water — would not be enough to support the population. The PTI would have to formulate long-term policies to address the population boom and issues correlated to population issues especially the housing, sewerage, drinking water, education, health and employment.

Under duress, Imran Khan had to address the issue of **TERRORISM FINANCING** especially in the context of Financial Action Task Force [FATF] observations which had put Pakistan on the grey-list. The caretaker government in early 2018 missed the deadline to address the concerns raised by the forum. The PTI government had to struggle to keep Pakistan off the 'black-list' or the country could have faced worst sanctions.

PTI ON THE LITMUS TEST 2018:

Keeping aside the usual outrages of the defeated political parties in news conferences, the new prime minister had to focus on implementing his wide-ranging reform agenda that prioritised the economy. Pakistan's external deficit was mounting, its foreign exchange reserves dwindling and the value of its currency depreciating. The opposition parties didn't opt to challenge the results so the PTI was not harassed and distracted by the expected turmoil that could follow. Here the military's support to the new elected government was needed which was, of course, available to Imran Khan.

Imran Khan proceeded to form the coalition government with members of the MQM and the PMLQ. The day after the election, despite reservations over the results, the PMLN conceded defeat more because their own selected Pakistan's Election Commission had rejected reports of alleged rigging.

The new government's litmus test was as to how it would deal with the extremist outfits which was an on-going threat to the national security. Imran had once attracted controversy for describing top *Tehreek e Taliban Pakistan* [TTP] commander Waliur Rehman as 'pro-peace' when he was killed by US forces in 2013. He **once advocated for opening a Taliban office in Pakistan**, arguing that if the US could open offices for the Afghan Taliban in Qatar, the Pakistani Taliban should also be permitted to do the same. He had also termed the killing of Taliban leader Hakimullah Mehsud by the US in a drone strike *'deliberate targeting of peace process'*.

Feeling Khan's loud voice behind them, the TTP nominated Imran Khan to represent them in mediation talks which Mr Khan had eventually refused. Similarly, the PTI government in Khyber PK gave a grant worth Rs:550 million to Madrasa of Maulana Samiul Haq in Akora-Khatak. Ahead of the polls of 2018, PTI had joined hands with Maulana Fazlur Rehman Khalil, who was on the US terror watch list then.

During the whole elections period, the Western media continuously attacked on the military establishment in Pakistan just on the basis of sponsored reports of pseudo-NGOs and organisations. Some foreign think-tanks opined that there could be imminent political turbulence in Pakistan around elections. Some were genuinely worried that how the military would respond if Pakistan landed in crisis amidst elections. Controversies were, of course, there that the country was still being threatened by the Pakistani Taliban [TTP] and the Islamic State like insurgents.

The reality was that Pakistan's that election [of 2018] alarmed the two major international powers most interested in this geographic area: the

United States and China. The Trump administration's South Asia policy was critically depending on Pakistani support. The US government had struggled to elicit much in terms of strategic cooperation during the earlier two corrupt ruling regimes. In 2018's scenario the onset of a new political regime in Pakistan could make such cooperation more unlikely to continue.

The Chinese, on the other hand, were worried how the Pakistani new political arena would affect the One Belt / Road projects passing through Pakistan. The Chinese wanted a strong government that would focus on the completion of these projects right away. Measuring the nervousness involved, China was in much stronger position than the US policy makers.

Referring to an article titled as '**The Rise, Fall and Rise Again of Imran Khan**' in **The New York Times** [NYT] dated 26th July 2018:

> "*Imran Khan, who has fiercely criticized American counterterrorism policy in a region plagued by extremism, appeared composed on the election-day (25th July 2018) to become Pakistan's next prime minister. He said he would fight corruption at the highest levels, improve relations with China, seek a **mutually beneficial relationship** with the United States and create a just welfare state along the lines of what the Prophet Muhammad (PBUH) did centuries ago.*
>
> '*We're going to run Pakistan in a way it's never been run before,*' *he said; he would never live in the prime minister's mansion.* **In a country of so many poor people, I would be embarrassed to stay in such a big house.**"

For years, Mr. Khan had tried but failed to take the reins of the government, which struggled with poverty, economic stagnation and instability and which was increasingly torn between its two biggest allies: China and the US. But this time around, he found a powerful ally in Pakistan's military.

In those months, army and intelligence officers *pressured, threatened and blackmailed politicians* from rival parties steadily thinning out Mr Khan's competition. Members of rival parties accused election officers of fraud, saying many ballots had been counted in secret, guarded by soldiers. '*The way this stage has been set, it would have been a surprise if he didn't win,*' the critics held.

Friends and foes describe Mr Khan, 65, as relentless, charming, swaggering and highly unpredictable. In 1992, Mr Khan captained Pakistan's cricket team to a World Cup victory over England; a moment of immense Pakistani pride. Later, he turned to Islam and the Sufi sect, which he said helped lend purpose to his life. Then he entered politics. <u>Pakistan in the late 1990s was a mess: Its Machiavellian spy services were working with the United States and, at the same time, supporting the Taliban and Osama bin Laden</u>. The country was poor, troubled and divided — probably, still the same today. Mr Khan seized the elections on a single issue: governance; see a glimpse of an interview (2018) to the NYT:

> *"In Pakistan, the main problem is not extremism, we are a governance failure. And in any third world country, the moment the governance collapses, mafias appear."*

Imran Khan had a focus on corruption - repeatedly urged that a few political dynasties had shamelessly enriched themselves while governance weakened and the country grew poorer. But Khan's shouts for reform were not taken seriously at first. The Justice Movement he founded in 1996, he could win only one seat (in 2002) in Parliament — of his own. However, he seemed adept at not letting the gossip pages distract him, and he kept hammering on about corruption. At last, *'the Panama Papers'* helped him in 2016-17. Evidence began to build that Mr Sharif had stolen millions of dollars from public coffers in Pakistan to buy expensive apartments in London, in the names of his children.

Mr Khan capitalized on this and called for Nawaz Sharif to resign. The Supreme Court removed Mr Sharif from the PM office, and just two weeks before the election, Nawaz Sharif and his daughter were sentenced by the court and imprisoned. Few would disagree that corruption is still out of control in Pakistan. Many observers saw the same thing in Sharif's downfall but a bit more selective, possibly more threatening and disturbing.

> *[By taking away crippled Nawaz Sharif from political field, the superior judiciary cleared path for Imran Khan to take over. BUT, on the other side <u>Nawaz Sharif had also clashed with the army chiefs</u>, even some of those he had chosen time and again; then he was taken as thorn in military's palm.]*

Imran Khan, on the other hand, was someone the military bosses seemed they could work with. In the run-up to the election, the military pushed even harder for Mr Khan. Human rights groups, academics and members of other political parties said security officers threatened politicians to defect to Khan's side - several did, in fact. *Even otherwise, Mr Khan was genuinely popular;* especially amongst youngsters who lionized him as a sports hero. As elections loomed, Khan's wave swept Pakistan. His face was everywhere — on banners, lamp-posts and torn flags flying from the sputtering rickshaws that flit in and out of traffic. His supporters were the most energized and confident with his PTI's symbol: a cricket bat.

Even during tabulations on the election-day, Khan's PTI was far ahead, though still falling short of an outright majority in Parliament. According to results on state television (PTV), Khan's party had 120 seats - **BUT for Khan it was not ideal:** Domestically, the challenges were overwhelming. Pakistan's electricity grid was disintegrated, its infant mortality rate was among the most distressing in Asia, its currency was sliding, and its debt — especially to China — was ballooning. So many Pakistanis were unable to find jobs that every year, countless young men set off on a desperate exodus to the Middle East to work as street cleaners, luggage handlers - and anything alike.

Internationally, Pakistan was in a pinch. China had extended it billions to build roads and other infrastructure, which at (that time) current growth rate was impossible to repay. At the same time, President Trump had cut hundreds of millions of dollars in foreign aid. *"They have given us nothing but lies & deceit, thinking of our leaders as fools,"* Mr Trump said of Pakistan in a tweet in January that year. *"They give safe haven to the terrorists we hunt in Afghanistan, with little help. No more!"*

Khan deeply disagreed and replied in an interview with **TIME** magazine:

> *"To blame Pakistan for that disaster is extremely unfair. The moment the US went into Afghanistan; everyone knew what was going to happen. It was the history of Afghanistan* (citing the defeat of occupying Soviet troops in the 1980s). *Just as with the Soviets - the longer the Americans stayed, the more resistance would grow. Pakistan has borne the brunt of the war on terror."*

[To know more about America's departure from Afghanistan, see **History of A Disgraceful Surrender** [2021] by Inam R Sehri, published by GPH Surrey (UK) in 2022; pages-356]

In Khan's view, it was a misguided strategy that killed thousands of people in his country and deprived Pakistan of billions of dollars in lost business. For years, he remained a particularly vocal critic of American drone strikes. Magically, all those positions played well with many Pakistanis. So did Khan's then support for the country's strict blasphemy laws; Pakistan was socially conservative, no doubt.

Mr. Khan had successfully rebranded himself as a populist alternative to Pakistan's political elite, whom voters seemed more than ready to discard and abandon. But his life, in many ways, was not different from that of most Pakistanis. His attendance record as an elected member of the National Assembly, Pakistan's Parliament, was not exemplary. Media analysts wondered how long Mr Khan's friendship with the military would last – as *'he is known to have erratic behavior and a very unpredictable personality.'*

100 DAYS AGENDA ANNOUNCED:

The first 100 days of Imran Khan's premiership had taken a symbolic significance after his party, *Pakistan Tehreek e Insaf* [PTI], announced a '**100-day Agenda**' months before the July-2018's general election in Pakistan.

The said First 100-days plan included:

- The creation of a **new province in Southern Punjab,** with complete autonomy, making it an agricultural hub and accompanied by an economic package; young people would be provided with job opportunities by setting up food processing industries.

- Reconciliation with **alienated Baloch leadership** for renewed development of the province including; also, implementation of job quota reserved for Baluchistan.

- **Development of Karachi** - to make it a mega-city with suitable Package with 6-point agenda which included improving law and order, strengthening of local government, operations against extortionists and 'China cutting mafia', a housing infrastructure plan, setup of a public transport system, and culmination of militant sections of political parties.

- **Poverty alleviation** with creation of 10 million jobs with other suitable steps.

- Betterment of the overall economy; the **manufacturing sector would be revived**, small and medium-sized businesses would be developed fast, and the private sector would be assisted in **building five million houses**.

- Jumbo development **package for FATA**; other provinces to contribute 3% of their share.

- Reformation of **tax administration**, development of **progressive tourism**, the transformation of **state-owned enterprises**, and overcoming of the energy challenges.

- Improvement of the **agriculture sector** through increasing profitability and access to finance for farmers; would also be provided value-added incentives, **livestock sector**, and produce-markets.

- Improvement of **National Water Policy** with prompt actions.

- Revamping of the **National Security Plan** by creation of four National Security Organizations.

All national and foreign media & newspapers dated 18-21st August 2018 are referred for more details on above points.

That before-election MANIFESTO was considered a benchmark to predict the early success of Mr Khan's government. He won the elections on 25th July 2018, was sworn in on 18th August 2018 as the 22nd Prime Minister of Pakistan – just a day after getting the parliament's vote of confidence.

INAUGURAL ADDRESS OF PM KHAN:

On **19th August 2018**, PM Khan addressed the nation formally on television in which he laid out the basis of his POLICIES & AGENDA for his government. In that address, he announced many austerity measures which included reduction of PM house employees and bullet-proof vehicles, conversion of PM house into a university, conversion of governor houses into public benefit buildings, cut-down on foreign visits of the PM & ministers, malnutrition of children and reduced spending on state-luxuries.

Most points were reiterated as an explanation of the 100-Days Agenda which was told to the general populace before the Elections-2018.

More new points were added as extended program for Pakistan as a welfare state and prosperous economic giant in the region. See the details here:

- PM Khan announced that he would not live in Prime Minister House and would **cut down the staff of PM House** from 524 people to 2 only; also, that he would **only keep two vehicles** out of the current 80 vehicles available for use by Prime Minister and the rest would be sent to Auctioneers; also, that he would not own any business while in office of the premiership.

- He promised to **reinforce the Zakat System** in whole of Pakistan.

- PM Khan announced that his government would take **measures to increase exports**; also, that he would feel ashamed to ask for monetary help from other nations and global financial organizations; rather would adopt austerity measures to get rid of the debt.

- PM Khan announced to **strengthen the tax collection system.**

- PM Khan requested overseas Pakistanis to help Pakistan in that time of great need by keeping money in Pakistani banks and by sending money via banks instead of remittances through illegal *hundi-means.*

- PM Khan announced to keep interior ministry to himself to keep Federal Investigation Agency [FIA] directly under his control so he would oversee the efforts to curtail money laundering; also, to create a task force to bring laundered money back to Pakistan.

- PM Khan offered National Accountability Bureau [NAB], the help of the federal government to curtail the corruption.

- PM Khan announced to form a task force to **improve government hospitals** so poor people of the country could get the same high-quality care as rich within Pakistan.

- PM Khan felt the crisis of water in major cities and promised to work on **completing Diamer-Bhasha Dam,** and also to help farmers on methods to save water during irrigation.

- PM Khan announced that we would not invite people from other countries to take care of **Pakistan's sanitation needs** rather would create our own sanitation system – citing that in the state of Medina how educated prisoners of war were given incentives upon teaching the uneducated people.

- PM Khan reiterated to **convert PM House** into a world-class research university; also, to **improve the government school system** so the people would not have to opt for private schools to give quality education to their children; also, to bring the **madrassah system at par** with the rest of the education system so it would produce quality citizens.

- PM Khan announced in his inaugural address to the nation that Pakistan wanted peace with all the nations in the world including India.

- PM Khan announced that his government would create initiatives **to plant a billion trees** to combat global warming and heat-waves; parks and playgrounds would be built additionally.

- PM Khan promised to build **four tourism sites every year** for the development of tourism; also promised to develop **international standard beaches**.

- PM Khan said that he specifically tasked his human rights ministry to work towards **ending sexual abuse towards children**.

- PM Khan stressed on the creation of a **new province in Southern Punjab**. Giving an example of Khyber PK's former government, he announced that the police system would be reformed in Punjab and Baluchistan in a similar manner and they would request the Sindh government to do the same.

- PM Khan said that he would have a meeting with Chief Justice of Pakistan [CJP] and together they would **reform the judicial system** so that every case would be decided in less than one-year time.

- PM Khan urged civil service to provide services to the common man with due respect & dignity.

- PM Khan announced to **create a new local government system** and not to provide development funds to members of parliament.

- PM Khan announced to appoint a former IGP Nasir Durrani as an advisor in Punjab Government so that he could bring same **reforms** in **Punjab Police** as he did in Khyber PK as Inspector General of Khyber PK Police during 2013-18.

CABINETS & POLICIES ANNOUNCED:

To carry on the above functions, PM Khan announced most of his team at national and provincial levels before he took oath as prime minister except a few. On 18th August 2018, after taking oath as prime minister of Pakistan, Khan announced his 21-member federal cabinet with their portfolios, one Azam Khan as his secretary and nominated Arif Alvi, a PTI MNA from Karachi, for office of the President of Pakistan.

On 19th August 2018; his nominee, **Usman Buzdar**, a new political figure on the arena, having no experience except belonging to the far remote area of Dera Ghazi Khan, was elected as Punjab's Chief Minister despite criticism. Odd voices surfaced mainly due to his less prominent background and allegations of a criminal case against him in 1998. Mr Khan justified Buzdar's selection, stating that Buzdar belonged to a poor district with *'no water, electricity or hospital'* and that he would be *well acquainted with how people live in those areas.*

On 20th August 2018; CM Buzdar's cabinet took the oath of office. PM Khan appointed former official of NAB Mirza Shehzad Akbar as his special assistant for accountability. On the same day PM Khan nominated one Ehsan Mani [*his old buddy from London and an Accountant by profession*] as Chairman of Pakistan Cricket Board after conveying Najam Sethi to resign. Five days later, Mr Khan nominated Ehsan Mani and Asad Ali Khan as members of the Board of Governors of Pakistan Cricket Board.

Same day, PM Khan ordered his finance minister Asad Umar to bring back the laundered money from oversees. He gave 2-weeks deadline to the task force which was created to bring back the country's stolen wealth from overseas and to come up with a detailed plan. This high-powered task-force comprised of FIA officers under the command of Spl Assistant Shehzad Akbar.

> [*Later,* **on 5th September 2018,** *it was decided in a cabinet meeting that efforts would be made to recover money illegally stashed abroad by Pakistanis, mainly due to corruption. Khan was in the process of ratifying a treaty with Swiss authorities to exchange information of Pakistani-owned bank accounts there. A whistle-blower law was*

> to be enacted whereby individuals and firms who helped in trailing and recovering illegal money abroad would be awarded 20% of the recovered amount.
>
> Financial Action Task Force [FATF] was a high-powered task force comprised officials of the Federal Investigation Agency [FIA], National Accountability Bureau [NAB] as well as intelligence agencies.]

Asad Umar also said that workers of Pakistan International Airlines [PIA] and Pakistan Steel Mills [PSM] would not be sacked.

On the same day, as part of the anti-corruption measures, Mr Khan's cabinet decided to put Nawaz Sharif and Maryam Nawaz on Exit Control List [ECL] barring them to leave the country. The cabinet also issued a directive to bring back Ishaq Dar, Hussain Nawaz and Hassan Nawaz - to face the court proceedings in pending cases against them.

On that day, Mr Khan also instructed his ministers to discontinue the overseas medical facilities which used to be funded by the government treasury. It was also decided to auction the bulletproof and extravagant vehicles belonging to the prime minister house. The decision was made to avoid unnecessary tours by government officials including the prime minister. Foreign Minister Shah Mehmood Qureshi was asked to attend the annual UN's General Assembly session in September 2018 instead of PM Khan.

On 21ˢᵗ August 2018: After reviewing a ten-year report of Capital Development Authority [CDA], PM Khan announced to end corruption in CDA; he also issued directive to solve water crisis in Islamabad. Furthermore:

- *The cabinet decided to eliminate discretionary funds for members of parliament including ministers and the prime minister.*
- *The cabinet also decided that no announcements of projects of public benefit would be made during public rallies like previous prime ministers used to do.*
- *Also directed that no tea or coffee (not even water bottles) would be presented to attendees during official meetings whatsoever.*
- *PM Khan would not use a special plane for international visits and the benefit of travel via first-class would be taken away from ministers, the prime minister, the president, and the chief justice of Pakistan; all would travel via economy or club class for their official tours, inland & abroad.*

Next day, two new special assistants to prime minister were inducted including Iftikhar Durrani on media affairs and Naeemul Haque on political affairs. Meanwhile, PM Khan's government launched a probe to audit all *metro bus projects* initiated by the previous PMLN government, including the established metros in Lahore, Islamabad and Multan, the upcoming *Green Line of Karachi,* and the *Orange Line Train of Lahore*; the objective was to evaluate the levels of transparency of the projects during the contracts made and how the funds were spent.

Same day, the cabinet decided to commence a major tree plantation project. A task force was created to launch a cleanliness drive in the country. The cabinet was informed about the first phase *launch of 10-million tree tsunami drive,* and that 1.5 million saplings were to be planted on 2nd September instant. That day, PM Khan arrived in Haripur and planted a sapling to commence the *'Plant for Pakistan drive'*; his aim was to bring Pakistan at par with Europe in terms of cleanliness during his term.

During the next two days, the PM gave his consent for the nomination of Ameer Khan Jogezai as Governor of Baluchistan; Shibli Faraz was nominated leader of the house for the Senate of Pakistan; approved the appointment of Anwar Mansoor Khan as Attorney General of Pakistan. *BUT, just a day after, PM Khan took back his decision of making Ameer M Khan Jogezai as governor of Baluchistan.* However; a 23-member Punjab cabinet and a 15-member Khyber PK cabinet was formed under guidance and approval of Mr Khan on the same day. PM Khan also appointed the FM Asad Umar as the boss of forthcoming Economic Coordination Committee [ECC].

On 28th August 2018; PM Khan decided to appoint Shehryar Khan Afridi as minister of the state for interior; appointed M Suleman Khan as Director General Intelligence Bureau [DG IB]; appointed Jahanzeb Khan as Chairman of the Federal Board of Revenue [FBR] and Mehr Khaliq Dad Lak was appointed as DG National Counter Terrorism Authority [NCTA].

During those days, *an extensive media controversy* had erupted regarding PM Khan not following his own announced austerity measures by using a helicopter for his daily travel between prime minister house and his Bani Gala residence. Also, over the FM Asad Umar's statement that the government was weighing its options regarding a fresh bailout package from the International Monetary Fund (IMF); Pakistan had gone to the IMF 12 times previously. Point to be remembered here that Imran Khan had announced at numerous occasions in open public gatherings that *'Pakistan will NOT go to the IMF any more'*.

Meanwhile, PM Khan's government announced its first reduction in petroleum prices. While going ahead with austerity measures, the *PM House set date for auction of 102 luxury vehicles including 27 bullet-proof ones.*

In the next move, PM Khan formed an **18-member Economic Advisory Council** [EAC] to advise on matters of economic policymaking. The council included financial experts associated with international universities such as Atif Mian from Woodrow Wilson School of Princeton University, Asim Ijaz Khwaja from John F. Kennedy School, and Imran Rasul from University College London. However, on 7th September 2018, the government asked Atif Mian to step down being an Ahmadi after bowing before a vicious campaign in social media. In solidarity with Mian, two other overseas-based economists in the EAC, Asim Khwaja and Imran Rasul, also announced they were resigning from the committee.

> [*An article in* **daily DAWN** *dated* 10th September 2018 *stated the actual reason behind Mian's removal lay in 'internal dissent' from religious parties who had threatened nationwide sit-ins against the appointment; while on the same day Chinese and Saudi dignitaries were to arrive in Islamabad. The government was compelled to take the decision to avoid an 'ugly' situation during the foreign dignitaries' visits, as well as due to political pressure from some opposition parties. Overall, it was termed 'unfortunate' and some cabinet members felt 'depressed' after the EAC lost three of its top thinkers.*]

During the 1st week of September 2018, the federal government deployed nine senior officers of the civil service to Baluchistan on long-term assignments, where they were to expedite works being carried out under the *China Pakistan Economic Corridor* [CPEC] projects. Next day, Mr Khan directed the concerned government departments to take proactive measures in preventing money laundering through illegal methods such as *hawala & hundi*. A committee was constituted to make existing financial laws stronger, and propose amendments to these laws where required.

Suddenly then, PM Khan approved a 46% increase in natural gas rates as advised by Oil and Gas Regulatory Authority [OGRA] considering it necessary given the pressure faced by the government over existing subsidies to the gas sector. The government also announced the end of the Prime Minister's Laptop Scheme and other loss-bearing schemes of the previous government. *The cabinet also gave its final approval to end discretionary funds for ministries and their divisions.*

It was in a federal cabinet meeting held on 5th September 2018, where such policy decisions were made with PM Khan in the chair. The meeting decided to abolish discretionary funds of all ministries estimating that with this move, over Rs:80 billion would become available to the national kitty.

Meanwhile, Special Assistant to Prime Minister on Accountability Shehzad Akbar held a press conference after the cabinet meeting and said:

> *"Initially we will target 100 big fish to retrieve their ill-gotten wealth stashed in foreign countries.* The whistle-blower law would be enforced immediately through an ordinance offering a reward worth 20 per cent of the recovered amount .... The names of informants would be kept confidential. Another ordinance on mutual legal assistance would be promulgated which would help remove bottlenecks in the way of seeking information regarding illegal wealth from foreign countries."

The Ministry of Foreign Affairs [MoFA] was asked to send a high-powered delegation to Switzerland to expedite ratification of a treaty on exchange of information on bank accounts. The treaty had been dumped in files since 2012 intentionally by the previous rulers, instead of being ratified. The prime minister issued directives to immediately ratify the treaty so that the government could get information regarding transfer of corruption money from Swiss banks to Pakistan.

Initially, PM Khan himself monitored the progress of that task force and other relevant departments in this regard *but the whole plan went THUSS...* because the Special Assistant in-charge of this plan, Shehzad Akbar, himself joined hands with Sharifs and Zardaris and turned the whole exercise at 180-angle while allegedly remaining special guest of the Sharifs in London.

- Still there is no dearth of *Mir Jaffers & Mir Sadiqs* in Pakistan.

During the same week, FM Asad Umar chaired a meeting of the **National Executive Committee**, which was formed to monitor the country's anti-money laundering measures and countering of finances to terrorist organisations, as mandated by the Financial Action Task Force [FATF] which had grey-listed Pakistan months earlier. Umar said implementation of the relevant measures would ensure Pakistan would successfully meet international standards under the FATF action plan.

Another week after, the PTI's Punjab government inducted nine more ministers, three extra advisers and five special assistants; the federal government also announced to expand the cabinet adding four more ministers - Omar Ayub Khan (with energy portfolio), Ali Zaidi (with maritime affairs portfolio), Muhammad Mian Soomro (with Privatisation Commission portfolio) and Murad Saeed, whose post was then undetermined but later he got the most important portfolio – Communication. This brought the number of total federal cabinet members to 24 till then.

On 17th September 2018: In all, 102 luxury and surplus vehicles parked on the lawns of PM House Islamabad were put to open auction, out of which 61 were sold off during the daylong activity as part of PM Imran Khan's austerity drive; the auction brought Rs:200 million to the national kitty. Out of 102s auction-lot, six bulletproof vehicles and 55 other vehicles were sold during the daylong exercise; 20 low-priced vehicles were not included in that day's auction because of low bids, while 21 armoured vehicles could not attract buyers' attention due to their high prices. The auction of these 21 most expensive luxury cars was to be held after correction of custom & taxes anomalies. *After that day; no auction news about state cars ever surfaced during PM Khan's tenure.*

... ABOUT MORE REFORMS & INITIATIVES:

Elaborating the media policy, the information minister Fawad Chaudhry announced on 21st August 2018 that government was ending political censorship from state-run media outlets such as *Pakistan Television Corporation [PTV] and Radio Pakistan* so they could produce content with complete freedom instead of just singing praise for the government. The PTI government also proposed to merge the *Pakistan Electronic Media Regulatory Authority [PEMRA]* and Press Council of Pakistan into one top body called as the Pakistan Media Regulatory Authority [PMRA]. There was also a plan to strengthen the cyber laws under the aegis of the Federal Investigation Agency [FIA]; two days later, a committee was formed to complete this assignment.

On 27th August 2018; the government directed FIA *to banish the VIP* protocol at airports which used to be usually given to elites including military officials, judges, senior bureaucrats, journalists, legislators, and politicians. *All previous governments decided about this measure but could never implement it – and astonishingly, the PTI govt also failed to get the directive implemented during its whole tenure of 3+ years.*

Next day, the cabinet gave ninety days to the task forces to come up with plans to fulfil their assigned obligations; the prime minister was to review their performance every fifteen days. It was also decided that the government would work with the opposition parties to bring about a consensus on the **creation of South Punjab province** so that a constitutional amendment could be tabled after ensuring two-thirds majority support in the parliament. The advisor Arbab Shehzad was also asked to work on speeding the process of the remainder of tasks for the *merger of Federally Administered Tribal Areas [FATA] into Khyber PK.* On 6 September 2018; task forces were set up separately to oversee the ongoing merger process which ultimately met success – FATA was merged into Khyber PK.

Aleem Khan announced that he would present a recommendation for a new local government system in Punjab to the prime minister on 1st September 2018, under this new system, local governments would get more financial and administrative powers.

Meanwhile, talking about election mismanagement, PTI's MNA Azam Khan Swati revealed that the government had decided to investigate allegations related to election mismanagement; he blamed NADRA for the failure of RTS on election day and exonerated Election Commission of Pakistan [ECP]. MNA Swati made the *appointment of the Chairman NADRA controversial* and recommended for his termination.

Immediately thereafter, Prime minister directed the Punjab government to take action against groups and mafias involved in encroachment and occupation of public properties. During a high-level meeting, he ordered to revamp local body system effectively, reform police system, reform the civil services and federal bureaucracy in line with a proposed government programme, remove barricades from Lahore city, and audit ongoing and completed projects for comprehensive transparency – HOWEVER, none of those directives could be turned into reality or effectiveness during the PTI's government in saddles.

During the next federal cabinet meeting held on 5th September 2018; the PTI cabinet discussed policies relating to health, education, and water supply at the federal level. A task force on education, led by education minister Shafqat Mehmood, was set up to explore how to bring out-of-school children into education – *BUT the federal minister miserably failed to take any step towards this foremost necessity. Not a single school could be added afresh by the PTI under this sector and the Literacy Rate of Pakistan remained stagnant throughout PTI's tenure.*

Same day, PM Khan ordered not to terminate any government employee or contractor except by a court order. Also, the federal cabinet indicated to abolish the National Commission on Government Reforms [NCGR], and replacing it with a newly-appointed task force which could bring about reforms in the government structure and civil service. An **Institutional Reforms Cell** was set up in the Prime Minister's office to serve as base of the task force, and the task force was desired to put forth its proposals on reforms in 90 days. Issues pertaining to provincial matters were to be placed before the Council of Common Interests (CCI).

> [*Till the ending of PTI govt on 10th April 2022, no report or proposal from the <u>Institutional Reforms Cell</u> had been surfaced on media pages; NOR any sort of reforms or change or improvement in government structure was seen. Not known if the proposals were drafted in this respect or placed before the Council of Common Interests (CCI) and if done so – then what remained their fate.*]

Same day, Governor of Sindh, Imran Ismail decided that Governor House Karachi would be open every day for the educational tours of students to show them the objects and articrafts used by Father Muhammad Ali Jinnah.

On **8th September 2018**; first phase of the anti-encroachment drive was implemented in Islamabad through the Capital Development Authority [CDA]; properties constructed on nearly two kilometres of illegally occupied lands were demolished and taken down. Similar drives were being expanded into Karachi and Lahore, under the directives of the local governments there. Same day, Railway minister announced a train service between Rawalpindi and Mianwali, the ancestral city of PM Khan, the service successfully commenced within a week.

Same day, the opposition (PMLN) threatened to launch mass protests against the government if it sought to abolish the existing local government system. Next day, Governor of Punjab, Ch Mohammad

Sarwar also opened the Governor Houses at Lahore and Murree for the public on every Sunday (10 am to 6 pm). Later, on 1ˢᵗ October 2018, the Governor of Khyber PK, Shah Farman also opened the Governor House Peshawar for the public.

On 10ᵗʰ October 2018; PM Khan launched the *Naya Pakistan Housing Program* under which the government intended to construct five million affordable houses for homeless people, and provide those homes within five years. Also announced that a *National Financial Regulatory Body* would be set up within 60 days to assist with the program's financial model and help arrange finances for the project. The law ministry had to remove all legal hurdles being faced by the construction industry. At the same time, a housing colony was announced for federal government employees known as the *Federal Government Employees Scheme* – in coordination with the Punjab government; details of which were not provided to the media then.

Scenario 244

ECONOMY DURING KHAN's REGIME

FACTS ABOUT COMPARATIVE PUBLIC DEBT:

Ishaq Dar, the former Federal Finance Minister during Pakistan Muslim League Nawaz [PMLN] government during 2013-18, wrote in daily 'the-News' dated 29th October 2018 that:

> "A lot of rhetoric by the incumbent government [the new regime of Imran Khan's PTI] has been flashed publicly through the media about the public debt, perhaps to divert the public attention from their incompetence, mis-governance and anti-public policies which all is quite visible in the first seventy days in office. As the said budget deficits are duly approved by the Parliament, the whole process is transparent and is the responsibility of the Parliament and there should be no hidden surprises for anyone."

Dar claimed that when the PMLN government started its term in June 2013 with Nawaz Sharif as Prime Minister, it inherited multiple challenges like large fiscal deficit, rising debt burden, unfavourable balance of payments, low foreign exchange reserves, poor growth in tax revenues, a shrinking tax-base, swelling current expenditures, a gigantic circular debt, which was unravelling the energy sector, flight of capital, weakening exchange rate and perilously declining investors' confidence.

In June 2013, on the external front, the major development partners had virtually ended their support on the face of rapidly weakening economic indicators. State Bank of Pakistan [SBP] forex reserves, which stood at $6 billion in June 2013 fell to $2.8 billion in February 2014; it was a highly precarious, volatile and explosive situation to steer the economy and stabilise the external financial position. The reserves were depleting and the currency was fast depreciating, which touched around Rs:111 to US Dollar in November 2013 thus fuelling inflation and raising the cost of debt servicing. On assuming office in June 2013, the new PMLN government introduced structural reforms with stabilisation measures within few days of its first Budget for 2013-14; but those reforms could not bring an iota of upwards change in the economic situation of the country.

The PPP government [2008-13] had entered into a front-loaded Stand-By Arrangement with International Monetary Fund [IMF] in 2008 with a total loan of $11.5 billion but left the programme after receiving an amount of $7,455 million against implementing first four of twelve phases of structural reforms due to its inability to implement the remaining agreed economic reforms. Out of the said PPP loan, PMLN had to repay $4.6 billion in its tenure and therefore entered into an Extended Fund Facility [EFF] with the IMF, agreed in July 2013, with an estimated amount of $6.4 billion leaving a net-intake of IMF loan of $1.8 billion in its tenure.

During the ending months of PMLN in 2018, the total public debt was Rs:30,000 billions on 30th June 2018 as quoted by the new PTI government; however, the PMLN's Ishaq Dar termed it factually incorrect and according to him the correct figure was Rs:23,051 billion as per detail below. He also claimed that Gen Musharraf's government 1999-2008 had increased the total public debt by 97%, in PPP's tenure 2008-13 it increased by 153% and the increase in PMLN's tenure 2013 -18 was 71%. However, no independent agency verified Dar's that statement of figures.

The PMLN government officials later admitted and told the media that the increase in total public debt during the year 2017-18 was Rs:3,416 billion of which Rs:1,978 billion was external debt – it was totally wrong statement because PMLN's Finance Minister had himself admitted earlier that the figure was Rs: 6,177 billion. They also explained that the increase in debt from Rs:19,635 billion to Rs: 23,051 billion, or from 46% to 71%, was very unfortunate, as PM Nawaz Sharif was disqualified from office. PMLN's new PM Shahid Khaqan Abbasi and his economic team had to face *huge unbudgeted financial demands* thus disturbing the whole economic discipline.

The PMLN also claimed that Pakistan's GDP grew from Rs:22,386 billion in June 2013 to Rs:34,397 billion in June 2018. Total public debt to GDP of Pakistan was 60.1% in June 2013 which rose to 61.4% by June 2017 and 67% by June 2018 due to additional extra-ordinary security-related expenditure for war against terrorism [*Operation Zarb-e-Azb*] etc.

PMLN later issued statement that despite PTI's political *'Dharnas'* spread over exactly 126 days, their fiscal policies in its tenure achieved an increase in the federal taxes collection by 100%, enhanced GDP Growth from around 3% to 5.8%, claiming the highest in previous 13 years; managed lowest inflation in the last forty years in addition to increase in foreign remittances from $13.9 billion to $19.4 billion; and rise in national foreign exchange reserves from $7.5 billion in February 2014 to $21.4 billion by 30th June 2017.

Former Finance Minister Ishaq Dar claimed that he had repeatedly offered PTI and other opposition parties to agree on a 'Charter of Economy' in order to keep Pakistan's economy free from politics but unfortunately none came forward. Also, that *the people of Pakistan had suffered enough in PTI's first seventy days after PTI's take over through massive devaluation of Rupee, decline in Pakistan Stock Exchange Index [PSX] and sky-high increase in cost of living with unprecedented hike in prices of essential commodities, gas, power and gasoline.*

However, in Pakistan it's always an impossible task to dig out the real facts from released ministerial figures in any organization – especially when headed by Ishaq Dar calibre accountants.

Referring to *Dr Farrukh Saleem*'s essay on media pages dated 7th October 2018; '*…..as per the World Bank estimates, the public procurement in Pakistan amounts to 19.8 per cent of country's GDP - $60 billion a year'.* Mostly it is through the abuse of public office for private gain [*see* World Bank's definition of corruption]; the 'leakages' amount to a low of $18 billion a year to a high value of $36 billion.

Pakistan Public Regulatory Authority [PPRA] held that '*….we do not need any borrowings from the World Bank or the IMF if we can save this money'.* According to the US based **International Narcotics Control Strategy Report,** the practice of money laundering cost Pakistan more than $10 billion a year – and for two decades this plundering is going on un-interrupted. Dr Farrukh Saleem held that:

> '…… *Pakistan's gross external financial need this year [2018] is $26 billion while the* **leakages** *in public procurement are potentially more than that. Our [Pakistan's] external debt is $95 billion while the past 10-year money-laundering cost stands at $100 billion. So, we have a potential surplus.* **Conclusion: Minus leakages and minus money laundering, we are a surplus country.**'

The real *tabdeeli* [change] started from the day Imran Khan took over as prime minister [PM]. For the first time in Pakistan's turbulent financial history, there was a PM whose top priority was anti-corruption. Similarly, for the first time in Pakistan's chequered history, there was a chief justice [Saqib Nisar] whose top priority was anti-corruption – thus for the first time in country's 71-year history, the head of government and the head of Supreme Court shared the same agenda and opted to reach the same goal.

On top of the things; for the first time in the Federal Investigation Agency [FIA]'s inconsistent 43-years history, the agency was moved to unearth the money laundering scams. The details appeared shocking: the number of fake bank accounts unearthed within two months' Imran Khan rule were 77; the number of individuals named were 334 [including PPP's chief Asif Ali Zardari and his sister Faryal Talpur MNA]; and the money thus laundered amounted to hundreds of billions – and more revelations were coming every day.

The modus operandi of money launderers was simple; political bosses and bureaucrats were routinely facilitated by bankers open fake bank accounts. The two then managed out contracts worth hundreds of billions to their favourite contractors. In return, contractors deposited the negotiated percentages into those fake bank accounts operated in fake names - then through trusted money-changers that black money used to be transferred to Dubai – for onward investments in London, America and Europe.

No doubt that the FIA's conviction rate always remained low at about 6%; and that NAB lacked the capacity to prosecute white-collar criminals – thus the powerful public-office holders remained Scot free and un-convicted. However, with the new regime of PM Khan, the process had taken a start – and that was encouraging for the poor populace of Pakistan.

IK NOT DESTROYED PAK-ECONOMY – FACTS:

'Destroyed' would be too harsh. Pakistan's economy has always been this way, bubbles of unequal growth, followed by high inflation and recession, and net decline. A few Pakistanis get richer; most are worse off.

However, Imran Khan could be blamed for being *'not the best'*; as Nawaz Sharif did nothing to resolve the country's perennial tax deficiency either, nor the bloated state expenditures. NS in his last stint was well aware that this face-off with a much larger and stronger neighbour [India] was bleeding the country dry. Pakistan was (*and still is*) like a child trying to grow with a millstone round its neck; no matter how much nutrition or exercise he got, the stone would ensure he never reaches full potential. NS knew this but allegedly the army advisors, the institution that mostly benefited from this millstone directly, made sure he couldn't progress towards resolution.

Mr Khan had grand ambitions, and sincerely too, but to reach the position he needed experienced team which he couldn't identify and engage; his PTI couldn't break through the thick wall of status quo. More generally, Imran had the best intentions, unaccompanied by the nous and grey matter which could turn them into reality. He posed but NOT skilled at everything; his mostly ineffective leadership didn't know how to build strong teams, nor could he prioritize, understanding that single 5-year term was not enough to address the plethora of issues he had inherited.

Imran Khan didn't follow the viable option to target one or two of the most fundamental problems, and to first work out a practical plan for solution – it was governance and management which Imran had never done before. In his speech to the nation, right after being sworn in, he listed over 50 separate challenges his government was going to take on. Mostly he meant what he said but the historians and intelligentsia knew he was going to fail.

He was an outstanding sportsman, but that also meant his life experience was that of a narrow specialization, where his personal talent was always enough overcome other deficiencies. He was a successful captain because he knew the game so well himself, and he led by example, plus the simple fact that everyone on a cricket field was bound by clear rules without exception. On the other hand, even as captain he was known for his lack of empathy for his players and his refusal to change his mind despite better advice.

As a cricket player, supreme self-confidence and refusal to surrender served him well, and these qualities helped him achieve the PM position. Unfortunately for Pakistan, what he never had was a subtle mind and genuine intellect, nor an ability to win over even adversaries, qualities which any reformer of Pakistan must have in order to navigate the treacherous tides of the nation's politics, where the strongest party was the military establishment perpetually in power – and since decades.

Referring to **THE EXPRESS TRIBUNE** dated 19th May 2022: During the last year of Imran Khan's government, Pakistan's economic growth rate accelerated to 6% – the highest pace in previous four years – helping to increase the size of the nation's economy to $383 billion besides jacking up per-capita income even after devastating Covid-19, it was a miracle for Pakistan.

The provisional Gross Domestic Product (GDP) growth rate for the year 2021-22 was estimated at 5.97%, announced by the Planning Ministry after a meeting of the National Accounts Committee. The broad-based growth was witnessed in all the sectors of the economy. The GDP was the monetary value of all goods and services produced in a year. That nearly 6% growth rate was higher than the official target of 4.8% and far higher than the estimates of the Ministry of Finance, State Bank of Pakistan, International Monetary Fund, World Bank and the Asian Development Bank.

The economic growth rate during the last two years of the PTI rule was slightly better than the PMLN's last two years but both the governments failed to address structural problems of Pakistan's economy. An attempt had been made to downplay the growth figures in the last year of the PTI government but the authorities dropped the plan after some reports appeared in media. *The details showed that the massive surge in imports and consumption greased the economic growth rate,* which had already triggered a serious external sector crisis – an identical pattern witnessed in 2018 when the country had fallen in the lap of the International Monetary Fund [IMF].

The 6% growth rate at the end of the PTI government was the highest in four years. Last time, the country attained a 6.1% growth rate in 2017-18 –when Shahid Khaqan Abbasi was the PM, which had also been driven by consumption and imports and took the country back to the IMF. During 2017-18 and 2021-22, Pakistan's growth was largely financed through foreign savings, which was highly unsustainable.

The agriculture sector was provisionally estimated to grow by 4.4%, nearly 1% better than the previous year. On the back of the Large-Scale Manufacturing sector, the industrial sector grew at the rate of 7.2%, lower than the previous fiscal year. The growth in the services sector was slightly better than the previous fiscal year, standing at 6.2%. The mining sector witnessed contraction. Had the annual imports remained at the projected level of $55 billion in the last fiscal year of Khan's era, the overall economic growth rate would have remained around 5%. The better crop production also supported the higher growth, except for wheat whose output decreased by one million metric tons to 26.4 million metric tons.

The size of the economy reached nearly Rs:67 trillion in 2021-22; about Rs3 trillion higher than the estimates. In dollar-terms, the volume of the economy in 2021-22 stood at $383 billion, according to the Planning Ministry's documents. Similarly, the per capita income that had been estimated at $1,676 in the last fiscal year increased to $1,798 – a surge of $122 or 7% per person. In rupee terms, per capita income jumped from Rs:268,223 in 2020-21 to Rs:314,353 in 2021-22 - although, the final growth rate of GDP for year 2019-20 had contracted by 0.94% due to COVID-19's world-over attack.

IMF – 'KASHKOL' REVIVED:

It was one of the major slogans of Imran Khan and the PTI, before and after the elections 2018 that *'WE'LL NOT BEG IMF'* – a key point in their manifesto, too. BUT, just within one year, the PTI's economic team had started Staff-Meetings with the IMF in May-June 2019 to get a bail-out package; see a media report dated 13th May 2019 as a reference; the opening lines were:

> *"Pakistan has secured a $6bn bailout from the International Monetary Fund (IMF) as the country battles to stay off an economic crisis. The funding, which will get approval from the IMF's management in the first week of July 2019 would be provided over three years. The agreement comes after months of negotiations and marks the latest in a string of bailouts from the fund."*

Pakistan was apparently facing an economic crisis with short supplies of foreign currency reserves and stagnating growth. In a statement, the IMF said *"Pakistan faces a challenging economic environment, with lacklustre growth, elevated inflation, high indebtedness, and a weak external position. The funding programme would support the authorities' strategy for stronger growth by improving the business environment, strengthening institutions, increasing transparency, and protecting social spending"*.

IMF bailout funding is typically provided under strict conditions, and some analysts had timely warned that any fresh IMF injection could harm PM Imran Khan's pledges to build a welfare state. Since he was sworn in August 2018, Mr Khan had been aggressively pursuing help from friendly countries in order to reduce the size of the bailout package that Pakistan needed from the IMF. The country was likely to face a potential balance of payments crisis - where a nation struggles to meet external debts or pay for critical imports - due to a stagnating economy.

The IMF had put its forecasts that Pakistan's economic growth would slow to 2.9% the said fiscal year from 5.2% in 2018. In February 2019, the central bank had only $8bn left in foreign reserves. Abdul Hafeez Shaikh, an economic advisor to PM Khan, was upset as the foreign loans had exceeded $90bn then, and exports had registered a negative growth over the past five years. *"So, Pakistan will get $6 billion from the IMF, and in addition we will get $2 to $3 billion from the World Bank and Asian Development Bank in the next three years,"* said Mr Shaikh to the media.

PTI had successfully paved the way for a multi-billion-dollar bailout, marking the 22nd such occasion but attracted a vibrant public debate. Primetime news anchors and columnists pondered upon the dilated impact of the devalued rupee, higher interest rate, more taxes and lower government spending. However, there were two substantially more critical questions: *First, why did Pakistan keep getting into a dire-enough condition that we needed an IMF bailout? And second, what could the country do so that it could avoid such situation forever?*

All the politicians knew the correct answers but never bothered for just solutions - some policy directions and reforms to increase domestic productivity.

In 2013, Pakistan got an IMF loan which did what it was meant to do — averted a balance of payments crisis, stabilized the economy and allowed the economy to leverage the stability for more borrowed capital; the country was able to pay for its imports. *There was an increase in foreign reserves to overvalue the rupee,* which essentially meant that Pakistan had subsidized imports by making them cheaper. It also made country's exports more expensive BUT helped boost the consumption of mainly imported goods, which brought economic growth; thus, the GDP.

Then, it was looking good only on papers - this created a bad set of incentives for the economy as the people had found more profit in acquiring import licenses rather than investing in capacity to export, or simply moving their investment towards non-tradable sectors. *For example, the growth in real estate that lured many textile firms to move investment away from expanding their manufacturing capacity and made huge investments in the property market – no one could export lands.*

In 1995, Pakistan exported about $11.6 billion of goods and services — that was about $95 for each Pakistani. By 2017, our exports jumped to just over $21 billion, or $108 for each Pakistani. In contrast, Bangladesh pushed its per-capita exports from about $20 to about $164 during the same period.

Pakistan needed real increase in exports – NOT just on-paper-exports to get the duty drawbacks by certain rogue exporters. The answer was by increasing domestic productivity — it needed people, money and materials — to produce goods or provide a service. Pakistan's growth model had mainly focused on the accumulation of physical assets, such as buildings and roads, but not the broader investments needed to increase productivity. Even the agriculture sector was unable to sustain an increase in productivity; more agricultural loans were floated in routine rather than enhancing the efficiency in using those inputs.

> *The PTI govt initiated work on 13 special economic zones in July 2020 in Punjab.* There were only three Special Economic Zones when PTI government came into power; the PTI government issued notifications for *seven Special Economic Zones.* The Second Special Economic Zone of the Punjab **'Quaid-e-Azam Business Park'** project was launched on 19th July 2020, whereas, one special economic zone had already been kicked off in Faisalabad.

Quaid-e-Azam Business Park was planned to cover an area of 1536 acres of land besides generating employment opportunities for more than 500,000 people. Accommodation facility for industrial workers were to be provided over 200 acres of land. The project was expected to gain great significance due to its proximity to the National Highway and Motorway; 653 industrial units were included in Quaid-e-Azam Business Park. This business park was declared a special economic zone by the Pakistani government then.

No doubt it was mega-project to give boost for the national economy; especially in those days when the whole world was facing economic difficulties due to Covid-19 outbreak. First time in the national history, tax relief of Rs: 56 billion was given to the business community in Punjab but it was in the backdrop of coronavirus pandemic.

FY20 REMITTANCES UP - RECORD $23bn:

The foreign remittances and inflows in June 2020 grew significantly compared to May (2020) when the country received around $1.866bn, rising despite the negative outlook due to the impact of coronavirus.

See the **State Bank of Pakistan's report** (SBP) for the last quarter of 2019-20 here; all print and electronic media dated 14th July 2020 is referred.

Pakistan received record $23 billion in remittances during 2019-20 while the inflows jumped by 51 per cent year-on-year to $2.466bn in June (2020). Despite economic slowdown caused by the Covid-19, the remittances in the last quarter of the fiscal year 2019-20 i.e. March-June increased significantly helping the country get more than expected inflows.

> [*'Workers' remittances rose by a significant 50.7pc during June to reach record high of $2.466bn compared with $1.636bn in June 2019. On a cumulative basis, workers' remittances increased to a historic high level of $23.120bn during FY20, witnessing a growth of 6.4pc over $21.739bn during FY19.'*]

Major chunk of the remittances was from Saudi Arabia at $619.4 million, USA $452m, UAE $431.7m and UK $401m recording increases of 42pc, 7.1pc, 33.5pc and 40.8pc respectively as compared to May (2020). Meanwhile, despite 0.98pc growth, the remittances from UAE were second highest in terms of total inflows reaching $4.662bn in FY20 – up by 6pc comparing with last year's figures.

The remittances from the Gulf Cooperation Council countries were up by 2pc to $2.162bn while inflows from Malaysia were down 8pc to $1.426bn in FY20. The growth in remittances from Malaysia was 35pc in FY19. The SBP added:

> *"The significant increase in remittances during June can be taken as seasonal inflows in the month of Ramazan coupled by zakat and charity funds collectively increased the inflows during the last fiscal year.... Supportive government policies in terms of extension of Reimbursement of TT Charges Scheme (**Free Send Remittance Scheme**) to small remitters by reducing threshold amount from $200 to $100.*
>
> *Financial institutions were motivated to use effective marketing campaigns with particular focus on digital channels for sending and receiving remittances to promote the use of legal channels."*

On 19th July 2020; Khyber PK govt told the media that the Executive Committee of National Economic Council (ECNEC) accorded approval to two very vital projects for the province including **Khyber Pass Economic Corridor and Swat Motorway Phase-II**. The people of Khyber

PK were thankful to the Federal Government and PM Imran Khan for approving the said two very important projects for the province. Khyber Pass Economic Corridor project was to be constructed with financial support of the World Bank that would cost an estimated amount of $460 million; while under Swat Motorway project, a four-lane-80km Motorway was planned from *Chakdara* to *Fateh Pur*.

PLUS POINT also, the **CURRENT ACCOUNT DEFICIT** (CAD) showed decline by **78pc in 2019-20;** Shahid Iqbal's analysis published in daily **DAWN** on 22nd July 2020 is referred. The CAD had narrowed to $2.966 billion in FY20, compared to $13.434bn in the previous fiscal year. It was mainly on account of significant decline in imports, record high remittances and foreign direct investment during the period under review.

The said massive decline also helped PTI government improve its foreign exchange reserves through a sharp reduction in the import bill. It had intervened through increasing duties and taxes to cut down the import bill in order to reduce the trade deficit. According to SBP data, the current account deficit in FY20 fell to 1.1pc of GDP compared to 4.8pc in FY19.

Details showed that exports in the fiscal year under review fell by 7.2pc to $22.505bn - mainly the fall was due to cancellation of exports orders since March when Covid-19 hit international markets and exports came to a halt. The SBP data further showed that the imports fell by $9.45bn or 18.2pc to $42.419bn. The fall in imports helped the government narrow the trade deficit — major driver behind the large current account deficit booked in FY18 and FY19.

The deficit in balance on trade of goods during FY20 was $19.914bn compared to $27.612bn (deficit) in the previous fiscal year. Similarly, the deficit in balance of trade in services fell to $2.835bn from $4.97bn in the corresponding year. The overall deficit in balance on trade of goods and services fell to $22.749bn compared to $32.582bn in FY19; a decline of $9.833bn. *The numbers showed that the government succeeded in bringing down both the trade and current account deficits.*

The pressure on forex reserves also eased after the G-20 deferred Pakistan's debt repayments due in that calendar year. However, about 30pc increase in imports in June FY20 was seen which was alarming for Pakistan's weak economy. *Pakistan's economy was expected to stabilise; the growth was the next target for PTI government.* Stabilisation policies — which included fiscal and monetary policies — remained what they were. The PTI govt opted to stabilise the economy around its underlying productivity growth rate. As Paul Krugman, a Noble Laureate economist, held that *"productivity isn't everything, but in the long run it is almost everything."*

The critics had serious doubts that during 2019-24 Pakistan's economy could grow as was projected by PTI government. The economic growth started falling down for a while because some drastic actions were taken by PTI government through FBR. The cases against political prisoners also terrified from industrialists to a common man and nobody was interested to spend a single rupee as an investment. The inflation was going upward and people were just passing the time with high hopes. In fact, *the population growth overwhelmed the economic progress.*

BUT, suddenly the PTI's policies started giving fruit; see the following:

> *"Over the first four months of fiscal year 2019-20, **the country's trade deficit decreased significantly by 33.5pc**. Trade deficit fell from $11.7 billion recorded from July-October of FY18-19 to $7.8bn during the same period this year; it was due to a fall in imports, which recorded a decline of 19.3pc. Exports, meanwhile, saw a meagre rise of 3.6pc and grew from $7.3bn to $7.5bn.*
>
> *During the month of October, trade deficit fell by 32pc and was recorded at $1.97bn as opposed to last year's $2.9bn. Exports during the same month of the current fiscal year increased by 6pc, rising from $1.9bn to $2bn. Imports fell by 17pc and were recorded at $3.9bn as opposed to $4.8bn from last year;"* **Reuters Report** published on 2nd November 2019 is referred.

PAK-ECONOMY UP BEYOND EXPECTATIONS:

For years 2021-22, Pakistan's economic growth rate was projected at 3.94pc - beyond expectations with all major macro-economic indicators showing positive trend amid the Covid-19 pandemic; it was as compared to a revised negative 0.47pc in 2019-20. See the media reports dated 22nd May 2021:

> *"The growth figures came as a surprise as the State Bank of Pakistan (SBP) had estimated GDP growth at 3pc, while the finance ministry's projection was slightly on the lower side. The growth projection of*

multilateral donors — the IMF and the World Bank (WB) — was between 1.3pc and 1.5pc for the fiscal year 2020-21 but the PTI's policies worked miraculously.

For a number of years, the services sector was a major reason for economic growth in the country and, this time again, it witnessed a growth of 4.43pc this year."

However, the **agriculture sector** posted a trivial 2.77pc growth, while industrial output grew 3.57pc. The surge in growth was partly explained by the low-base of last year when the economy contracted due to effects of the Covid-19 pandemic. Figures defied IMF & WB projection and exceeded even SBP's estimates. *The said figures were framed in the 103rd meeting of the National Accounts Committee, chaired by Planning, Development and Reform Secretary, to review the Gross Domestic Product.*

Provisional estimates for the fiscal year 2020-21 for GDP and Gross Fixed Capital Formation (GFCF) were presented on the basis of the latest data available for six to nine months. PM Khan took to Twitter, saying *'the higher GDP growth reflects the success of his government's economic policies while managing the Covid-19 pandemic. Our V-shaped recovery is balanced between three major sectors — agriculture, industry and services.'*

The country's GDP size then stood at Rs:47.709 trillion for 2020-21, compared to Rs:41.556tr of the previous year, showing a growth of 14.8pc. But contrary to that, the GDP size surged to $296 billion in 2020-21 against $263bn in 2019-20, an increase of $33bn or 12.54pc. The size of the economy grew in dollar terms as the rupee strengthened against the greenback — the highest-ever increase in the previous years.

The per capita income was calculated at Rs:246,414 for 2020-21, compared to Rs:215,060 in 2019-20, showing a growth of 14.6pc. The per capita income in dollar terms had jumped by 13.4pc to $1,543 during that fiscal year from $1,361 last year. The per capita income had posted a growth due to a combination of GDP growth and strengthening of the rupee against the dollar. The growth in GDP in a period in which Covid-19 posed a huge challenge to the economy was extremely gratifying and proof of success of the PTI government's economic policies.

AGRICULTURE SECTOR, as said above, grew by 2.77pc during the fiscal year 2020-21 against 3.31pc in 2019-20. The growth of important crops that year was 4.65pc in the backdrop of the historic highest-ever production of wheat, rice and maize. Sugarcane registered the second highest-ever production. *The growth in production of wheat, rice, sugarcane and maize stood at 8.1pc, 13.6pc, 22pc and 7.38pc, respectively.* However, cotton witnessed a negative growth of 22.8pc, which also resulted in a 15.6pc decline in cotton ginning. Other crops, including vegetables, fruits and green fodder, showed a positive growth of 1.41pc.

LIVESTOCK SECTOR registered a growth of 3.1pc, which was a deviation from its historical growth, primarily because of shrinkage in demand for dairy and poultry. Forestry growth declined to 1.4pc from last year's 2.29pc.

INDUSTRIAL SECTOR *witnessed a positive growth of 3.57pc the said year as against a negative growth of 3.77pc previous year.* However, value-addition in the mining and quarrying sector had declined by 6.5pc. *The large-scale manufacturing (LSM) sector, which was driven primarily by QIM data (from July 2020 to March 2021), showed an unprecedented growth of 9.29pc.* Major contributors to this growth were textile (5.9pc), food beverage & tobacco (11.73pc), petroleum products (12.71pc), pharmaceuticals (12.57pc), chemicals (11.65pc), non-metallic mineral products (24.31pc), automobiles (23.38pc) and fertiliser (5.69pc).

The electricity and gas sub-sector had declined by 22.96pc mainly due to lower allocation of subsidies by the government to power distribution companies, low increase in output and a higher proportional increase in intermediate consumption.

CONSTRUCTION ACTIVITY had increased by 8.34pc mainly due to an increase in general government spending and private sector construction-related expenditures. The wholesale and retail trade sector grew by 8.37pc primarily because of an increase in marketable surplus. The *transport, storage and communication sector* declined by 0.61pc. The finance and insurance sector showed an increase of 7.84pc. The remaining components of services — housing, general government and other private services — witnessed a positive growth of 4.01pc, 2.20pc and 4.64pc, respectively. PTI's Finance Minister Shaukat Tarin had unveiled the Pakistan Economic Survey 2020-21 at a press conference in Islamabad on 10th June 2021.

Shaukat Tareen further said that the **INFLATION** measured by the Consumer Price Index (CPI) was recorded at 8.6pc during July-April

FY2021 against 11.2pc during the same period of previous year. The government had targeted inflation of 6.5pc for FY21. This was achieved due to the government measures for maintaining price stability. Inflation in perishable food items increased 0.1pc against an exorbitant increase of 34.7pc during the same period of the previous year.

Federal Board of Revenue (FBR) **Tax Collection** came in at Rs:3,780.3 billion, registering double-digit growth of 14.4pc during July-April FY2021 against Rs:3,303.4 billion in the same period of previous year. The PTI govt had set a revised target of Rs:4,691 billion for FBR for the full fiscal year.

Under **Current Account** heading: during FY2021, while the world was reeling from the economic impact of the pandemic, Pakistan's external sector appeared as a key buffer for resilience. During July-March FY2021, current account posted a surplus of $959 million (0.5pc of GDP) against a deficit of $4,147m last year (2.1pc of GDP). The main driver of improvement in current account balance was the robust growth in remittances. The inflows accelerated posting a year-on-year growth of 26.2pc during the period under review.

Trade Deficit: During July-March FY2021, export of goods grew by 2.3pc to $18.7bn as compared to $18.3bn the same period of previous year; import of goods grew by 9.4pc to $37.4bn. Consequently, the trade deficit increased by 17.7pc to $18.7bn as compared to $15.9bn of the previous year. Thus, Pakistan's total debt had increased nominally in the last 9 months; Rs:1.67 trillion in FY21 to reach Rs:38 trillion - out of that Rs:25 trillion was local debt while around Rs:12.5 trillion was foreign debt.

Employment levels almost came back to pre-Covid time; the economic survey revealed. Before the start of the Covid-19 pandemic, 35pc of Pakistan's population or 55.7m people were employed; the number decreased by around 20 million to 35m after lockdowns were imposed. In July 2020, the government announced [a] package for construction sector. Thus, opening of sectors in which daily wagers were working along with fiscal stimulus and monetary measures made economy recover. As a result, people started working again and the total number of employed people rose to 52.5m or 33pc of the population. In the start, the provinces doubted [the federal policies] too but because of them, 52m people came back to work in October 2020 and only 2.5m people were left unemployed then.

PTI's MANIFESTO – ECONOMIC BETRAYAL:

However, contradicting the said (above) Economic Survey presented by the PTI's FM Mr Tareen, some critics raised loud voices; see the analysis of *Dr Ikramul Haq* & others dated 29th October 2021 on daily **DAWN** and allied media pages:

> *"In its manifesto, PTI made commitments to introduce reforms and transform governance through accountability to the core of government, empowering people at the grass root level through local government, depoliticizing and strengthening police, reforming the criminal justice system, and providing speedy access to justice. They also submitted their commitment to bringing reforms in civil services, institutionalize e-governance, delivery through legislative reforms, ensuring freedom of the press – BUT No achievement seen......"*

{However, one can see the intelligence of the critic that instead of commenting on Economy related performance, he relied on general narration of administrative clauses like police & criminal justice system etc......}

The said critics elaborated that the *Chapter IV of the manifesto* explained about the road to inclusive economic growth by introducing reforms in Federal Board of Revenue (FBR), creation of 10 million jobs, implementing policy framework to build five million housing units, making Pakistan business friendly and facilitating rapid growth of the Small and medium Enterprises (SMEs), transformation of key economic institutions, fixing energy challenges and ensuring that China Pakistan Economic Corridor (CPEC) would be translated into a game-changer. Apart from those tall claims, the PTI also undertook in the manifesto providing easy access to finance for citizens and industry, boosting tourism, building of knowledge economy by utilizing Information Technology (IT). BUT, *by looking at their (till then) 38 months' performance, Pakistan experienced a negative form of governance.*

The learned critic held that the PTI coalition government failed to introduce *performance review mechanism for ensuring check and balance on the cabinet members* as well as public sector institutions (*that objection was not Economy related strictly either*). BUT he forgot the known legal maxim *'he who comes into equity must come with clean hands'* - the basic guiding principle of accountability went ignored for his own person. To some extent, **Dr Ikramul Haq** truthfully mentioned:

"….. some members of federal cabinet are facing corruption allegations. Pakistan has witnessed increase in corruption under the present (PTI) Government. Resultantly, the mantra of corruption is losing its effectiveness and contrary to government's claims, Pakistan in 2020 slipped seven positions downwards on corruption perception index as compared to its position in 2018.

Some cabinet members are also named in various scandals. The famous Sugar Crisis caused unprecedented price increase as exporters of sugar gained benefit in two ways: first they were able to get subsidy and secondly allowed to make profit from the rising sugar prices in the local market (increased from Rs 55 per kg in December 2018 to above Rs 100 per kg in 2021). Despite **Report of the Sugar Inquiry Committee** wherein the role of various ministers has been questioned recommending action against them, no enquiry is made for the alleged corruption.

The unprecedented decision of the (PTI) Government to allow sale of subsidized wheat for the poultry sector was taken at the policy level. The entire process was completed within a span of only three days, from submission of application by the Poultry Association to the Minister of National Food Security & Research (MNFS & R) on 19th November 2018, summary moved by the Secretary MNFS&R on 20th November 2018 and the ECC's decision allowed 0.2 million tons on 22nd November 2018."

This had been a saga of failures at the miscellaneous policies and administrative governance levels where massive embezzlement in public procurement was further compounded due to inept handling by the provincial food departments, and collusive malpractices of their officials and private stockists. Planned shortage of wheat had harshly affected the common man while on the other hand had enriched the poultry business owners by giving them subsidized wheat and later raising the prices of poultry products. The nation suffered on account of maladministration but no economic failure was involved in the said media article.

On another count, the PTI govt approved price hike for hundreds of local and imported medicines ranging between, 262% to 400% as reported in the media with the name of a PTI minister in circulation but no action was taken against him. Rather, he was awarded with a powerful party position. On economy front, the rupee against the USD reached record level of 176 (- *after April 2022, it went the record lowest of Rs:300 within six months*). Claims of reforms in FBR could not materialize as had been failed in previous regimes of the PMLN and PPP. Bailouts from friends instead of investment served no useful purpose – as had been happening during other parties' regimes previously.

> {**One Friday night**, on 6th November 2021, *27-year-old Asadullah, who used to sell old shoes on a cart, set himself on fire in the Pakistani city of Karachi. His relatives, blamed the state of an economy where rampant inflation was hitting those least able to cope. In comments to local media, they said Asadullah used to get calls from his wife and parents asking him for money, but he could not afford to pay the rent and meet his own expenses and sending money back home was no longer possible.*}

An alleged economic meltdown was putting the Pakistani prime minister, Imran Khan, under immense pressure and bringing the *threat of unrest as record inflation – the fourth highest in the world* – the price of sugar was higher than petrol. However, in an address to the nation in ending days of October 2021, Khan blamed the opposition for past mistakes and inflation in the international market for the miseries of the people in Pakistan. He also announced a 120bn-rupee relief package providing subsidies on essential food items. The economic analysts said it was not enough – *'The package is a drop in the ocean and will do little to help the mass of ordinary people. The pressure on Imran Khan will continue to mount because we have seen further price hikes, such as of fuel and sugar, after the announcement of the package.'*

The critics of the PTI maintained that inflation was imposing a crushing burden on ordinary people because it came at a time of high unemployment and stagnant wages. *Prices of some essential items, such as fuel and electricity, were unprecedentedly high – could be due to after-effects of Covid-19 when the whole world was suffering the same like high-tides of inflation.* The Pakistan Democratic Movement (PDM), an opposition alliance, announced a campaign against the PTI govt and the inflation rates the country was witnessing. A long march against inflation was also announced as a part of the campaign from Lahore to Islamabad.

The agenda of the said campaign remained that ordinary people of the country would struggle to afford basic necessities if prices were not brought down. Low level shopkeepers witnessed a fall in the number of customers as prices went up. No one was worried about inflation to daily wage workers, who were unable to afford buying food for their families.

People in neighbourhoods believed that three years ago, a sack of sugar (50kg) cost about 3,000 rupees (£13) but then it was more than 7,000 rupees (£30). A federal officer complained, while saying: *'I could run my kitchen for 60,000 rupees (£261) three years ago and now I can't do it for 90,000 rupees (£393);'* daily **THE GUARDIAN** of UK dated 9th November 2021 is referred.

Scenario 245

COVID-19 PANDEMIC IN PAKISTAN

On 26th March 2020; the **COVID-19** pandemic virus was confirmed as reached Pakistan, when two cases were recorded; a student in Karachi who had just returned from Iran and another person in the Islamabad Capital Territory. By 17th June 2020; each district in Pakistan got recorded at least one confirmed case for COVID-19 virus. Despite being the world's 5th-most-populous country, till then Pakistan had only recorded the world's 29th-highest death toll (at approximately 23,087) and similar highest number of confirmed cases (at approximately 1,011,708). However, these figures didn't include undercounting of COVID-19 infections in the country. Pakistan till then had experienced three different waves of COVID-19.

The nation's first wave of COVID-19 began in late May 2020, peaked in mid-June when daily new confirmed case numbers and daily new death numbers reached high points, then ended in mid-July. The first wave was marked by a low death rate, and passed very suddenly as case and death rates began to drop very quickly. After the first wave, Pakistan's COVID-19 situation subsided daily new death numbers and testing positivity rates in the country stabilized at low levels. Cases and deaths began rising again, though, in early November 2020, culminating in the country's second wave. This wave was low in its intensity, mainly affected the southern province of Sindh, and peaked in mid-December 2020.

The country's third wave began in mid-March 2021, when testing positivity rates, and daily new confirmed cases and deaths began to skyrocket. The third wave mainly affected the provinces of Punjab and Khyber PK. This wave peaked in late April 2021, and then, positivity rates, daily new case numbers, and daily new death numbers started falling. Pakistan's most populated province, Punjab, saw the highest raw number of confirmed cases (334,000) and deaths (9,770). Sindh, had seen the second-highest number of confirmed cases (308,000) and deaths (4,910). Khyber PK confirmed 80,300 cases and had seen 745 deaths, while having the lowest fatality rate in the country.

The country was put under a nationwide lockdown from 1st April 2020 and extended twice until 9th May. Upon its end, the lockdown was eased in phases. After the first wave, the country battled COVID-19 by using *'smart lockdowns'* and enforcing the state SOPs vigorously.

On 9th **January 2021;** Islamabad got its first coronavirus vaccination Centre after the government established the facility in *Tarlai* area of the federal capital. Next day, the government's National Command and Operation Center (NCOC) opened registrations for frontline healthcare workers, who received the first doses of the COVID-19 vaccine. Staff in both public and private health facilities were vaccinated,

On 16th **January 2021;** *AstraZeneca*'s COVID-19 vaccine was approved for emergency use in Pakistan as the Chinese vaccine was awaiting approval from the Drug Regulatory Authority of Pakistan (DRAP). Pakistan had adequate cold chain facilities for most kinds of vaccines. Two days later, The Drug Regulatory Authority of Pakistan (DRAP) approved the *Sinopharm* BIBP vaccine for emergency use; meanwhile, China agreed to provide half a million doses of the Chinese *Sinopharm* vaccine free of cost to Pakistan on immediate basis. On 31st January 2021, it was announced that 17 million doses of the *AstraZeneca* vaccine were being provided to Pakistan in addition. Next day, Pakistan received the first consignment of vaccine doses from China.

EFFECTS OF GLOBAL DETERIORATION:

The COVID-19 pandemic was undoubtedly the biggest global challenge the world had faced in recent memory. Well over 100 countries worldwide instituted either a full or partial lockdown, following in the footsteps of Asian and European countries. The pandemic had caused both demand and supply shocks to vibrate through the global economy. In Pakistan, there was day-by-day growing fear over how a state with extremely limited resources would deal with this pandemic, especially due to the fact that in the past Pakistan had failed to contain infectious diseases like polio, hepatitis and tuberculosis. As per state statistics, till then, the COVID-19 virus had caused 30,379 deaths, with 1,530,145 confirmed reported numbers of cases.

On 13th **March 2020;** PM Khan held 'the first cabinet meeting for COVID-19' after the first confirmed case in Karachi. The federal government devised a National Action Plan for COVID-19. This plan was a policy document illustrating the fundamental principles for outbreak preparedness, containment and mitigation. The administration took swift actions authorized by the Ministry of National Health Services, Regulations Coordination (MNHSRC) to take necessary measures. The MNHRSC formulated guidelines to tackle the disease, such as priority testing; social distancing; the establishment of quarantine facilities; Standard Operating Procedures (SOPs) for *Ramazan*, Eid, gatherings, ceremonies and marriage; and guidelines for the reopening of educational institutions, tourism, air transportation, etc.

By mid-March 2020, as cases of local transmission started multiplying rapidly, particularly in densely populated cities like Karachi, Lahore and Peshawar. Sindh province was the first to impose a stringent lockdown on 23 March 2020; it restricted public movement and barred the opening of non-essential businesses. The other three provinces followed in Sindh's footsteps but imposed far looser restrictions, arguing that a complete lockdown would be fatal for people living below the poverty line. Thus, all provinces except Sindh, especially Punjab, allowed many businesses to reopen.

Quoting the 18th Constitutional Amendment, many party leaders showed their political mileage gaining behaviour, even during a calamity; thus, caused an inter-provincial rift, which, in turn, emerged as the biggest obstacle for promulgating a unified policy to curb the spread of the virus. Nonetheless, finally, on 14 April 2020, Imran Khan implemented a nationwide lockdown for 15 days initially. However, restrictions on several non-essential industries, including construction, textile industry, small and medium-sized enterprises (SMEs), were relaxed.

On 24th March 2020; *considering the massive economic disruption due to COVID-19, the **PTI govt announced an economic bailout package of PKR 1.2 trillion** as a part of its immediate response to COVID-19.* Key fiscal measures included:

- *Import duties on health equipment eliminated*

- *PKR 200 billion allocated to provide financial support to daily wage workers*

- *PKR 150 billion allocated to be distributed amongst low-income families*

- *PKR 100 billion allocated for tax relief for the exporters*

- *PKR 100 billion allocated for support of SMEs.*

The bailout package also allocated <u>PKR 280 billion for procurement of wheat, PKR 50 billion to utility stores</u> to ensure the provision of essentials at subsidized rates, <u>PKR 70 billion to provide relief in fuel prices, PKR 15 billion to support food</u> and health supplies, <u>PKR 110 billion to subsidize electricity prices</u>, <u>PKR 100 billion as an emergency</u> contingency fund and <u>PKR 25 billion to the National Disaster Management Authority</u> (NDMA) to buy essential equipment to deal with the pandemic.

The provincial governments also announced various economic initiatives, broadly revolving around tax relief, speedy upgrading of the healthcare system and cash grants to low-income families. The provincial government of Punjab gave a PKR 18 billion tax relief package as well as a **PKR 10 billion cash grant program**, whereas the provincial government of Sindh commenced a PKR 1.5 billion ration distribution program for the poorest of the poor.

The said economic stimulus package was remarkable, many of the items listed in it were made part of the federal budget but interestingly, the bulk of the allocated money remained unutilized, which was later presented as a new allocation.

While the IMF had lauded the bailout package given by the PTI government to help the economic sector to recuperate from the COVID-19 shock, it pegged the package to be 1.2% of the GDP. Furthermore, in response to the pandemic and to give business people much-needed relief, the State Bank of Pakistan (SBP) made a series of revisions to the benchmark interest rate. Prior to COVID-19, in January 2020, the SBP retained the interest rate at 13.25 percent, which it stated was necessary due to high inflation rates. However, in a period of just five months, from mid-march to June, the SBP drastically reduced the interest rate by 625 basic points to 7 percent.

While this move was applauded by most businessmen, economists remained sceptical as to whether it would be able to generate economic activity as the pandemic prolonged. Generally, states across the globe wanted to end their lockdowns, enforced to curb the spread of the pandemic, as soon as possible to begin the economic rejuvenation process. However, states that were facing numerous economic challenges before the pandemic, like Pakistan, were facing tremendous pressure to lift the lockdown. A substantial part of Pakistan's population was engaged in the informal economy; thus, a long lockdown would have had a detrimental effect on a large segment of the society.

The areas of south-western Baluchistan and north-western Khyber PK, which were adjacent to the borders, got badly affected as borders remained closed for many weeks. Major economic generation of both these areas comes from the services industry related to cross-border trade; thus, economic hardships were faced by the locals. According to Rafiullah Kakar, the Director of the Strategic Planning and Reforms Cell, Government of Balochistan, the lockdown inflicted a loss of PKR 60–90 billion on the province.

On 23rd April 2020; in the federal health ministry, immediate structural adjustments commenced complementing the pandemic response. The PM Khan's team launched a PKR 595 million Pakistan Preparedness and Response Plan (PPRP) to help contain and quash the COVID-19 outbreak. The PPRP aimed to strengthen Pakistan's capacity in prevention, preparedness, response and relief, as well as its health system, within nine months - by December 2020. The PTI called for all stakeholders to join hands, use their expertise and forces and exploit all available resources to help execute an organized response at the federal and provincial levels. The following were the key determinants of the PPRP:

1. Increase and enhance emergency response systems to ensure a collective society approach

2. Initiate large-scale COVID-19 public awareness campaigns

3. Establish necessary facilities to curb COVID-19: mass testing, contact tracing and isolation wards

4. State-of-the-art surveillance mechanism to determine the origins of the virus outbreak and monitor virus outbreak trends

5. Implement health measures to ensure effective social distancing to curb the transmission rate

6. Ensure that laboratories should be equipped with polymerase chain reaction (PCR) testing kits to adequately test and detect the virus

7. Upgrade the health system to deal with the surge in patients, especially ensuring an ample stock of medical supplies

8. Provision of emergency food rations and cash transfers.

Further, to ease Pakistan's external economic burden, many international economic institutions came forward to provide the direly needed economic assistance in the form of loans, aid and grants. On 2nd April 2020, a US$200 million economic stimulus package for Pakistan was approved by the World Bank. Furthermore, on 16th April 2020, the IMF approved a US$1.386 billion financial assistance package for Pakistan so that Pakistan could resolve the urgent balance of payment crisis that had emerged due to the COVID-19 outbreak. Also in April 2020, the Islamic Development Bank (IDB) agreed to give Pakistan a US$650m financial package to fight against the pandemic.

In addition, on 19th May 2020, the Asian Development Bank (ADB) gave a US$300 million emergency assistance loan to Pakistan. Surprisingly, these support packages and loans were issued to ease the economic blow of pandemic; however, the budget report of the fiscal year 2020 showed that the country had experienced negative growth. The dependency paradigm repeatedly claimed that international financial institutions, which were / and are dominated by the developed world, never helped the developing countries in good conscience, and that it was at most a show staged by the developed world to glorify its sincerity to help resolve the problems of the developing states; what a pity state of affairs.

In Pakistan's case, to help battle COVID-19, a similar approach was adopted by international financial institutions by providing economic assistance which was very low compared to the amount required to stabilize Pakistan's economy. In short, the mitigation measures adopted by the PTI regime were able to provide relief to the masses despite huge limitations.

On 1st APRIL 2022; Minister for Planning & Development Asad Umar announced CLOSURE of the National Command and Operation Centre (NCOC) operations, partly because of all-time low COVID-19 indicators and partly because of high level of vaccination.

DECISIONS IN WAKE OF COVID-19:

On 26th March 2020; in the wake of coronavirus threat, Islamabad High Court (IHC) ordered to release *twenty-four under trial suspects in various corruption-related references filed by the National Accountability Bureau (NAB)*. Divisional bench of IHC comprising CJ Athar Minallah and Justice Amir Farooq ordered to release such suspects being tried in fake bank accounts case, *Modharba* and *Karke* references. Amongst the released persons in custody, some big names were: Mustafa Zulqarnain, Khawaja Suleman, Hussain Lawai, Liaquat Qaimkhani and Dr Dansha; Hussain Lawai, who was said to be a close aide of former president Asif Ali Zardari, facing investigation / ennuiry in a Rs:35 billion money laundering case, was arrested by the Federal Investigation Agency (FIA) on 6th July 2018.

The court issued order in the wake of spread of the epidemic coronavirus in the country. The NAB prosecutor had opposed the decision; Justice Athar Minallah remarked that sentence for such offences against them was not more than fourteen years but they were in risk of their lives in the jail. The judge also said that '*under trial suspects are considered innocent until the trial concluded.*' The court then issued orders for the release of such 24 prisoners. The IHC had earlier granted bail to 408 prisoners imprisoned at Adiala Jail under minor offences amid coronavirus fears.

On 31st March 2020; the Economic Coordination Committee (ECC) of the Cabinet under Chairmanship of Advisor to PM on Finance Dr Abdul Hafeez Shaikh approved the relief package of Rs1.2 trillion including Rs 100 billion supplementary grant for the Emergency Relief Fund to combat COVID-19 Virus. Adviser Finance Dr Shaikh held that the PTI govt was keen to fulfil the necessary requirements for different relief measures already announced by the PM Khan for the public relief in the Corona Virus Pandemic.

The approval to fiscal stimulus package of Rs:1.2 trillion also included Rs: 100 billion Supplementary Grant for the **Residual-Emergency Relief Fund** in terms of Article 84(a) of the Constitution for mitigating the effects of COVID-19. The ECC also approved special package for relief to 12 million poor families **through cash assistance under the Ehsaas Program**. It was aimed to provide cash grants under the regular **Kafalat program** and Emergency Cash Assistance on the recommendation of the district administration. The assistance was initially provided for four months and besides the BISP beneficiaries it was one-time dispensation. The cash was to be provided in one instalment of Rs:12000 through Kafalat partner banks i.e Bank Alfalah and Habib Bank Limited after biometric verification.

The partner banks were asked to make arrangements through branchless banking networks *to disburse cash*. *Rs:72.9 billion of additional funds* through technical supplementary grant were given to BISP under '**Ehsaas Cash Assistance Package in Response to COVID-19**'. After Ministry of

Industries and Production presented a comprehensive proposal regarding the targeting parameters, implementation mechanism, cash assistance per family per month and financial phasing of the program, ECC approved *Rs:200 billion of cash assistance for the daily wagers* working in the formal industrial sector and were laid off as a result of COVID-19 outbreak.

It was estimated that around three million workers could fall in the said category and they were to be paid a minimum wage of Rs.17500 per month. The estimated cost of that *provision for daily wagers was around Rs: 52.5 billion a month*. ECC directed that immediate consultation with the provincial labour departments should be carried out for providing timely assistance to those who were in need.

The ECC also approved Rs:50 billion for Utility Stores Corporation (USC) to provide essential food items to the vulnerable section of the society at subsidized rates. USC prepared an initial plan to deliver 9 essential food items @ Rs:3000 for a family of 2+4 people through Pakistan Post Foundation Logistics Division. USC further planned to procure essential items within 2-3 weeks; USC also engaged with BISP to obtain data for targeted assistance and again came back to the ECC with a detailed proposal for reaching out to the poor families for effective use of this package before making any expenditure from that amount.

- *The ECC also approved Rs:75 billion for FBR to enable them to payback the sales tax and income tax refunds, duty drawbacks and customs duties which was due for the last 10 years. The amount was given to help 676,055 beneficiaries by improving their liquidity position.*

The ECC also allowed reducing different taxes and duties on import and supply of different food items for alleviating the adverse impact of COVID-19 on different segments of the society. *Rate of advance tax on the import of different pulses was reduced to 0% from 2%.* individuals and associations of persons providing tea, spices, dry milk and salt to USC without a brand name were to pay 1.5% withholding tax instead of 4.5%. Individuals and companies receiving payments from USC for supplying ghee, sugar, pulses, and wheat flour were to be charged 1.5% withholding tax instead of 4.5% earlier. *ACD (additional customs duty) @ 2% on soya bean oil, canola oil, palm oil and sunflower oil (and on those four oil seeds) was also exempted.*

- *The ECC also approved the supplementary grant of Rs:30 billion to Ministry of Commerce to payback duty drawbacks to textile*

> *exporters in the said financial year to improve their liquidity position. ECC was briefed that SBP was working on payment of claims worth Rs:49 billion out of which around 40 billion were to be paid by June 2020.*

The ECC approved supplementary grant of Rs:6 billion for Pakistan Railways to meet its expenses. Pakistan Railways had suspended its passenger train services around the country since 19th March 2020. The approved amount was utilized for paying salaries to 70,000 employees, repairs, paying for utilities and performing disinfectant sprays on platforms and inside trains for proving safe journey to the passengers. Those days, Pakistan Railways was earning only 1/6th of its monthly income through coal freight and the rest of its transport activity was suspended.

On 3rd April 2020; while announcing package for the construction industry, PM Imran Khan told the media that it was important to strike balance between lockdown and coming up economic recession. He said:

> *"In Pakistan, on one hand, you have the corona-virus and on the other hand, you have to deal with hunger. A lockdown imposed only in Defence or Gulberg will not be successful; the success of lockdown will depend on whether the poor will get food at their home or not."*

The PM cited China's example, saying that authorities had locked down Wuhan but that measure went successful as the government provided food to people at their doorsteps. '*We, as a nation, will fight [this disease] but no one can say what will happen in the next two to three weeks.*'

STATE-WRIT FLOUTED BY THE CLERGY:

> *"The history of the clergy classes of the world is replete with peculiarities. Its retrogressive policies and conservative approaches towards social issues has always proved that this class is bereft of foresight. Its inflexibility hindered the development of sciences throughout the Middle Age while also roasting critical thinking that is crucial for any healthy society. Its abandonment of logic and reason led to fatal ramifications for nations.*
>
> *The sins of this so-called sacred class do not end here. It not only gave a superstitious colour to every natural calamity, disease and pestilence but also came up with bizarre recipes to cure the ill. From epilepsy to*

plague and cancer to HIV, it described every disease as a divine wrath which could only be tided over through rituals etc."

journalist Abdul Sattar's essay in **daily THENEWS** dated 31st March 2020 is referred.

It's on record that some sections of the Hindu clergy in India had asked their followers to drink cow's urine to cure the coronavirus AND when some from the religious right in Pakistan had urged their followers to eat pigeons' flesh. But for students of history, the phenomenon was not much surprising; it was what a large section of the clergy has been doing throughout the history. From the inquisition in Spain to the persecution of scientists in Europe (and) to the tormenting of rationalists in the Islamic world, it becomes clear how the said class of clergy in all religions think.

Such attitude often added to the miseries of people. For instance, the covid-19 outbreak in Iran would not have been as worse had the clergy of Iran not tried to impose its religious mind-set on vast majority of their people, leaving them *in a state of denial first and ignoring the advice of Iranian health experts.* Even advanced America, facing an impending humanitarian catastrophe, was not immune to the eccentricities of the reactionary class. An incumbent of the Oval Office was an ardent supporter of evangelical Christians whose worldly view was not much different from their ideological brothers and sisters living in other Christian atates of the world. Their stubbornness prompted them to reject all pleas of precaution and restraint.

Journalist Abdul Sattar, in above cited reference, wrote details of Pakistani clergy-men's apathy and indifference:

> *"This was what the religious clergy did in Pakistan. Despite the request of the Punjab government,* **the Tableeghi Jamaat held their massive congregation in Lahore** *attracting tens of thousands of people. Some estimates suggest more than 100,000 people attended the gathering between 11-13th March 2020, initially meant to last until 15th March. Gulf News put the number at 250,000 while insiders of the Tableeghi Jamaat claimed more than 500,000 attended the 'spiritual gathering'. The event was believed to be one of the major factors contributing to the spike in coronavirus cases across the country then. A number of people who returned to Sindh, Islamabad and other parts of the country carried the virus with them. Some of them had caught virus immediately after while others were forced to be quarantined.*

> *The activities of this organization were not confined to this gathering only. <u>They continued their weekly gatherings (called Shab-e-Juma) across their mosques in the country besides holding a three-day congregation (called Seh Roza) in every major city until got to be admitted in nearby hospitals.</u> Annual regional gatherings in areas like Bajaur also remained reportedly unabated while the three-day long congregation ended on <u>22nd March 2020</u> in Mardan, which was one of the worst corona-affected areas of Khyber PK province.*
>
> *<u>The Jamaat also formed preaching teams in Lahore and elsewhere, sending them to various parts of the country.</u> One such team roamed about several streets of an area in Islamabad forcing the authorities to lock down the vicinity after the members of the Jamaat tested positive for corona. The Sindh government had to quarantine over 40 people, including foreigners, in Sukkar after it was learnt that they had attended the religious gathering in Lahore."*

Pakistan reported its first case of corona by the end of February 2020 (*it was an unofficial report while officially reported TWO CASES appeared in media during mid-March 2020*). Merely a 16,000 gathering of the preaching group in Malaysia towards end of the same month had sowed the seeds of a health catastrophe there. Perhaps at the time when the World Health Organization (WHO) was deliberating over the hazards of the outbreak, the people were busy appeasing the powerful clergy by turning a blind eye to the preparations for this massive gathering.

The global health body declared it a pandemic on the day this huge gathering kicked off, *making a mockery of the state's writ which was otherwise throwing vegetables of push-cart sellers, beating up young men riding a bike and employing sledgehammer tactics against the weak.* But it chose to ignore the flood of humans **in Raiwind** likely to wreak havoc with the lives of thousands of Pakistanis besides putting the health system of the country into confusion and dismay.

The said gathering at **Raiwind** (Lahore) raised several important questions. The *Tableeghi Jamaat* projects itself as a law-abiding organization, then why did it not cancel the event? *Why did the prime minister appease Maulana Tariq Jamil instead of demonstrating the resolve of the state by having the event cancelled?* Tableeghis from Palestine and Kyrgyzstan had caught corona-virus or not - the event and its fatal ramifications were enough to convince our clergy for suspension of all types of gatherings.

What was done couldn't be undone; the government had to make hectic efforts to test mostly those who attended the gathering and quarantined them. It didn't mean that only one religious group was responsible for the outbreak and the impending catastrophe. A *Barelvi* cleric announced a huge gathering in Lahore, assuring no one would be affected while some *Shia* organisations in Karachi insisted on taking out mourning processions too. *All such groups could have received a clear message from the state – instead an announcement of PKR 1.2 trillion Covid-Package from a debt-ridden poor country.*

- A COGENT POINT TO PONDER: *Why the PTI govt, like all previous govts in such situations, immediately resorted for announcing CASH-DISTRIBUTIONS TO THE POOR worth billions – simply because the CORRUPT BUREAUCRACY kept the same mind-set in all governments. Was it the time to clear ALL PENDING CLAIMS OF EXPORTERS, FBR FILERS & COMMERCIAL TRADERS while front desks staff at hospitals and health facilities were without PPEs; doctors and nurses were losing their lives who had caught the deadly virus? They didn't need media applause but proper protection.*

Additionally, all political leadership, Senators, Law-makers, Generals, High Judges, high bureaucrats and Corporate-Managers & Administrators could have donated their salaries & perks to the fight against corona. Millions were suffering because of the lockdowns including those employees who were laid off by their employers.

COVID-19: PAKISTAN's ECONOMY:

Due to COVID-19 outbreak, the economy of Pakistan was in a trouble like other countries *but there was no threat of it collapsing*. It changed with the pandemic; the country's economy came up virtually on the brink of bankruptcy as, unlike other states, Pakistan didn't possess the required resources to provide the much-needed huge bailout packages to maintain and sustain its already crippled economy.

Over the years, Pakistan's GDP growth rate had never been that remarkable but there was consistent improvement. However, after Pakistan took the latest International Monetary Fund (IMF) programme in 2019, which had conditions like substantially reducing the current account deficit, its GDP growth took a massive hit. In the fiscal year 2018, Pakistan's GDP growth was approximately 5.5 percent, which came down to 3.3 percent in the fiscal year 2019, and the majority of the economic experts, as well as institutions, had projected that for year 2020, Pakistan's GDP growth rate would further fall to 2.4pc. After COVID-19 took Pakistan into its grasp, forcing major disruptions in the country's economic activities, the result was that *for the second time in Pakistan's history, after 1951–1952, it experienced a negative GDP growth rate; –0.4 percent for the fiscal year 2020.*

The dependency paradigm could explain Pakistan's constant average GDP growth rate and its dependence on global financial institutions. After COVID-19 took over the world, the international financial institutions did not have the required resources to bail out countries like Pakistan; thus, their economic conditions rapidly deteriorated. Furthermore, *with COVID-19 came with a huge wave of unemployment and poverty,* meaning more misery and hardship for the masses. In the fiscal year 2018, Pakistan's unemployment rate stood at 5.8 percent – showing an improvement from the year before. However, as COVID-19 struck Pakistan, *in few months, 3 million people lost their jobs, and the unemployment rate rocketed to 9.56pc for the year 2020;* //www.ncbi.nlm.nih.gov (PMC10014452) dated 13th March 2023 is referred.

Also, *millions of people were pushed into poverty due to COVID-19 in Pakistan; to be exact 18 million people; the poverty population increased from 69 million (31.3 %) in 2018 to 87 million in 2020.* The Western economic / developmental model followed by Pakistan was more or less responsible for such a staggering unemployment rate, as predicted by the dependency paradigm. Pakistan was unable to develop and implement, as had been its history, a tailor-made development scheme as per its complex ground realities; as advocated by dependency theory, the unemployment crisis couldn't be controlled in an effective manner.

In addition, not only did COVID-19 greatly disrupt global trade, but also it had profound implications on Pakistan's exports and imports, adversely affecting its overall economy. In the fiscal year 2020, Pakistan's exports shrunk to US$22 billion, which was US$1.51 billion less than in the fiscal year 2019, representing a 6.36pc decrease [*Ref: Trend Economy, 2021*]. Meanwhile, in the fiscal year 2020, Pakistan's imports also decreased by 8.56 percent as compared to in the fiscal year 2019 – US$45 billion in 2020 and US$50 billion in 2019, showing a net difference of US$5 billion. If the relationship between the developed and developing world were cooperative in nature, then during COVID-19 special subsidies could have been given to Pakistan to help balance its trade deficit and manage its current account deficit. However, no support was given by the developed world, thus reiterating the stance of dependency theory that *'the developed world economically exploits mostly the developing / underdeveloped world.'*

Resultantly, COVID-19 considerably slowed down economic activity in Pakistan. For the fiscal year 2020, initially, the government set a tax collection target of PKR 5.5 trillion. Interestingly, even before COVID-19 emerged as a threat, Pakistan's tax collection target was revised twice; in December 2019 to PKR 5.2 trillion, and in February 2020 to PKR 4.8 trillion. However, *none of these targets were met, especially after COVID-19 hit Pakistan, only PKR 3.9 trillion revenue was collected* – identical to the amount collected in the previous three fiscal years. On the contrary, Pakistan's spennding increased by PKR:2.1 trillion, further coercing the already stressed and strained economy.

Moreover, COVID-19 significantly challenged the living standards of the common person in Pakistan, as a record inflation rate was witnessed and the per capita income dropped remarkably. In the fiscal year 2016, the inflation rate in Pakistan was at an all-time low of 2.86 percent, with low inflation years in the preceding years - 4.15 percent in 2017, 3.93 percent in 2018 and 6.74 percent in 2019 - until COVID-19 hit and disrupted life and the inflation rate jumped to a staggering 10.74 percent in the fiscal year 2020.

During Covid-19, the *per capita income in Pakistan fell drastically from US$1625 in the fiscal year 2019 to US$1325 in the fiscal year 2020.* Since its independence, time and again, Pakistan's economic agenda has been more or less dictated by the West-led international financial institutions. Dependency theory states that the policymakers of the developing / underdeveloped world intentionally implement an economic system, at the behest of the developed world, that safeguards the interests of the developed world at the expense of their own citizens, hence the persisting underdevelopment and dismal economic conditions of Pakistan.

Pakistan's public finances remained unsafe and risky during that whole decade. However, the COVID-19 situation greatly increased the country's difficulties when it came to debt servicing. *In the fiscal year 2018, Pakistan's total debts and liabilities were US$95.2 billion, with the exchange rate at Rs:121.54, whereas in the fiscal year 2020 these debts soared up to US$112.8 billion, while the exchange rate was at Rs: 162.2.* The enormous increase in the exchange rate coupled with taking more loans means that Pakistan had slipped into the debt trap – taking new loans to pay back old ones. Strikingly, the then prevailing paradigm predicted a vicious cycle that the developing world found itself trapped in, being largely dependent on the West. The famous proverb that beggars can't be choosers explains Pakistan's helplessness vis-a-vis its economic affairs then.

The COVID-19 virus infected Pakistan's economy through three transmission channels. It affected the aggregate demand, owing to the steps taken to contain the transmission of the virus, which not only slowed down the economy but also substantially increased the unemployment rate. These layoffs decreased the disposable income of many households, thus causing a demand shock across the economy. Consequently, the aggregate demand considerably shrunk, not only adversely affecting Pakistan's economic outlook but also altering the lifestyle of the common person.

In short, Pakistan's economy was undoubtedly in turmoil even before the COVID-19 crisis emerged. However, the COVID-19 situation exacerbated the situation since most, if not all, economic parameters, such as GDP growth rate, unemployment rate, inflation, per capita income, debt, tax collection, poverty and trade (imports / exports), showed a substantial decline.

WORLD-OPINION ABOUT COVID-19 IN PAKISTAN:

> *It was said that PTI govt's one misstep – lifting lockdown too soon – had placed **Pakistan among the twelve countries hardest hit by coronavirus – but it was not the whole truth**. Provinces could make their own health decisions and focus on helping citizens in need – and they did so as their resources allowed them.*

See an **ANALYTICAL REPORT** from *//www.crisisgroup.org* dated 6th August 2020:

> *"Hoping to mitigate COVID-19's economic toll, Imran Khan's PTI government lifted a countrywide lockdown in May 2020 (mainly because) **the public, misled by the clergy and mixed messaging from the religious mercenaries, disregarded precautions during religious festivities and ceremonies**.*
>
> *Climbing infection rates could overwhelm ill-equipped health systems and hinder economic recovery. (Even then) citizens are*

seldom denied health care or basic aid though the economy was shrunk; public tolerated the short-comings, though potentially threatened their social order.... The federal government also permitted the provinces to devise their own local strategies guided by medical experts...."

On 9th May 2020; Imran Khan's PTI government almost completely lifted a nationwide lockdown it had imposed in late March to counter COVID-19; Pakistan subsequently saw a little surge in cases. The government justified the easing of nationwide restrictions on economic grounds; indeed, the lockdown's toll on the most vulnerable, workers and the poor were brutal indeed. Yet signs of economic recovery since it was lifted were few, while the virus continued to threaten the ill-equipped and under-funded health systems. Rising anger and alienation among citizens were negligent – not sure if the ruling PTI had liaison with their political rivals on its coronavirus strategy.

The govt's mixed messaging aside, misinformation from some religious leaders overtly showed that many Pakistanis were flouting and disobeying the public health advice at their own will. Pandemic's health risks led to widespread public disregard for social distancing procedures. *The removal of restrictions on communal prayers in mosques though increased the risks of new virus clusters – but the populace was happy. Many clerics advocated religious practices that undercut physical distancing and other preventive measures; they told worshippers that piety alone, and not health practices, would determine their fate.* Officially lifting of the lockdown on 9th May 2020, in fact, encouraged public complacency - many believed that the pandemic was over in Pakistan.

PTI government's adoption of what it called **SMALL LOCKDOWN STRATEGY** was logically explained. The strategy entailed removing restrictions in specific areas within cities or regions where the authorities assessed that case rates were relatively low. But poor data and low testing rates had hampered efforts to *track, trace and quarantine*, which were essential to curbing the virus. With COVID-19 spreading in densely populated cities such as Karachi, Lahore and Peshawar, limited closures were unlikely to prevent contagion – but it worked well. While city hospitals were better prepared to deal with the pandemic, they were able to deal with the surge, though with difficulty, as the *Eidul-Azha* was ahead. Next month of Muharram was more dangerous in the wake of large mourning processions; people were ready to accept the consequence – but not ready to take care of state instructions.

The virus had also spread to rural regions, where the health infrastructure was weaker. The federal government's centralized decision-making people often refused to share authority with their political opponents. Islamabad's pandemic policies, devised by the top political and military leadership, prevailed over provincial preferences, with court rulings strengthening centralized control. The Pakistan Peoples Party (PPP)'s govt in Sindh, the sole opposition-led province, had promoted rigorous restrictions, for instance, and they were able to implement them in a befitting manner.

Anger at the government and social tensions could mount had the citizens sensed that the PTI government was not adequately looking after their health and wellbeing. While COVID-19 left PTI government few good options, there was no big harm to lives and livelihoods as compared to the rest of the world. Prime Minister Khan's fears about the toll of lockdowns were well justified. Yet the economy was unlikely to start moving. Adapting the *smart lockdown strategy* devotedly saved the people from pain of a prolonged lockdown while still saving lives. However, emergency assistance to families under the poverty line and unemployed workers remained uncertain.

The PTI's critics held that there were some slip-ups at the earlier stage of Covid-19 in Pakistan but it was misunderstood for being a poor country ruled by an inexperienced party. In February (2020), the government refused to repatriate hundreds of Pakistani students in Wuhan, China, fearing they would spread the virus; in itself, the decision was quite sensible. The government had to quarantine hundreds of students, might be in overcrowded & unhygienic conditions, but helped the international community.

The first major cluster of locally transmitted infections occurred when CM Buzdar's Punjab government delayed a decision to cancel the Sunni preaching group *Tableeghi Jamaat's major annual congregation (ijtema)*, scheduled for five days from 11th March. The organizers though had cancelled the *ijtema on the 3rd day*, but till then an estimated 100,000 believers, including around 3,000 foreigners, had already set up their camps together. After its cancellation, most participants left, but a few hundred stayed on at the organization's headquarters. Later, they were allowed to leave for their home provinces without being tested or isolated. (***The episode has already been discussed in detail in earlier paragraphs.***)

The world media alleged that the PTI government was slow to respond when the pandemic spread. The first cabinet meeting devoted to the subject was held on 13th March 2020, 15 days after the first confirmed case in Karachi. At a time when political consensus was most needed in forging a national response to the pandemic, the PTI's relationship with the two major opposition parties remained strained, as before. By mid-March, cases of local transmission began to mount in densely populated cities such as Karachi, Lahore and Peshawar. Not known if the two opposition parties had offered to cooperate to counter the pandemic. The PTI govt, however, chose to sideline parliament – mostly known for futile debates on non-issues.

On 23rd March 2020; Sindh's PPP government was the first to impose a province-wide lockdown. PM Khan, who himself held the federal health portfolio, initially ruled out a countrywide closure, saying it would adversely affect the poor and working class; SMART LOCK-DOWN STRATEGY is referred. The military weighed in, supporting a lockdown and deploying troops countrywide to assist civilian administrations in enforcing it. Hours after the prime minister's address, the federal govt reversed course, agreeing to impose a nationwide shutdown, which it subsequently extended until ending May 2020.

The 3-party-controlled provinces, Balochistan, Khyber PK and Punjab, also imposed lockdowns. Yet, apparently guided by the prime minister's aversion to those measures, they opted for looser restrictions, particularly in Punjab, which soon allowed several types of businesses to reopen. Inter-provincial coordination remained poor, echoing friction between PM Khan and his political opponents. The main bodies responsible, set up in mid-March, reflected the government leadership's preference for a centralized approach.

On 13th March 2020; the National Security Committee, the apex civil-military body, set up a *National Coordination Committee for COVID-19*, chaired by the prime minister and including Army Chief Gen Bajwa, the four provincial chief ministers and senior military officers. **The National Command and Operation Centre**, which was tasked to send the committee recommendations on pandemic policy, was headed by the federal minister for planning and included relevant federal and provincial ministers and also several senior military officers. The stated objective of setting up those two bodies was to bring the federal and provincial governments and military leadership together. *In principle, responsibility for the health sector should have remained with the provinces, not the capital.* In practice, however, the top political leadership in the center controlled pandemic policy, in coordination with the provincial concerns.

On **14th April 2020:** Prime Minister Khan extended the nationwide lockdown for another two weeks but had also relaxed restrictions. Several non-essential industries, including construction, reopened. Khan said there was '*98 per cent consensus among all provinces and the center on the reopening of some sectors*' - yet the Sindh government disagreed. Judicial intervention, however, strengthened the center's control over pandemic policy. In a *suo moto* hearing on the virus crisis in mid-April, the Supreme Court called for a uniform policy, warning Sindh not to close businesses and services that generate revenue for federation.

The critics also alleged that PTI government's mixed messaging about the pandemic left the public confused about its gravity. Early in the crisis, in a televised address on 17th March 2020, Prime Minister Khan had downplayed health risks; saying *'There is no reason to worry'* - since 90pc of the infected would have mild flu-type symptoms and 97pc would recover fully. The brave Pakistani people, however, liked their leaders' courage and valor.

A mid-April 2020 decision to reopen mosques for communal prayers was taken ill by the rest of the world whereas the people in Pakistan took it just as their routine activity. In the beginning, provincial govts had barred mosques from holding communal prayers; could go open only for administrators and staff. The police were tasked with enforcing the restrictions in major cities but clerics mostly violated the orders and state instructions.

Islamabad's police registered cases but made no arrests when Lal (Red) mosque's hardline clerics openly violated restrictions. Clerical leader Abdul Aziz released footage of large congregations attending Friday prayers. When the police tried to barricade the mosque's entrance, female madrasa students blocked the road. The PTI government hesitated in taking action against the Lal Masjid clerics, fearing a repeat of the bloody July 2007 standoff, when a military operation against heavily armed jihadists in the mosque had left 100 militants and eleven soldiers dead.

On **18th April 2020;** President Arif Alvi agreed with major religious leaders to *reopen mosques nationwide for communal, including taraweeh prayers* – but under certain health & safety precautionary conditions - including social distancing. Justifying the decision, Prime Minister Khan said he was heeding popular demand; saying: *"Pakistan is an independent nation, Ramadan is a month of worship, and people want to go to mosques. His government would not forcibly tell them not to do so"*.

Thus, thousands prayed in packed mosques, ignoring health measures and creating new hot-spots of viral infection. Many clerics rather stressed worshippers to demonstrate piety by praying shoulder to shoulder, warning that the pandemic is a punishment for erring Muslims' sins. As a result, many who regularly used to attend mosques either believed they would not contract the virus or that prayer would protect them. *Many also chose not to get tested or treated due to religious and social stigma attached to the disease – AND* the fact remains that the FAITH really worked in Pakistan then.

On 9th May 2020; the federal government ended the lockdown. Prime Minister Khan insisted that the decision was taken with the provinces' consensus. The Punjab and Balochistan governments warned against lifting restrictions BUT the judiciary again weighed in. On 19th May 2020, *during the coronavirus suo moto case hearings, the Supreme Court noted that provinces were constitutionally bound to follow Islamabad's directives.*

- *The PTI's federal government said it would lift the lockdown in phases but* by mid-June the country was almost fully open for business. *Schools remained closed but all markets and shopping centres were operating and restrictions on most non-essential businesses had been removed. Borders with Iran and Afghanistan were re-opened, domestic and international flights resumed, and several train services started up again, as did local public transport. Punjab re-opened its shrines that attracted large number of visitor daily.*

Prime Minister Khan's justifications for lifting the lockdown were twofold: the burden on the poor & working class, and the adverse impact on the national economy. Announcing the National Coordination Committee's decision to cancel the closures on 7th May 2020, he said:

> *"We are doing it because people are facing extreme difficulties. Small business owners, daily wage earners and labourers are suffering. We fear that small and medium-sized industries might vanish completely if we don't lift the lockdown".*

A week earlier, the federal minister heading the National Command and Operation Centre said the government's revenues were otherwise falling by 30-35pc. The pandemic had seriously compounded Pakistan's already grave economic challenges. Pakistan's economy was in dire straits - large-scale manufacturing declined, exports fallen, the budget deficit widened and unemployment had increased. Remittances, a vital source of foreign exchange, were likely to shrink as thousands of workers in the Gulf had come home. The GDP contracted by 0.38 percent for the fiscal year 2019-2020.

The PTI government's goal in lifting the lockdown was to get the economy moving but very little there was. Till about four months later, signs of economic recovery were still crawling. The federal government provided emergency assistance to families in need, including food subsidies and support, but being a poor country that aid was barely enough. *The Ehsaas emergency cash program provided financial assistance to an estimated twelve million families who were living under the poverty line* - AND had extended the program to provide a similar amount to four million unemployed workers all over the country.

Prime Minister Khan held: '... *the cash disbursement program can only be a temporary solution, which is why the lockdown was lifted. There's no way the government can give out handouts to feed people for that long*'. At the same time, the government's financial resources were strained to move ahead smoothly. As unemployment was further up, more citizens were falling under the poverty line day by day.

It was (and still is) a hard fact that Pakistan's under-funded health care system remained ill-equipped to deal with an unprecedented public health emergency like Covid-19. Medical professionals repeatedly called for a stringent nationwide lockdown then but the government, concerned about the economic costs, had to ignore their advice. Professional bodies of doctors countrywide had issued similar calls for a nationwide closure to contain the disease's spread both before 9th May and afterward – but economy didn't allow the state to follow the developed world's norms.

As per figures available on foreign media, by 9th May 2020, when the lockdown was lifted, the total number of cases was around 29,000 and the death toll was 637. About six weeks later, the total number of cases and the death toll stood three times multiplied – but the PTI govt didn't bother as it had no funds to match the SOPs of the western states. In early June, the World Health Organization's country head in Pakistan recommended imposing targeted and intermittent two-week-on - two-week-off lockdowns. Health experts quickly supported his recommendation. But the prime minister's health adviser said: '... *the WHO has assessed Pakistan's situation through a health lens and that the PTI government has to make tough policy choices to strike a balance between lives and livelihoods.*'

AND the smart lockdowns were launched and stressed; the government eased or removed them altogether in low-risk areas. In mid-June, provincial governments imposed two-week lockdowns in city-areas such as Karachi, Lahore and Peshawar. The government argued that such limited lockdowns could contain virus spread without economic hardship. According to Pak-official statistics, the daily number of confirmed cases had declined considerably since mid-July. However, <u>by 2nd August 2020,</u> *Pakistan had around 280,200 registered cases and nearly 6,000 deaths, ranking 13th amongst COVID-19 affected countries globally* (in terms of total cases) – however, the figures were far less than in European countries.

The *smart lockdown's track, trace and quarantine strategy*, which involved tracing and isolating virus carriers and their contacts and placing viral hot-spots under quarantine, was allegedly hampered by poor data and low testing rates. *According to the National Command Operation Centre, testing capacity had increased to over 70,000 by early July;* however, the then coming-up religious holidays had threatened another uptick. The affected people were more during Ramadan in June - Eidul Fitr contributed to the first surge of infections as massive crowds went for shopping in markets and large congregations prayed in mosques. This time, case numbers were increasing substantially in smaller cities and rural regions due to weaker health facilities there.

A little later, placing the onus of preventing contagion on citizens appeared at the heart of a new strategy – *'Living with the Pandemic.'*. A rethink was urgently needed – but government's weak financial position was in everyone's mind. However, it was felt that the parliament could play a more active role, particularly with regard to fiscal and other assistance for the most vulnerable sections of the population. The military leadership was already in as an equal partner in the pandemic response. Yet citizens always hold the elected leadership accountable had the pandemic response faltered.

SCENARIO 246

FAIZABAD *'DHARNA'* CASE VERDICT (2019)

Historically **Dharna** is a Hindi word for a non-violent sit-in protest to receive fast justice, state response or payment of a debt. The word originates from the Sanskrit word Dharna. In the time of all India, when there was the colonial system, Dharna was used as a popular form of public protest to express strong disagreement, disapproval and opposition to some action or something. It was also used as part of Mahatma Gandhi's *Satyagraha* form of civil disobedience and protest during Indian Independence Movement.

BACKGROUND OF 2017's *DHARNA* CASE:

On 8th November 2017: Thousands of green-turbaned religious foot soldiers of the *Tehreek-e-Labaik Pakistan* [TLP] managed to paralyse Islamabad and Rawalpindi by blocking the main link between the twin cities inter-provincial traffic. They were led by one Khadim Hussain Rizvi, a religious leader whose entry in the federal capital was banned by the government then.

The Faizabad sit-in was a worrying example of the state and government being held hostage by a religious group largely ambiguous. Hundreds of thousands of commuters use the Expressway to enter the federal capital from areas on its periphery every day. Even on the best of days, a minor accident or blockade can result in miles-long traffic jams. Sit-in of religious zealots over a change in law that had already been reversed was made an issue.

The government and city administration started out by deploying huge containers on main roads to block the influx of protesters. This threw traffic into a tailspin. By the morning of 9th November, patients were unable to get medical attention, students could not attend classes and people could not make it to their workplaces and offices. The city governments of the two districts were totally incapacitated. The point to mention is that demand to reverse a change in the law pertaining to the finality of prophet-hood had already been accepted and the PMLN government had made it the respective law.

However, the TLP group was vying to raise its public profile. TLP had joined electoral politics and bagged over 7,000 votes in the by-polls for NA-120 following Nawaz Sharif's disqualification. Since the PMLN was concerned about religious parties like TLP causing a dent in its vote bank, it refused to acknowledge the group's legitimacy by either negotiating with them or confronting them directly - but its policy of waiting for the protest to fizzle out did not work either. The PMLN government then invited representatives of the TLP for talks after a violent clash between protesters and the police which had left several people injured.

The PMLN government's inaction was seen as a sign of weakness by its opponents. In the opinion of many politicians, the crisis could have been easily averted with strict administrative measures. There was a clear distinction between a legitimate political cause for which the Constitution grants you the right to protest AND illegitimate political causes which cause chaos in society. PTI's *'dharna'* in 2014 had paved the way for religious groups to march to the capital to protest and press for their demands in a peaceful way. The violent protest over the hanging of Mumtaz Qadri, who had assassinated Punjab governor Salman Taseer in the near past, had also paralysed the capital and caused massive inconvenience for the public.

Those were the days when the clergy was disconnected from society and the real community problems. In its fight to preserve orthodoxy, it openly went against the interests of ordinary people. The protesters, in such situations, do not even see themselves causing any trouble to commuters. In this particular event, TLP leader Khadim Hussain Rizvi also urged while addressing protesters at Faizabad:

> *"Our sit-in and protest should not be blamed for the trouble of the city's people ... it's the government which is responsible for blocking roads and creating problems.*
>
> *We have only one demand: remove (PMLN's) Law Minister Zahid Hamid from office as he is the one responsible for amending the affidavit that contained the clause about the finality of Muhammad (PBUH)'s prophet-hood. If you don't remove Zahid Hamid, we don't care if the whole assembly dies."*

On 16th November 2017; the National Assembly gave nod to 'The Elections (Amendment) Bill 2017', seeking restoration of the *Khatm-e-Nabuwwat* [finality of Muhammad (PBUH)'s Prophet-hood] clause to its original form. On the same day, The Islamabad High Court [IHC] ordered the said religious group (TLP) to end its sit-in on the Faizabad Intersection — the main link between the twin cities – but the high court orders couldn't be implemented by the police and city administration – the sit-in stayed as such.

On 19th November 2017: Government's second deadline to call off Faizabad sit-in ended, protest continued and the PMLN govt had to approach scholars to conciliate Faizabad protesters. The government convened a grand meeting of leading clerics in an effort to find a peaceful solution to the protracted sit-in that had paralysed the twin cities of Rawalpindi and Islamabad for the two weeks. Next day, Islamabad police arrested a suspect allegedly carrying 2kg of explosive material near Faizabad Interchange which caused considerable unrest among the state institutions. On the other hand, the IHC issued show-cause notices to the district administration Islamabad and interior ministry officials over their failure to implement the court orders (of 16th November) to disperse the sit-in.

On 21st November 2017: The Supreme Court of Pakistan [SCP] took *suo motu* notice (No.7/2017) regarding the *Tehreek-e-Labaik Pakistan*'s [TLP]'s Faizabad *Dharna* (sit-in) when the Islamabad High Court [IHC] had seized the matter in Syed Pervaiz Zahoor case (WP No. 3914/2017).

On 24th November 2017; the Islamabad administration issued a final warning to the protesters, occupying the Faizabad Interchange to clear the roads or face 'strict action'. Next day, the Police and Frontier Corps personnel launched crackdown but got retreated within hours. Perhaps the Army Chief Gen Bajwa had telephoned the then Prime Minister Shahid Khaqan Abbasi and advised him *'to handle the Faizabad sit-in peacefully as violence is against national interest and cohesion'*. The PMLN Government called out Pak-Army to break up Faizabad sit-in, but military said: *'it can't use force against our own people'*.

Next day, the law enforcement personnel used tear gas and water cannons to disperse the protestors, but *failed and gave up after 173 of them suffered serious injuries* – the law enforcement personnel were not allowed to use firearms and were provided only with anti-riot equipment. Two days later, Law Minister Zahid Hamid resigned following an agreement between TLP and the PMLN govt; Khadim Hussain Rizvi called off the sit-in.

The PMLN government had invoked Article 245 of the constitution and sought the assistance of Pak-Army but before the army could be deployed, the matter was resolved between the govt and the protestors on the night of 26th November 2017. The TLP leadership there, received payment from men in uniform AND dispersed. The moments were captured on videos and remained available on social media for weeks. The footage went viral. It was indeed *'rare evidence'*, as a BBC report suggested, of what seemed to be a *'soft spot of the military'* for religious groups whose support had been often mobilized against mainstream political parties. See below:

> @omar_quraishi at Twitter on the same evening of 27th November 2017 at 7:39pm with 35 sec video and text: *Turns out the full context of this clip is as follows: The DG Rangers was visiting the protest site & was told that these are v poor activists who couldn't afford to return to their homes outside ISB - that's why at the start a man also says "Let us help them" - money is for that…*

Referring to the BBC dated 29th November 2017; the demonstrators blocked a main road in Islamabad for three weeks until the military brokered an end to the protest after a botched police operation. The law minister then resigned meeting a key demand of the protesters who had accused him of blasphemy. The deal was seen as surrender by the civilian authorities under pressure from the military.

> [In the captured video of 27th November 2017, Director General of the Punjab Rangers Maj-Gen Azhar Navid Hayat was seen giving envelopes containing 1,000-rupee (£7) notes to participants in the protests, who were described as having no money to pay their bus fare home. *'This is a gift from us to you,'* the General was heard telling one bearded man. *'Aren't we with you too?'* He then went on to pat another protester on the cheek and offered a reassurance that, *'God willing, we'll get all of them released'* - presumably making a reference to some arrested protesters.
>
> *'This is all we had in one bag. There's some more [money] in the other,'* Gen Hayat said, before the footage ends.]

The above video was shot by **Dawn News TV's** reporter Shakil Qarar on his mobile phone. He said it was run on the Dawn News website but no idea how footage without the Dawn News logo ended up on social media. There was no immediate reaction from the military, which knew more about each politician's role and lust in Pakistan.

No politician from the governing party (PMLN) or the opposition (PPP, PTI & JUIF) commented and *TV channels refrained from running the footage,* perhaps reluctant to annoy the Pak-Army. The **Nation** and **Dawn** daily newspapers did cover the story but did not headline it, and it got a back-page mention in the Urdu-newspaper **daily Jang**. However, there was fierce reaction from some Pakistanis on social media.

Omar R Quraishi, a Samaa TV journalist, asked *'whether it was a good use of taxpayers' money'*. The said sit-in came to an end after 21-days; the PMLN government was forced to accept TLP's demands after a futile operation to break up the sit-in went skewed and sparked violent protests across the country. This *Dharna* could have been avoided had the government kept the political environment cordial and amiable instead of following the politics of abusive syndrome for political opponents and nabbing them through NAB; PMLN's weakness had played more vital role.

In this charged atmosphere, religious extremists affiliated with the TLP roamed the streets, inciting and committing acts of violence. Under those circumstances, taking a stance against the establishment, questioning the executive, critiquing mainstream political parties including the PTI, and even scrutinizing the judiciary was an extraordinary act in politics, given the formidable forces aligned against such dissent.

That *Dharna* Case engulfed a prolonged and quarrelsome sit-in staged at Islamabad's Faizabad interchange. The protest itself started out as a political stand-off, but soon evolved into a litmus test for the resilience of democratic institutions, the sanctity of the Constitution, and the boundaries of freedom of expression.

At that time, Nawaz Sharif, a three-time elected prime minister, had been disqualified, and preparations were underway for his imprisonment. Political parties were undergoing significant changes, with one being dismantled and another; the PTI however, was enjoying robust public support. *Much of the superior judiciary and media had largely aligned with the establishment's narrative.* Even the elected PMLN, led by Shahid Khaqan Abbasi at the Centre and Shahbaz Sharif in Punjab, refrained from challenging the establishment's dominance; said to be extended to religious extremists, too – but remained a matter of open media discussions for long.

In November 2017, the situation in Islamabad had been simmering for three weeks before it erupted into violence and ultimate defiance of the Islamabad High Court [IHC] orders. Many blame the government for allowing the protesters to grow in number and build a countrywide momentum for their movement. When the ICT authorities moved, they did not appear to have a good plan. The police failed to arrest leaders of the protest, and when trouble started to spill into other cities, they resorted to a controversial policy of blocking all live news channels and social media websites.

> {...*but the situation was not unprecedented in this country; it's a routine matter here. This is Pakistan where corruption scandals had been invariably used to topple governments through courts, and there were instances when religious hordes had stormed urban centers to undermine the legitimacy of the respective governments. Many suspected that those moves came with the tacit support of the military; but the military always denied.*}

25th November (2017)'s police action against the protesters was launched under cool but worried circumstances. Since the PMLN was known for having considerable standing with right-wing religious voters in Punjab province, many believed the protest by the ultra-right-wing TLY and TLP was aimed at attracting some of that support towards then freshly ousted PM Nawaz Sharif. The military stepped in later when its chief spokesman tweeted to say the army chief had told the new Prime Minister, Shahid Khaqan Abbasi, that '*...the issue of protesters should be resolved by avoiding violence from both sides ...*'

The said directions raised many eyebrows. Dawn newspaper in an editorial comment said it had '*oddly equated the (PMLN) government with the protesters*'. Others raised concerns over the timing of this tweet, saying: '*...it would embolden the protesters*'. Hours after the tweet, the government enlisted the army's support in aid of civil administration but security experts were of the view that the military could only secure state buildings and installations against possible attacks, and that regular army troops were unlikely to physically confront the protesters.

Much late, on 25th instant, police fired tear gas and rubber bullets to disperse protesters, hence its initial reluctance to move against the protesters came up understandable. Nearly the same timing - top judiciary jumped in. Islamabad High Court declared the highway sit-in illegal earlier and during the last week it issued contempt notices to top administration officials for failing to clear the protesters. Later the Supreme Court also initiated hearings in the case, asking the government to restore the people's right to freedom of movement in occupied areas. It was just unexpected and unprecedented.

Initially, the media coverage of the protest was minimal due to small number of the protesters and also because road blocks by obscure religious groups trying to register their presence had become a routine affair in Pakistani politics. However, six people were believed to have died in the protests and hundreds were injured, including of police. Last day's escalating events changed the whole scenario; pressure was felt by the both - the government and the military. Aside from the blocking of Twitter, Facebook, Instagram, YouTube and other social media websites, television channels were made off-air and their live streaming pages were suspended.

Schools were also ordered closed for two days – 27-28th Nov 2017 - in the province of Punjab, which was home to more than 50% of the country's population; also, the ruling party [PMLN]'s home base.

TOTAL ADMINISTRATIVE FAILURE:

In Faizabad *Dharna* Case, the government, Islamabad administration, police and other law-enforcing agencies totally failed in removing the protesters from Faizabad, and despite using thousands of officials from multiple agencies, the protest site was kept occupied by more protesters than before; all operations went in vain. For many, the *halwa-eating maulvis* proved better at planning a protest and putting up resistance than the law enforcement agencies and administration had estimated.

Experts blamed the PMLN govt's delayed reaction for the chaos and instability; one mentionable crack-down was ultimately done on 26th November 2017. However, others felt the problem was more complicated. One Brig (R) Asad Munir, attributed the govt's failure to ill-planning; see below:

> *"They should have blocked all the routes to the sit-in to avoid chances of more protesters reaching the site at the time of the operation. In the morning, there were just a few hundreds of them – as most people tend to go away at night and return in the morning. Had the supporters been arrested as they tried to reach the sit-in a day before (it was Friday) morning, the situation would have been completely different. More important, Khadim Hussain Rizvi, the leader of the protesters, should have been arrested as early as possible by using teargas - the most effective weapon in protests.*
>
> *For such operations, law enforcement personnel in reserve should be three times as many as the men deployed; but here there was no*

such arrangement. Hence, once the force was exhausted, it became impossible to control the situation."

A veteran media-cum-political analyst Imtiaz Gul said:

".... the state's delay allowed the protesters to make plans for a counter-protest across the country. This is why country-wide protests were witnessed after the operation began. Due to such strong and widespread demonstrations, it has become very difficult to address the situation without involving the armed forces.

The most serious mistake was not arresting Rizvi in the morning, when there were just a few hundred participants at the sit-in. It is strange that the law enforcement agencies focused on the workers rather than arresting the leadership.

The electronic media should have been approached earlier and explained why it should not cover the operation (where was PEMRA by the way). The live coverage simply helped fuel the anger across the country and more people headed for the protest site. The military should have been called in earlier."

A former IGP, Tahir Alam Khan, who had served in Islamabad earlier, felt that the operation revealed the lack of coordination between police officers and personnel. High-ranking officers should have led the operation, but they didn't bother. The govt should have focused first on controlling the protests across the country before launching another operation to clear Faizabad. Referring to Zahid Hussain's analysis Published in **daily DAWN** dated 22nd November 2017:

*"What more troubling is that the flames of bigotry are sweeping across other parts of the country creating a dangerous confluence of religion and politics. The controversy over the missing oath that has apparently been exploited by the newly formed **Tehreek Labbaik Ya Rasool Allah** [TLY], (surely an off-shoot of TLP) to whip up religious sentiments has turned into more of a political issue bringing the beleaguered government under severe pressure."*

Cleric Rizvi's show started with just few hundred zealots blocking Islamabad's main highway; then turned into its 3-week demonstration and with thousands more crusaders in, the blockade virtually brought the administration to its knees. Pampering and pleading failed to move the defiant clerics; even the court order to end the siege fell on deaf ears.

The paralysis of the state bestowed the fanatics with a lot greater consent they didn't deserve.

The repeated extension of deadlines and seeking the help of religious leaders to end the stand-off demonstrated the helplessness of the administration amidst of political crisis. It was the fear of a blowback that limited the option of using force. The political fallout of the 2007's Lal Masjid military operation and the 2014's Model Town police action kept haunting the embattled PMLN govt and their buddy Islamabad administration. On the other side, giving in to the irrational demands of a politico-religious group weakened the state authority further. The authorities had not learnt from the consequences of the policy of conciliation and pacification in such situations.

There was certainly no outpouring support for that unruly sectarian mob; *in fact, there was huge public outrage over the blockade.* But initial indecisive and hesitant planning on the part of the administration encouraged some other groups to join the siege, making the situation much more volatile. Certainly, it was much easier for law-enforcement agencies to remove a few hundred protesters when they started to block the road. Nor it could be taken as a spontaneous move when the protesters led by Mr Rizvi marched into Islamabad travelling all the way from Lahore. There was a clear plan behind the siege. It was quite intriguing why the Punjab government did not stop the TLY supporters despite the fact that the issue of the missing clause about the finality of Prophet Muhammad (PBUH) had already been resolved.

Evidently, some senior members of the ruling PMLN also played a role by stoking the controversy because of political expediency. Some opposition leaders, from PPP, PTI and JUIF, could have jumped into the fray for their own vested political interests; <u>reportedly the newly formed TLY enjoyed tacit support of some intelligence agencies to undercut the PMLN vote bank</u>. All these factors created a monster and stoked the flames of bigotry that burnt down their own homes. The filthy language used by these clerics and the open incitement to violence made the lives of minority religious communities and of moderate Muslims more vulnerable to mob violence. The slightest perceived allegation of blasphemy could cost anyone his / her life.

The speeches of Rizvi and his fellow clerics were being live-streamed on social media; one could see and understand the kind of venom being spewed in the name of religion - they were merchants of hate - holding the nation captive. It was pathetic that the law minister had to prove his allegiance to faith and beg forgiveness for an oversight for which he was not directly responsible. The demand for his resignation was not just about his person but the sanctity of parliament. Conceding to that demand to end the sit-in further strengthened the extremist forces who were manifestly above the law.

One couldn't understand the administration's irresolute response despite the order of the Islamabad High Court to clear the siege. The order declared that no group could be allowed to infringe upon the rights of the people or disrupt the administration. Indeed, it was primarily the responsibility of the government to protect the rights of the people and uphold the rule of law. But the issue of extremism was also the concern of the state and other stakeholders. The use of religion as a policy tool by the state and its confluence with politics divided the nation along sectarian lines and fueled bigotry; it was a serious challenge to the ruling regime of the PMLN.

> {SUMMARY: *The agitators claimed that during the passage of the Elections Act 2017, the Khatm-i-Nabuwwat oath was deliberately modified as part of a larger conspiracy. The amendment to the oath was deemed a clerical error by the government and was subsequently rectified through an act of Parliament.*
>
> *The government had attempted to negotiate in vain with the protesters to end the sit-in several times. Finally, it launched an operation to disperse the protesters, in which at least six people were killed and scores others injured. After the botched operation, the government decided to call in the army for help. Negotiations were undertaken with protesters once again, and the government accepted a number of their demands in return for ending the protest. The agreement document bears the signatures of then interior minister Ahsan Iqbal, TLP chief Khadim Hussain Rizvi, and Gen Faiz Hameed among others.*}

SC JUDGMENT ON SIT-IN CASE:

On 5th February 2019: The Supreme Court of Pakistan issued a bold and strongly-worded 43-pages judgement in 2017's Faizabad sit-in case, in which it observed lapses on the part of the govt, media, the Pakistan Electronic Media Regulatory Authority [PEMRA], intelligence agencies, the armed forces, and the Election Commission of Pakistan [ECP]. Below are excerpts from the judgement given by Justice Qazi Faez Isa in the said *suo motu* case:

- *The leaders of the dharna intimidated, hurled threats, abused, provoked and promoted hatred. The media provided unabated coverage to the TLP.* Anyone having a grouse against the government joined in. The report submitted by Inter-Services Intelligence [ISI] under the title 'Public Support' and subtitle 'Political Parties / Personalities' listed the following: 1) Sheikh Rasheed Ahmed (Chairman AML), 2) Ejaz-ul-Haq (PML-Z), 3) PTI Ulema Wing Islamabad released audio message & 4) Sheikh Hameed (PPP).

- Inflammatory speeches were delivered by irresponsible politicians. Some unscrupulous talk-show hosts incited and provoked citizens.

- *The free publicity made TLP, a little-known political party, into a phenomenon.* Basking in the limelight, TLP's leadership became ever more intransigent, abusive and aggressive.

- With each passing day, as they grew in strength and number, they became delusional and alleged that people would be rendered objects of Divine displeasure (which is a criminal offence) unless they followed the chosen path of the TLP. Protests turned violent and spread to other cities.

- As per the unanimous view of all the intelligence agencies, *TLP wanted to maximize political mileage* for itself.

- The ambitious leadership of a fledgling political party projected itself as the defender of the Muslim faith.

- *They provoked religious sentiment, stoked the flames of hatred, abused, resorted to violence and destroyed property worth Rs:163.95 million.*

- The report submitted by the Ministry of Interior [...] also disclosed that *the requisite permission to take out a rally or to stage a sit-in (dharna) was not obtained by the TLP* and that TLP's leadership repeatedly broke their promise to relocate to the designated protest areas, namely, Democracy Park & Speech Corner.

- The report of the Inspector General of Police Islamabad (IGP Islamabad) corresponds with the reports of the Intelligence Bureau (IB) and the Ministry of Interior, and highlighted the illegal actions of the protesters, including causing the death of a seriously ill eight-year-old child.

- The ISI report did not negate the reports submitted by IB, Ministry of interior and IGP Islamabad.

- *Abusing, threatening and attacking people undermine their right to live a life of 'dignity'* (guaranteed under Article 14 (1) of the Constitution) which requires enforcement.

- When shops and businesses are forced to shut, when people cannot pursue their vocation, when poor daily workers are denied the possibility of earning a livelihood their right to work (guaranteed by Article 18 of the Constitution) requires enforcement.

- When property is damaged or destroyed, the right to hold and enjoy property (guaranteed under Article 23 of the Constitution) requires enforcement.

- *The right of assembly, the freedom of association and the freedom of speech cannot be exercised by infringing the fundamental rights of others.*

- *Without obtaining permission public meetings cannot be held on roads. Nor can a road be used as a camping ground or to assemble on it indefinitely.*

- Roads are for vehicular use and pavements are for the use of pedestrians to enable the travelling public to move freely, which is their fundamental right.

- *TLP's leadership created hatred amongst the people, they abused, threatened and advocated violence; and this was broadcast by some private television channels.*

- *ISI's report identified Channel 92 as a television channel supporting TLP* and stated that its owners had supplied food to the protesters occupying the Faizabad Interchange.

- PEMRA, however, did not take action under the Pemra Ordinance against any of its licensees for violating the terms of their licenses.

- *PEMRA abdicated its statutory duty, a duty which it was legally obliged to fulfil.*

- *PEMRA also failed to protect the legitimate rights of its licensed broadcasters.*

- *Broadcasts by Dawn and Geo television channels were stopped / interrupted; complaints stating this were acknowledged by Pemra.*

- *Dawn and Geo were particularly targeted in the Cantonment and Defence Housing Authority areas of the country*, which too was confirmed by Pemra.

- It did nothing to protect the interests of its licensees nor took action against those cable operators who were responsible.

- On 19th March 2018 and on 24th April 2018, information was sought from Pemra as to who was responsible, but *Pemra professed ignorance (on the subject questions)*.

- The Council of Pakistan Newspaper Editors [CPNE] has *alleged "media repression", "that editors and journalists are forced to self-censor their work amid pressure from certain quarters"* and it *"appealed to all state and non-state actors to refrain from such unconstitutional practices"*.

- It seems that *Dawn*, the oldest English language newspaper of the country, which was founded by Quaid-i-Azam Muhammad Ali Jinnah, was targeted the most.

- *Overt and covert censorship is unconstitutional and illegal.* Nebulous tactics, such as issuing advice to self-censor, to suppress independent viewpoints, to project prescribed ones, to direct who should be hired or fired by media organizations is also illegal.

- No one, including any government, department or intelligence agency can curtail the fundamental right of freedom of speech, expression and press beyond the parameters mentioned in Article 19 of the Constitution.

- Those who resort to such tactics under the mistaken belief that they serve some higher goal delude themselves.

- Pursuant to the judgement in Air Marshal Asghar Khan's case, *the involvement of ISI and of the members of the armed forces in politics, media and other 'unlawful activities' should have stopped.*

- Instead, when *TLP's dharna participants received cash handouts* from men in uniform, the perception of their involvement gained traction.

- The Director General of the Inter-Services Public Relations (ISPR) has also taken to commenting on political matters: "History will prove the 2018 general elections were transparent."

- The armed forces, and all agencies manned by the personnel of the armed forces, including ISI, Military Intelligence (MI) and ISPR serve Pakistan, and thus all its citizens. They must never be perceived to support a particular political party, faction or politician.

- *If any personnel of the armed forces indulge in any form of politicking or tries to manipulate the media, he undermines the integrity and professionalism of the armed forces.*

- The report submitted by *ISI did not disclose the "source of livelihood, place of work, address, funding of their organizations, etc" of the TLP leadership.*

- Subsequently, we had inquired whether they paid income tax or had bank accounts. ISI responded by stating that it did not have the mandate to gather such information and therefore was unable to provide answers to our queries.

- The learned AGP was thus asked to inform us about the law / rules / regulations governing ISI and its mandate. The learned AGP tendered a document (in a sealed envelope) which spelled out ISI's mandate, but requested that the mandate of ISI should not be disclosed.

- He did not give any reason for such secrecy except that this was also the practice in other countries but did not cite the example of a single one (country).

- We, therefore, ascertained whether other countries maintained secrecy about the mandate of their intelligence agencies. The United Kingdom, the United States of America, New Zealand, Australia, Canada and Norway have laws governing their intelligence agencies, and all these laws also disclose their respective mandates.

- *We are disappointed in the manner in which the government handled this aspect of the case; by ignoring an issue it does not go away.*

- The perception that ISI may be involved in or interferes with matters with which an intelligence agency should not be concerned with, including politics, therefore was not put to rest.

- Article 17(3) of the Constitution requires political parties to account for the source of their funds and Section 211 of the Elections Act, 2017 demands that details of election expenses be provided.

- *The Election Commission of Pakistan [ECP] confirmed that TLP did not account for its funds and election expenses, but, surprisingly, professes its helplessness because the law according to it is cosmetic in nature.*

- The ECP should disabuse itself that constitutional and legal provisions are cosmetic. The responsibilities placed on the ECP by the Constitution and the law must be fulfilled, they are not optional. The Constitution also empowers the Election Commission to get requisite information from any executive authority.

J Qazi Isa's verdict came at the peak of a peculiar hybrid experiment, with a new prime minister cementing the *'same page'* between the executive and the establishment. Apparently, the judiciary itself had become an active participant in this collaboration barring very few judges. Notably, Justice Shaukat Aziz Siddiqui of the IHC, had previously been removed from office by the SJC when he exposed pressure from the establishment and the ISI. The intelligentsia held it as a bold judgement but no one was sure if the directions of the apex Court would be implemented any time sooner or ever.

{The Supreme Court of Pakistan [SCP] had taken *suo motu* notice (No.7/2017) regarding the *Tehreek-e-Labbaik Pakistan* [TLP]'s Faizabad *Dharna* (sit-in) when the Islamabad High Court [IHC] had seized the matter in Syed Pervaiz Zahoor case (WP No. 3914/2017).}

Referring to *Saad Rasool*'s analysis in **daily 'Nation'** dated 10th Feb 2019:

"Justice Isa, in his prolific writing style, starts the judgment with a brief background of the events that transpired in the wake of 'change in the wording of the declaration' related to finality of the Prophet (SAWW), enacted through the Elections Act, 2017. He notes how the resulting dharna effectively paralyzed the cities of Islamabad and Rawalpindi as a result of which public's movement was restricted or altogether stopped and commuters could not get to courts, schools, colleges, universities, their place of work, et cetera. Simultaneously, the judgment observes that leaders of the dharna intimidated, hurled threats, abused, provoked and promoted hatred, while anyone

having a grouse against the government supported them and the media provided unabated coverage to the TLP. In the circumstances, the Court took cognizance of the issue under Article 184(3) of the Constitution, declaring that the matter undisputedly was one of public importance and required the enforcement of the fundamental rights of nearly every citizen."

[The underlined words are verbatim from J Qazi Isa's said judgment]

The judgement of the IHC had concluded that a right to protest was a qualified right that needed to be balanced with other citizens' fundamental rights, adding that there were designated places for protests in Islamabad - **Democracy Park and Speech Corner [Parade ground]**.

The opinion of the Supreme Court in this *suo moto* case was authored by J Qazi Isa with his own pen. In addition to answering a question concerning enforcement of entrenched fundamental rights, the verdict adequately attended the question of public importance to assume SCP's jurisdiction under Article 184 (3). Right to protest is not an entrenched fundamental right in Pakistan's Constitution, thus the Court observed:

"The Constitution does not specifically stipulate a right to protest. The right of assembly, the freedom of association and the freedom of speech cannot be exercised by infringing the fundamental rights of others. Without obtaining permission, public meetings cannot be held on roads. Nor can a road be used as a camping ground or to assemble on it indefinitely. Roads are for vehicular use and pavements are for the use of pedestrians to enable the travelling public to move freely, which is their fundamental right."

By framing the issue of TLP's protest as one due to which the *'country effectively came under lockdown'*, the apex Court, justified assumption of jurisdiction under Article 184(3) of the Constitution as the protest that infringed rights of other citizens. A similar conclusion was made by the IHC in its orders which were not implemented by the Islamabad Admin and Police due to unknown reasons.

MOVE TO REMOVE J FAEZ ISA:

On 20th **April 2019**; the Executive Committee of the Punjab Bar Council (PbBC) at Lahore passed a resolution against Supreme Court's J Qazi

Faez Isa, terming the remarks given against Pak-Army in the Feb 2019's judgment as *'uncalled for'* and *'against the independence of judiciary'*.

On **24th April 2019**, an emergency meeting of the Executive Committee of the Pakistan Bar Council (PBC) disapproved the Punjab Bar Council's (PbBC) Executive Committee resolution passed four days earlier (dated 20th April 2019). The Executive Committee of PBC met under the chairmanship of Hafiz M Idris Sheikh; and the meeting was attended by its members including M Ahsan Bhoon and Azam Nazeer Tarar. PBC's vice chairman Syed Amjad and a member Syed Qalb-i-Hassan also attended. The PBC held:

> *"Senior lawyers believe that the PbBC's executive committee move was made in a haste and most members were not taken into confidence over it. It might have been an attempt to satisfy 'certain quarters (related with Pak-Army desks). PbBC's Executive Committee resolution is a deliberate move to divide the judiciary and create and environment against a judge before fixture of review petitions on Faizabad sit-in judgement, authored by Justice Isa wherein certain observations were passed regarding intelligence agencies."*

It was noted with concern that Ministry of Defence in its review petition had contended that the said judgment would adversely affect the morale of the armed forces and the directions to the Chiefs of Armed Forces of Pakistan (to take action against personnel who violated their oath) were ambiguous. The ruling PTI govt in its review petition had also contended that the judgment on Faizabad Sit-in case was sufficient to invite the *'verdict of professional misconduct'* against Justice Isa in terms of Article 209 of the Constitution. [*However, Imran Khan later withdrew its petition and refilled another one with the request to expunge the disturbing remarks*].

The resolution to remove Justice Qazi Faez Isa for *'criticizing the army and the ISI'* in Faizabad Sit-in case verdict indicated that there were clamps on freedom of speech within the superior judiciary in Pakistan. The 'Faizabad sit-in (Nov 2017)' was one of the major events in the political landscape of the country which highlighted several boiling issues within the country's society, Parliament, Bars and the Establishment.

Peeping into the backdrop history, the sit-in was a reaction to a trivial issue raised by a religious party, which blocked a major junction of the twin-city for days, resulting in rioting and terror spreading on the streets throughout the country. The Supreme Court had taken up a *suo motu* case, and the verdict was delivered on 5th February 2019. However, in April 2019, a six-member executive committee of the Punjab Bar Council came up with a resolution to remove Justice Qazi Faez Isa – who had authored this verdict. The committee said Justice Isa *'criticized the army and the ISI'*. For many, this was a unfair claim, and they believed that the true loyalties of the then Punjab Bar Council committee rested elsewhere.

The verdict was issued by a 2-member bench of the Supreme Court of Pakistan [SCP] comprising Justice Isa and Justice Mushir Alam, and it gave facts and details of the sit-in staged by the *Tehreek e Labbaik Ya Rasoolallah* [TLY], an off-shoot of the *Tehreek-e-Labbaik Pakistan* [TLP] at the Faizabad Interchange in the federal capital, Islamabad. In its verdict, the court had directed the federal and provincial governments to monitor all elements *'advocating hate, extremism and terrorism and prosecute the perpetrators in accordance with the law'*. More courageously, it gave a bold statement telling all institutions of the state, including its agencies and media guru PEMRA, to stay within their mandate as required by their oaths.

Further background; the TLP had objected to the language of one of the election laws then placed on media pages after revision. The parliament resolved the misgivings and mis-understandings but the TLP continued its protest, and in the first week of November 2017, they occupied the interchange – one of the main points connecting Islamabad and Rawalpindi. They also demanded the removal of the then law minister and called for the resignation of the govt itself. The verdict, authored by Justice Isa read that:

> *"...the leaders of the dharna intimidated, hurled threats, abused, provoked and promoted hatred; the media (also) provided unabated coverage to the TLP. Instead of ideally giving lukewarm coverage to the group of hooligans, most of the media – especially broadcast media – chose to play a sensationalist role.*
>
> *Some unscrupulous talk-show hosts incited and provoked citizens,"* further read the detailed verdict. *"The free publicity made TLP, a little-known political party, into a phenomenon. TLP's leadership became ever more intransigent, abusive and aggressive. With each passing day, as they grew in strength and number, they became delusional and alleged that people would be rendered objects of Divine displeasure (which is a criminal offence) unless they followed the chosen path of the TLP."*

The SCP had invoked jurisdiction under Article 184 (3) of the constitution with regard to protecting the fundamental human rights of citizens, because by then the protests had turned violent and spread to other cities; further details are given below under separate sub-headings.

Additionally, the worst hit was those who were in dire need of medical treatment. Ambulances, doctors, paramedical staff and others providing emergency services, including firefighters, bomb disposal squads and rescue services, were prevented from rendering emergency assistance. The impact reached its height with an eight-year-old boy dying when he failed to reach the hospital in time – as the sit-in prevented the ambulance from moving.

Meanwhile, the media continued its sensationalist fury. The ISI's own report identified **Channel 92** as a channel supporting the TLP and stated that its owners had supplied food to the protestors occupying the Faizabad Interchange; the PEMRA remained inactive. At one point, the verdict said:

> "The perception that ISI may be involved in or interferes with matters with which an intelligence agency should not be concerned with, including politics, therefore was not put to rest."

The verdict also referred to the *Asghar Khan Case*. The late Air Marshal Asghar Khan was concerned that the ISI and some armed forces personnel were pursuing a political agenda. He expressed these concerns to the Supreme Court, which took cognizance of the matter under Article 184 (3), as it was a matter of public importance regarding the enforcement of fundamental rights. The decision in Air Marshal Asghar Khan Case declared that:

> "Involvement of the officers/members of secret agencies i.e. ISI, MI, IB, etc. in unlawful activities, individually or collectively calls for strict action being, violative of oath of their offices, and if involved, they are liable to be dealt with under the Constitution and the Law."

Again, these thoughts surfaced at the time the *dharna* participants received cash from a military officer. With regard to the ISI and other agencies, the decision concluded that:

> "All intelligence agencies (including ISI, IB and MI) and the ISPR must not exceed their respective mandates. They cannot curtail the freedom of speech and expression and do not have the authority to interfere with broadcasts and publications, in the management

of broadcasters / publishers and in the distribution of newspapers. The Constitution emphatically prohibits members of the Armed Forces from engaging in any kind of political activity, which includes supporting a political party, faction or individual. The Government of Pakistan through the Ministry of Defence and the respective Chiefs of the Army, the Navy and the Air Force are directed to initiate action against the personnel under their command who are found to have violated their oath."

It was this kind of tough cross-questioning and speaking of mandates that the Punjab Bar Council (PbBC) took offence to. They claimed that Justice Isa had violated laws by targeting intelligence agencies in the Faizabad sit-in case. PbBC's resolution had said: *"He (J Qazi Faez Isa) should not have 'mocked' the state institutions ... the Pakistan army."*

The sentiments were, however, not greeted warmly across the board. In fact, it seemed as if those behind the resolution were in a minority, not even fully supported by some members of their own council. One Punjab Bar Council member held that the executive committee did not represent the whole house of the council, neither did it have the mandate to pass such resolutions or interpretations of judgments. Meanwhile, the Sindh Bar Council [SBC], including the Karachi and Hyderabad Bar Associations, instantly condemned the resolution.

> *"We must express our severe disappointment with the six members of the PbBC who were elected to be the voice of the legal fraternity but have chosen, instead, to become puppets of the puppet master; adding that such a resolution was only trying to sabotage the unity of the legal fraternity."*

Within a day, the Pakistan Bar Council [PBC] – the body that regulates the affairs of the legal fraternity – rejected the resolution and described it as uncalled for, and an unnecessary one that transgresses the independence of the judiciary. Senior members *of the late Asma Jahangir Group* stepped forward to publicly disown the PbBC's resolution against Justice Qazi Faez Isa. The Human Rights Committee of the PBC also stood by the latter group to reject the said resolution; it's chairman held:

> *"It's just something foolish, as there are no justifiable grounds to think of removing him. Definitely, there are factions within the judiciary but there is a tangible presence of those who are standing with Qazi Isa. Different institutions of the country are given their limits by the constitution of Pakistan. But unfortunately, many of us do not bother*

to even give the constitution that kind of respect."

Meanwhile, review petitions were moved by the PTI, the Ministry of Defence, Intelligence Bureau [IB], Election Commission of Pakistan [ECP], Sheikh Rashid Ahmed, the Pakistan Electronic Media Regulatory Authority [Pemra], Ijaz-ul-Haq and the Muttahida Qaumi Movement [MQM]. One of the review petitions by the Defence Ministry pleaded to set aside explicit or implicit adverse observations implicating the armed forces and or the ISI, in particular the declaration to the armed forces (*details are sited elsewhere in this essay*).

In fact this was not the first time that J Qazi Faez Isa had been targeted including challenging his appointment, move after a carnage in Quetta in which 70 lawyers were killed in a blast in the court there AND try to entangle him for strengthening the narrative of RAW and India etc – but, his truthfulness and integrity prevailed. Such incidents indicated there were hidden forces seeking to influence him and pressurize the judiciary.

DHARNA POLITICS IN PAKISTAN:

Truthfully, in Pakistan along with use of other forms of protests and strikes, sit-in got more popularity. The *Dharna* tactic in this country was first used in 1958 by the first Chief Minister of the NWFP Late Abdul Qayyum Khan against Prime Minister Feroze Khan's administration to remove his President Iskander Mirza. It is part of the history that Pakistan National Alliance [PNA]'s *Dharna* helped Gen Ziaul Haq to oust PM Zulfiqar Ali Bhutto [ZAB] and PNA used mosques to stimulate the masses. Unfortunately, *Dharnas* always served as latent aid to overthrow the democratic governments. Qazi Hussain Ahmed, the then JI Amir, had also organised *Dharna* against PPP government in 1993; murder cases were registered against the then Interior Minister late Gen Naseerullah Babar and the Commissioner Rawalpindi.

On 9th March 2007; Gen Musharaf deposed the then Chief Justice Iftikhar M Chaudhary along with sixty other judges and dissolved the judiciary which led to a nationwide lawyers' long march. For more details see:

JUDGES & GENERALS IN PAKISTAN VOL-II,
(2012) Scenarios 44-47, Pp496-550; GHP Surrey UK
- Available at AMAZON in paperback and as eBooks;
also at https://www.inamsehri.com/

Later in 2009, during PPP government, Nawaz Sharif of PMLN along with Imran Khan of PTI and Qazi Hussain Ahmed of JI planned a sit-in protest in the name of *'Restoration of Judiciary'*. It was handled effectively before it could enter Islamabad; timely political wisdom and dialogue worked out and successfully averted the situation. Iftikhar M Chaudhry was reinstated as the Chief Justice of Pakistan.

There was another *Dharna* in 2013 when Pakistan *Awami* Tehreek [PAT] under Dr Tahirul Qadri marched from Lahore and staged a sit-in against PPP's government in front of the Parliament Islamabad which was also successfully averted; PAT was brought to the table through dialogue resultantly the said sit-in ended amicably. On the other hand, during PMLN Government, the PAT Lahore's *Dharna* was not dealt with political negotiations, resultantly turned into a war Zone **on 17th June 2014** taking the lives of dozens of PAT workers. The lesson was that aggressive political moves might lose chances of a peaceful settlement and can take many innocent lives when mobs go unruly, disobedient and disorderly.

Thus, the history of *Dharnas* and lockdowns in Pakistan have mostly resulted into victory of politicians but failure of democracy and the state institutions. Such tactics mostly bring political instability and discourage economic growth. Consequently, the political instability further reduces economic growth and escalates inflation and mis-trust for the ruling party.

Then comes up the sit-in of November 2017 held by one Khadim Hussain Rizvi owning a sister organization of the *Tehreek e Labbaik Pakistan* [TLP]. It's details are available on these pages along with a little details of a landmark judgment dated 5th February 2019, penned down by Justice Qazi Faez Isa. The honourable Court noted therein that despite all efforts by the government (*including use of tear gas and water cannons on 25th November 2017*) the protestors could not be disseminated that day. However, next day, after negotiating an accord with the PMLN government AND after receiving *'payment from men in uniform'* they dispersed.

J Qazi Faez Isa's judgment deliberated upon a wide spectrum of issues:

1. History of past dharnas / protests, and how the concerned parties had never been proceeded against;

2. The overall ambit and scope of *'Right to Protest'*, under our constitutional dispensation;

3. Failure of the Election Commission of Pakistan [ECP] to proceed against matter relating to funding of TLP;

4. Impotence of PEMRA in cracking down against hate speeches;

5. Prohibition of hate-mongering within the ambit of the Islamic tenor of our Constitution;

6. Need for a defined legal / statutory **'mandate'** of the intelligence agencies.

Justice Isa was absolutely correct in pointing out that due (stern) action could be taken against those responsible for causing public inconvenience, and also that those in control of the cold-blooded Karachi massacre of 12th May 2007 must be prosecuted. For details of Karachi carnage, see:

JUDGES & GENERALS IN PAKISTAN VOL-II, (2012)
Scenario 45, Pp513-524; GHP Surrey UK
- Available at AMAZON in paperback and as eBooks;
also at https://www.inamsehri.com/

It is equally imperative to say that the TLP *dharna* of Nov 2017 was entirely unjustified after the govt had already enacted the requisite statutory amendment to redress their grievance. However, what required deeper and serious attention was the manner in which the apex Court defined the ambit of one's constitutional right to protest, and the consequences of 'abusing' such right. Specifically, its direction that *'protestors who obstruct people's right to use road and damage or destroy property must be proceeded against in accordance with the law and held accountable.'*

The judgment of the SCP, in its section titled **Previous Protests and TLP Dharna**, recounted two previous incidents of public protest:

1) "12th May, 2007 Karachi Massacre" during the Lawyer's Movement, and

2) "2014 dharna by PTI-PAT" at Islamabad.

Justice Isa in his judgment noted that:

> "...*perpetrators of the May 2007 event were not punished and even after a judicial Inquiry Commission had rebutted PTI's allegations, no adverse consequences followed*". Consequently, emboldened by this lack of consequences, participants of the TLP dharna ignored the law (e.g. DC's imposition of section 144 Cr.PC.), destroyed property worth 163,952,000 rupees and caused nearly all economic activity in the country to come to a virtual standstill, which per day, caused a GDP loss of 88,786,180,821 rupees, and should be compensated by someone (the perpetrators)."

However, the serious minds pondered that who would start calculating the total damage done to the economic activity in Pakistan, as a result of the Lawyer's Movement? What about the blocking of Mall Road on every Thursday, for almost two years? And, of course, the consequent hindrance in getting to the Courts, or hospitals or schools? What about the constitutional right to *move freely* on GT Road, during the 2009 lawyer's Long March? The Bar Councils could have been be charged this bill?

Taking words from Saad Rasool, referred *elsewhere above*, while on the point of past protests, what about the one Nawaz Sharif did, in his 'GT-Road Rally'? Should that bill, including loss of GDP, be charged to the former Prime Minister? Perhaps through some apex judgment in the future, the honourable Court could clarify whether there was a constitutional distinction between protests / dharnas / rallies that were short-lived, and those that lasted for longer? If so, how long a period of disruption could be taken as *'tolerated'*. BUT then what about the time when a group of blind government employees had blocked the Mall Road in Lahore? Should their protesting be measured in terms of their ability to pay?

At another point, referring to J Qazi Isa's judgment again, that the '... *right to assembly cannot be used to bring about a revolution or insurrection'*. Very respectfully, it required further clarification from the apex Court that *'why can a protest not aspire to become a revolution?'* World history is depleted with many such examples of successful revolutions.

On 6th April 2019; PPP co-Chairperson Asif Ali Zardari urged his party's supporters to *'march towards Islamabad'* and oust the government. According to the PPP leader, the accountability cases against him were part of an agenda to revoke the 18th amendment to the Constitution, which was passed by the PPP government in 2010. Otherwise, PPP has traditionally championed democracy and adherence to law & order but such a statement was disappointing. Mr Zardari didn't clarify what the purpose of such a long march was; the demand of *'ousting the government'* was outrageous, and against all legal realms.

If the march was meant to register a protest against a possible pushback of 18th Amendment, that could be done through political dialogue avoiding disruption of normal state business. Besides, there was no move or announcement by the sitting govt indicating challenge to the 18th amendment.

Later it transpired that Zardari's battle cry during his rally was just a bluff made in a wave of enthusiasm, - not a move for an actual long-march. Indeed, the economic inactivity that the PPP used to complain then got more terrible. Also, it appeared that PPP were (still) haunted by the politics of sit-ins. PTI's dharna of 2014, which was harshly criticised for civil disruption and law & order violation, in fact, paved the way for a political culture of waging protests to fulfil demands which could have been better fulfilled in via political discussions on the table and negotiations. The PPP could have acted gracefully; raising such divisive rhetoric always bring negative results.

AZADI MARCH OF JUI(F): Coming back to the *Dharna* science in Pakistan. In 2019, it became (serious) joke like a *lunger-gup* amongst seasoned politicians even. The date of Maulana Fazalur Rehman's *Dharna* titled *'Azadi March'* was near around and every coming day was making the PTI government nervous. <u>PM Imran Khan was advised by intelligentsia that he should keep his ego aside and personally talk to the opposition leaders of various parties AND invite them to a talk & dine evening</u>. It was a nice suggestion to defuse the political uncertainty in the country; but the PM was un-necessarily proud. The political scenario could have been different and the upcoming political move of Maulana Fazalur Rehman could have gone frustrated had the PM Khan understood the political intrigues in power-corridors.

The news of JUIF's sit-in had created uncertainty and chaos in the minds of the general populace of Pakistan; particularly it was scarier for the citizen of Islamabad based on their past bad memories of sit-ins when businesses were halted, roads blocked, markets deserted and the schools closed. The previous *Dharna* of 2017 was still alive in the minds because an eye-opener judgment of J Qazi Isa was in place since February that year.

RE-SURGENCE OF FAIZABAD CASE:

On 21st September 2023: Just a week after taking oath of his new office, Chief Justice of Pakistan [CJP] Qazi Faez Isa fixed review petitions against the Faizabad Dharna Case judgment, wherein the Inter-Services Intelligence [ISI], Intelligence Bureau [IB] and Military Intelligence [MI]—and Pak-Army's media wing, the Inter-Services Public Relations [ISPR], were directed not to exceed their constitutional mandates. A 3-judge bench of the apex court—led by the chief justice himself and comprising Justice Aminuddin Khan as well as Justice Athar Minallah —took up the petitions on 28th September 2023 against the 6th February 2019's verdict.

The pleas were not taken up during the tenures of the last three chief justices, namely Asif Saeed Khosa, Gulzar Ahmed and Umar Ata Bandial. During the hearing of Justice Isa's case related to an inquiry into three UK properties in the name of his wife and children, his counsel Muneer A Malik had told the apex court that the judge's observations in the Faizabad sit-in judgment—*'an inconvenient truth'* – prompted the PTI-led federal government to file a presidential reference against him.

Eight review petitions were filed against the Faizabad sit-in case verdict by various political parties and organizations including the PTI, MQM-P, Election Commission of Pakistan [ECP], Pakistan Electronic Media Regulatory Authority [Pemra], IB and the ISI. The review petitions were part of a coordinated exercise as all were saying that [the] observations in [the] SC judgment demoralized the armed forces. Surprisingly, the content of the review petitions filed by the PTI and MQM was the same. Both the parties had accused Justice Isa of *'misconduct'* for giving his observations against the establishment.

The ISI challenged the SC verdict through the then Attorney General for Pakistan Anwar Mansoor Khan saying that:

> "It (the verdict) would adversely affect the morale of the armed forces. It contended that the court's observations would gather the impression that the armed forces and the premier intelligence agency were responsible for *'unconstitutional acts like sit-ins / dharnas'*. It added that the verdict displaced the image of the armed forces defending the country against the menace of terrorism with that of those *'mired in politics, manipulating elections, subverting free speech, muzzling the press and funding extremists'*. The ISI also contended that the

> *observation about the involvement of the armed forces in politics was vague as there was no evidence to back it up.*
>
> *Likewise, there was no evidence to suggest that the ISI was involved with either the Faizabad sit-in, outcome of the 2018 general elections, abridgment of free speech, or intimidation of or censorship of the press. Also, that observations and findings created the impression that the armed forces, in violation of their oath of office, have been found by the court to be involved in politics and other unlawful activities. Further, the apex court's observations created the perception that the armed forces were busy pampering rather than checking those who resorted to abuse, hate and violence.*
>
> *These are disturbing allegations unsupported by any credible and admissible evidence without identifying any person. Yet, the chiefs of armed forces of Pakistan have been directed to take disciplinary action against unnamed individuals who the court suspects of being so involved."*

In their review plea / petition, it was also contended that such remarks (given in the judgment against the military agencies) would be exploited by external foes in their propaganda war against Pakistan's armed forces. Their [external foes'] politicians and media had in the past exploited such allegations to their advantage and would use the said SCP verdict to allege that *'the highest court of Pakistan is of the view that the armed forces are harbouring extremists'*. It continued that the armed forces could counter propaganda but their task would become unenviable when the judgment of the highest court of Pakistan supplied ammunition to the enemies of the country.

The intelligence agency also submitted that to promote their own interests and further their designs, several hostile foreign intelligence agencies had created a 'false perception' against Pakistan and its armed forces of aiding and supporting extremist organizations in the region.

The ISI also objected to the court's observations of halting TV transmission in the cantonments and defence areas; adding that:

> *"[The] armed forces have zero tolerance policy when it comes to violation of oath by their officers. An allegation that an office of the armed forces has violated his oath of office is always inquired into. If the allegation is not devoid of basis, disciplinary proceedings are initiated. However, no action is possible in the absence of any credible evidence*

and that too against unnamed officers for their alleged involvement in un-particularized incidents on unspecified date[s]."

The full court formed a committee comprising Justice Minallah and Justice Muhammad Ali Mazhar to take up the task of chalking out standard operating procedures (SOPs) for the live telecast of court proceedings.

Justice Isa, in his 2019 Faizabad Dharna judgment, had written that the Constitution emphatically prohibited members of the armed forces from engaging in any kind of political activity, which included supporting a political party, faction or individual. *'The government of Pakistan through the ministry of defence and the respective chiefs of the army, the navy and the air force are directed to initiate action against the personnel under their command who are found to have violated their oath,'* read the 43-page verdict authored by incumbent CJP Isa.

CJ Isa, in his Faizabad Dharna judgment, had also held that:

> "Pakistan is governed by the Constitution … obedience to the Constitution and the law is the inviolable obligation of every citizen wherever he may be and of every other person for the time being in Pakistan."

On 26th September 2023: The Intelligence Bureau [IB] and PEMRA moved the SCP for the withdrawal of its review petition against the judgment delivered in the said sit-in case over four years ago, stating that it did not want to pursue the case anymore. The withdrawal application came just two days before the hearing of the review petitions by a 3-member bench led by Chief Justice Qazi Faez Isa and comprising J Aminuddin Khan and J Athar Minallah.

COURT COMMISSION's REPORT:

On 6th May 2024; CJP Qazi Faez Isa expressed his dissatisfaction with the report submitted by an inquiry commission formed to investigate the *Tehreek-i-Labbaik Pakistan*'s (TLP) 2017 Faizabad sit-in, remarking that the probe body was not even aware of its responsibility. The bench — headed by Justice Isa, and also including Justice Irfan Saadat Khan and Justice Naeem Akhtar Afghan — presided over the hearing that day, which was broadcast live on the Supreme Court website and YouTube.

In that February 2019's judgment, adverse observations were made against several government departments, including ISI & MI of the Pak-Army for causing inconvenience to the public as the 20-day sit-in had paralysed life in both Islamabad and Rawalpindi. Pleas were subsequently moved against the verdict by the Ministry of Defence, the Intelligence Bureau (IB), the PTI, Pakistan Electronic Media Regulatory Authority (Pemra), the Election Commission of Pakistan (ECP), the Muttahida Qaumi Movement (MQM), AML chief Sheikh Rashid and Ijazul Haq. However, most of the petitioners withdrew their pleas, prompting the CJP to ask *'why is everyone so afraid to speak the truth'*.

During a previous hearing, former Pemra chief Absar Alam had made revelations on the interference of intelligence agencies and *'media coercion'* during the Faizabad sit-in. Although the primary objective of setting up the Faizabad Commission was to fix responsibility for the failures that led to the TLP sit-in spiralling out of control, the Commission's report had stopped short of placing the blame directly on any individual's shoulders. During the hearing that day (6th May 2024), CJP Isa had to express his dismay at the report compiled and submitted by the Commission, noting that it was not according to the Terms of Reference (TORs).

CJP Isa inquired whether the Attorney General of Pakistan (AGP) had seen the report submitted by the Election Commission of Pakistan (ECP), to which the latter replied in the negative. Inter-alia, he told the apex court that Gen (rtd) Faiz Hameed had told the Commission that it was not the ISI's responsibility to look into the financial support of terrorists.

While scrutinising the report, CJP Isa pointed out that while one paragraph said it was not the ISI's responsibility, another said no evidence was found of TLP being financially assisted. Justice Isa asked the AGP to reflect on how much loss the country had suffered because of the Faizabad sit-in. *'Kill, vandalise and leave; what is this? I cannot comprehend what level of mind prepared this report. The commission does not even know what its responsibility was.'*

The Commission, led by retired IG Syed Akhtar Ali Shah and also comprising former Islamabad police chief Tahir Alam Khan and additional interior secretary Khushal Khan, was constituted to ensure compliance with the 2019 SC judgment. The TORs were to investigate the causes and subsequent events leading to the omission and commission of acts not in accordance with the law. It included proposed drafting rules and SOPs to regulate the working of intelligence agencies since the involvement of the army or its affiliated agency in civilian matters adversely affected the fair image of the institution.

The CJP asked about the whereabouts of other Commission members. The chief justice asserted furthrt:

> "The right to protest is a part of democracy but the right to kill is not. Those who do so must be taken to task. What sort of report is this? There is no mention of TLP workers in the report. Were the TLP workers called? They weren't; truth might have come forward if TLP workers had been summoned by the Commission. The statements of those who sent breakfast and food are on the record."

"This is a grade-five [student's] statement that is being filed in the SC," CJP Isa quipped while referring to the report. However, the Commission's report said that since no one from the then-premier, former law and interior ministers, and the former Punjab chief minister had accused intelligence agencies of facilitating the protesters, nor was any evidence furnished to this effect, the commission could not connect any organisation or state official with the TLP sit-in – and that was the end of the court business that day.

The IB's review petition had urged the court to set aside the adverse observations made against the department, adding that it was the premier civilian intelligence agency responsible for state security. It had contended that the impugned order created a "bad impression" on the public that the IB was involved in unlawful activities and politics, after transgressing constitutional boundaries. It had said the observations made in the verdict were based on "vague facts" and that during the sit-in, the department was in close contact with the federal and Punjab governments and forewarned them about the plans and intentions of the TLP, with a view to foiling their attempt to storm/lockdown Islamabad.

Meanwhile, in response, the defence ministry had requested the court to set aside the explicit or implicit observations about the armed forces and/or the Inter-Services Intelligence (ISI). The ministry's petition had said that a host of factors could affect morale. However, it said, what was fatal was the belief amongst the rank and file that their officers while acting like "self-proclaimed saviours" were violating the fundamental rights of citizens and instead of serving "Pakistan and thus all its citizens", supporting a "particular political party, faction or politician".

"...When the source of such remarks is the highest court in the land, it can promote fissiparous tendencies and has the capacity to destroy the ability of the armed forces to act as a cohesive fighting force," the review petition had argued. It had further said there was no evidence before the court to suggest that the armed forces or ISI were, in any manner, involved with either the sit-in or a particular outcome of the general elections of 2018 or the abridgement of free speech or intimidation or censorship of the press.

In its petition, the ECP contended that it had comprehensively applied and enforced the Constitution, law and code of conduct by issuing a letter to the TLP on Aug 16, 2017, asking the party to provide details of its bank account and even had issued notices to it with a warning to cancel its registration.

Daily life in Islamabad was disrupted for about 20 days when protesters belonging to religio-political parties occupied the Faizabad Interchange which connects Rawalpindi and Islamabad through the Islamabad Expressway and Murree Road, both of which are the busiest roads in the twin cities.

Scenario 247

QAZI FAEZ ISA's………..

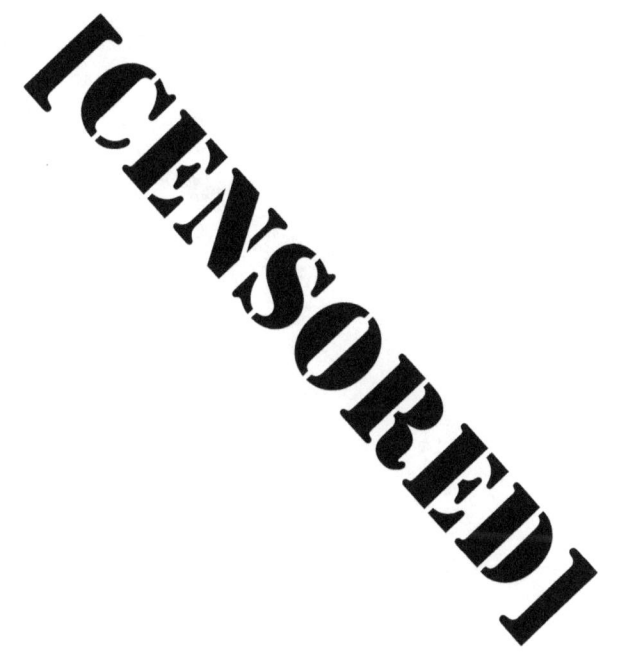

Scenario 248

FOREIGN POLICY IN KHAN's TIME

A Point to Ponder:

In January 2022, the total cost of PM Khan's foreign trips during his 3-year tenure till then was $530,000. The amount pales in comparison to *Zardari's single visit* to New York City in 2012 which cost the national kitty $1.1 million then and the $901,250 spent on *Nawaz's single visit* to the same city in 2016; 'PM Imran's 47 foreign trips.... Report' at nation.com.pk dated 4th January 2022 is referred.

PRE-ELECTION (2018) LANDSCAPE:

On 25th July 2018: The general election in Pakistan was a defining moment in the country's history. This was the third election held since the restoration of civilian rule in 2008. The contest was clearly between the outgoing ruling party PMLN of Nawaz Sharif and the PTI led by Imran Khan. In that decade, the PPP, which had been a leading political party since 1960s, saw a sharp decline - then reduced to a regional party in Sindh. Its last charismatic leader Benazir Bhutto was assassinated in Dec 2007, but neither her husband Asif Zardari nor her son Bilawal had shown any crowd-pulling appeal.

The other major party PMLN suffered a major setback when its leader Nawaz Sharif was disqualified by the Supreme Court of Pakistan in July 2017 and later sentenced to 10 years in jail by a NAB court, on the charge of corruption. His daughter Maryam Nawaz, who was being groomed as his successor, was also in jail on similar corruption charges, and disqualified from holding public office. During the trial, Nawaz Sharif tried his best to discredit the judiciary to convince his followers that he was being framed for political reasons.

Nawaz Shharif's narrative was that the establishment, his code word for the army, his old nemesis, pressurized the courts to act against him. He often claimed himself the great champion of democracy, conveniently forgetting that he himself rose to power during Martial Law regime of

Gen Ziaul Haq. Nawaz Sharif and his colleagues in PMLN were very confident that the masses would turn up in huge numbers to show their rejection of the court verdict; but got deeply disappointed. His party won lot many seats in 25th July's elections, but couldn't stage a comeback to power.

Another important political development was that Imran Khan, the PTI leader, emerged as the next Prime Minister of Pakistan. A former cricketing hero-turned politician, he was able to garner increasing support, particularly among young voters, *on the twin slogan of change and an end to corruption.* There was no doubt that the erstwhile ruling parties, in cahoots with dishonest bureaucrats, were guilty of massive corruption. They robbed the country ruthlessly and amassed assets in Western countries and Dubai through illegal commissions on government projects and large-scale money laundering. Their corruption was the major reason for the on-going economic crisis in Pakistan, on account of burgeoning debt burden that resulted in depreciation of Pakistani rupee at an unprecedented low.

In addition to corruption, these leaders mainly from Sharifs, Zardari & *ulema* (religious tycoons)'s family dynasties, were guilty of misrule and poor economic planning. They gave preference to some glitzy mass transportation schemes like white elephants, while denying funds to projects needed to fulfill the required needs of industrial development, basic education, health, sanitation, clean water and power.

Most of the above said politicians were driven by a lust for power and money; sold loyalties for the sake of their offices. The moral fiber of bureaucracy got eroded; when civil servants are not selected on merit nor allowed to function honestly, or picked up on the basis of nepotism, it would result in entirely bad governance and massive corruption. Imran Khan could fill the bill, but also miserably failed due to the crooked & non-cooperative bureaucracy AND corrupt practices of some of his own team of advisors and cronies.

At the time when IMRAN Khan took reins of the country as Prime Minister in August 2018, Pakistan was facing grave challenges in foreign policy, while plagued by a serious economic crisis allegedly. Priority had to go for handling the economic challenge first as a collapsing economy seriously impairs a country's ability to keep adequately good relations with other countries.

Pakistan is basically a sound country with good resources; its people are talented and the armed forces are disciplined and highly trained, while it possessed nuclear power, too. But it needed political stability under a clean and forward-looking leadership. Education and health needed high priority. Economic growth alone could provide jobs. The alarming growth of population had to be checked since decades. If other Islamic countries like Iran and Bangladesh could achieve success in this area, why can't Pakistan? Eradication of terrorism and extremism were not only nation's internal need but would also help improve our external ties.

For economic progress and internal reforms, Pakistan needed peace and international cooperation. In his policy pronouncements, Imran Khan had emphasized his intention to take Pakistan out of its economic mess, created by former governments through corruption, misrule, and self-serving economic priorities – coupled with negative or hostile relationship with our neighbouring countries. During the past 70 years, the US had given over $75 billion in aid to Pakistan, which was mostly in shape of military weapons and army officer's training – NO INFRASTRUCTURE OR DEVELOPMENT PROJECT for the general populace ever.

Pakistan got the US weapons for defense against Communist aggression, but it became an essential tool of corruption through its military and bureaucratic hands. While negotiating or accepting deals, the civil and military leadership NEVER thought that sovereignty should come first; Gen Ayub Khan's book FRIENDS NOT MASTERS was a true slap on the face of that collective Western imperialism - but was not pondered by any.

Imran Khan's stance remained that *'USA has turned Pakistan into a client state and that we have been fighting America's wars';* additionally, that the US was always found demanding that Pakistan should *'do more'* in the war against terror. Let us examine the facts. In international relations, convergence of interests brings two countries closer. Imran Khan's arguments were contradicted by numerous anti-nationalism factors like why Pakistan always opposed Israel; why befriended China in 1950s when the US had hostile relations with it; why developed ties with Gaddafi and Khomeini who were hated by the US; why developed Pak-nuclear bomb, then refused to roll it back and carried out nuclear explosions - all these 'actions' of Pakistan were against US agenda. In 1978, Soviet military intervention was seen in Afghanistan, Pakistan felt it as a grave threat to its own security thus Gen Ziaul Haq started giving aid to the Afghan Mujahidin. When the US jumped into Afghan-War, Pakistan openly opted to support the war; since its closest friends, Saudi Arabia and China, were also supporting the same.

PM Khan made the above statement because in Afghan War Pakistan sacrificed its 80,000 civilians and Army-men, destroyed its $165+ billion business etc and what the US and its allies lost – only nearly 2400 heads in total during long 20 years. Still we had to be blamed for NOT DOING MORE; the US got the most humiliating defeat of the modern times. For more details see:

'THE HISTORY OF A DISGRACEFUL SURRENDER [2021]'
by *INAM R SEHRI*, 360 pages, published by GHP Surrey UK IN 2022

Imran Khan was right in saying that political negotiations should be held to end the Afghan war but the real issue was to persuade the Taliban to agree to a political compromise - in fact the Taliban didn't want to join such negotiations. What was the fault of Pakistan or the new PTI government if the Taliban were not coming to the negotiation table?

Later, Al-Qaeda declared a Jihad against Pakistan and Pakistani Taliban [TTP] began a vicious campaign of terror. Pakistan was alleged that terrorists use sanctuaries in Pakistan to conduct operations in Afghanistan; Pakistan strongly denied the said charge.

KHAN CONFRONTED THE US:

The PTI's new government had two issues in the basket then. It entered into a spat with the US on what Secretary of State Pompeo had discussed with Imran Khan. Secondly, the Foreign Minister misunderstood the Indian position on talks, necessitating a clarification by the Foreign Office. The PTI government's objective to seek better relations with India was laudable, but no high hopes could be raised. As for Iran-Saudi differences, any mediation could only be attempted with Riyadh's approval.

Before taking over the premiership by Imran Khan in Pakistan, the military-to-military relationship was going ideal during the US President Trump's unpredictable behaviour for Pakistan. The western media and media anchors on Pak-TV channels were frequently discussing the development and the apprehended consequences; the US publication **'THE DIPLOMAT'** dated 18th August 2018 is referred in this context.

Over the last two decades, one area of cooperation that remained off-limits to any bilateral rows was Washington's intent to offer *coveted training programs for Pakistani military officers.* During Trump administration, the change didn't become a factor that could shift Pakistan's regional security policy because Washington had already conveyed to Pakistan that the military training component of US aid would remain in place despite the suspension of the security assistance package. Traditionally, the US military had sought to protect such educational programs from political tensions, arguing that direct military-to-military ties were strategic in nature and were crucial for future alliance building purposes.

However, the Trump admin, in its latest attempt to put pressure on Pakistan, started to close various training programs for Pakistani military officials. Many nationalist think-tanks in Pakistan were happy over Trump's decision to shut down military training programs – because it openly manifested that Washington's influence would further reduce over Pakistan. However, the policy couldn't be implemented due to certain internal factors within American high offices – and then US elections of 2020 took away Mr Trump.

It was, perhaps, the backdrop that Pakistan had to sign a military training agreement with Russia; the Pakistani military officials were planned to receive training in Russia's military institutes. Security cooperation between Islamabad and Moscow had expanded over the previous few years. Among other things, **Washington's heavy-handed approach toward Pakistan was, in fact, considered as the reasons driving it away from the United States.** The decision further isolated Washington's remaining pockets of influence in Pakistan.

Moreover, an attempt to isolate Pakistan militarily at a time when the United States was trying to directly engage the Afghan Taliban didn't bode well for any effort to revive the Afghan peace process - Pakistan had big stakes in the Afghan peace process then. On the whole, it was not clear how Pakistan's national security establishment viewed the decision. Islamabad and Washington's direct line of contact for the military-to-military relationship had suffered a serious blow – the analytics could guess.

On 27th August 2018: Shah Mahmood Qureshi, the new Foreign Minister, held his first press conference and talked about the new government's foreign policy putting *'Pakistan first'* and emphasizing a focus on national interests. He briefly touched upon Pakistan's relations with its neighbourhood, the US and China, and outlined the government's visions and road map in the months to come. During his first visit to Pakistan's Foreign Office on 24th August 2018, PM Khan had emphasized that *'he would pursue an independent and proactive foreign policy with no compromise on national interests, seek relations based on parity, and bridge the trust deficits in regional relations'*.

Three days later, PM Khan once more emphasized that his government would not accept any unfair demands by the US; adding that his government would cancel any agreements made against national interests by previous governments. Next day, the Pentagon cancelled $300 million aid to Pakistan, supposedly due to a lack of *'decisive action against militants'*. The suspension was in addition to another $500 million worth of Coalition Support Funds which had been withheld earlier in the year under the Trump administration and was done to build up more pressure on Pakistan. Basically, this money was not an aid - it was a due right of Pakistan as reimbursements for the losses suffered by the country in the war on terror.

US's 'DO MORE' MANTRA – NO MORE:

On 3rd September 2018; at his office, PM Khan held a one-on-one meeting with Gen Bajwa mainly in connection with US-Pakistan relations - the meeting came ahead of US Secretary of State Mike Pompeo's scheduled visit to Pakistan on 5th September 2018.

US Secretary of State Pompeo was in Islamabad only for five hours but only to repeat their *mantra* of 'DO MORE'. The hard fact was that US-Pakistan bilateral relations were at an all-time low in those days; a serious trust deficit, made worse by President Trump's bullying style. However, the US needed Pakistan to keep open the supply route for its forces in Afghanistan and in helping to secure a face-saving exit from the longest war in its history.

During those days, it was an attempt to isolate Pakistan militarily at a time when the US was trying to directly engage the Afghan Taliban in an arena of the Afghan peace process. Pakistan had big stakes in the said process and an eventual settlement had to incorporate Pakistan's concerns. In that context, the ongoing targeting of an ally country's security apparatus was taken as a deliberate effort to create more distrust among both countries' national security institutions; both were directly engaged in Afghanistan politically and militarily since two decades long span.

BUT it was Washington's choice – might be a blessing in disguise for Pakistan. The US had shown cold shoulders to the significance of 'military diplomacy' during those times and it was considered a good omen then.

> *"In 2004, Rumsfeld was asked about **military diplomacy** as a variant of soft power he feigned ignorance. Four years later, his successor Robert Gates however admitted that the trials of the US in Afghanistan and Iraq were proof that military strength was not sufficient to secure peace. He admitted that in the global war on terror, soft power and military diplomacy were far stronger instruments than hard power;"* an old essay of Raashid Wali Janjua dated 11th July 2016 in daily **'the News'** of Pakistan is referred.

In pseudo-democracies like in Pakistan where the political leadership, instead of asserting civilian control in defense and security spheres, leaves a yawning gap to be filled by military leaders, military diplomacy comes to the rescue of the state by default. Why a democratic government used to abdicate vital foreign policy and security fields to the bureaucracy remained a riddle that needed unraveling in the interest of national security. Giving outlines of his foreign policy, PM Khan said:

> *"If any country needs peace right now, it is Pakistan. We want to have good relations with all neighbours. It would be very good for all of us if we have good relations with India".*

PM Khan offered dialogue on the core issue of Kashmir and promised that if ***'India takes one step forward; he would take two steps....'***. He stressed the need for peace for Afghan people who had suffered the most in the War on Terror [WOT]. He wanted to have open borders with Afghanistan one day. He also indicated that he wanted to improve ties with Iran.; and Saudi Arabia was a friend who had always stood by Pakistan in difficult times.

RELATIONS WITH SAUDI ARABIA:

During last week of August 2018, the Inter-Services Public Relations [ISPR] issued a note that during his meeting with Pak-Army Chief Gen Bajwa at Mina, Saudi Crown Prince Mohammad bin Salman conveyed his wishes and support for the new elected government in Pakistan. The expression of solidarity and support by Saudi Arabia was in continuation of the goodwill gestures demonstrated by the Kingdom and its leadership ever since the 2018 General Election in Pakistan.

Ambassador of Saudi Arabia to Pakistan Nawaf bin Said Al-Malki was the first foreign diplomat to have a meeting with Imran Khan even when the poll results were still pouring in and that was reflective of deep relationship of the Kingdom with Pakistan. Like China, Saudi Arabia too kept relationship with Pakistan based on mutual respect and people-to-people contacts and remained immune to political changes in Pakistan. There were reports in the media that Saudi Arabia was ready to provide meaningful assistance to Pakistan in overcoming its economic and financial challenges at a time when the US was implementing plans to squeeze the country and was even threatening to block any moves to get bail-out package from the International Monetary Fund [IMF].

Saudi Arabia, was always seen in the forefront be it political or diplomatic support to Pakistan or economic and financial cooperation. On 7 September 2018: Saudi Arabia's minister for information and culture Awwad Alawwad arrived Pakistan and met his counterpart, Fawad Chaudhry. The two discussed extending the current Pakistani-Saudi cooperation in all fields, particularly economic development and the media sector. The Saudi minister also met PM Khan, in addition to the political and military leadership. Pakistan expressed its support for ongoing Saudi reforms, including the Vision 2030.

18-19th September 2018: Imran Khan's visit to Saudi Arabia was fruitful; the kingdom alone could help Pakistan bail out from its payments-crisis, as Islamabad needed $10+ billion to meet its immediate obligations. As an opposition leader, Imran Khan had insisted on Pakistan keeping out of the Yemen war and also opposed Gen Raheel Sharif's appointment as head of IMCTC. The Saudi stance on both issues was the opposite. Imran Khan was the new Prime Minister with great responsibilities. Pakistan's foremost need was to overcome the economic crisis - a testing time for mutual diplomacy.

> *[Since 1950s, Pakistan always kept a huge commitment to provide security to Saudi Arabia; but the fact remained that Riyadh had given far more aid to other countries which did much less. Just talking about recent times, in 2014, Saudi Arabia gave an aid package of $25 billion to Egypt. In June 2018, Saudi Arabia, Kuwait and UAE pledged $2.5 billion to Jordan to help it come out of its financial crisis, plus annual support for its budget for five years. UAE gave Egypt $3 billion after the coup in 2013 and provided $4 billion in April 2016. The last Saudi aid to Pakistan was $1.5 billion in 2013. PM Khan had these comparative figures in mind when he talked to Saudi Crown Prince Muhammad bin Salman during his visit to Pakistan after the change in Pakistan government in 2018.]*

Maxim lies that international politics is a ruthless pursuit of national interests, much beyond one's emotions, illusions and ego-traits.

22-23 October 2018: At the invitation of King Salman bin Abdul Aziz and the Crown Prince Muhammad bin Salman, PM Imran Khan again visited Saudi Arabia to participate in the Future Investment Initiative [FII] Conference. Amongst other bilateral discussions, far-reaching decisions on bilateral economic and financial cooperation were also agreed. After inauguration of the FII Conference, a Pakistan-specific session was organized, in which PM Khan underlined Pakistan's priorities towards optimizing the economy and attracting foreign investment – but no positive or practical response received.

Saudi Arabia's $6 billion pledge reduced the size of bailout package from the International Monetary Fund [IMF]. For $3 billion loan, a memorandum of understanding [MoU] was signed between the two Finance Ministers under which Saudi Arabia had to place a deposit of USD three billion for a period of one year as balance of payment support. It was also agreed that the Kingdom of Saudi Arabia would also provide a one-year deferred payment facility for import of oil, up to USD three billion and this arrangement would be in place for three years, to be reviewed thereafter.

Crown Prince Muhammad bin Salman also agreed with PM Khan's suggestion to reduce visa fee for Pakistani workers, which was a significant step towards enhancing the country's workforce in Saudi Arabia, as well as facilitating travel of people from both the countries. In the meantime, a visit of the Saudi delegation had evaluated the possibility of investing in a petroleum refinery in Gwadar Pakistan. Saudi Arabia confirmed its interest in this project. Saudi Arabia also expressed interest in development of mineral resources in the country. For this purpose, the Federal Government and the Government of Baluchistan consulted each other to invite a delegation of the Kingdom for feasibility assignments.

Later, another all-weather friend and trustful, **Saudi Arabia** had a soured story like the Chinese. The deterioration of relations started when Pakistan's Foreign Minister Shah Mahmood Qureshi, in a televised interview criticized Saudi Arabia and the OIC's (Organization of Islamic Countries) inaction over Kashmir and threatened to create a new Islamic bloc. It was during that time, Mahatir Muhammad, the then PM of Malaysia invited PM Khan to an Islamic Summit, seen as an alternative to the OIC. PM Khan backed out at the last moment due to the pressure from both the establishment and Saudi Arabia.

Saudi Arabia demanded the repayment of 1 billion USD from a 3 billion USD Soft loan back from Pakistan as the mistrust between the two heightened. Even UAE demanded its 1 billion USD loan back making Mr Khan and his government realize the consequence of challenging Saudi leadership in the Islamic world by trying to create new OIC like block.

Even though relations remained tenacious between the two, Saudi Arabia had agreed to bail out desperate Pakistan with a 4.2 billion USD assistance package. In the history of Pak-Saudi relations, never such stringent clauses of the assistance deal were seen where a country was barred to use its $3 bn credit in State Bank of Pakistan (SBP) and instead had to pay a 4% interest for just keeping this amount in its bank and that too only for a year. Also, if default in this agreement was committed the right of jurisdiction and arbitration over the matter would be presided by the Saudis. Only at a notice of 72 hours, Pakistan would pay the entire sum or the assets that were negotiated under that would seize to exist as part of the agreement.

The above provisions could give the world's financers an idea of how far the relations between Saudis and Pakistan had gone bad.

MOST SIGNIFICANT CHINA GOT ANGRY:

On 7th September 2018; China's foreign minister Wang Yi arrived Pakistan, on a 3-day visit to discuss bilateral relations and the ongoing economic projects under the multi-billion **China-Pakistan Economic Corridor [CPEC]**. Wang met with Qureshi, as did their respective delegations, and also met PM Khan and army chief Gen Bajwa. Following their meeting, the two foreign ministers held a press conference during which both announced the two countries had agreed to deepen their ongoing strategic cooperation. FM Qureshi reiterated that CPEC was a vital instrument of Pakistan's socio-economic development and both sides touched upon their bilateral trade, poverty alleviation efforts, cultural links, job creations and other developments.

Previously, PM Khan had made many references for matching the Chinese model of rapid social and economic development in Pakistan. The Chinese delegate also offered clarification on China's One Belt-One Road projects in Pakistan under the aegis of the CPEC, and said the projects were not *debt but rather investments* that would unleash huge economic benefits to the Pakistani economy. CPEC projects had created 70,000 jobs in Pakistan till then and added to economic growth by one to two per cent.

An article in THE FINANCIAL TIMES dated 9th September 2018 claimed that Pakistan was planning to renegotiate the terms of agreements existing under CPEC, especially those that were perceived to be tilted away from Pakistan's favour; the report quoted Abdul Razzaq Dawood, the cabinet member for commerce, textiles and industry stating:

> "The previous government did a bad job negotiating with China on CPEC — they didn't do their homework correctly and didn't negotiate correctly so they gave away a lot. Chinese companies received tax breaks, many breaks and have an undue advantage in Pakistan; this is one of the things we're looking at because it's not fair that Pakistan companies should be disadvantaged".

However, this report was swiftly refuted by both Pakistani and Chinese government sources; Dawood said he had been quoted *out of context* in many parts of the report, on which he would be adding clarification in detail.

The Chinese Foreign Minister's visit reaffirmed the strong bonds of friendship between Pakistan and China. Imran Khan reiterated that friendship with China was a cornerstone of Pakistan's foreign policy. He assured that his government was committed to the implementation of CPEC. The Chinese Foreign Minister gave out specific information about the progress already achieved and a willingness to address any concerns about CPEC projects.

Simultaneously, PM Khan held that China had given Pakistan a huge opportunity through CPEC. He wanted to learn from China how it brought 700 million people out of poverty, as also its anti-corruption measures. With USA he wanted to have a mutually beneficial relationship, which until then had been a one-way situation NOT as the version that America gave aid to Pakistan for fighting their war. Imran Khan's speech was carried live by CNN and BBC and was largely applauded at home and abroad for its balanced and reconciliatory stance.

However, Pakistan had never been so isolated even in the worst of its times; whether it was China, the US, the EU, or Saudi Arabia; every ally or its strategic partners alike had distanced themselves from Pakistan after the Afghanistan debacle. The Taliban and Afghanistan were not the only issues that resulted in the said isolation, the multiplicity of Pakistan's interest had resulted in mutual distrust among all its partners and friends.

The relationship **with China,** its all-weather ally, and 'Iron brother' saw some rough tides when a story unearthed about the corruption scandal of Chairman CPEC Authority, Lt-Gen Asim Saleem Bajwa (retd) was forced to resign due to the pressure from the Chinese. The increase in the assaults over Chinese citizens by fringe Pakistani groups and the freedom fighters of Baluchistan too made China revisit its commitments under this project. The incident at Dasu Dam Project, its handling by Pak authorities irked the 'Iron brother' to an extent that all major projects under CPEC came to halt and China had to ask a compensation of 38 million USD for the families of the deceased. This demand was a pre-requisite or to put in another way, a confidence-building measure to restart operations.

- More on **China's CPEC** discussed in a separate scenario.

KHAN's FOREIGN POLICY: ISOLATED:

Apparently, Imran Khan's victory in July 2018's election reaffirmed belief in essential values: decency, compassion, honesty, equality and self-respect. It was, no doubt, a vote for rule of law, for democracy and constitutional governance. The victory speech made by Imran Khan was an uplifting moment in Pakistan's history. He displayed his vision of a new Pakistan, free of corruption and ending oligarchic rule. However, the general populace was seen disappointed and disgruntled when *his 50+ cronies, an army of ministers and advisors, couldn't deliver the fruit* later as had been manifested by the PTI and Imran Khan through their key points at their *'agenda before the election'* and after holding the govt, they betrayed the nation by doing nothing as per their manifesto.

In the 2nd week of September 2018; Pakistan's PM Khan hosted Foreign Ministers from Japan, Iran, USA, China and Turkey. Since getting oath a month earlier, Imran Khan had telephone conversations with leaders of India, France, UK, China, Iran, Saudi Arabia, Turkey and others. In addition, Foreign Minister Shah Mahmood Qureshi was also sent to Kabul; immediately after he left for New York to attend the annual UN General Assembly session where he met some of his counterparts including of the US. On his first foreign visit, PM Khan proceeded to Saudi Arabia to see King Salman and Crown Prince Muhammad bin Salman – a positive start with an intensive diplomatic activity from a new government.

It was favourable diplomatic recognition by the international community of Pakistan's importance as a state whose policies could affect the region and beyond. Each of the visits by the five foreign ministers [FM] to Islamabad had its own background and significance. Japanese FM Kazuyuki Nakane signed an agreement for economic development assistance; it has been a major trading partner of Pakistan.

Iranian FM Jawad Zarif was an early visitor to Islamabad, perhaps by intention. He met top Pakistani leaders and delivered a letter from President Rowhani to PM Khan inviting him to attend the Asian Cooperation Dialogue Summit in Iran in October 2018; the very next month. PM Khan thanked Iranian Supreme Leader Khamenei's support for Kashmiris' struggle for self-determination [*though Iran officially avoids any mention of Kashmir*]. Notable thing was that Pakistani FM Qureshi supported 'Iran's principled stance on the nuclear deal issue', pitting it against the US which had withdrawn its commitment. The American sponsored intelligentsia in Islamabad was worried about the possible harm due to this explicit support for Iran to Pakistan's relations with USA and Saudi Arabia, in their back-drop of cold war with Iran. However, PM Khan never bothered on such issues.

Iran and Pakistan share an embattled border and PM Imran Khan's visit to Iran — which came just a week after 14 persons were killed, reportedly by an Iran-based armed group; most of the world appreciated the gesture. Because, Islamabad blamed Tehran for that attack in or at Baluchistan; Tehran had also blamed Pakistan for a suicide attack in which 27 members of Iran's Revolutionary Guards were killed on 14th February 2019 — just when Pulwama incident occurred in India.

KASHMIR ISSUE IN PM KHAN's TIME:

After getting premiership, PM Khan's first speech on foreign-policy was not welcomed in India. It was unhappy to see Nawaz Sharif defeated who was regarded as pro-India. It was a satisfying factor that religious parties, including some advocating anti-India militancy, lost ground in 2018 elections. However, as expected, India didn't reciprocate meaningfully to Imran Khan's offer of friendship. Modi's BJP regime had thrived domestically by its anti-Pakistan policy. It was unlikely for India to change direction or show any accommodation on Kashmir issue or its solution.

Prime Minister Narendra Modi addressed the 74th session of the United Nations General Assembly (UNGA) in New York on **27th September 2019** evening. While PM Modi did not mention Kashmir or Pakistan in his speech, PM Imran Khan spoke about the Kashmir issue in his speech. While addressing the UNGA, PM Modi said:

> "India has been so ahead on the global goals that the country has now become an inspiration for the world. When a developing nation successfully carries out the biggest cleanliness drive of the world and provides more than 11 crore toilets to its people just within 5 years, that system gives a message of inspiration to the entire world. My focus is to drive India's development."

Pakistan's Prime Minister Imran Khan too addressed the UNGA later that night. The salient features of his speech were:

> "If the conventional war starts with a country which is four times bigger than Pakistan, what will we do? This is what I ask myself a lot of times. But I say this; we will fight but think what happens when two nuclear countries fight."

"Nuclear war is not a threat; it's a fair worry."

> "There are millions of Muslims in India. PM Modi, do you know what they must be thinking. If there's a bloodbath, Muslims will become radicals. You are forcing Muslims into radicalisation. They will pick up arms."

> "Has PM Modi thought what would happen when the curfew in Kashmir is lifted? Do you think people in Kashmir would accept that you have withdrawn the special status? Thousands of children in Kashmir have been put under detention. They, too, will come out on the streets after the curfew in the state is lifted and the Army will shoot them. We also hear about pellet guns being used by the Indian Army. But whatever happens in Kashmir after the curfew is lifted, there will be another terror attack like Pulwama and Pakistan will be blamed."

> "PM Modi's whole life is RSS which is inspired by Adolf Hitler, Benito Mussolini. RSS believes in the ethnic cleansing of Muslims. RSS goons butchered hundreds of Muslims. This is arrogance. This makes people do cruel things. Something PM Modi has done. Arrogance has blinded PM Modi."

> "When Pulwama happened, India immediately blamed us. We asked them for proof but they instead sent their aircraft. PM Modi's election campaign was also based on a lie. During elections, PM Modi campaigned saying 'I have taught Pakistan a lesson' was a lie."

"When I came to power, my priority was Pakistan would be a country which would try to bring peace. The Mujahideen groups, which were trained by Pakistan and funded by US, were called terrorist groups by the Soviet. Come 9/11, Pakistan joined the war against terrorism. Now that we joined the US which occupied Afghanistan, these groups turned against us. 70,000 Pakistanis died in this war. When we came to power, we dismantled what was left of these groups. I know India keeps accusing us that there are military groups but these are not. The UN officials can come and check themselves."

"Islamophobia since 9/11 has grown at a pace which is alarming. The human community lives together, there should be an understanding. But Islamophobia is dividing the world. Muslim women have been asked to take off their Hijab in other countries. A woman can take off her clothes in other countries but cannot put on Hijab."

"Some countries are not serious about climate change. When my party came to power, we planted a billion trees but one country cannot do everything."

PM Imran Khan's speech at the United Nations General Assembly [UNGA] started shortly after 8:30 pm; meanwhile, PM Modi did not stay in the hall to listen Imran Khan's speech. He further elaborated the following eye-opening issues that:

"We all know that marginalisation leads to radicalisation. We must address this issue... Western leaders' equated terrorism with Islam."

"In all human communities, there are radicals, there are liberals, and there are moderates. All human communities ... no religion preaches radicalism. The basis of all religions is compassion and justice, which differentiate us from the animal kingdom."

"Terrorism has nothing to do with any religion. No one did research that before 9-11, the majority of suicide bombers in the world were Tamil Tigers. They were Hindus – [but] No one blamed Hinduism. And quite rightly what does Hinduism got to do with what desperate people were doing in Sri Lanka?"

"We all know, we've seen films about Japanese 'Kamikaze' pilots at the end of the Second World War doing suicide attacks. No one blames their religion."

"There is a misunderstanding in the West regarding Islam, which is causing Islamophobia in the world. There are 1.3 billion Muslims in this world. Millions of Muslims are living in the US and European *countries as minorities. Islamophobia, since 9/11 has grown at an alarming pace."*

"Why did Islamophobia grow. Why did it start? - Because certain western leaders equated terrorism with Islam, calling it Islamic terrorism and radical Islam. What is radical Islam? There is only one Islam. This Islamic radicalism has been the main reason behind Islamophobia. This has caused pain to Muslims."

"If a conventional war starts, anything could happen. But supposing a country seven times smaller than its neighbour is faced with a choice: either you surrender or you fight for your freedom till death. We will fight and when a nuclear-armed country fights to the end it will have consequences far beyond the borders, it will have consequences for the world."

"So it's important to understand this: The Prophet lives in our hearts. When he is ridiculed, when he is insulted, it hurts... We human beings understand one thing: The pain of the heart is far, far, far more hurtful than physical pain. And that's why the Muslims react [to insults against the Prophet].... having lived in the West, people didn't understand this."

"We need to explain that, look, in a human community; we must be sensitive to what causes pain to another human being. We have in the western society, and quite rightly, the Holocaust treated with sensitivity, because it gives the Jewish community pain. That's all we ask: Do not use freedom of speech to cause us pain by insulting our Holy Prophet. That's all we want."

As part of his **'Mission Kashmir'** to draw global attention on the issue, Pakistan Prime Minister Imran Khan urged the Kashmir Study Group during a meeting with its leaders to highlight the situation in Jammu and Kashmir, which he said **'poses a grave threat to regional peace and security'**.

> [PM Khan had met with the founder of Kashmir Study Group, Farooq Kathwari, who called on him in New York. Kathwari had earlier served as member of the US President's Advisory Commission on Asian Americans.]

However, in the light of country's past, and skipping the details about SEATO and CENTO agreements, it was after 1979 when US President Jimmy Carter authorized the CIA for covert operations, Pakistan became the capital for Islamic Radicalization and the epicenter for Afghan jihad.

The critical analysts held that Pakistan's obsession to remain firm in the western camp was very much reflected in its early foreign policy that advocated for joining US-led Western Bloc. However, everything took a turn when the US announced its withdrawal and <u>by 15th August 2021</u>, Kabul fell to the Taliban. The humiliation and defeat of the American-led campaign in Afghanistan were solely attributed to the deconstructive role of Pakistan. Albeit, the failure of the US in Afghanistan was mostly due to its mishandling of the situation but for the US and the West, Pakistan remained the best scapegoat for many of those failures directly or indirectly.

Since old days, Pakistan's multiplicity of interest in Afghanistan and Kashmir and engaging both at the same time did prove a tactical victory but it had to endure heavy losses as well. On the eastern side, it lost Siachin and till Kargil it was involved in the arms race, thereby impacting its dependent economy. Over the years, India's prevention of cross-border infiltration through enhanced counter-terror grid, ground Information, and public outreach campaign both by forces and civil administration all synergized as a combined effort in combating terrorism in the valley. On the diplomatic front India ensured that Pakistan pays in cash & kind, mainly in human loss.

Pakistan has been on FATF's grey list for financing terror. *Even during Imran Khan's era, practically, every supporting country of Pakistan lost interest in Kashmir Issue due to India's pro-active foreign policy.* The effective counter to the fake narrative and propaganda peddled by Pakistan had helped India to expose it on the global stage and also bring the issue of terrorism in Pakistan to the diplomatic tables for discussion. However, the spat between India and Pakistan was not new; most of the losses for Pakistan had been at the western front as it had to host 30 million (*unofficial figure touched 60m*) Afghan refugees which continued to pour-in accompanied by Drugs, Kalashnikovs and explosives in Pakistan.

The formation of new radical jihadi movements like TLP and many others led to the rise of extremism in (till) present-day KPK's former FATA region and Northern-Areas of Baluchistan. Kidnapping, extortion, and human trafficking increased over the Durand line making the internal security vulnerable. As the destabilization continued even after Pakistan's associates were in Kabul, the threat of spillover effect like TTP (*Teherik-e-Taliaban Pakistan*) of the unfinished conflict further rigged the economy and socio-political set up in Pakistan. The exponential rise in radicalism was just the beginning of impending doom. For more details, following book is once again referred:

'THE HISTORY OF A DISGRACEFUL SURRENDER [2021]'
by *INAM R SEHRI*, 360 pages, published by GHP Surrey UK IN 2022

India was the only 'other' part of the Kashmir issue. India never really cared about Pakistan at least after 2014; India seldom did, but Pakistani rulers and media often seen raising their voices against India - utter waste of energy, money and time; Mr Khan's govt was no exception. The fact remained that *Pakistan couldn't manage support of 56 members in the UNHRC - failed to get hold of 16 members to table a resolution against India in 2019.*

PM Khan offered to hold talks over Pulwama attack after 6 days of the attack, but PM Modi made it clear that *'this is not the time for talks now'*.

MOSCOW VISIT OF IMRAN KHAN:

Few Pakistani politicians could think it promising to find themselves in Russia on the day the modern world changed forever. But <u>on 23rd February 2022</u>, hours before news broke that Vladimir Putin had invaded Ukraine, Khan emerged from an aircraft in wintry Moscow. *'At what a time I have come! So much excitement!'* Khan said to Igor Morgulov, Russia's deputy foreign minister, who welcomed him at the airport. His excitement and liveliness at this awkward juncture were captured by world media on camera. The optics, many in Pakistan held, were terrible.

Khan could not have known that within 12 hours of his arrival, Putin would announce the invasion. But before he left Islamabad, hoping to make trade deals, he knew that tensions between Moscow and Kyiv were at an all-time high. Just that week, US intelligence agencies had warned that Putin was moving troops close to the border with Ukraine and soldiers had received orders to invade. An official at the US National Security Agency called his Pakistani counterpart and urged caution; though apparently there were no significant trade deals to be made between Pakistan and Russia during that trip. **Khan was in the wrong place at the wrong time.**

How did he get there? In fact, Pakistan had been trying to click up Russia for the last 10 or 15 years; everyone knew the US-Pakistan relationship ebbs and flows… [*The Russians don't trust Pakistan because of this (special relationship), and see the Pakistani military as too 'pro-west'*].

In Imran Khan, however, Putin saw a leader who could be trusted more than those in the uniform or his counterparts, because of his unorthodox thinking. They were waiting for this for 20 years. Later, at an Oxford Union address in October 2022, Khan explained that:

> '... he went to Russia *in the national interest. Russia could supply us cheap oil – also, that he (Imran Khan) wasn't anti-America but that he suspected the Biden administration wanted a more pliable stooge'.*

During his visit to Moscow on 23rd February 2022, the Prime Minister Imran Khan had conveyed to Russian President Vladimir Putin that the military conflict between Russia and Ukraine, could be averted through a diplomatic solution. A communiqué issued after the meeting stated that PM Khan stressed that conflict was not in anyone's interest and that developing countries were always hardest hit economically in case of such conflicts.

During 3-hours long meeting with the President Putin Mr Khan reaffirmed the importance of *Pakistan-Stream Gas Pipeline as a flagship economic project between the two countries and also discussed cooperation on prospective energy-related projects.* While the PM and his National Security Advisor Moeed Yusuf were meeting President Putin and his team, the rest of the cabinet members were seen strolling in Red Square. Astonishingly, there was no interaction with the press following the meeting between the two heads of government. A readout on the Kremlin's official website simply read: *"The leaders of the two countries discussed the main aspects of bilateral cooperation and exchanged views on current regional topics, including developments in South Asia."*

As anticipated, nothing concrete had been agreed upon or signed that could be touted as a major successful takeaway from the visit. The two press releases of both meetings also didn't mention any such agreement or even the signing of a Memorandum of Understanding (MoU). The main purpose of coming to Moscow was that Pakistan needed regional connectivity, mutual trade and Gas-Pipeline. Minister for Energy Hammad Azhar was of the view that whatever agreements were signed on several energy projects, eventualities like possible sanctions on Russia in the backdrop of the Ukrainian war would be dealt with under legal cover.

In a cautious response to PM Imran Khan's visit to Moscow, the US, on the same day prompt, reminded Islamabad that every responsible country must voice concern over Russia's invasion of Ukraine. On Mr Khan's Moscow visit, US State Department spokesperson Ned Price said:

> "We're certainly aware of the trip, and the points I said earlier about the PRC (China) in some ways apply here. We've communicated to Pakistan our position regarding Russia's further renewed invasion of Ukraine, and we have briefed them on our efforts to pursue diplomacy over war. (Further) The US has had a longstanding partnership and cooperation with Pakistan and we view our partnership with a prosperous, with a democratic Pakistan as critical to US interests.
>
> The US had a similar expectation from Pakistan on the question of Ukraine. We certainly hope, when it comes to those shared interests – the aversion of a costly conflict, the aversion of a destabilizing conflict, that every country around the world would make that point clearly in unambiguous language in their engagements with the Russian Federation."

In fact, the US had taken the timing of the visit as an indirect endorsement of President Putin's policies – and indirectly asked the Pakistani government about its intent. It was perhaps in response or anticipation to the above given America's point that the Pakistani information minister (Mr Fawad Hasan), in his measured interaction with the media in Moscow, said:

> "**Pakistan was moving ahead while keeping the complexity of the situation in mind.** We are also in contact with the US and the PM is also likely to visit Europe soon as well; In these circumstances, postponing the planned trip to Russia would have been difficult."

News published in print media and extensive TV discussions on 25th February 2022 are referred.

SHAH M QURESHI's LAST ADDRESS AS F M:

On 10th April 2022: As the parliamentary session began after adjournment, FM Shah M Qureshi took the floor once again and lambasted the fact that lawmakers switched their loyalties for material-gain; while asking:

> "Are those powers who have sworn to uphold the Constitution not seeing this bazaar? The nation was well aware of how votes were bought and sold during last year's Senate elections. We raised objections [...] we presented those videos in the Election Commission of Pakistan (ECP). The PTI kept knocking on the ECP's doors for a year. After this struggle, the arguments were concluded. [But] despite the lapse of a year, the judgement is reserved and we have not gotten justice.".

The foreign minister was true as the *'blatant attempts for changing the regime'* were not hidden; '...history will expose those who have run this entire drama [...] the pen of the historian does not forgive anyone. Pakistan is standing at the crossroads of history. The nation has to decide whether we will live with our heads bowed or with our heads held high.'

Qureshi said he wanted to take the house into confidence; that the process for the prime minister's visit to Russia was set in motion two months before it was scheduled. Adding further that:

> *"We called and consulted Pakistan's seasoned diplomats, academics and some media persons at PM House regarding the pros and cons of undertaking the visit. It was decided with mutual consultation (with the then Army Chief Gen Bajwa especially) that it would be in Pakistan's interest to go ahead with it. **We are a sovereign state. We do not want to bear the yoke of slavery.**"*

The fact remained that prior to the visit to Russia, the US National Security Adviser (NSA) called his Pakistani counterpart with one very brief message: ***Don't go.*** Qureshi questioned how a sovereign state could be stopped from a bilateral visit in this manner.

FM Qureshi added that once the decision to go was made, Pakistan decided to give its input on the Ukraine war. Pakistan is a country that believes in the United Nations charter and self-determination and we never supported the use of force; thus, our response in the UN General Assembly was different. He also highlighted how Pakistani citizens were evacuated from Ukraine as the Russian invasion began. *'We made what efforts [we could]. There was talk of humanitarian assistance, I sent it myself.'*

Qureshi also talked about the then meeting of the Council of Foreign Ministers (CFM) of the Organization of Islamic Cooperation (OIC) where the Afghan issue, the Kashmir issue and the Ukraine issue were raised [...]. Pakistan built consensus among 57 countries of the Islamic ummah; also, that the Islamabad Declaration would go down in history.

Talking about the *'threat letter – CYPHER'*, the foreign minister held:

> *"If the opposition members still have questions about that document, I will give a briefing in parliament. Let's go for an in-camera session and let the ambassador to the US tell us whether he stands by what he sent. **Is it not a threat if you are told that there will be very bad***

> consequences if you do not desist, that Pakistan will be forgiven if the no-confidence motion is passed but will be isolated if the motion fails?"

Mr Qureshi, the foreign minister, also talked about **India's** *'accidental fire of a missile'* into Pakistan.

> *"There was no loss of life but when we asked them for an explanation, they said it was accidental. Will India tell this to the UN Security Council (UNSC)? He had written to the UNSC and said the accidental fire could have led to an **'accidental war'**. It is such a dangerous game that India has played. Where were the standard operating procedures and the protocols?"*

Talking about the China-Pakistan Economic Corridor (CPEC), Qureshi said - the PTI government felt that this was a project that would enhance regional connectivity and lift millions of people out of poverty. PTI government's foreign policy called for good relations with every country and to increase Pakistan's diplomatic space; and didn't want to be hostile with any country.

Once again, Mr Qureshi rejected the claims that the **'threat letter – CYPHER'** was fake, adding that the meeting in Washington took place on 7th March 2022.- and the very next day the no-confidence motion was submitted against the prime minister Imran Khan. Look at how these things coincided - calling for holding an in-camera session.

Turning to the opposition, he said that they had been calling for elections for the last three-and-a-half years. He called on lawmakers not to push Pakistan into a constitutional crisis and to go for fresh elections; urging:

> *"They used to say the elections were not fair and said that Imran Khan was selected. Now when the prime minister said let's hold elections and see what the nation wants, they are not ready for it – we call for the nation to decide - **why are you scared of the nation?**"*

Scenario 249

SHARIFs IN FOCUS DURING PM KHAN's TIME

THE VIDEO SCANDAL:

On 6th July 2019; Pakistan Muslim League Nawaz [PMLN]'s Maryam Safdar released a controversial videotape at a press conference alleging that <u>the country's judiciary acted under compulsion and pressure to convict her father Nawaz Sharif</u>. In the video, Accountability judge Arshad Malik was seen <u>allegedly admitting</u> that he was *'blackmailed into delivering a verdict against former PM Nawaz Sharif in a corruption case <u>on 24th December 2018</u>*. The particular verdict was given in Al-Azizia Case in which Mr Sharif was found guilty of corruption charges and sentenced to seven years in prison.

In the audio, recorded separately from the video, the judge pointed out the defects in his own judgment and shared the points that Sharif would be able to argue in the appeal then pending before the Islamabad High Court. The foreign media analysts contended that the independence of the Pakistani judiciary was [once more] eroded to the extent that such an ugly scenario had popped up. In the country, Maryam stirred Pakistan's entire political and judicial system through her press conference.

The PTI government rebutted Maryam's claim vehemently that the audio-video was fake and was concocted to malign the judge and the NAB as an anti-corruption state institution. The electronic media and the press of the country got a hot issue inviting the intelligentsia for and against and started discussing the scandal on air and in open.

A month earlier, a similar scandalous video was <u>aired</u> on TV channels and social media having secretly recorded a conversation between the NAB Chairman [Justice retired Javed Iqbal] and a woman, the wife of another convicted criminal. In the video, the NAB Chairman expresses a sexual desire to meet the woman separately. However, the Chairman neither acknowledged or commented on it nor resigned as per expectations of many.

[*Such intimidations remained in circlulation throughout the judicial history of this country. In the 1990s, the Nawaz government was caught calling Lahore High Court's Justice Malik Qayyum to enhance 'full doze' of the verdict against Benazir Bhutto. Later, in 2007, Gen Musharraf summoned the then Chief Justice of Pakistan Iftikhar Chaudhry demanding his resignation.*]

Coming back to the video in question, the judge Arshad Malik told a PMLN worker [Nasir Butt, who allegedly had a strong part-affiliation history, too] that there was no evidence of corruption, money laundering or kickbacks against Nawaz Sharif, but he (the judge) was forced to rule against him. At one point, Malik also said that someone had a video of him of a very personal nature and it was ready to be released. The dialogue played was: **he would not be able to 'sustain pressure' and might even 'commit suicide'**.

PMLN's Maryam Safdar also claimed that she's in possession of more such tapes that could prove her father was convicted in a fraudulent trial - she demanded that Nawaz Sharif be released immediately in the light of that tape video. The aspiring next prime minister was so ignorant of the laws of the land that no government executive could release any convict on the basis of such tape releases or press conferences – <u>one has to go through due process of law in the respective courts</u>.

However, following her press conference, Judge Malik immediately released a statement refuting Maryam's claims while saying that:

> "I want to clarify it there was neither any direct or indirect pressure on me nor was there any greed. I decided all these cases on the basis of evidence."

It appeared that the said videotape scandal had put the legitimacy of Nawaz's conviction under question for a while. If it was a fact that he actually admitted to being under duress could completely vitiate a trial. However, separate issues related to the videotape cropped up - mainly an issue about privacy; as **judge Arshad Malik was recorded in a video without his consent**. More so, the evidential value of the tapes was subject to forensic tests.

Maryam Safdar's critics and a sizable number of media houses argued she could have taken the tapes to the judiciary and not released them through a press conference. Most of them contended that Maryam's prime motive behind releasing those videotapes was political and not legal. And she was successful in scoring high points. Imran Khan's government initially okayed to facilitate an investigation looking into the legitimacy of these tapes but finally declared it a matter relating with the judiciary. Meanwhile, certain TV anchors were reprimanded for being un-careful for airing the uncertified version of the said video-tape. Some channels were made off air for some time, too.

The scandal also rattled the Pakistani judicial establishment. Following Maryam's press conference, the Acting CJ of the Islamabad High Court [IHC] had a 45-minute exclusive meeting with the Pakistan's Chief Justice Asif S Khosa to find out some solution of the video-tape issue. Two options appeared: Either the Islamabad High Court could take the matter forward or the Supreme Court could initiate proceedings *suo-moto*.

BUT the intelligentsia had the dismal and bleak history of Pakistan's judiciary in mind. In 1997, Supreme Court Justice Malik Qayyum had convicted former Pakistani PM Benazir Bhutto and her husband Asif Ali Zardari in a corruption case on explicit instructions of PMLN leadership. It was later found that Justice Qayyum had colluded with the executive and the ruling had to be overturned. *In 2001, the judge was sent home disgracefully and un-ceremonially by the Supreme Court of Pakistan.*

ACCOUNTABILITY JUDGE SENT HOME:

On 12th July 2019; Maryam Safdar called for the verdict against her father Nawaz Sharif to be expunged following the Islamabad High Court's [IHC] decision to remove Accountability Judge Arshad Malik from his post. In numerous tweets, Maryam held that the matter was not about the removal of a judge, instead - it was about suspending the verdict that the judge had issued. See her tweets:

> *"The clear meaning of the removal of the judge is that the judiciary has accepted the truth. If this is the case, how can a verdict by this judge be maintained?*
>
> *A judge [...] was found guilty of misconduct and being removed from his post; how can the subject of his misconduct be punished?*
>
> *Is it enough to only remove the judge? Certainly not.*
>
> *Now this matter is not restricted just to Nawaz Sharif. I am turning to the judiciary for justice. I will keep waiting."*

On 13th July 2019; after consultation with the Supreme Court amid deepening political and judicial crises, the Islamabad High Court [IHC] removed accountability court judge Arshad Malik while the apex court fixed a petition seeking a thorough probe into the video for hearing on 16th July 2019, three days later. The admin stopped the judge from performing judicial duties.

Prior to this, Judge Malik had called on acting CJ of the IHC, Aamer Farooq, twice within that week and submitted a letter to him along with an affidavit claiming that he was blackmailed owing to another *'damaging but manipulated immoral video in a compromising position, recorded somewhere in Multan'*.

> [In his affidavit, judge Malik claimed that Nasir Butt and Nasir Janjua of the PMLN used the manipulated immoral video to blackmail him time and again. He also claimed that his two acquaintances Mahar Jilani and Nasir Janjua met him in February 2018 and informed him that his appointment was made on their recommendations.
>
> On 13th March 2018, Judge Malik was posted as the Accountability Court judge a couple of months after being transferred to the IHC from Lahore High Court. When Nawaz Sharif's trial in Al-Azizia and Flagship Investment was transferred to his court, he was approached multiple times by associates and supporters of the PMLN supremo, the judge said.]

However, Mr Malik said in spite of all those attempts, he was determined to decide the reference purely on merit and subsequently convicted Nawaz Sharif in Al-Azizia reference but acquitted him in Flagship Investment reference on 24th December 2018. After their failed attempts, they showed him the immoral Multan video when he was posted there in the past. The judge submitted that:

> '.....due to fear of the 'Multan video' he met Nawaz Sharif at Jati Umra on 6th April 2019, Hussain Nawaz in Saudi Arabia on 1st June 2019 and Nasir Butt pressurized him to get his assistance in preparation of grounds for appeals in Al-Azizia and Flagship references.'

After perusing the affidavit, the IHC addressed to the law ministry stating that the releasing of videos, issuing of press release by the registrar accountability court-II Islamabad and affidavit submitted by the incumbent judge narrating his version required his immediate removal. Judge Arshad Malik's affidavits were also enclosed. The IHC's recommendations were strong enough saying that *'he may be removed / relieved from his duties by the competent authority forthwith so that he can be repatriated to his parent department, i.e. Lahore High Court, Lahore.'*

The IHC registrar office also stated:

> *"This letter may be treated as consultation of the Chief Justice of this court as required under section 5A (4) of the National Accountability Ordinance, 1999. An early action in this regard shall be highly appreciated."*

Shortly after this development, the Federal Ministry of Law, in compliance with the IHC directions, barred Judge Malik from serving as an accountability court judge. It also expressed the hope that NAB would initiate proceeding against those who used the video to blackmail the accountability court judge.

On 16th July 2019: In another significant development, the SC started hearing that petition moved by one Ishtiaq Ahmed Mirza, a lawyer and a social activist. During the hearing of the case by a three-judge SC bench, the CJP regretted that the conduct of Judge Malik had caused all honest, hard-working and dedicated judges to bow their heads in shame. The CJP also wondered why the Federal Investigation Agency (FIA) had failed to conduct forensic examination of the video. The entire country, except the FIA, had copies of the video. The CJP questioned why no party had moved any application before the IHC to place the video as evidence in the appeal pending against the ex-PM's conviction.

While reading out a report furnished by the FIA on the video scandal, the then Attorney General (AG) told the honourable bench that the video of Judge Malik was made by (another) accused Mian Tariq Mehmood of Multan between the years 2000 and 2003, when the former was posted as additional District and Session's Judge in Multan.

According to the FIA report, Shahbaz Sharif had expressed ignorance about the video, claiming that (only) Maryam Safdar could give any clarifications. Other PMLN leaders Kh Asif, Ahsan Iqbal and Atta Ullah Tarrar also adopted a similar stance. Significantly, Maryam also attempted to disassociate herself from the details and specifics of the acquisition, origins, source, recording, dissemination, release and timing of the said audio / video. She placed the entire responsibility and burden upon accused Nasir Butt.

In an affidavit, Judge Malik said that at a social gathering attended by both accused Nasir Janjua and one Maher Ghulam Jilani, the former took him aside and implored him to give verdict of acquittal in both the references. The judge also claimed he was again approached by the two accused *Janjua and Jilani offered him Euros equivalent to Rs:100 million and telling him that the foreign currency worth Rs:20 million was readily available in their vehicle outside.* Also, that accused Nasir Butt met him and threatened him regarding revelation of the video by accused Janjua.

After a couple of days, accused Mian Tariq visited the judge's house and showed him the video. When Judge Malik was asked if accused Janjua had ever personally showed the video to him, the former replied in the negative. However, the judge maintained the version and accusations in his affidavit and complaint as correct.

On 23rd August 2019; the Supreme Court wrapped up all the petitions on video links involving judge Arshad Malik, saying that *'We find that it may not be an appropriate stage for this court to interfere in the matter of the relevant video and its effects' since the criminal appeal was lying subjudice before the Islamabad High Court* [IHC]. The verdict was authored by the CJP Asif Saeed Khosa himself. His written remarks in the judgment included:

> "His admitted conduct emerging from that press release and the affidavit stinks and the stench of such stinking conduct has the tendency to bring bad name to the entire judiciary as an institution.
>
> His sordid and disgusting conduct has made the thousands of honest, upright, fair and proper judges in the country hang their heads in shame."

However, the five issues addressed by the top court were that:

- Relevant forum for consideration in Nawaz Sharif Case
- Establishing video as 'genuine piece of evidence'
- If genuine, how will video be proven before court of law?
- Effect on the Nawaz Sharif Case
- Conduct of judge Arshad Malik

On 7th September 2019; a trial court of Islamabad acquitted three people accused in Accountability Judge Arshad Malik's video scandal as the country's premier investigation department, FIA, had failed to produce any evidence against Nasir Janjua, Khurram Yousuf and Ghulam Jilani. They were arrested on 2nd September after a Cyber Crime Court had turned down their plea for extension in bail before arrest. A report by the FIA had cleared them of all charges whatsoever.

On 5th Oct 2019; Former PM Nawaz Sharif requested the IHC to review the evidence linked to a controversial video and statement of judge Arshad Malik before deciding the PMLN supremo's appeal, then pending before that court, against his conviction in the Al-Azizia case.

A sad note: It also remains a fact that Pakistan's superior courts keep a history of undertaking to resolve all sorts of contentious political cases; more often quite un-necessarily. The Supreme Court has written several controversial opinions legitimizing military coups, legitimizing several political office holders knowing that they were not truthful and honest - blatantly ignoring the evidence on record - FAKE DEGREES case and swallowing the bank loans of billions smilingly are here as reference.

Due to acute politicization, Pakistan's high courts didn't enjoy a reputation of judicial integrity; the lower courts being more corrupt. The administrative courts like Banking, Labour, and Customs and to great extent the NAB courts too, are particularly vulnerable to political pressure. The media and the politicians accuse, though only in whispers, the military establishment for most political convictions BUT in fact both segments allege the army just to hide their own shortcomings and corrupt practices.

Unfortunately, there is no easy solution for fixing the degradation of judicial ecology in Pakistan. No anticorruption agency like NAB or FIA can initiate action against any judge; even the parliament or its committee cannot do so. The only door open to this effect is a constitutional provision of the Supreme Judicial Council [SJC] – AND the irony of fate is that since 1973, only one judge could be proceeded against successfully by the SJC made under that provision while tens of cases are either lying pending or suffered their own death due to ineptness of the said body / Council.

Referring to an essay by L ALI KHAN in *jurist.org* dated 11th July 2019:

> *"A culture of military coups, election tampering, corruption, horse trading in the national and provincial legislatures, ethics-free politics, obsessive patriotism that treats critics as traitors, these and other factors vitiate the dynamics of justice. Under these social burdens, good faith judicial neutrality appears unavailable. Much like politicians, judges and Generals are perceived to have been forced into partisanship."*

Article-II of the Judicial Code of Conduct states that '.... *a Judge should be God-fearing, law-abiding, abstemious, truthful of tongue, wise in opinion, cautious and forbearing, blameless, and untouched by greed*'. However, in practice not an iota of the above adjectives is adhered to. This rule, under the current epidemic of scandals in fact presented a very dismal scenario of Pakistan's judiciary – the details of Judge Arshad Malik be taken as a fresh episode confirming that attitude.

SHAHBAZ SHARIF AT MAIL-ON-SUNDAY:

On 14th July 2019; an investigative report appeared in the British newspaper **DAILY MAIL** accusing former Punjab chief minister Shahbaz Sharif and his family of allegedly embezzling millions of pounds out of £500m aid lent by the Department for International Development [DFID] for 2005 earthquake victims. However, Mr Sharif refuted the report declaring it a fabricated and defamatory story tarnishing his political image. He termed it as part of propaganda launched by the then Prime Minister Imran Khan against the PMLN in the name of sham accountability.

When the report was published, Shahbaz Sharif was the leader of Pakistan's main opposition party, Pakistan Muslim League-Nawaz (PMLN) and, before losing power in 2018, spent ten years as mighty chief minister of the country's biggest province, Punjab – home to 110 million people. For years he was renowned as a Third World poster boy, who spent millions for the uplift of his province. However, the investigative report claimed that Shahbaz and his family were embezzling tens of millions of pounds of public money and laundering it in Britain. The investigators were convinced that some of the allegedly stolen money came from DFID-funded aid projects.

On the other hand, Shahbaz's London based son Suleman immediately denied the allegations against him and his family, saying they were the product of a 'political witch-hunt' ordered by Pakistan's PM Imran Khan and his PTI.

> [**Transparency International:** *Pakistan comes just 117th in the world integrity index and 'corruption is a major obstacle' there. DFID admits it is 'well aware' that Pakistan is a 'corrupt environment'. However, since 2014, DFID has given more aid to Pakistan than any other country – up to £463 million a year.*]

During the first week of July 2019, **The Mail on Sunday** (**MOS**) – which had campaigned against Britain's policy of spending 0.7 percent of national income, then about £14 billion a year, on foreign aid – was given exclusive access to a high-level probe ordered by PM Imran Khan. Interview of key witnesses held on remand in jail were allowed where a UK citizen Aftab Mehmood, claimed that:

> "......he laundered millions on behalf of Shahbaz's family from a nondescript office in Birmingham – without attracting suspicion from Britain's financial regulators, who inspected his books regularly."

During 2018; the Daily Mail had also disclosed corruption cases against Pakistan's former prime minister Nawaz Sharif, who had built up a London property empire worth £32 million. Convicted of corruption, he was then serving a seven-year jail sentence but *due to weak justice system of Pakistan, he managed to flee from there on the basis of false medical reports.*

The **Mail on Sunday** further revealed that:

- Certain legal documents divulged that Shahbaz's son-in-law named Imran received about £1 million from a fund established to rebuild the lives of earthquake victims – to which DFID gave £54m from UK tax-money;

- There were alleged thefts from DFID-funded schemes to give poor women cash to lift them out of poverty and to provide healthcare for rural families;

- Stolen millions were laundered in Birmingham and then transferred to Shahbaz's family's accounts by UK branches of banks including Barclays and HSBC;

- Self-confessed Birmingham money-launderer Aftab Mehmood told the MOS that he had his accounts audited every three months by Her Majesty's Revenue and Customs – who failed to notice anything abnormal;

- Britain's National Crime Agency worked closely with Pakistani investigators to unearth the scam to full extent while the members of Shahbaz's family were enjoying refuge in London;

- Aware of how widespread corruption is in Pakistan, DFID has been running a £1.75 million project designed to 'reduce the exposure to fraud and corruption' of UK aid. DFID admitted that, till then, it referred just one individual to the Pakistani authorities for trying to steal UK funds.

A night before the article published in the MoS, former International Development Secretary Priti Patel, who is widely tipped to rejoin the Cabinet if Boris Johnson becomes PM, demanded an inquiry. She told the MOS while specially referring to the background of poverty in Pakistan:

> "We spend millions on anti-corruption initiatives and yet it seems clear that Britain is still a money-launderers' paradise. It's vital we now co-operate with the Pakistani investigation, to ensure those allegedly responsible come up against with the full force of the law."

Indeed, this was how the investigation into Shahbaz and his family began. After winning election on a pledge to combat corruption, Imran Khan set up a special team to deal with it, the Asset Recovery Unit, headed by a UK-educated barrister. They examined a series of suspicious transactions running to many millions and shown that Shahbaz's family's assets grew enormously during the years he was in power.

A confidential investigation report, seen by the MOS, said the family was worth just £150,000 in 2003 but by 2018 their total assets had grown to about £200 million; the family's legitimate income sources could not account for their richness. The money, was channelled from abroad – via several elaborate money-laundering schemes, in which Britain played a central role. Then laundered payments were made to Shahbaz's children, his wife and his son-in-law Ali Imran. But Shahbaz *'was the principal beneficiary of this money-laundering enterprise, by way of spending, acquisition of properties and their expansion into palatial houses where he lived.'*

One of the most audacious schemes was focused on Birmingham. The report listed 202 'personal remittances' from the UK and the United Arab Emirates (UAE) into the bank accounts of Shahbaz's wife, two sons and two daughters.

Under Pakistani law, before the recipients could accept these payments into their accounts, they had to sign 'due diligence forms' saying they had been sent as 'investments' by people they knew personally. Some details here:

- 'We noticed that someone called Manzoor Ahmed had sent a series of 13 payments from Birmingham worth £1.2 million to Shahbaz's wife Nusrat and his sons Hamza and Suleman.' He was traced through his identity card, whose number was on the forms; he turned out to be '*a small home-based tuck shop owner' in a remote village, who scraped a living selling poppadoms*. Needless to say, he had never had £1.2 million, nor ever travelled to England.

- Another man who was said to have sent about £850,000 to Shahbaz's family from Birmingham via HSBC was Mehboob Ali, a Lahore 'street hawker', who lived from taking tiny commissions from collecting old banknotes and changing them into new ones. When I met him in Lahore, he was visibly terrified. He said: 'When I discovered my identity had been stolen, my life overturned. I never met any of these people. *'Now I try to live by selling glasses of lime juice and it's hard to feed my family.'*

Sending money to Shahbaz's family apparently from these and other poverty-stricken 'investors' was managed via a Briton Aftab Mehmood, the proprietor of Usman International, a money-changing firm in the Sparkbrook area of Birmingham. He explained how the money-laundering worked:

> "*I would just receive a fax from Pakistan with the names of the people I had to wire money to. I knew who they were: they were famous. It wasn't my business to ask where the money came from. I simply transferred it, and I did it through the proper channels.*
>
> *'I was audited by HMRC every three months. They wanted to make sure I wasn't money-laundering. I always passed with flying colours. That meant I had no problem with the banks."*

The investigators held that the money had been taken as kickbacks and 'commissions' from government-run projects and delivered by 'cash boys' in bulging sacks to the office of Mehmood's Lahore contact, Shahed Rafiq. In jail, *Rafiq confirmed this, adding: 'I don't know where the cash came from. It was just business.'* The last part of the scheme was clever. How did Rafiq ensure that when Mehmood wired money to the accounts in Pakistan, he had funds to pay accordingly.

The answer was that Mehmood's company in Birmingham also did legitimate money transfers and had thousands of clients who wanted to send money to relatives in Pakistan. When and if asked to send £100,000 to one of Shahbaz's sons, he would simply wait until he had funds from UK customers who wanted to send equivalent sums to Pakistan. Then, instead of wiring the money to his customers' relatives, he would send it under the names of fake investors to Shahbaz's family's bank accounts. <u>In Lahore, Rafiq would give the relatives the stolen money which had been brought by the cash boys; the payments made by this method totalled £21 million – but were merely the tip of the iceberg.</u>

Investigators traced a further £9.1 million from 'ghost' investors who didn't exist but fake loans and investments in family companies continued in routine; their value touched a further £160 million. Having established the scale of the money-laundering, the investigators moved into phase two – finding out where and how the laundered funds were stolen. Shahbaz's son, Suleman said:

> *"This is a witch-hunt against my family. It is similar to what happened at Guantanamo Bay, and under apartheid in South Africa. There is a clique around Imran Khan which is trying to shut out the opposition and they are picking out my family members in order to harass them."*

One case was in the court till the newsbreak – a guilty plea by *Ikram Naveed, the former finance director of ERRA, <u>Pakistan's Earthquake Relief and Reconstruction Authority</u>, set up after the devastating quake of 2005, which had received £54 million from DFID between then and 2012, both for immediate relief and long-term schemes to rebuild victims' lives. [*Naveed is described in Pakistan as the 'right hand man' of Ali Imran – Shahbaz's son-in-law who is married to his daughter Rabia.]

Naveed pleaded guilty and confessed in November 2018 to embezzling about £1.5 million from ERRA during the period DFID was funding it, of which he passed on almost £1 million to Ali Imran. Naveed said half of this was transferred directly from ERRA's accounts – a claim confirmed by banking records. Ali Imran was summoned to answer questions from investigators, but he failed to appear – because he was in London, and refused to speak to them. He didn't respond to a request for comment from the MOS. Other family members, who had received laundered millions, had also sought refuge in Britain, including Shahbaz's son, Suleman.

DFID REPORT ON ERRA PERFORMANCE:

An internal DFID report, drawn up in 2008, had warned that ERRA 'had yet to develop effective and transparent accountability systems.'

Nevertheless, DFID continued pumping millions into ERRA. The report stated that DFID aid to ERRA was not 'earmarked', but paid into its general budget. DFID's funding was aimed at: *'The UK's financial support to ERRA over this period was for payment by results – which means we only gave money once the agreed work, which was primarily focused on building schools, was completed, and the work audited and verified.'*

Under the Pakistan National Cash Transfers programme, for which DFID had provided nearly £300 million since 2012, giving payments of £100 a month to mothers in poor families. Before Imran Khan became prime minister, inquiries had begun into payments to *'ghost claimants'* which were being siphoned off – but the investigation was shut down while Shahbaz's party was in power. It was reopened, and investigators were conducting a fresh survey of how the money was spent, and whether women who got the stipend actually existed; the Mail on Sunday [MoS] wrote.

A further investigation was then under way into alleged thefts from maternal and child health programmes. Meanwhile, Mr Shahbaz was summoned numerous times to answer investigators' questions, while his son, Hamza, was being held for questioning in custody.

When asked about the payments Suleman allegedly received from the poppadom seller and other questionable sources, he said: *'The law allows foreign remittances and each and every penny I received came through proper banking channels, cleared by the State Bank of Pakistan. [The investigators] are just releasing funny stories in the media. I deny their version. I have done everything according to the law.'*

However, Asset Recovery Unit's chief Shahzad Akbar held that his investigations had already uncovered evidence of money-laundering on a vast scale, much of it conducted via the UK; it appeared that (perhaps) very large sums may had been stolen from aid and development projects financed by the British taxpayers. MoS reporter ended with a very disappointing note from investigators including the main 'Mir Jaffer' of PM Khan named Shahzad Akbar:

> 'We are working closely with the **National Crime Agency** and the **Home Office**. We are grateful for this assistance and we hope it will ensure that theft and money-laundering of this magnitude will never happen again.'

According to **Daily Mail report,** Shahbaz Sharif visited Downing Street when David Cameron was UK's prime minister, held talks with successive international development secretaries – Andrew Mitchell, Justine Greening and Penny Mordaunt – and hosted Boris Johnson when he was foreign secretary. However, they were convinced that the allegedly stolen money came from DFID-funded aid projects. The Mail on Sunday (MoS) revealed:

- *"Legal documents allege that Shahbaz's son-in-law received about £1 million (Rs:198.7 m then) from a fund established **to rebuild the lives of earthquake victims** – to which DFID gave £54 million from UK taxpayers;*

- *Inquiries were launched into alleged thefts from DFID-funded schemes **to give poor women cash to lift them out of poverty** and to provide healthcare for rural families;*

- *Stolen millions were laundered in Birmingham and then allegedly transferred to Shahbaz's family's accounts by UK banks including Barclays and HSBC;*

- *Self-confessed Birmingham money-launderer Aftab Mahmood told the MoS that he had his accounts audited every three months by H M Revenue and Customs – who failed to notice anything was amiss;*

- *Britain's National Crime Agency is working closely with Pakistani investigators and Home Secretary Sajid Javid is discussing the possible extradition of members of Shahbaz's family who have taken refuge in London."*

Aware of how widespread corruption is in Pakistan, DFID has been running a £1.75 million (PKR 347.7 m then) project designed to **'reduce the exposure to fraud and corruption' of UK aid** - But the Pakistani authorities were trying to steal UK funds. The former International Development Secretary Priti Patel, keeping the above said investigations in mind, had also felt disturbed – thus her remarks (noted in earlier paragraphs) are on record.

Duncan Hames, policy director of Transparency International told that: 'First you identify suspicious transactions in the banking system and then you follow the money trail back to discover where they came from.' Indeed, this was how the investigation into Shahbaz and his family began. The Asset Recovery Unit of Pakistan had examined a series of suspicious transactions running to many millions and shown that Shahbaz's family's assets grew enormously during the years he was in power. Unit's report listed 202 'personal remittances' from the UK and the United Arab Emirates into the bank accounts of Shahbaz's wife, two sons and two daughters.

LEGAL NOTICES TO DAILY MAIL ETC:

On 26th July 2019: PMLN President Shahbaz Sharif sent a legal notice to British Publication *The Mail* on Sunday (MoS), online news site Mail Online, and its *journalist David Rose*, about an article published on 14th July 2019, detailed in above lines. A London-based legal firm Carter-Ruck Solicitors had acted on behalf of the Sharif family; a formal legal complaint was also issued against the news outlets and investigative journalist Rose for the said *'gravely defamatory story.'*

The story published earlier this month claimed that Sharif, the former chief minister of Punjab, had embezzled funds provided by UK's Department for International Development (DFID) for the rehabilitation of the 2005 earthquake. It quoted Assets Recovery Unit Chief Shahzad Akbar and a few other individuals — none of whom were in an official position.

Thus, the story was quickly refuted by the PMLN and the party had insisted that it was published *"on the behest of [Prime Minister] Imran Khan"*. It was also rejected by DFID, that said the body's robust systems had protected UK taxpayers from fraud. *'The article is gravely defamatory of Mr Sharif, including false allegations that he misappropriated UK taxpayers' money of DFID aid intended for the victims of the devastating 2005 earthquake in Pakistan,'* the press release read. *'I am utterly appalled by these allegations,* the press release quoted Sharif as saying.

The statement further said that at no stage were the allegations properly put to Sharifs in advance of publication. Shahbaz Sharif pointed out that — among other matters —at the time of the earthquake in 2005, I was not even in Pakistan but living in UK in exile. He claimed that the story was part of a *'politically motivated campaign'* initiated by Mr Khan and his aide Akbar. *'No allegation has been proven. There is no evidence of kickbacks,'* Shahbaz's son Suleman was quoted as saying in the report.

JOURNALIST DAVID ROSE RESPONDED:

BUT, simultaneously, Journalist David Rose re-affirmed what he had said in his reporting at **MAIL-ON-SUNDAY** [MoS]:

> "We were also able to interview key witnesses held on remand in jail, including a UK citizen Aftab Mehmood. He claims he laundered millions on behalf of Shahbaz's family from a nondescript office in Birmingham – without attracting suspicion from Britain's financial regulators, who inspected his books regularly."

Moreover, hours after Shahbaz Sharif's legal team released the press note, Journalist of the MoS David Rose took to Twitter, saying:

> *"I'm only going to make one comment on Shahbaz Sharif's recent statements. He [Shahbaz] complains the earthquake was in 2005 before he became CM. But according to evidence already aired in a Pakistani court, the alleged thefts from the quake relief fund were in 2009 and 2011. Refutation?"*
>
> **David Rose@DavidRoseUK**
> 11:38 AM - Jul 26, 2019

Later, **on 23rd August 2019:** British journalist, David Rose exposed a series of tweets directed towards him and the news publishers by PMLN President Shahbaz Sharif. Shahbaz Sharif, taking to the website Twitter, had claimed that the British news publisher and the journalist associated with them, i.e., David Rose had failed to respond to his legal notice sent prior citing defamation and libel. To this, Rose had responded that he had already answered it via his twitter message dated 26th July – (as given in above paragraphs)

On 9th October 2019: LONDON office of Pakistan's daily THENEWS wrote:

> *"A journalist from Daily Mail UK, David Rose has once again come up with claims of still not receiving any lawsuit from the former Punjab chief minister and the Opposition Leader in the National Assembly Shahbaz Sharif against his story exposing alleged thefts from the earthquake relief funds."*

David Rose, in his fresh Twitter message – once more said:

> *"Hello Pakistani friends. A lot of you have been asking if Shahbaz Sharif has commenced a lawsuit against me and my newspaper yet. He hasn't..... Sources tell me that investigations by NAB [National Accountability Bureau] and the Asset Recovery Unit into allegations against Shahbaz Sharif have continued with same vigour since my article was published. **This may explain why he hasn't filed a lawsuit:** they have been keeping him busy."*

DAILY 'THE MAIL' IN COURT AT LONDON:

In fact, the said libel suit against the MoS admin and journalist David Rose was formally launched <u>on 31st January 2020;</u> it was launched at the London High Court then. The disclosure of formal court action was made at a press conference at the chambers of British law firm Carter-Ruck by Alasdair Pepper and Antonia Foster, who were representing Shahbaz. Shahbaz was present with his lawyers at the press conference where the announcement was made. Further, that the Mail Publications were in receipt of the claim form.

Mr Pepper had however, confirmed that tweets by David Rose had also been made part of the defamation claim. On the other side, David Rose said he would not be making any comments for the time being. A source at the Daily Mail confirmed that the publication's lawyers had received the legal claim from Shahbaz Sharif's lawyers. Whereas, the DfID had already rubbished the claims made by newspaper as *"false and without any foundation."* Shahbaz Sharif's lawyer said the UK government had also flatly contradicted the Mail's claim. On the very day of the publication, the UK's Department for International Development (DFID) responded to the Mail on Sunday.

The Carter Ruck lawyer said that (astonishingly) PTI's Federal Minister for Education *Shafqat Mahmood had supported refutation of the Mail's claim*. He was referring to a press conference held at the Dorchester Hotel a week ago by Shafqat Mahmood in which, answering questions, he said that Britain's aid programme to Pakistan was by and large well managed and run properly under the previous PPP and PMLN governments. PTI's federal minister also held that: *"Shahbaz Sharif seeks withdrawal of the allegations and an unreserved and unambiguous apology from the Mail's publisher – AND that any sums awarded to him in damages will be paid to charity."*

It remained a mystery that why PM Khan's Special Assistant on Accountability Shahzad Akbar was not made a party in the claim against Daily Mail although Shahzad Akbar had incited Shahbaz Sharif to sue him as well. Addressing the media, Shahbaz Sharif said:

> *"The article was a politically motivated campaign against him and his family by the incumbent government of Pakistan (PTI). He was determined to prove that allegations against him were false, baseless and politically motivated to malign him. He regretted that the Mail publications made allegations without any proofs. It was clear that the Mail journalist was*

used by the PTI government by **granting the journalist exclusive access to some of the tampered results** of a high-level probe ordered by PM Khan; including a **confidential investigation report** and unusual access to interview key witnesses held on remand in jail.

They (the PTI) couldn't compete with the PMLN in anything."

Shahbaz Sharif held further that the Transparency International (TI)'s report had frightened the PTI government, which was in turn; attacking and victimising political opponents; wondering at the clarification issued by the TI Pakistan while the report had been released by the main chapter of the NGO in Berlin. He termed PM's Special Assistant Shahzad Akbar as a *"sycophant - there was not even a shred of evidence against him"*. Mr Sharif added that:

> "DfID had done a great job in training the youth of Pakistan and providing them healthcare. He said that instead of thanking DfID and the British authorities, the Pakistani government was defaming them. Little did they realise that while trying to hit me, they [government] are bringing a bad name to Pakistan."

DfID had separately refuted the claims made by The Mail on Sunday (MoS). It was understood that the case was going for trial before a judge at the Royal Court of Justice and the due date to get trial was between nine months to a year those days.

Regarding **hearings** at the Royal Court of London, Daily Mail took much time to submit a defense of Rose's story. On 20th April 2020, Justice Nicklin issued the initial order for the listing hearing window running from 21st April 2020 to 31st July 2020. On 7th May 2020, Justice Nicklin issued a second ruling that extended the due dates. On 20th October 2020, Justice Nicklin issued the first order, merging the claims of Shahbaz and his son-in-law Yousaf.

On 28th January 2021; Justice Nicklin issued another order pertaining to the preliminary issue trial. The verdict and order were delivered on 5th February 2021. Justice Nicklin ruled at the hearing at the London High Court in favour of PMLN President Shahbaz and his son-in-law. *Justice Nicklin determined that the Mail on Sunday's article carried the highest level of defamatory meaning for both Shehbaz and Yousaf.*

On 18 February 2021, Justice Nicklin issued the directive with relation to certain deadlines. On 15th March 2022, The Daily Mail filed its defense. Following negotiations to resolve the dispute after March 2022 between Daily Mail and PM Shahbaz, it was made apparent to the premier's legal counsel that the publication would issue an apology and take down the item under his conditions. On 26th September 2022, Justice Nicklin issued an order and scheduled a joint case management meeting.

> *Three days prior to this hearing, Shahbaz pulled his request for a delay. According to the regulations, the court was not informed that the lawyers for Daily Mail had been secretly negotiating with Shahbaz's lawyers for several months, proposing to apologize. Shahbaz Sharif was persuaded by his legal staff that there was no use in submitting more paperwork as the newspaper had already agreed to apologize and remove the defamatory and misleading piece.*

Daily Mail publishers and Shahbaz's lawyers signed an agreement of settlement with Tomlin Order in the second week of December 2022 after which *Daily Mail* removed the defamatory article and apologized to the prime minister and his son-in-law. It was promised that the Daily Mail would never repeat the false allegations at any forum and has already worked with Google to remove all articles carrying *Daily Mail's* article. REFERRING TO THE PAKISTAN'S DAILY TIMES DATED 9TH DECEMBER 2022:

> *"British publication The Mail on Sunday (MoS) and news site Mail Online apologised to Prime Minister Shehbaz Sharif for an **error in an article it published on 4th July 2019** – in which it had accused the premier of **stealing British foreign aid money**. The said news story, written by investigative journalist David Rose, has now been removed from the publication's website and other platforms.*
>
> *The article had claimed that Shahbaz had embezzled funds provided by UK's Department for International Development (DFID) for the rehabilitation of the 2005 earthquake while he was chief minister of Punjab. It had quoted former accountability chief Shahzad Akbar and a few other individuals – none of whom were in an official position. The story was quickly refuted by the PMLN."*

SHAHBAZ SHARIF IN HOT WATERS [*via* NAB]:

On 4th December 2019; the National Accountability Bureau (NAB) immobilised 23 properties belonging to Shahbaz and his sons Hamza and Suleman, over claims they had acquired assets beyond their known sources of income and committed money-laundering.

The properties under radar of NAB were also owned by wives of Shahbaz Sharif including Nusrat Shahbaz and Tehmina Durrani. As per NAB orders, the NAB directed the Lahore commissioner to freeze 13 plots, owned by Hamza Shahbaz in Johar Town Lahore and Judicial Colony. In this regard, secretary Judicial Employees Cooperative Housing Society, Lahore, was directed to freeze the transfer and sale of four plots (49. 50, 51, 52), owned by Hamza Shahbaz in the Judicial Employees Cooperative Housing Society Lahore, each plot measuring more than one kanal. The Lahore Development Authority (LDA) was asked to freeze nine plots of Hamza in K-Block, Johar Town. A letter was also written by NAB to DG Galiyat Development Authority, Abbottabad, to freeze a property measuring 9 kanals in Nishat Lodges Dunga Gali, owned by Nusrat Shahbaz, wife of Shahbaz Sharif.

Secretary Model Town Lahore was asked by NAB to freeze two more properties, owned by Nusrat Shahbaz in Model Town Lahore including the famous 96-H and 86-H. The Defence Housing Authority (DHA), Lahore, was also directed to freeze two properties owned by Tehmina Durrani located in its Phase-V. Furthermore, the bureau had also frozen a cottage and a villa in Pir Sohawa and two more plots in Chiniot.

Previously, the NAB Lahore had ordered for freezing various industries of Shahbaz Sharif family, including Chiniot Power Limited, Ramzan Energy Limited, Al-Arabia Sugar Mills, Crystal Plastics Private Limited, Sharif Dairy Farms Private Limited and Sharif Poultry Farms Private Limited.

On 28th September 2020: Leader of the Opposition in the National Assembly Shehbaz Sharif got arrested by the NAB after the Lahore High Court (LHC) rejected his interim bail in money laundering case. A two-member bench of the LHC heard the case, while lawyers representing the former Punjab chief minister presented their arguments after a three-day pause.

On 11th November 2020: PMLN president Shahbaz Sharif and others were indicted in a money laundering case by an accountability court in Lahore. The suspects, however, pleaded not guilty. Speaking to media outside the courtroom, Shahbaz dismissed the NAB cases as baseless and termed them politically-motivated.

The former chief minister Punjab was accused of accumulating assets worth Rs:7,328 million in connivance with his co-accused family members, *benamidars*, front persons and close associations and for developing an organized system of money laundering. NAB had nominated a total of 20 individuals in the reference – Shahbaz's wife Nusrat, his sons Hamza and Suleman, and daughters Rabia Imran and Javeria Ali. <u>NAB accused the PMLN president of corruption creating fake sources of income to justify the assets acquired beyond known sources of income</u>.

The PMLN president was previously arrested <u>on 5th October 2018</u> in another case pertaining to Ramzan Sugar Mills and Ashiana Housing Scheme. He was in the anti-graft watchdog's custody when the inquiry into money laundering was authorised. <u>On 14th April 2021</u> the LHC released him on bail in that money laundering reference.

On 12th October 2022: Shahbaz and Hamza were acquitted on all charges of corruption and money laundering by the Special Court Central in Lahore; the money laundering charges were filed in 2020.

Judge Ijaz Hassan Awan of the Special Court Central in Lahore announced the verdict in front of the prime minister's legal team, who had earlier during the hearing requested a one-day attendance exemption. The family was charged during the administration of former PM Imran Khan. The Federal Investigation Agency (FIA) in Lahore filed corruption and money laundering charges against Sharif and his two sons, Hamza and Suleman, in November 2020, <u>accusing them of laundering Rs:16.3 billion through 28 bank accounts, which had no names for the account holders</u>, between 2008 and 2018. Suleman was not tried since moving to London.

The case in Special Court in Lahore *was totally baseless and politically motivated;* said Sharif's lawyer Amjad Pervez - there was no immediate comment from the prosecutor.

> [In Pakistan, one may salute **its unique centuries old judicial system**. When Imran Khan was prime minister, he got hold of the NAB to dig out massive corruption of billions against his political opponents, even against the top notch Shahbaz Sharif – also being the leader of the opposition in parliament. When Shahbaz Sharif became the prime minister of the country in April 2022, he got hold of the same NAB to declare the same cases baseless and without evidence. Revengefully, Imran Khan was sent to jail on various counts – AND the same courts declared PM Shahbaz Sharif and his family innocent.

> *All elements of targeting political opponents are used just in routine by filing legal / illegal cases against them, apparently to keep them entangled in court proceedings and away from the governance fields.]*

SHAHZAD AKBAR: ADVISOR TO PM KHAN:

On 24th January 2022; about three months before the PTI Chief Imran Khan was voted out from premiership, PM's advisor on accountability and interior, Shahzad Akbar resigned from his post as pressure had mounted more on PTI's ruling coalition on a wider range of issues. The former deputy prosecutor for the National Accountability Bureau (NAB), Akbar was appointed as the Special Assistant to PM Khan on accountability in August 2018.

Later, in December 2019, he was also given an additional portfolio of *Adviser to the prime minister on Interior Affairs*. In July 2020, the barrister was promoted and made Adviser to the prime minister on Accountability and Interior *with the status of a federal minister*. The intelligentsia and media gurus had an opinion that simply Mr Akbar looted the state-kitty with salaries in pounds, allowances and perks – did nothing in fact.

Akbar hoped that the ongoing process of accountability against Sharifs would continue under the leadership of PM Khan as per the manifesto of the ruling PTI. *'I will remain associated with the party and keep contributing as a member of the legal fraternity – but it suddenly ended* (as if 3years+ were not enough to dig out / fabricate cases against only one family)', Akbar held his stance.

On 17th August 2022: Shahbaz Sharif's federal cabinet placed the names of 10 people, including former PM Khan's close aide Shahzad Akbar, on the Exit Control List (ECL); BUT Mr Akbar had already left for Dubai on 17th April 2022, a week after Imran Khan's removal five days after the Islamabad High Court (IHC) had suspended FIA orders placing his name on the stop list (ECL). The government was intentionally not disclosing the names of those who were placed on the ECL and struck off; however, Shahzad Akbar's name was placed on the ECL at the request of the NAB.

On 25th September 2023: An alleged acid attack on an ex-adviser to the former Pakistani prime minister Imran Khan at his home in Hertfordshire was reported in news. There were claims by a senior Tory MP that: *'... it was carried out by an agent of the country's feared intelligence* *agency...;'* INDEPENDENT of UK dated 26th September 2023 is referred.

Shahzad Akbar, who sought refuge in Britain after leading Pakistan's efforts to combat corruption and becoming an outspoken opponent of the regime, told *The Independent;* he was lucky not to lose his sight in the said attack on Sunday afternoon. He was saved by his spectacles, which were badly damaged. Mr Akbar described how the attack was launched in front of his four-year-old daughter, and left him with acid burns on an arm and the top of his head.

NAWAZ SHARIF's PLATELETS PROBLEM:

On 29th October 2019; Nawaz Sharif was granted bail by the Islamabad High Court [IHC] on medical grounds in connection with Al Azizia and Chaudhry Sugar Mills corruption cases. *The ailing Pakistani leader was serving a seven-year imprisonment in the Al-Azizia case in Kot Lakhpat jail of Lahore.* Besides that, he was remanded to the NAB custody in Chaudhry Sugar Mills case. Nawaz Sharif had continuously been complaining about his deteriorating health especially that his platelets counts were going alarmingly low.

> [*Nawaz Sharif was prime minister of Pakistan from 1990 to 1993, then again from 1997 to 1999, and finally from 2013 to 2017. He also appeared as the country's richest industrialists.*
>
> *In 2018 - following the Panama Papers Leak Case - he was found guilty of corruption, relating to his family's ownership of upmarket London apartments. He was given a 10-year prison sentence, **but was released two months later** when the court suspended the sentences, pending a final judgement.*
>
> *But in December 2018 he was **jailed in corruption cases again**, this time for seven years, in relation to his family's ownership of steel mills in Saudi Arabia. He however, denied wrongdoing **and accused the military of conspiring to end his political career** BUT never provided any money trail or business background logic for his huge financial empire.*
>
> On 24th December 2018, *an accountability court, headed by Judge Malik Arshad, had sentenced Sharif to seven years in prison in the Al-Azizia Steel Mills Corruption Case while acquitted him in the Flagship Case.*]

On 2nd November 2019; Muttahida Qaumi Movement [MQM] founder Altaf Hussain claimed via twitter that former Prime Minister Nawaz Sharif has been given polonium, the drug which slowly poisoned Yasser Arafat, famed Palestinian President, to death in 2004.

> *"Lower platelets count in Nawaz Sharif's body! A known fact is that 'Polonium' (a radioactive element) is used to eliminate enemies. It acts as a slow poison and destroys platelets. Only specialized radioactive laboratory can verify it. The international laboratory must examine it."*

However, no one in Pakistan believed Altaf Hussain's hypothesis.

The 69 years old Nawaz Sharif was admitted to the Services Institute of Medical Sciences [SIMS] in Lahore on 22nd October 2019 but after few days, precisely on 6th November 2019, he was shifted to his residence – Jati Umra where an Intensive Care Unit [ICU] was set up under the supervision of Sharif's personal physician Dr Adnan Khan and the doctors were bound to be present in the ICU round the clock. Sharif's daughter Maryam Safdar, who was also undergoing treatment at the same hospital, too was moved to his house from the hospital. Maryam was also granted bail in the Chaudhry Sugar Mills Case, wanting for money laundering trails.

The medical board that treated the 3-time prime minister recommended his treatment abroad keeping in view complications of his disease. However, it remained a fact that doctors provided the best treatment to Nawaz Sharif in Pakistan. The medical board consisting of four senior and leading hematologists diagnosed N Sharif with immune thrombocytopenia [ITP] disease - a disorder that could lead to easy or excessive bruising and bleeding.

On 12th Nov 2019; PM Imran Khan's Cabinet decided to allow Nawaz Sharif to go abroad for medical treatment if he would agree to sign surety bonds making a commitment that he would return after the treatment and undergo jail sentences against him. The Cabinet meeting, chaired by PM Imran Khan himself, approved removal of Sharif's name from the Exit Control List [ECL]. It was a conditional release permission to which PMLN supremo agreed and opted to go to UK for treatment. PM Khan looked at the case of Sharif on *"human grounds and decided to allow him get treatment out of Pakistan"*. The surety bond money was agreed as to be equal to the fine imposed by the courts while convicting him – about seven billion Pak Rupee.

The anti-corruption watchdog, National Accountability Bureau [NAB], some of the Cabinet members, especially Minister for Water Faisal Vawda and Minister of Science Fawad Chaudhry, and key-party members blatantly opposed to giving any concession to *'Convicted in Jail'* Sharif – however, PM Khan prevailed while deciding on pure humanitarian grounds.

The **BBC** on **19th Nov 2019** passed sarcastic comments that:

> '.... The Lahore High Court lifted a travel ban on Saturday and the government rubber-stamped the decision on Monday.'

Fact remained that Imran Khan's government had been reluctant to release Nawaz Sharif without signing a surety bond for money equivalent to court's fine due on him. He wanted Nawaz Sharif - who had served less than 12 months of a seven-year prison sentence till then - to sign an indemnity bond worth $44m [£34m] before allowing him to go abroad. However, the equally dubious judges allowed him to travel without signing the bond.

Till the last moments of his departure, Nawaz Sharif consistently said he had no wish to leave the country, preferring to stay and fight for his political survival; but media termed it his hypocrisy of highest order. After Nawaz Sharif's flight in a family aircraft sent by the Qatari rulers, an uproar remained hanging in the whole Pakistan press & media that - how much 'factually ill' Nawaz Sharif was? Sharif had agreed to return within four weeks, or when doctors would declare him fit to return. His brother Shahbaz - who later travelled with Nawaz Sharif - signed a court document that said:

> "If at any stage, the federal government has credible information that Nawaz Sharif is living abroad despite his fitness to travel, a representative from Pakistan's High Commission would have a right to meet with his physician(s) to verify or confirm about his health – (but nothing like commitment prevailed)."

Thus, Nawaz Sharif stayed in UK till mid-2023 and had run his PMLN party remotely and very successfully.

Scenario 250

MADINA MODEL – NAYA PAKISTAN OF PM KHAN

Before moving to the merits of **Madina Model of Imran Khan** in Pakistan (2018-22), have a glance over the then prevailing facts about Islam & Muslims in other Islamic states.

George Washington University's *Prof Hussain Askari* researched how Islamic countries are Islamic. By looking for the countries that follow the rules of the state and society in Islam, it was found that those who follow the Islamic rules in their daily life are not Muslim countries. The study (astonishingly) found that:

- "... the most Islamically compliant country is New Zealand followed by Luxembourg. Then came Ireland, Iceland, Finland, Denmark sixth and Canada in seventh position. Malaysia is 38th, Kuwait is 48th, Bahrain is 64th, and surprisingly Saudi Arabia is at 131st position. In this study published in GLOBAL ECONOMY JOURNAL, Bangladesh's position is below the Saudi Arabia.

- ... that Muslims are very careful about prayer, fasting, Sunnah, Qur'an, Hadith, hijab, beard, dress but do not follow the laws of Islam in state, social and professional life.

- ... that Muslims listen to more religious sermons nasihat (sane advice) than anyone else in the world, but no Muslim country could become the best country on the globe. In the last sixty years, Muslims have heard the Friday sermon at least 3000 times.

- ... Notably, a gentile Chinese businessman said, Muslim businessmen come to us with orders to make number two fake things and say to put the label of such and such a famous company. Later, when I told them to eat with us, they said, It is not halal, so I will not eat it. Is it halal to sell counterfeit goods?

- ... A Japanese new Muslim said: I see non-Muslims in western countries following the rules of Islam, and in eastern countries I see Islam but no Muslims. Alhamdulillah, I have already accepted the religion of Allah knowing the difference between Islam and Muslims.

- *... Islam is not just prayer and fasting, it is a way of life and a matter of communication and fellowship with others.* A person who prays fast and has a scar on his forehead can be a hypocrite in the eyes of Allah.

- ... Islam has two parts, one is the public declaration of faith called 'Iman', and the other is the subject of faith called 'Ehsaan' - which is realized by following justly correct social norms. **If both are not practiced together, Islam remains incomplete which is happening in every named Muslim country.**

- ... Observance of religious prohibitions is one's personal responsibility and is a matter between Allah and the servant. But adherence to social norms is a matter between one servant and another. Lord Bernard Shaw once said:

> "Islam is the best religion and Muslims are the worst followers".

MADINA- CONCEPT OF MR KHAN:

On 26th July 2018; during his victory speech made at his Bani Gala residence that was broadcast via a video link, Imran Khan claimed victory and termed the elections 2018 *'historical'*, saying that he had been finally given a chance to change the fate of the country. In his address, Imran Khan promised a state which would take care of the underprivileged, with the new government's policies focused on enabling poor and the less fortunate prosper. He said:

> "A country is not recognised by the lifestyle of the rich, but by the lifestyle of the poor. I want to share the kind of Pakistan I envision, the type of **state that was established in Madina**, where widows and the poor were taken care of."

Imran Khan assured his opponents that there would be no political victimization and vowed to cooperate with them to investigate complaints of voting irregularities. Mr Khan said his model was the **First Islamic State in Madina,** as also the vision of Pakistan's founder Jinnah. He said accountability will start with him. **'We will set an** *example of how law is same for everyone.*' He held that the biggest challenge for Pakistan was the economic crisis then. It never had such a huge fiscal deficit: the economy was going down because of dysfunctional institutions. His recipe for economic revival was ending corruption, helping small businesses and creating jobs. He promised to work to build a welfare state in Pakistan where uplift of downtrodden would get high priority.

Important decisions were made in a federal cabinet meeting held at PM Office on <u>5th September 2018</u> with PM Khan in the chair. The meeting also decided to abolish discretionary funds of all ministries estimating that with this move, over Rs:80 billion would become available to the national kitty.

Amongst other decisions, the government would <u>establish an orphanage</u> in the federal capital to offer shelter to homeless beggar women and children and provide assistance to Pakistanis languishing in prisons of foreign countries so that they could be reunited with their families.

Much later, <u>on 17th January 2022</u>, Prime Minister Imran Khan himself explained the true spirit of Islamic Civilization by writing an article for media in his own name; titled as '**Transforming Pakistan: Powerful, crooked politicians accustomed to being above law**'; saying that in Islamic civilization, the manifestation of our spiritual principles happened in the Prophet's (SAW) Medina. He wrote:

> "*The rise and fall of nations are different from the rise and fall of civilizations. Nations can be raided, redrawn or re-imagined exogenously but civilizations cannot be killed from the outside, they only commit suicide.*
>
> *The core of every civilization is its spiritual principles; when they die, the civilization dies. In Islamic civilization, the manifestation of our spiritual principles happened in the Prophet's (SAW) Madina. Besides many other important principles, there were five very important guiding principles upon which the state of Medina was built.*
>
> *These principles are unity, justice & rule of law leading to meritocracy, strong moral and ethical foundation, inclusion of all humans in progress and prosperity, and finally, the quest for knowledge. To help revive the spirit of the covenant of Medina,* **<u>National Rahmatul Lil 'Alamin Authority</u>** *(NRA) has been formed.*

- *The first principle which laid the foundation for **Riyasat-i-Madina** was of unity.*

- *The idea of unity (Tawhid) comes from the Quran and in a sense, the entire religion is based on that. From unity of God to unity of mankind, it is the most fundamental principle of Islam.*

- *Remember that our Prophet (SAW), who was mercy for all mankind, unified people of diverse ethnic and religious backgrounds into a single community. Besides Muslims, there were Christians, Jews, Sabeans and other groups who were all woven into a unitary communal whole under the state of Madina.*

- *The second founding principle was Rule of Law which resulted in justice and meritocracy. The Prophet (SAW) made it clear that no one was above the law. He said that nations perish when two sets of laws exist, one for the rich and another for the poor:*

- *"O people, those who came before you were destroyed because if a person of high status committed theft among them, they would spare him, but if a person of lower status committed theft, they would apply the punishment upon him. By Allah, if Fatima, the daughter of Muhammad (SAW), were to steal, I would have cut off her hand." [Sahih Muslim 1688]*

- *If one looks at the world today, one can easily witness that most successful states also have the most robust application of the rule of law. Besides several Western nations, one witnesses those East Asian economies that have recently prospered, strictly practiced this principle. Japan, China, South Korea are good examples. Whereas in those nations where rule of law was subverted, seem to be sinking into poverty and chaos. In many countries of the Muslim world, despite the prevalence of tremendous resources, there is less progress, which is attributable to lack of rule of law. Another good example is South Asia. In today's India, the apartheid rule of law has immediately brought about poverty and countless insurgencies that threaten the union of their country. In Pakistan, not adhering to the rule of law has led to siphoning off of billions of US dollars which has imposed collective poverty on our public. The pattern of politics and development in many countries of Africa and Latin American suggest the same. The so-called banana republics are the way they are because of lack of rule of law. This cause-and-effect relationship between rule of law and socio-political harmony cannot be emphasized enough.*

- *The third founding principle of **Riyasat-e-Madina** was of an ethical and moral transformation of the people – the concept of **Amr-bil-maroof-wa-nahi-an-al-munkar** (doing good AND forbidding evil); the Holy Quran declares it as defining mission for Ummah:*

- *You are the best community that has been raised for mankind. You enjoin good and forbid evil and you believe in Allah. [Sura Aal-e-Imran; 3:110].*

- *Enjoining what is good and forbidding what is evil is a collective duty that leads to moral transformation of a society. Nobody would dispute this principle, but there are elements in our society that are of the opinion that ethical development of people should be left to the people, the state should remain neutral about good and evil as conceived by religion. This approach is quite outmoded and problematic because it handcuffs the state from performing its ethical and moral duties and allows adversaries of the country to come in with handfuls of money and subvert our values using our own educational systems and channels of information. NRA will endeavour to engage in **amr bil maaroof** by teaching **seerat-al-nabi** (SAW) to our youth in schools and universities in the hope to raise the level the ethics and morals in our society.*

- *The fourth founding principle was of inclusive development through creation of a welfare state where society takes care of its poor and vulnerable and everyone is a stakeholder in the development of society and state. State of Medina was first recorded welfare state of mankind where the state took responsibility of its weak. Since we must emulate the example of our Prophet (SAW), our citizens should learn to be strict with themselves and generous with others.*

- *Keep in mind, however, that in recent times the idea of welfare state has been coloured by the Western European experience. Indeed, the West created impressive welfare systems from 1950s to 2010s, of which the most impressive were the Scandinavian ones. However, most of the Western welfare states were not sustainable environmentally because these were very high consumption societies that produced enormous waste. If the whole of non-West were to copy these welfare states, then our pattern of production, consumption and waste would resemble theirs, and by some estimates it would require us six more planet earths to act as sinks that would absorb our waste. Such a welfare state is neither possible nor desirable. Since Islam is the middle path, only moderate prosperity and consumption would be ideal, just enough to fulfil our basic needs with dignity and honour, with health care & education.*

- *And finally, a knowledge-based society that doesn't confound literacy with knowledge. Literacy may lead to illuminative knowledge that may guide us to good behaviour, but some of the highest crime zones of the world also have very high literacy rates. One must not lose sight of an important historical fact that nearly all scholars of early and medieval Islam had deep roots in spirituality.*

- *Hence literacy alone may not be sufficient for a happy society. Knowledge with spiritual transformation from cradle to grave is important. All sources that impact human behaviour should disseminate knowledge which produces self-control, self-discipline, patience, forbearance, tolerance and a spirit of service.*

- *Lastly, in the light of our ideals, we have embarked on the road to the welfare state with some great initiatives. Despite tight financial means, we allocated unprecedented amount of money to our initiatives such as the **Ehsaas Program** which was launched back in 2019. Ehsaas Programme is a social safety and poverty alleviation programme necessary for the vulnerable groups in society. This was one of our key initiatives towards building a state that cares about the welfare of our citizens. By far, one of the greatest programs in history of Pakistan is the **Sehat Sahulat Program** which offers our citizens universal health coverage. This is not just to protect vulnerable households from sinking into poverty who often borrow money for medical treatment, but it also leads to a network of private sector hospitals all over the country, thus benefitting both the public as well as the private sectors in the field of health. Just Punjab government alone has allocated Rs:400 billion for this. The Sehat Sahulat Programme is an important milestone towards our social welfare reforms. It makes sure that some low-income groups in Pakistan may have access to their entitled medical health care quickly and honourably without financial obligations.*

- *In the wake of global economic hardship brought about in the post-Covid era, we have not neglected the fast-transforming educational arena. Our **Ehsaas scholarship** program would ensure that talented students within the under-privileged and poor strata of society would get a chance to pursue decent education that would augment their chances of getting better livelihoods. This program combined* with all our other scholarships amounts to six million scholarships worth Rs:47 billion. This too is unprecedented in the educational history of Pakistan.

- In conclusion, I will reiterate that the most urgent of all challenges facing our country right now is the struggle to establish the rule of law. Over the last 75 years of Pakistan's history, our country has suffered from elite capture, where powerful and crooked politicians, cartels and mafias have become accustomed to being above the law in order to protect their privileges gained through a corrupt system. While protecting their privileges they have corrupted state institutions, especially those institutions of the state that are responsible for upholding the rule of law. Such individuals, cartels and mafias are parasites who are not loyal to our country and defeating them is absolutely necessary in order to unleash the real potential of Pakistan.

[Imran Khan - the Prime Minister of Pakistan]

MADINA MODEL PROJECTED IN UN:

See an extract from **Statement by the Prime Minister of Pakistan, Imran Khan to the Seventy-fifth Session of the UN General Assembly delivered on 25th September 2020**:

- Mr. President, Secretary General Guterres, Excellencies, Ladies and Gentlemen…..

- "Since my government assumed office, our consistent effort has been to fundamentally transform Pakistan. **We envisage 'Naya Pakistan' to be modeled on principles of the State of Madinah, established by our Holy Prophet Muhammad (PBUH).**

- …. A just and humane society where all Government policies are directed at lifting our citizens out of poverty and creating a just and equitable dispensation.

- …. our foreign policy aims to have peace with our neighbours and settle disputes through dialogue.

- …. (Ref: Prof Noam Chomsky) mankind is at even a greater risk than it was before the 1st and 2nd World Wars in the last century, and this is because of the increased threat of nuclear war, Climate Change, and sadly the rise of authoritarian regimes.

- .... we believe that the driving force in international relations must be cooperation, in accordance with the principles of international law, and not confrontation and force.

- .... the COVID-19 pandemic has illustrated the oneness of humanity. Locking down to control the pandemic has triggered the worst recession since the Great Depression in the last Century. This has hit the poorest countries the hardest as well as the poor in countries.

- .... Despite financial constraints, my government (PTI) deployed an unprecedented EIGHT (8) billion dollars for our health services; plus support the poorest and most vulnerable households **with direct cash payments through 'Ehsaas program'**; and then subsidies to the small businesses.

- .... We have not only managed to control the COVID-19 and stabilize our economy, but most importantly, we were able to protect the poorest segment of society from the worst fall out of the lock down.

- .... Today, Pakistan's response is cited among the success stories in controlling and responding to the pandemic. It was obvious that developing countries would need fiscal space to respond to, and recover from, the COVID crisis.

- .... The IMF has estimated that developing countries will need over US$ 2.5 trillion to respond and recover from the crisis. Money that could be used towards human development is siphoned off by corrupt elites. The loss of foreign exchange causes currency depreciation that in turn leads to inflation and poverty.

- .... If this phenomenon is unaddressed, it will continue to accentuate the inequality between the rich and the poor nations, and eventually will spark off a far bigger global crisis than the present migration issue poses.

- .... There are robust anti-Money Laundering and anti-Terrorist Financing regimes. This year, I must again reiterate the threat posed to mankind due to Climate Change. Unprecedented fires in Australia, Siberia, California, Brazil; unprecedented flooding in various parts of the world; record temperatures even in the Arctic Circle. This should make us all worried for our future generations.

- .... Pakistan's contribution to carbon emissions is minimal, but it is one of those countries most affected by climate change; yet, we have decided to take the lead through our extremely ambitious program to plant 10 billion trees in the next three years.

- .... The pandemic was an opportunity to bring humanity together. This Assembly should declare an **'International Day to Combat Islamophobia'** and build a coalition to fight this scourge – scourge that splits humanity.

- .... There will be no durable peace and stability in South Asia until the Jammu and Kashmir dispute is resolved on the basis of international legitimacy. Kashmir has been rightly described as a **'nuclear flash point'** (by most concerned policy making powers).

- .... A comprehensive reform of the United Nations, including the Security Council, is essential to promote greater democracy, accountability, transparency and efficiency. Pakistan will continue to participate actively in this process and endeavour, with other Member States, to build a (peaceful) world....

It was an honour for Pakistanis that their leader Mr Khan had mentioned his governance program based on Madina Model before the UN General Assembly – but it remained limited to its mention in TWO LINES only – no details or special steps to implement that said program. Rest of his whole speech had encompassed the points related with country's foreign policy. He mentioned various aspects like India's RSS vs Muslim genocide, the US presence in Afghanistan, Indian atrocities in Kashmir valley, formation of new Palestinian state and UN's desired roles in similar areas of the globe – BUT nothing about his NAYA PAKISTAN or the MADINA MODEL of governance in detail.

'NAYA PAKISTAN' OF IMRAN KHAN:

Prime Minister Imran Khan said: 'Naya Pakistan shall soon resemble the 7th century state of Madina; referring to an article appeared on media pages of 18th December 2018 (also given in above paragraphs verbatim).

Beginning with his public addresses and party meetings, Imran Khan used to repeat his vow on no less than 11 separate occasions (till Dec 2018). Although all Muslims acknowledge the Madina state as a model of perfection, Khan mostly left unsaid just *how closely Naya Pakistan would be raised as Madina.* Was he achieving classlessness & equality and welfarism as the goal? Was the Madina Model state also a template for Pakistan's political and judicial reconstruction – replacing its 200 years old PPC, CrPC and Evidence Act etc and associated Police Rules of 1934?

To create a prosperous welfare state was a commendable and universal objective. Serving the needs of their citizens without prejudice, a few modern states already had operational systems in place. To join them, just five minutes of serious contemplation could tell Mr Khan what was needed to be done in Pakistan. The ideal plan could be:

- …. elimination of large land holdings through appropriate legislation;

- …. effective collection of land and property taxes based upon prevailing market values;

- …. setting up of summary courts to impart quick & visible justice

- …. making the courts, *kutchehry, patwar khaney* and police stations transparent through quick punishments for wrong-doers;

- …. making meritocratic appointments in state departments;

- …. enhancing primary & high school bases to get 100% literacy rate;

- …. developing skills in technical education institutions as its central goal – so that the people should work instead of putting them to expect CASH DISTRIBUTIONS – making them beggars;

- …. making peace with Pakistan's neighbouring states using nationalistic approach – respecting PAKISTAN-FIRST;

- …. choosing trade over aid both at domestic and abroad levels;

- …. letting politicians and bureaucracy prove their worth – would leave no option for soldiers to help civilians.

- .... Making appointments in higher judiciary through merits – not via selections by CJs, CJPs, their law chambers or superior bars.

- .... Dragging land-lords into TAX-NET; could be *10% Khums* – the Islamic levy as per Khilafat days..

That were the BASIC jobs to be initiated in NAYA PAKISTAN - pretty hard! The successful implementation needed no less than a revolution, bloodless or otherwise. But Imran Khan wanted to match the Madina state as a political entity through SLOGANS only, it was NOT possible – nor would be now. Modern states keep geographical boundaries BUT for the Madina state, borders were irrelevant — where you lived didn't matter. Was it Imran Khan's goal to adopt the Madina state's laws and / or letting it survive as a political voice.

Built around a tribal accord, *Misaq-e-Madina*, citizenship required only that an individual should submit to the authority of the Holy Prophet (PBUH). What elements were chosen by Imran Khan to achieve his goals – *unfortunately it was only a wishful thinking nothing beyond.* How PM Imran Khan could reconcile diamond-like notions of the Madina state *vis-à-vis* **Pakistani nation of proven liars.**

Time has increased territorial affiliations. Everywhere, inside and outside Islam, large national armies protect borders and nationalism competes fiercely against religion as a contradictory force. Imran Khan's pledge to grant citizenship to 1.5 million desperate Afghan refugees was potentially a BIG DANGER, and the later developments after August 2021 proved Khan wrong.

Human rights activists were thrilled but delighted during his rule; but, once the adverse reactions set in, Khan's U-turn followed. He was not to be blamed alone – he had no sane or seasoned advisor in his 52-members team or so-called cabinet.

Moving on: **what about judicial matters?** Could laws of the Madina state apply in Naya Pakistan – what set of laws Khan got passed from his parliament; none. What powers and procedures he got approved from the national assembly or senate for the respective courts to adopt those Islamic Legislative reforms – NOTHING. To remind Mr Khan that the Misaq-e-Madina lists 63 rules for determining *diyat* (blood money); ransoms to settle tribal feuds; life protection for Muslims and Jews; apportioning of war expenses; etc. Which of his advisors had Mr Khan engaged to make out such rules / laws for his Naya Pakistan – for his nation of LIARS & FRAUD?

Justice is an ever-evolving concept in every culture and religion; for example, 2,000 years ago, Aristotle had argued that some individuals and races are 'natural slaves' better to be enslaved than left free. Among today's Muslims, apart from the militant Islamic State groups and a few others, no one defends slavery. In Pakistan too, owning slaves is a criminal offence – but most of us keep them in our homes and at our lands.

The notion of equality is accepted by nearly all societies now, or give lip service, to the idea that all people are equal before the law. Blood money, common in earlier times, also takes on a very different flavour. Pakistanis were outraged when a smirking Shahrukh Jatoi emerged from jail after murdering 20-year-old Shahzeb Khan in cold blood. Jatoi's wealthy parents had purchased his pardon through *diyat*, probably by pressuring Khan's family. Months earlier, CIA contractor Raymond Davis had been released after the families of the two men he had killed were paid $2.4m as blood money.

The world of yesterday and the world of today bear no comparison. At the Holy Prophet's times, things were nicely negotiated for all warring Arabian tribes. Then, joblessness and lack of housing were non-issues; air pollution and load-shedding hadn't been conceived; and white-collar crime was awaiting invention centuries later. No police or standing army existed in the Madina state. There were no jails. However, Imran Khan never shared with Pakistanis that how would he conceive about such things TODAY (means during his governance period).

It was easy to see why certain religious slogans appealed to the popular imagination in Imran Khan times. In a country that was (and still) deeply unequal and plagued by huge class asymmetry, people yearned for an unblemished past when everything was perfect. But when Khan like leaders promise to take us there, how seriously one could take it? <u>The masses had responded favourably when Gen Ziaul Haq had raised a similar slogan in the 1980s — that of **Nizam-e-Mustafa**. Disappointment soon followed. Imran Khan's Madina slogan was NOT different at all.</u>

MADINA MODEL AFTER 3 YEARS:

On 25th June 2021: Terming the federal budget a step forward towards the country's transformation into the state of Madina, the then Finance Minister Shaukat Tarin said the government had rejected the directives of the International Monetary Fund (IMF) regarding further hike in gas and electricity tariffs. Concluding budget debate in the National Assembly he said PM Imran Khan had stabilized the crippling economy by taking some *bold steps* and contrary to the expectations of even IMF and the World Bank, the country's GDP growth rose up to four per cent in the fiscal year 2020-21. Despite three waves of Covid-19 and crippling economic situation, PTI took many sagacious decisions like imposition of smart lockdown and as a result the wheel of the industry continued to run and the country didn't suffer much.

The FM Mr Tarin hinted at starting focus on sustainable growth and uplifting the lot of poor people.; adding that the government was taking steps which would directly give some relief to the poor. The government had chalked out a strategy to provide affordable houses to four million families. Similarly, Rs:500,000 agriculture loans were to be given to the farmers and in urban areas interest-free loan of similar amount for the individuals to enable them to start small businesses.

Under another direct relief plan, the government was issuing health card to each Pakistani. The government would also impart skill training to one person in a poor family so that the skilled person could support his/her family. Record 40 percent increase had been made in the allocations for the Public Sector Development Program in the budget 2021-22 as its volume had been increased from Rs:630bn to Rs:900bn. The finance minister vowed to bring down fiscal deficit to zero. *'We (PTI) have already reduced fiscal deficit from 7pc to 6.3pc and the current primary deficit — 3.8pc — will be reduced to 0.6pc,'* the federal finance minister claimed; GOOD IT WAS.

Rs:30bn were earmarked for construction and housing sector. The PTI government was also determined to take maximum advantage of the China-Pakistan Economic Corridor (CPEC). *'We (PTI) have addressed all concerns of China and now CPEC will take off,'* the FM added – but it proved total failure at the end because we had not taken the TTP and BLA insurgents seriously. An amount of Rs:260bn were allocated for *Ehsaas program to provide CASH assistance to poor families* – that was TOTAL CORRUPTION like prevailed in PPP & PMLN because the CASH is distributed ONLY ON LISTS not in actual; all money goes to US & Dubai via distributors.

Mr Tarin said Pakistan was facing major structural issues in the power sector as the government had to pay Rs::900bn on account of capacity payments for electricity that was not even being utilized; causing an enormous increase in the circular debt. However, he acknowledged that making improvements in the power sector remained a big challenge for the government.

SOCIAL MEDIA CRITICS ON MADINA MODEL:

On 17th January 2022: PM Khan in an article: *'Spirit of Riyasat-e-Madina: Transforming Pakistan'* which he had written for various newspapers; said:

> "We have embarked on the road to the welfare state with some great initiatives. Despite tight financial means, we allocated an unprecedented amount of money to our initiatives such as the Ehsaas Programme which was a social safety and poverty alleviation programme necessary for the vulnerable groups in society.
>
> The **Ehsaas scholarship program** initiative would ensure that unprivileged, talented students would get a chance to pursue their meaningful ambitions in education."

In his article, PM Khan wrote that the most urgent of all challenges facing the country was the struggle to establish the rule of law. *"Over the last 75 years of Pakistan's history. The country had suffered from elite capture, where the powerful and crooked politicians, cartels and mafias had become accustomed to being above the law in order to protect their privileges gained through a corrupt system."*

The premier while giving examples of China, Japan and South Korea said if one looked at the world, one could easily witness that the most successful states also had the most robust application of the rule of law. *"In Pakistan, not adhering to the rule of law has led to siphoning off of billions of US dollars which has imposed collective poverty on our public."* The article appeared at a time when the government was already facing severe criticism due to unprecedented inflation. After the article, Twitter got flooded with mixed reactions; some said the PTI government was trying to sell religious-card while others were showing support. See some scripts below:

- 'Your model of riyasat e madina has failed khan sahab' — Faryal Khan (@FaryalFKhan) January 17, 2022

- "Inflation and unemployment are on the rise. A large number of patriots are facing this thing. Profiteering of profiteers is on the rise. The looters are returning. Talking about my consciousness up to my *age, it feels like living in a forest. Still, I hope that someday* 🙂 " — Muhammad Usama محمد اسامہ (@its_usamaislam) January 17, 2022

- "*One of the cheapest and easiest things in politics is to sell religious card. Though i am supporter of pm iK. But selling religious card in country where population of us Muslim is 99 percent could be disastrous.*" — Bilal Ahmed (@BilalAh51795966) January 17, 2022

- "*This govt has absolutely nothing to do with Riyasit Madina. People of Pakistan are suffering in every corner of the country. In riaset madina, hazrat Umer was responsible for even a thirsty dog. Do not abuse this word please.*" — Hammad Khan (@hmdkhan) January 17, 2022

- "*Excellent! People of Pakistan really need to raise in character which is the biggest problem face by us. Guiding principles like rule of law and justice are a must to be implemented. We can never prosper without raising ourselves morally.*" — Ghessan Mushtaq (@ghessanm) January 17, 2022

- "*Where this state of Madina goes: when people freeze to death, when ordinary citizens take law in their own hands and become judges and witnesses at the same time? Actions are needed to implement state of Madina in true sense. Only verbally nothing can be achieved*" — Ishaq Ahmaad (@IshaqAhmaad) January 17, 2022

- "*Riyasat-e-Madina is complete and perfect model for life style but yours goodness is to implement the legislations and our responsibility is to follow it.*" — Waqas Ali Jafri (@WaqasAliJafri) Jan 17, 2022

Imran Khan was charmed and captivated with the working of the state of Madina of the Prophetic era of the early 7th century. There was no doubt that governance and administration of justice in the city of Madina was a great progressive achievement of the Muslims of those times. *The governance of the city state of Madina was exemplified by justice, truthfulness, simplicity, fairness, tolerance, communion and equality before the law in an age where the great Roman and Persian Empires treated their common subjects as slaves and possessions.*

The companions of the Prophet considered love of money as the root cause of all evils and never accumulated ill-gotten money. Do we have those kinds of people in our focus now and how and by whom the

Madina Model could be modeled in 2018-21's Pakistan? Looking at Pakistani print & electronic media and hearing news of corruption and plunders by those who were responsible for wellbeing and progress of the people and who were guardians of the State, it was feared that the country could be subjected collectively to God's fury and annoyance.

From sociological point of view, in the time of the state of Madina, the population was very small. The entire Muslim population of Madina and its surrounding areas was less than a million. Life was simple and was not as complex as it is today. *Education and military services were for the purpose of propagation of Islam's message of justice and social transformation.* Hence, service in education and military department were voluntary without any regular daily or monthly remunerations. There was no concept of paid teachers and soldiery.

Given the prevailing situation of Pakistan in Khan's rule, it was very difficult to replicate the Madina model exactly in the same way as it was some 1400-year ago. From where PTI's Pakistan could bring those upright and honest people to run the affairs of the present large-size States on Madina model! *<u>The best way to match the Madina Model was to get inspiration from the founding principles of the state of Madina such as rule of law, equality before the law, justice, liberty, fraternity, brotherhood, simplicity</u> and strict adherence to the Islamic laws both in our individual and collective lives.*

Islam, in the times of state of Madina, was considered a complete code of life with equal importance given to rights of God (*huquq-ullah*) and rights of the people (*huququl-ibaad*). To achieve the tranquility and grandeur of the Muslim predecessors *(aslaaf)*, one would need to strengthen the educational systems to inculcate the ethics and morals of Islam in youth. Who could prepare many generations of students with virtues of caring, compassionate, tolerant, honest, simple, chivalrous and magnanimous individual to enable the general populace to build a model of Madina's state?

> *<u>Imran Khan and his PTI could have invented and adopt the qualities of good governance, brotherhood, pluralism</u> and social justice from the Madina Model – BUT in Pakistan, Imran <u>Khan was not prepared to sit on the table with PMLN & PPP's leadership declaring them corrupt. Could Imran Khan's Madina state model afford such hatred and humiliation</u> as a part of his personal trait or behaviour.*

Till such time PTI achieve its objective of honest human resource development to enable the junta to build Madina-type state, **Mr Khan** *could have searched and study the successful functioning of states in contemporary times and copy their best practices.* Unfortunately, in terms of justice, rule of law and fair play, some Muslim States in Africa and Asia and especially Pakistan, remained far behind in changing their centuries old rotten laws and procedures. Did Imran Khan's parliament ever thought or tried to adopt immediate (summary) punishments for murder, hurt and theft etc as are visualized in Islam EVEN TODAY.

Imran Khan and the PTI's Pakistan needed to look somewhere else particularly toward Saudia, Iran, China or Japan for best practices in governance and statecraft. Scandinavian countries such as Sweden, Denmark, Norway and Finland and Switzerland, Spain, United Kingdom and Portugal in Europe could offer best clues about the importance of rule of law, equality before the law and good governance for overall national progress and development.

On Madina Model, one media comment termed it *'Simply, a combination of syasi (political) and mazhabi (religious) dramas.'* - June 28, 2020 at 3:33 pm at twitter.

NAYA PAKISTAN HOUSING PROGRAM FAILED:

One candid opinion prevailed that Pakistan would be democratically stronger after Imran Khan's exit as political parties in the GDP (then opposition) had all experienced the hybrid system in one way or another and were set to chart new territories in its wake. Others disagree: *The turmoil of March-April 2022 underscored the volatility of parliamentary democracies in Pakistan.* More broadly, the turmoil was an unfortunate distraction for a country dealing with soaring inflation, worsening economic stress, and extreme terrorism challenge. Ultimately, it's the Pakistani public that lost their stakes whereas the political leaders—whoever they were – feeling easy by their personal perspectives.

Much of the promises of Imran Khan have been discussed on the previous pages of this dissertation. On another count: The vision of former PM Khan for the NAYA PAKISTAN HOUSING PROGRAM was *"...to deliver five million housing units with allied amenities to needy citizens, especially focusing on the financially underserved and middle-income communities, as a measure of comprehensive socio-economic uplift."*

That's written on the official website of Naya Pakistan Housing and Development Authority (NAPHDA) expressing the raison d'etre of the

Naya Pakistan Housing Program. The creation of 10m JOB OPPORTUNITIES was also subject to the provision of 5m houses. Because construction of 5m houses would have to run the wheel of construction and other allied industries of building materials and ultimately led to the creation of more job opportunities. The PTI government, to meet the above objectives, formed the NAPHDA. The generation of construction activity in the country that could provide stimulus to over 40 housing and construction-related industries was written as an objective on its official website.

However, it was unfortunate that out of 5m only around 59,000 housing units were worked upon across the country out of which 20,000 had been completed under the Naya Pakistan Housing initiative at the end of the Khan's government. In a news report, a NAPHDA spokesperson confirmed before the media that *only the Akhuwat Foundation provided 17,000 housing units* to the deserving ones and around 3000 apartments were erected with the collaboration of the Workers Welfare Fund. A whole host of reasons, from rising prices of building materials to lack of digitization of land records resulted in the project's dismal & failure.

Moreover, the NAPHDA, which was made to fulfil this dream by the PTI government, *didn't deliver a single housing unit to anyone by itself.* The former prime minister himself conceded that according to his 'flagship program', 5m houses weren't supposed to be constructed by the government, but by the private sector. The government just had to support the private sector in this regard. One wonders if that was the case, then why the NAPHDA was made and blessed. Besides, a National Coordinating Committee of Housing Construction and Development was announced to review the progress of developments every week.

Notwithstanding, there were multi-faceted shortcomings of the Naya Pakistan Housing Program of the PTI government. These shortcomings jeopardized the workability and sustainability of that flagship program, despite a *lucrative construction package in 2020* and sizable growth in housing loan disbursements by the banking sector.

On 3rd April 2020 Prime Minister Imran Khan announced a set of incentives for the construction sector in Pakistan, saying that his main objective was to employ the labourers so that they could be saved from *'hunger and the future difficult circumstances.'* The PM said that:

> "......Persons or entities who invested in the construction sector this year will not be asked about their source of income. The government has decided to agree to the demand of the construction sector and has

introduced the fixed tax. This [move] will bring down the amount of tax to be paid. Also, <u>if the investment is for the Naya Pakistan Housing Scheme, we will exempt 90% of the tax on it</u>.

The withholding tax on materials and services has been abolished in the informal sector. Tax will be collected only on steel and cement, mainly because these are the formal sectors.

The government will not collect any capital gains tax from any family that wants to sell its house. <u>A Rs:30 billion subsidies for the Naya Pakistan Housing Scheme will regulate economic activity and ensure houses for the poor were also built</u>.

The construction sector is being given the industry status and the formation of **The Construction Industry Development Board** *is underway; it is to promote the construction industry in Pakistan."*

The premier spoke about the **Corona-virus Relief Fund** solely for the benefit of the poor in Pakistan. <u>**The government started giving out cheques while about four million people had already been registered for the funds.**</u> However, the PM had reservations against people who, in the past, used calamities to hide their corruption. In tackling the coronavirus pandemic, PM Imran didn't force provinces to do anything after the 18th Amendment had been passed.

Next day; Association of Builders and Developers of Pakistan [ABAD] welcomed the incentive package for construction industry announced by PM Khan. It was termed as a historic package which could be a turning point for the economy of Pakistan. Since a while ABAD was demanding incentives for the construction sector because more than 70 allied industries were depending on the construction sector. The ABAD hoped that the government would also wave off the withholding taxes for the sector, and also to consider sales tax reduction in the provinces. ***Punjab and Khyber PK had already reduced sales tax to two percent;*** the other two provinces were in fact waiting for PM's interference.

Amidst fatal uncertainty of the post Covid-19 scenario, providing relief to the construction industry was widely criticised - that it was eventually to benefit the already-billionaire property tycoons and cement-factory owners. With PM Khan's close friends like <u>Aneel Musarrat of Manchester</u> [UK] and Aleem Khan in the property sector, it was evident that who would ultimately benefit from this relief package. Yet at the same time, doctors fighting the corona-virus were not provided adequate personal protective equipment [PPE]; young doctors had launched [on 6th April 2020] a strong protest against inadequate PPEs in Quetta and were brutally baton-charged by the police. On the other side private-school teachers, numbering around 1.5 million, were facing financial distress as they were not being paid their meagre salaries and there was no relief package for them.

First and foremost, the government's conception of the construction industry was incomplete, if not incorrect. The construction sector globally includes civil engineering, infrastructure projects and real estate developments both in the public and private sectors. But the general understanding of the construction sector within the PTI's state-package was limited to housing and real estate, that too mainly in the private sector. Moreover, Khan's government never considered that many infrastructural developments like highways, bridges, dams, rural housing and especially the public support development programs were also the allied requirements and vital to move the wheel of the overall construction industry.

Further, the basic necessity, the availability of land or its acquisition were never insights of the leadership when it came to power. As a result, the government did not get enough land during its tenure to launch low-cost housing and the numbers lingered at a few thousand under-construction flats at the end.

Similarly, the PTI government could have first started with the digitalization of properties and embarked upon master plans for cities. That would have enabled it to assess land records and figure out accessibility to land at the beginning. But unfortunately, this didn't happen and it stayed as one of the most significant obstacles faced by the governments, federal and Punjab.

Chairing a meeting of the National Coordinating Committee for Housing, Construction and Development in August 2020, PM Khan directed to ensure automation, digitization and simplification of procedures of land to facilitate investors and citizens. However, in December 2020, he admitted that *"...government departments are (running in) loss. They are in debt. They have land but they cannot benefit by selling it because they do not have land records."*

The provision of banking loans was an essential component of low-cost housing. The State Bank of Pakistan (SBP) had issued a government mark-up subsidy for housing finance to facilitate the provision of subsidized financing to low and middle-income individuals. Tax incentives and lower interest rates had encouraged participation in real estate businesses – NOT housing. However, tight standards and strict prerequisites for giving out such loans persisted as a major constraint during the majority of the cases. On the other hand, it was later revealed that banking loans were largely disbursed to the non-residential sector rather residential one – nepotism and acquaintances worked the best, of course.

Lastly, the continual price escalation of construction materials appeared as the main shortcoming that the PTI government was unable to contain. Due to the ongoing inflation rate and unstable dollar position in the market, the prices of construction materials increased enormously. Owing to the sharp uptick in prices, the Construction Association of Pakistan in an advertisement (in 2021) declared their inability to execute and continue construction on public sector projects. The builders and developers in the private sector stopped kicking off their real estate projects as well as bookings because of uncertainty in building material prices. The same situation persisted till ending of the PTI govt (April 2022) with the new regime in Islamabad.

RAHMATUL LIL ALAMEEN AUTHORITY:

On 10th October 2021: Prime Minister Imran Khan announced for National Rahmatul-lil-Alameen Authority (NRAA) as an ideological institution of the Government of Pakistan; it was set up under the Federal Ministry of Education & Professional Training. The ordinance to set up the authority was promulgated by President Arif Alvi on 13th October 2021. The authority was destined to conduct research on the prophetic biography and hadith to build the character of the youth. In addition, the authority was tasked to consult with relevant experts to make the biography of Muhammad [PBUH] a part of the academic curriculum – *and was also ordained with explaining Islam to the world.*

PM announced that this authority would be responsible for researching how best to disseminate lessons from the life of the Holy Prophet (PBUH) to the masses. The prime minister was addressing the *Ashra-e-Rehmat-ul-Lil-Aalamin* (PBUH) conference in Islamabad to kick off the ten-day celebration period till the 13th of Rabiul Awwal tht year. He said:

> *"I will be the patron myself but we have started searching for a person who has written books of tafsir, has great command [over religion] and is a scholar for the chairman. There will be an international advisory board above him on which we will bring the Muslim world's top*

scholars — we have looked at many names and are approaching them as well.

Islam was a religion of peace and humanity and the West did not understand it so the authority would also be tasked with explaining Islam to the world.

The scholars in the authority would be also be charged with monitoring the schools' curriculum and how the course on the Holy Prophet's (PBUH) biography was being taught and whether any changes were required to improve it."

Additionally, there were more subjects which the prime minister had pointed to like promoting Islamic research in universities, the strengths and weaknesses of Western culture, whether our divorces have increased and how monitoring the media and indoctrination of our own cartoons to teach our children about our culture. More emphasizing on that our Prophet (PBUH) had generated a perception that *'...education be given priority over money.'* The premier called for society to collectively tackle the issue of sexual crimes at priority.

However, from the same day, criticism and controversies started in print and social media. According to analysts, the purported purpose of the new authority was to get Pakistan out of a selectively portrayed cultural breakdown and moral crisis afflicting all aspects of social life. Pakistan has been, and still is, going through regressive conservative revivalism in television segments of religious televangelism. For decades, Pakistan has been in the midst of a large scale Barelvi and Deobandi revival with much more violence around the blasphemy law; Quranic study circles and spiritual movements like as Tablighi Jamaat and Al Huda are influencing the middle class and thus, associated beliefs and rituals of religious sectarianism were seen on increase.

Intelligentsia believed that the new authority established by Imran Khan was an extension of Gen Zia's legacy of deploying religiosity to achieve political gains, with the cover of resetting the system in the name of Islamic faith, the moves were to undermine the freedoms of expression, democratic processes in the country and encourage authoritarianism; *'Resettling the System'* in **daily DAWN** dated 15th December 2021 is referred for details.

See the **Friday Times** dated 8th December 2021; it opined that the appointed founder Chairman Ejaz Akram held and promoted controversial views against ethnic civil rights groups like the *Pashtun Tahafuz Movement* (PTM) and that Akram was critical of the concept of democracy. Akram advocated conspiracy theories (*espousing 9/11 for instance*), and regional expansionism and his concept of rule by fascist elites. Akram wrote that *'Belief in deep secularism, the idea of a republic, nationalism, capitalism, feminism, absolute freedom of speech, are all false consciousness that must be abandoned for things that work for us.'*

Due to the controversies surrounding the founder Chairman, Ejaz Akram had to resign after just two months into his formal tenure. In his place, a respected academic, Dr Anis Ahmad (Ph.D Temple University, USA), the then Vice Chancellor of a private *Riphah University* and formerly a Vice President of the International Islamic University Islamabad, was appointed as Chairman.

By establishing the NRAA, PM Khan had openly manifested that Pakistan was facing an acute form of a moral crisis; cultural breakdown was afflicting all aspects of social life AND Pakistanis, as a collective entity, had moved away from their roots. The latest step to stem the tide of this proclaimed moral decay had nothing to do with showing the real face of Islam to the outside world. Leaving aside the wholesale equivalence drawn between Pakistani culture and Islam, and the general ignorance of doctrinal and ritualistic differences that dot this society, Khan could think beyond rising divorce rates, breakdown of the family systems, and spread of *fahaashi* in entertainment – beyond *the growth of entertainment and fashion industries.*

- *In 20 years, <u>the divorce rate among population aged 15 and above has gone up from 0.34 per cent to 0.40pc in Pakistan</u> – then, was this topic worth for a prime minister to concentrate its energy **instead of taking its nation to 100% literacy, or providing technical education to most mid-order educated ones, or expanding infrastructure for industrialization, removing poverty by providing them adequate employments OR fighting population growth etc.***

Since the early 2000s, as against growth in fashion, *'fahaashi'* and entertainment segments, Pakistan also witnessed the concurrent rise of regressive themes in TV dramas; enhanced religious televangelism in media; spread of conservative and spiritual movements; anthropologist Ammara Maqsood's book *'New Pakistan's Middle Class'* is referred.

In nut-shell, PM Khan's politics of religiosity aside, the man he selected to head the said Authority (NRA), as part of his effort to build a *Riasat-e-Madina*, didn't believe in democracy; instead he preferred to prop up the *'elite of the elite'* to run the affairs of the state; his views about regional and global politics were extremely bizarre. Additionally, this body was mandated to monitor the country's education system and the media – what an anti-thesis to the education systems prevailing in Iran & Saudia, what to speak about comparisons with US, China or European states.

Such a sweeping mandate for the authority raised several questions about its objectives; widely alleged that it was an extension of Gen Zia's legacy of using religiosity to achieve political objectives. The appointment of Dr Ejaz Akram with his highly controversial views supporting authoritarianism reinforced worries on that count.

One could estimate that by selecting Ejaz Akram, Imran Khan had mistakenly opened another un-necessary war-front; profoundly unwantedly – Mr Akram called Pakistan's political leadership coward, stupid, and sold out for many decades; …that the *'only hope this country has now is if the whole principle and structure of governance is completely dismantled'*. He wanted the creation of a new system of governance led by an elite having an upright character coupled with much deeper understanding of ideologies, religions, civilisations, and principles of statecraft. He believed that only the military could clean up that 'mess'.

Dr Akram often stressed on correcting the 'direction of Qibla' - recalling Gen Zia's rhetoric of retrogressive laws in the name of faith. Since decades Pakistan suffered with bloodshed with the rise of faith-based extremism. Astonishly, people heard the same narrative from a person heading a body that was mandated to work for Imran Khan's vision of turning Pakistan into a 'Riasat-e-Madina'; Mr Khan attracted more hatred than applause in fact - where were we heading with that kind of worldview while aiming at monitoring of education and the media.

More troubling: that it was all being done in the name of faith. Imran Khan's vision of 'Riasat-e-Madina' was in fact an effort to further Gen Zia's obscurantist legacy – a great leap backward, the people believed.

SUDDEN DEATH OF NRAA: Unfortunately, the wholesome homework done for NRAA got finished because just six months later, PM Khan had to face the No Confidence Move (NCM) in April 2022 and his govt was packed. Even otherwise, it remained a fact that _**NRAA could not be activated after the government notified it in the gazette due to the lack of interest of the education ministry**_. The new PDM government had done away with the said Authority on 6th June 2022. Instead, the PDM government passed a new bill with amendments in the National Assembly and Senate on 9th June 2022. That amended bill was called **National Rehmant lil Alamin and Khatam-un-Nabiyyin Authority** [NRAKNA] but no attention was paid to activating the authority due to the lack of interest of the Federal Ministry of Education.

Scenario 251

CPEC DURING KHAN's PREMIERSHIP – FACTS

After the Kargal War, Pakistan once felt the need of having a military naval port so the Karachi-Gwadar Road (Coastal Highway) was built for defense purposes. Gwadar forms the crux of the CPEC project, as it was envisaged to be the link between China's ambitious One Belt, One Road project and its 21st Century Maritime Silk Road project. A lot more projects were to be developed around the port of Gwadar by December 2017.

CPEC – YEARS AFTER 2015:

Due to political short-sightedness of the leadership of Pakistan and external pressures on it, allegedly from the US and India, as of 2022, only three CPEC projects – $4 million Gwadar Smart Port City Master Plan, $300 million Physical Infrastructure of Gwadar Port and the Free Zone Phase-1, and a $10 million Pak-China Technical and Vocational Institute in Gwadar were declared completed whereas one-dozen projects worth nearly $2 billion remained undeveloped including water supply, electricity provision, expressway, international airport, fishing harbour and hospital among others. China provided 7,000 plus sets of solar panels for households in Gwadar till 2022. Another 10,000 sets of solar panels were under active preparation for the poor people in Balochistan for their general uplift.

The special economic zone in Gwadar was to be completed in three phases. By 2025, it was envisaged that manufacturing and processing industries would be developed, while further expansion of the zone was intended to be complete by 2030. **On 10th April 2016,** the Chairman of China Overseas Port Holding Company said in a conversation with *The Washington Post* that his company planned to spend $4.5 billion on roads, power, hotels and other infrastructure for the industrial zone as well as other projects in Gwadar city.

China had undertaken to grant Pakistan $230 million to construct a new international airport in Gwadar. The provincial government of Balochistan had set aside 4000 acres for the construction of that new Gwadar

International Airport which required 30 months for construction, the costs of which were to be fully funded by grants from the Chinese government which Pakistan was not obliged to repay – *but due to poor security situations China didn't opt to give start* to this most needed project.

The city of Gwadar was further to be developed by the construction of a 300 MW coal power plant, a desalinization plant, and a new 300-bed hospital which was to be completed in 2023. Plans for Gwadar city also included construction of the Gwadar East Bay Expressway – a 19 kilometer controlled-access road for connecting Gwadar Port to the Makran Coastal Highway. These additional projects were estimated to cost $800 million, and were to be *financed by 0% interest loans* extended by the Exim Bank of China to Pakistan – BUT zero progress seen in any project.

On 19th November 2020: A crucial meeting of the Joint Cooperation Committee (JCC) of China-Pakistan Economic Corridor (CPEC) was *further delayed after both the countries could not agree on the future roadmap for industrial cooperation.* Pakistani and Chinese authorities could not agree on a common agenda for holding the fifth meeting of the Joint Working Group (JWG) on Industrial Parks and Special Economic Zones (SEZs) in Pakistan.

There were nine JWGs of CPEC that dealt with every important sphere of economic cooperation. Till then, seven groups had met while meetings of JWG on industrial cooperation and Gwadar had not taken place. The working group meeting had to take place before convening the next JCC meeting, the 10th in sequence. In fact, the industrial cooperation was the lynchpin of the SECOND PHASE of CPEC.

Pakistan's Foreign Office had tentatively scheduled the 10th JCC meeting for the end of October but later delayed it to mid-November (2020). As per Federal Ministry for Planning & Development Islamabad, the JWG meetings were *almost completed* and both sides were considering whether to hold face-to-face meeting or meet remotely due to the Covid-19 situation.

Pakistan was also keen to make progress on an agreement *on financing the Mainline-I project of Pakistan Railways* during the 10th JCC meeting. Total cost of the project was $6.8 billion and Pakistan was seeking $6.1 billion in Chinese loan, according to a decision taken by the Executive Committee of National Economic Council (ECNEC) of Pakistan. *[JCC was the highest decision-making body of CPEC, co-chaired by Pakistan's minister for planning & development and the Chairman of China's National Development and Reforms Commission (NDRC)]*.

In 2014, Pakistan and China had announced that they would deepen their economic and strategic cooperation through CPEC, which was the pilot project of the trillion-dollar Belt and Road Initiative of the Chinese president. Pakistan and China were successful in showing progress during the first four years of CPEC implementation and implemented nearly $25 billion worth of projects. However, things started slowing down after 2018 and there had hardly been any progress in Khan's first two years regime. Due to some reasons, allegedly China delayed the finalization of agenda for holding the 5th JWG meeting on industrial cooperation – but it was NOT China, Pakistan's zero-security arrangements were responsible.

Pakistan's P&D ministry had forwarded the agenda and draft minutes to Chinese authorities in April 2020 but they responded back in November 2020. Also, that Pakistan was keen to sign the Framework Agreement on Industrial Cooperation as existing cooperation was only under a memorandum of understanding. Pakistan's Board of Investment (BOI) wanted to have meaningful bilateral cooperation in the industrial sector – however, the ball remained in Chinese court for the revised draft agenda – perhaps due to Covid-19 around AND Pakistan's failure to provide effective security to the foreign (Chinese) workers remained the main reasons for the said hang-up.

Under industrial cooperation, Pakistan wanted to develop nine prioritized SEZs but the pace of work remained very slow – in fact, no work got started by Pakistani authorities on industrial zones till that time. During the ninth JCC, it had been ***decided that Pakistan would provide infrastructure at zero point and one-window service to all SEZs*** – but the Pakistani bureaucracy was not able to give start to any (except a little job at the Rashakai SEZ in Khyber PK). Imran Khan's govt was not able to finalize procedural formalities for the provision of electricity, gas, water, roads and security to the other SEZs. Also, the successive govts had not approved an incentive package and it remained at the draft stage for five years (till 2020), including a part of PMLN's last governance.

See a comment at **//ORFonline.org** dated 25th November 2020:

> ".... Political fragility and increased interference of security agencies in the matters of civilian administration and even CPEC projects have made Beijing rethink on the CPEC's outcomes."

CPEC AUTHORITY – A WHITE ELEPHANT (?)

On 8th October 2019: President of Pakistan Dr Arif Alvi promulgated an ordinance for the establishment of the '**China-Pakistan Economic Corridor Authority** (CPECA)'. The process had started a few years back when it was decided to establish a high-level authority, with the highest autonomy and powers, to get expected results out of the CPEC.

Pakistan was then facing its worst economic crisis (as it's today in mid-2024) as the foreign debt had nearly crossed $100 billion. Pakistan had to approach the IMF for a bailout package and signed a 39-month restructuring program. Under that scenario, CPEC was considered as vital as oxygen for Pakistan's ailing economy. CPEC Authority was aimed at *accelerating the pace of CPEC-related activities, find new drives of growth, unlock the potential of the interlinked production network and global value chains through regional and global connectivity*. It was designed to cut off some bureaucratic hurdles and facilitate coordination amongst ministries and departments, paving ways for smooth execution of CPEC projects.

Pakistan had never been involved in such a mega initiative and had no such previous experience. Due to lack of experience and capacity, poor planning, and shortage of requisite human resources, Pakistan struggled to tap the full potential of CPEC. Nevertheless, the progress of CPEC projects remained satisfactory, and most of the early harvest projects were complete or nearly complete; the fruits of completed projects were being felt by all. The network of motorways and highways were playing a very important role in the transportation industry, and ultimately contributing toward the socio-economic development of the nation. Within couple of years, the GDP grew from 4.5 percent to 5.7 percent due to the CPEC initiatives.

To improve further, in August 2019, PM Khan announced that the government was establishing CPECA to ensure the timely completion of the corridor's projects – through ensured coordination amongst the departments concerned. *The timely completion of CPEC projects was the top-most priority of the PTI government* and CPEC was a clear example of joint efforts and partnership between Pakistan and China. Till then, there were complete consensus and harmony between the two nations.

The fact remains that President's Alvi's promulgation of the ordinance for establishing CPECA coincided with Khan's visit to Beijing from 7-9th October 2019. Khan was accompanied by a high-level delegation comprising important members of his cabinet. His visit included addressing the China-Pakistan business forum and CPEC was a major agenda. It had further strengthened the ideal existing understanding between the two countries. Pakistan's Minister of Planning Khusro Bakhtiar held it as '... *a meaningful engagement on all aspects of China-Pakistan relations taking CPEC cooperation to new heights.*'

Pakistan was ready for the second phase of CPEC, where the social sector, agriculture and special economic zones (SEZs) were the focus of rapid development of the economy. It was widely hailed that the establishment of the CPEC Authority would facilitate Chinese and Pakistani sides to expedite the projects and smooth execution. It was then considered instrumental in widening and speeding up of projects under CPEC. Pakistan was then definitely committed to make CPEC a success story and role model for the rest of the world. It was the flagship project and promises a far-reaching impact.

BUT *the things didn't move ahead as Imran Khan and his PTI team planned* – thus, the CPEC Ordinance had to lapse on 31st May 2020.

It was a little puzzling for the media gurus, some allegedly paid from foreign sources, to hear about the **CPEC Authority**. They took it as some sort of body to oversee all CPEC-related work for the government - creating a massive parallel bureaucracy that could significantly usurp powers from the provincial governments. Was that CPEC authority being devised to perform only functions related to coordination, or would it be empowered to make decisions on matters ranging from corporate governance, gas allocations, PSDP releases, power tariffs, custom duties and trade? True, that the PTI govt had no details of the plan till then.

However, the new experience was positive because *the said parallel bureaucracy* was being contemplated as one which was empowered to make final decisions on all matters related to and arising from CPEC-related investments. Of course, there were pitfalls; that one class of investor would receive white-gloved treatment whereas the others would be in queues.

Obviously, greater transparency remained a pressing priority, with the latest discussions on a CPEC authority being the best example of how decisions were being deliberated upon in actual situations. For just decision, the matter could be discussed in parliament and given an adequate public airing before sending it to the federal cabinet – IT DID HAPPEN THEN – a miracle in Pakistan's parliamentary history.

A NATIONAL Assembly panel, on 11<u>th</u> November 2020, *postponed the clearance* of the proposed China-Pakistan Economic Corridor Authority (Amendment) Bill, 2020, for discussion and voting by the lower house till the government could satisfy its members on the authority's legal status months after lapse (on 31<u>st</u> May 2020) of the ordinance that created it. The planning officials couldn't bring any plausible explanation for its existence or the expense incurred on running it without any law to protect its operations.

Among other things, the bill had sought to indemnify the actions of the authority since the expiry of the ordinance that had been promulgated a year ago (2019) and later extended in January (2020). The authority did not have a chairman at that moment but the panel could not be convinced when informed that *the 'incumbent chairman' of the technically defunct authority was just 'coordinating' without drawing any salary or perks since the expiry of the ordinance*. The planning ministry's written clarification was needed for transparency in the affairs of the CPEC Authority.

However, it was ironic that an agency that was created to inject momentum into CPEC projects and streamline the initiative's policymaking process was caught up in a storm because the government didn't put in the effort required for the timely passage of legislation; might be PTI govt didn't pursue the same due to transparency concerns. The delay in the passage of the bill required to give legal cover to the authority didn't send positive signals to China at a time when the multibillion-dollar CPEC initiative was expected to pick up momentum. With the tenth Joint Cooperation Committee meeting scheduled for later that month, the important decisions about the ML-1 and hydropower schemes, as well as the progress on the SEZs suffered a lot.

POLITICAL MESS AND CORRUPTION:

The fact remained that Beijing had sought to invest over US$62 billion in infrastructure and energy projects in Pakistan through the CPEC. The Chinese officials were of the view that the CPEC would create around 2.3 million jobs in Pakistan by 2030 and would provide an alternative pathway for exports and energy imports from West Asia to China, linking China's western provinces to key global sea lanes through

Pakistan's Gwadar port. However, political fragility, increased interference of security agencies and the army establishment in the matters of civilian administration and even CPEC projects made Beijing rethink on the CPEC's ultimate utility.

The calling card of criticizing the CPEC was being held by all the major opposition parties in Pakistan, which were later called Pakistan Democratic Movement [PDM] collectively. Over the previous seven years, the CPEC had also been abused as a political tool by the opposition parties in Pakistan to serve their ends; before being elected to form the government in 2018, the Imran Khan-led PTI was allegedly a staunch critic of the CPEC, too.

In 2018, the World Bank had cautioned the participating countries in the BRI projects about the impending debt risks, stranded infrastructure, social risks, and corruption. All those risks propounded by the World Bank were at least true for Pakistan - marred in recent years by continuing the political instability and growing interference of the US-sponsored forces and bureaucracy in Pakistan, especially after the alleged rigged elections of 2018 in favour of Imran Khan. It was alleged by the nationalist sects of intelligentsia that the active and retired top brass of the Pakistan army, who were appointed on crucial positions in the CPEC projects, had amassed huge wealth by mishandling the project funds; though no cogent proof of it was not available on record.

Fault lied with Imran Khan because his PTI government had refused to investigate the corruption charges in the CPEC projects. Former army official Lt Gen Asim Saleem Bajwa, then Chairman of the CPEC Authority, was also appointed to head the Prime Minister's media management team. In August 2020, according to media & news reports, Asim Bajwa had massed tones of undisclosed wealth during his tenure as the Chief of the CPEC Authority and acquired offshore assets in his wife and brothers' names; despite protests, Gen Asim Bajwa had refused to step down from post of the Chairman CPEC Authority. Chinese officials expected that about 80 percent of investments in the CPEC was lost to corruption and this leakage was difficult to avoid.

The critics also held that the inflow of Chinese investments had worsened the corruption in private-public partnerships and in the realms of privatization due to bad governance and conflicting roles played by the civilian governments, both of PMLN and PTI and the army establishment had full knowledge of it. At times, Beijing also used corruption to its advantage by exploiting the growing socio-economic weaknesses of Pakistan.

Growing corruption, promises of jobs not materializing, rampant exploitation of natural resources with no effective controls had triggered anti-state insurgency among the people of Baluchistan – who in turn targeted the Chinese deployments there. Pakistan army and Balochistan army-militia didn't provide enough security to the Chinese engineers and workers - thus, they were often attacked and killed by dissidents like of Balochistan Liberation Army [BLA]. Chinese authorities went discouraged by state of insurgency and extremism in Baluchistan – thus, planned to dump the whole set of CPEC projects finally – a great loss for the nation during PMLN & PTI govts both.

Pakistan kept on washing its hands off the worsening security situation in Baluchistan. Instead of passing summary-trial court procedures and death sentences like their neighbouring countries (Iran, Afghanistan, and China), they continued to accuse New Delhi of sabotaging its economic partnership with China. Through this way, the Baluchistan Liberation Army (BLA) intensified its demands for Baloch independence, blaming Beijing instead of India & US, for exploiting and making the province more volatile.

Even the Pakistani army admitted it often that Indian agencies were specifically targeting Chinese development projects of the CPEC and had sponsored about 700 people to harm CPEC projects. Such claims made by the Pak army made the Chinese even more cautious of their investments. *Global Times*, the CCP mouthpiece, once wrote that: *'Beijing will keep a close eye on how the (security of their men) issue unfolds in the future.'*

The above mentioned factors had forced the CCP to halt some of the CPEC projects. For example, *the Imran government had cleared US$ 6.8 billion for the Mainline-1 (ML-1) rail upgrade to double the speed of trains* on 6 August 2020. The ML-1 project was the costliest project of the CPEC, with 90 percent finances made available by the Chinese. However, Beijing was seen reluctant to make progress on its upgrade agreement till the end of his tenure. Same was the case with industrial cooperation where the Chinese were doubtful, given the security situation in Pakistan. The friendliness between China and Pakistan was to face more troubles in the coming months, especially given the bad economic situation because of Covid-19 and the wavering political environment in Pakistan.

[The fact remained that Imran khan was not opposing CPEC; he was just demanding that we should as nationalists get Pakistan's priorities

right in a way - not as subordinates of PRC but close partners working on the basis of equality. However, the intelligentsia held that working on ML-1 Railway and the SEZs were of prime importance for Pakistan. <u>During Mr Khan's days, the CPEC had slowed down, rather halted altogether because of the US wish and pressure through the Pakistan's rouge bureaucracy, civil and military, to discourage Chinese investments in the country</u>. The security situation was also made worse for Chinese workers at all places through BLA or other agents of US and India.]

CPEC – THE GAME CHANGER:

The China-Pakistan Economic Corridor (CPEC), one of the most ambitious components of Beijing's Belt and Road Initiative, was announced with great fanfare in 2015. Since then, it has consistently been held up as a *'game-changer for Pakistan's economy'*. But the road to completion was long and winding. Reports indicated that the pace of CPEC projects has been slowing down in Pakistan from the second year of operation. China was the only country that was heavily investing in Pakistan. The slowdown of CPEC thus didn't augur well for a cash-strapped country like Pakistan, which got plagued by countless issues, mostly concerning with security and protection of the Chinese on ground; **The Diplomat,** a US magazine, dated <u>16th Februay 2021</u> is referred for more details.

The CPEC was (and still is) meant to help Pakistan take off economically – BUT the program could not be kept up with its projected timeline. Numerous reports indicated that in years 2018-22 the pace of CPEC projects had been slowing down in Pakistan and the Chinese counterparts, despite their legendary patience, were not happy.

In Pakistan, there had not been a major development during nearly a decade in the CPEC operations. The lack of progress has been mentioned in numerous reports about CPEC being at a near standstill in the country. A **Bloomberg video report** dated <u>14th January 2021</u> on CPEC as an example of *'how China's flagship Belt and Road project stalled….'* had in fact stirred the confidence of the EU countries who were then keen to invest in Pakistan

The **Bloomberg video** discussed CPEC in general, with a particular focus on the port city of Gwadar. Interestingly, Gwadar, despite being the epicenter of multibillion dollar projects, lacked basic necessities like reliable access to water and electricity, let alone other facilities. Official circles in Beijing and Islamabad dubbed the said report as another piece of Western propaganda; but in fact, had pointed out several issues that had gone wrong, likely:

- City of Gwadar was being fenced off as a security measure then. The authorities had to stop work on the fence after much uproar by Baloch nationalist groups, including protests. They considered that *the fencing was part of a masterplan to separate Gwadar from Balochistan and bring it under direct federal control.*

- There were frequent and sporadic gun-attacks in Gwadar and elsewhere in the province to discourage Chinese investments in the province. *China wanted assurances for their security*; BUT sealing off an entire town for guaranteeing Chinese security was precisely the wrong approach – also, giving a wrong impression of Pakistan that could discourage future potential investments and business. By fencing a port town, it could have sent a message to the business world, including the Chinese, that the country was unsafe for investors at least.

- Security cooperation remained a key factor in Pakistan's relationship with China, as their economic ties lagged far behind military engagement; since 2015, their economic relations, focused on the CPEC had assumed new significance. The overall investment in the CPEC, originally envisaged at $46 was enhanced to $62 billion till 2022 – the largest single coordinated development initiative ever undertaken in Pakistan's history.

- Fair enough, fence construction in Gwadar was stopped. However, other local Balochis started feeling left out of development and got apprehensive about their future in Gwadar.

- After a brief pause, in year 2020 however, geopolitical developments in the region provided robustness to CPEC projects in Pakistan. As a result, two new deals for hydropower projects in Pakistan-administered Kashmir were signed in quick succession, along with an agreement on a special economic zone (SEZ) in Faisalabad. These moves gave cause for CPEC supporters to assert that the projects in the country were, once again, moving in the right direction. With the signing of the new deals, officials from both countries were content that CPEC had returned to its previous pace, which had noticeably slowed down since mid-2018 when PM Khan had assumed his office.

- Both Beijing and Islamabad were aware of the hurdles on the part of the successive Pakistani governments. The CPEC authority in Pakistan was created at China's urge to better coordinate CPEC projects among stakeholders from both sides. Run by a retired Gen Asim Saleem Bajwa, the new authority, had to plan and coordinate the smooth implementation of the CPEC projects, collectively worth $70 billion. But some independent analysts in Islamabad were of the view that the CPEC authority actually shifted the key projects from hands of the civilian govt to military authorities in Pakistan.

- The slowdown of CPEC in Pakistan provided an obvious opportunity to the opposition parties, especially the PMLN led by Sharifs. Opposition leaders had repeatedly criticized the PTI government for being responsible for stalled-out projects – a manifest of poor governance.

- Khan's government tried hard to overcome the opposition by focusing its attention on the CPEC projects' revival. In late December 2020, China and Pakistan held a meeting to increase the momentum of CPEC projects, and also availed an opportunity to proclaim that both sides *'were satisfied with the progress and committed to turn mega projects into a role model for the rest of the world to follow.'* Immediately after, the second meeting was held in China's Xinjiang region on 25th Dec 2020 – but again **THUSS..**

- The Imran Khan government, in fact, had strived hard to work hand in hand with their Chinese counterparts, hoping to overcome any damage done from past criticisms of CPEC. But unfortunately, PTI's wrongly selected team, their inefficiency and incompetence became the major cause of bottlenecks in the implementation of the multibillion dollar projects – and the position went worsened till Mr Khan's departure in April 2022.

US + INDIA BLOCKED THE CPEC:

The CPEC's major side-benefit was also supposed to harmonize inter-provincial relations in Pakistan. However, Balochistan – the home of CPEC's flagship project in Gwadar – felt left out; factors never analyzed seriously. Security remained the major issue. The presence of Chinese personnel onsite was proving to be an easy target for terrorists who opposed the project; Imran Khan government was blamed for slowing down the implementation of the CPEC – but it was not the whole truth.

> *"The causes of slowdown were much deeper – externally and diplomatically the CPEC had been under attack from India and the US through their covert financial assistance. The Indian objections were based ostensibly on India's unilateral claims over the Jammu and Kashmir state through which some CPEC road works were navigating. In reality, India took the project as China's geo-strategic advancement and influence in the Indian Ocean. India's ambition, backed by the US; thus, played a great (and successful) game in Balochistan for winding up the CPEC;"* Prof Sajjad Ashraf of **National University of Singapore**, in his thesis explained *'Why CPEC Faces Challenges in Pakistan';* **his paper dated 2nd June 2022 is referred.**

The United States remained the principal critic of China's Belt and Road Initiative (BRI) of which the CPEC was an essential component. The US believed that China's ultimate goal was to utilize Pakistan's strategically positioned deep-sea port, Gwadar, for energy security and its power projection into the Indian Ocean. In its global competition with China, the US wanted to deny the Chinese the said advantage. CPEC and BRI thus signaled a strategic and economic advantage for Pakistan and China.

Wary of China's expanding global role, *the US warned Pakistan against deeper engagement with China, while China challenged Washington over its support of India.* The growing US-Indian strategic relationship in the last decade is evidence of the US support of Indian naval power to counter the growing Chinese influence in the Indian Ocean. The US also accused China of *'debt trap diplomacy'* which allegedly allowed China to gain access to Pakistan's strategic assets.

The region of Balochistan is rich in minerals and it comprises 48 percent of Pakistan's land. There are multiple oil and gas pipelines in this region stretching from Russia and Central Asia. There are outside powers known to everyone (like the US & India) to support terrorist activity to subvert the CPEC projects; allegedly the CIA sponsored Afghans which remained controversial within Pakistan since years. Multiple connectivity links were being built between China's Xinjiang province and Gwadar port in Balochistan – that included three highways: western, central and eastern – but all remained in suspension since 2017 at least.

Notwithstanding the external reasons for delay in implementation of the CPEC there were essentially domestic issues that caused interruptions in its planning and execution. In Pakistan's dysfunctional democracy there was no self-analysis over why CPEC progress had stuttered from the initial fan-fare celebrations of 'go-up now.' As a part of political point scoring the then PMLN government in 2015 promoted the CPEC as a gift from China. All details were kept secret from the public, which led to suspicion over the project and its costs. Much of the funding was concessional loans from the Chinese commercial banks; PMLN kept it hidden – US played their tunes at it.

For China it was *'a partnership with shared responsibilities'* between the two. This duality of the concept itself led to conflicting implementation strategies. Consequently, Pakistan never handled the enterprise in its proper context. Almost all subsequent problems were directly linked to that ***faulty political sell by the then government***. Pakistan's declining capacity to share the costs later caused disappointment and delays. Thus, in 2022, Pakistan, like Sri Lanka, started feeling itself in serious economic trouble as a result of ignoring important timelines and adopting unsustainable policies that had prevented revenue generation.

Without the money coming in it was hard to pay back any investment. That was the quagmire Pakistan found itself in 2020-22. Critics of China's investment and the foreign ill-forces had fully understood that fact on the ground too. The dilemma boiled down to a different way of work between the Chinese seriousness and dedication as against Pakistan's chaotic democracy, lack of commitment and incompetence that caused bottlenecks in the implementation of the multibillion-dollar projects. The state machinery was not up to the task; neither during PMLN regime nor in Imran Khan's era – that's how the situation developed.

With stakes so high, China and Pakistan couldn't afford further delays but it happened. Mr Khan and the PMLN both had to play in the hands of its detractors. The US used it as an opportunity to criticize China. The project was critical for China in its drive for acquiring energy security – it was China's ambition of becoming the world's largest economy. Pakistan, apart from immense benefits accruing, should not have let the project be delayed further – but the dishonest and inexperienced politicians plus few tainted bureaucrats didn't want to understand the seriousness of the issues involved. Perhaps, the country was marching towards the fate of Sri Lanka then.

PMLN / PDM GOVT OPPOSED CPEC-A:

In the 3rd week of April 2022, just after TWO WEEKS of Imran Khan's departure, Shahbaz Sharif's PDM government decided in principle to scrap the China-Pakistan Economic Corridor (CPEC) Authority terming it 'redundant' and 'obstructive'. It decided to revert to the earlier arrangement of routing CPEC projects through the planning ministry to line-up ministries for execution for revitalizing the country's biggest, most prestigious bilateral economic development project. See a stunning open statement dated 23rd April 2022, made during a visit to CPEC Authority offices, from the *Federal Minister for Planning and Development Ahsan Iqbal* here:

> *"... (He) called for immediate removal of problems faced by the Chinese investors and contractors working on China-Pakistan Economic Corridor (CPEC) including swift processing of their visa cases. The authorities concerned are directed to prepare a structure so that **the CPEC Authority could be wound up and integrated into the Ministry of Planning and Development because it was in conflict with rules of business of the various ministries.**"*

The Minister held that the CPECA was dysfunctional and was in conflict with the role of line ministries. Under the rules of business, ministries had the basic roles in the implementation of policies and projects under the CPEC but a parallel organization only created duplication of work and lack of ownership. In fact, the CPECA's chairmanship had been given to newly sworn in federal minister Ch Salik Hussain of PMLQ who was not aware of any such move - but expressing that it was illogical to have a parallel set up.

Thus, in nut-shell, the PMLN had strongly opposed the creation of CPECA through an act of parliament or otherwise because it was unnecessary and superfluous as the planning ministry had discharged the role very diligently and effectively in the past. The opposition members had dissented to the act because it appeared to be a parallel Planning Commission with little utility and *become a white elephant*. PMLN's Ahsan Iqbal in his dissenting note had noted that more than $29 billion worth of investment had been channelized by the Planning Commission successfully without any authority and with the support of various ministries which could have continued for successful implementation of various decisions involved in the process.

The implementation of the decision (about shelving CPEC Authority Act), however, was made conditional to Chinese consent. Federal Minister for Planning, Ehsan Iqbal, held that he had multiple interactions with Chinese officials since the cabinet decision and:

> *"... they (the Chinese) seemed indifferent over structural settings on Pakistan's side as long contractual commitments are honoured and*

work on CPEC projects is accelerated. Chinese friends are happy to see our actions and the new momentum. They are not interested in details of how we implement CPEC. In their opinion that's Pakistan's internal issue."

The debate over the disbanding of the CPEC Authority largely depended on which side of the political fence one was sitting on. The planning minister further elaborated that:

"We are going back to the 2013-18 model of CPEC implementation which brought in investments worth $29 billion. Since the authority was created, not a single dollar worth of new investment has flowed in. Only projects in the pipeline continued but at a slower than anticipated speed. The CPEC Authority was a non-starter and proved to be a failure. Disbanding the CPEC Authority is pro-CPEC because the authority blocked progress by adding a new bureaucratic layer. All the good work on the CPEC happened before the authority was created. All it did was to stall the CPEC."

BUT there were arguments in favour of the CPEC Authority, too. – a very cogent voice, a sitting senator and member of the CPEC Parliamentary Committee had roared:

'How can a one-stop shop that resolves all issues pertaining to CPEC projects be a bad idea, especially in second phase where a higher robust engagement of Chinese private companies in multiple sectors is expected? - Can lethargic ministries and sub-federating units with their own set of problems be assumed more effective in dealing with investors?

Before anything else it's personal. Honestly, it's sad to see the nation's interests compromised to service the egos of political pigmies. How else can you explain channelizing energy in cancelling instead of building on at the current critical juncture?"

Mr Senator said narrating instances of PMLN's opposition at every step of the way in the National Assembly and the Senate. Another senior member familiar with CPEC affairs shared his insight:

"Initially even PTI legislators were reluctant to support CPEC Authority as it was seen as a move by the deeper establishment to assume the charge of the flagship Chinese One Belt One Road initiative. The resistance dissolved as the Chinese threw their weight behind such a platform."

PROPAGANDA: CPEC SLOWED DOWN IN KHAN's ERA:

NO; it wasn't. China quashed disinformation about CPEC slowdown….. Spokesperson Zhao said many livelihood projects were implemented in last three and a half years.

On 20th January 2022: Beijing said the CPEC framework was moving forward against a headwind posed by Covid-19 pandemic and promoting economic development and people's livelihood in Pakistan. Speaking at a regular briefing, Chinese Foreign Ministry Spokesperson *Zhao Lijian rejected reports that work on the CPEC, a flagship project of the Belt and Road Initiative, had slowed down over the past three and half a year.*

> *"So-called claim that little has been achieved and no program was approved over the past three and half years… [is] pure disinformation. Over the three and a half years under the framework, many livelihood projects have been approved and implemented, delivering tangible benefits."*

The Chairman Zhao and his colleagues shared the positive progress achieved in the CPEC framework with the media on many occasions, while saying: 'CPEC *as an important pilot project under the BRI framework follows the principles of joint consultation and contribution for shared benefits. Recently, we have seen President of Pakistan Dr Arif Alvi, Prime Minister Imran Khan and some media's positive comments on the progress made in the CPEC flagship project';* **APP's analysis** on all media papers and TV channels dated 21st January 2022 is referred.

Chairman Zhao also told that under the CPEC, agriculture working group, technical working group and technological and scientific working groups had been established. However, it was pointed out that ML-1 Railway project needed huge investment, and that the two sides were having consultation on it. About the Dasu dam project, he set aside the reports that the Chinese contractor had demobilized from the site and raised several demands as preconditions to resume the work; both countries were aware of the situation as it was going on. The Chairman also commented that the CPEC framework was an important platform and the said BRI flagship project had entered an important stage - going forward. The two countries were on one page for focusing on industries, science and people's welfare.

However, despite the above assurance and alike moves, the intelligentsia held that *'there was, in fact, a slow-down seen in CPEC projects'* – BUT it was not on the part of PTI govt or the Imran Khan's person. See the PTI govt's agitated reminder for the Chinese government dated 10th November 2021; daily **THE EXPRESS TRIBUNE** of the same day is referred:

Pakistan has requested China to remove obstacles in the way of completion of seven energy and infrastructure projects worth roughly $12 billion, Special Assistant to Prime Minister on CPEC Affairs Khalid Mansoor told the media.

> *"I have written two separate letters to the vice Chairman of National Development and Reforms Commission (NDRC) of China, urging him to remove barriers hindering the completion of these projects (Ref: Khalid Mansoor's talk with a group of journalists that day). The vice chairman's support had been sought for **six energy schemes and one infrastructure project – Mainline-I (ML-I) of Pakistan Railways.** The cost of energy projects is $5 billion and the estimated value of the ML-I scheme is $6.8 billion. We have requested China that the agreed projects should be taken to the development stage.*
>
> *Pakistan was also trying to resolve problems in connection with flexibility on the $6 billion loan terms that it wanted to secure from China for construction of the rail project - as the progress on the ground did not move at the pace agreed between the two nations. To finalize the loan deal with China for the ML-I project, Pakistan was waiting for a term sheet from China for the loan agreement. Pakistan would show flexibility on the interest rate, foreign currency component of the loan and tenor of the loan (Pakistan had earlier requested for a loan at 1% in US dollar but the Chinese side didn't agree).*
>
> *The government had approved the 1,733km-long Karachi-Peshawar ML-I projects at a cost of $6.8 billion, which the Chinese termed on the lower side. Pakistan offered China to arrange an all-Chinese competitive bidding for the said project and if bids would be higher than $6.8 billion, then the government would stand ready to revise PC-I of the project. The military had assured the provision of complete security to the project. The ML-I project was already facing a delay of over four years and the two sides had been discussing financing terms for the past two years.*
>
> *PTI govt was simultaneously found trying to save Gwadar power plant, Karot power plant, Kohala power plant and three other projects from the adverse impact of delay in power purchase payments to the Chinese*

sponsors. However, the Chinese were seeking sureties that those new power plants could also be stuck in circular debt – thus, Chinese were reluctant to move further whereas the PTI government was actively working to clear Rs:250 billion payments of Chinese firms on account of power purchase that were stuck in the circular debt (then).

The PTI government was paying Libor plus 2% cost to the sponsors of Chinese power plants on the amount that was delayed beyond a certain period. The only good thing was that China had not called (till then) the guarantees, which indicated that the Chinese were willing to work in Pakistan. However, it remains a fact that the deals were the need of the hour.

In fact, the CPEC was a quid-pro-co. Pakistan went to China to seek help to remove road and infrastructure bottlenecks and in return, China demanded road access to connect its western parts with the Gwadar port. Rather, going a step forward, the PTI govt had to adopt '*...expensive electricity was better than no electricity*' as the slogan at that time and the country was sustaining losses equal to 2.25% of the GDP.

The Chinese planners initially laughed at Pakistan's plan to end load shedding through Gaddani Power Park and establishment of coal fired power plants there. China then gave an alternate strategy and, one by one, dropped the Gaddani Power Park and two Punjab-based coal-fired power plants i.e. Rahim Yar Khan power plant and Muzaffargarh power plant.

Under the head of infrastructure, the lives of the residents had become comfortable due to the mass transportation projects during PTI's governance; Pakistan had handled $5 billion Chinese investment in a power company till that hour. The $53 billion investment had been envisaged under the CPEC and Pakistan had fairly dealt the phase-I of the CPEC successfully; 5,300 MW of new electricity generation capacity was added and an 880 km long transmission line had been laid. Power projects possessing a capacity of 3,500 MW were under implementation till the end of Khan's premiership - another 4,144 MW capacity projects were at the planning stage.

It was Pakistan's last chance to industrialize and the key was the development of Special Economic Zones (SEZs) under the CPEC. Under the CPEC, nine Special Economic Zones (SEZs) and a free zone at Gwadar were planned and four SEZs and the free zone were being developed on priority including one in Faisalabad."

On 24th **August 2022**; once again China's Consul General in Karachi, Mr Li Bijian rubbished reports that the work on the CPEC had slowed down during PTI tenure. *The said statement had come on media record about FIVE MONTHS after the departure of Imran Khan as the country's PM.*

Speaking to a local media outlet, Li Bijian ruled out reports claiming that work on the CPEC, a flagship project of the BRI, had slowed down over the past three and half a year. He had emphasized that '...*work was slowed down due to Covid-19 pandemic and security issues. So-called claims that work paused due to the previous govt. policies are baseless.*'

Chinese Consul General had also ruled out any disagreement between Pakistan and the Chinese governments; saying:

> "*China and Pakistan have always shared mutual trust, mutual understanding and mutual support, and are all-weather friends. The change in policies affects the investment and the same thing is being seen in CPEC projects - hopefully all persisting issues would be resolved in time*. There were security issues regarding Chinese officials in two provinces of Pakistan but we are satisfied with the measures taken by federal and provincial govts after recent incidents;" daily **PAKISTAN TODAY** dated 24th August 2022 is referred.

The impression of the CPEC slowdown under Imran Khan's government remained hard to contest. Some experts attributed it more to the pandemic Covid-19 that had paralyzed the world. Others did blame the PTI government that took too much time to digest the value and the politics surrounding CPEC after assuming power. Some business tycoons observed:

> "*Some faint light started flickering on the CPEC playboard after the induction of a top business executive as a special assistant to the prime minister in 2021. A nice pitchbook to lure private Chinese investors was developed and contact channels were opened to mend the ties. Just when things finally started looking up the regime change happened and things came to naught once again.*"

An angry senior officer in Pakistan's Ministry of Planning divulged:

> "*Ask the Chinese if you don't trust us. Check the Chinese media which made its displeasure public even during Imran Khan's tenure. They were upset over the statements of government ministers casting aspersions*

on the transparency of CPEC deals. They were uncomfortable with changes in the taxation regime, frustrated over delays in payments to power producers and opening of a revolving account and resented any further talks on sealed deals."

The CPEC Authority was established to locate new drivers of growth and unlock the potential of value chains through regional and global connectivity. The efforts of the authority got mobilized $1.5bn investment by medium-sized Chinese companies in Pakistan collectively. ***It got the cabinet approval of compliance in place of the approval regime for Chinese investors who were required to acquire 37 no-objection certificates for investment in Pakistan;*** daily **DAWN** dated 29th August 2022 is referred for complete details in that regard.

"A research publication of the CPEC Authority had projected competitive and comparative edge in seven key sectors including IT, textiles, footwear, agriculture, auto, pharma and furniture. It engaged 19 top Chinese firms with a potential collective investment of whooping $30bn in Pakistan;"

– BUT Imran Khan was no more in saddles then.

Scenario 252

PAKISTAN IS DRYING UP: WATER CRISIS

> "According to a recent report by the International Monetary Fund (IMF), **Pakistan ranks third in the world among countries facing acute water shortage.** Reports by the United Nations Development Program (UNDP) and the Pakistan Council of Research in Water Resources (PCRWR) also warn the authorities that the South Asian country will reach absolute water scarcity by 2025.
>
> No person in Pakistan, whether from the north with its more than 5,000 glaciers, or from the south with its 'hyper deserts,' will be immune to this [scarcity];" an article at **energyupdate.com.pk** dated 9th January 2021 is referred.

Researchers predicted that Pakistan is on its way to becoming the most water-stressed country in the region by the year 2040. It was not the first time that development and research organizations had alerted Pakistani authorities about an impending crisis - probably a bigger threat to the country than terrorism. Pakistan had once touched the *'water stress line'* in 1990 and again crossed the *'water scarcity line'* in 2005. Presumably, the situation continued to persist - still likely to face an acute water shortage or a drought-like situation in the near future, according to PCRWR, which is affiliated with the South Asian country's Ministry of Science and Technology.

Fact remains that Pakistan has the world's fourth-highest rate of water use. Its current water intensity rate — the amount of water, in cubic meters, used per unit of GDP — is the world's highest. This suggests that no country's economy is more water-intensive than Pakistan's. As per statistics with the IMF, Pakistan's per capita annual water availability is 1,017 cubic meters — perilously close to the scarcity threshold of 1,000 cubic meters. Back in 2009, Pakistan's water availability was about 1,500 cubic meters.

The bulk of Pakistan's farmland is irrigated through a canal system recovering only a quarter of annual operating and maintenance costs. Meanwhile, agriculture, which consumes almost all annual available surface water, is largely untaxed. Experts say that *population growth and urbanization are the main reasons behind the said crisis.* The issue has also been exacerbated by climate change, poor water management and a lack of political will to deal with the crisis. Michael Kugelman, South Asia expert at Washington's Woodrow Wilson Center, told DW in a 2015 interview:

> *"Pakistan is approaching the scarcity threshold for water. What is even more disturbing is that groundwater supplies — the last resort of water supply — are being rapidly depleted. And worst of all is that the authorities have given no indication that they plan to do anything about any of this."*

Water scarcity has been triggering security conflicts in the country, too. Experts held the economic impact of the water crisis would remain immense, and more people would be fighting for resources. Water scarcity in Pakistan has also been accompanied by rising temperatures. In May 2020, at least 65 people died from heatstroke in the southern city of Karachi. In 2015, at least 1,200 people died during a spate of extremely hot weather in the country - heat waves and droughts in Pakistan are a result of climate change, in fact.

During the previous decade, the monsoon season remained mostly erratic; the winter season had shrunk from four to two months in many parts of the country. On top of it, Pakistan could not save floodwater due to scarcity of dams. At the time of Pakistan's birth in 1947, forests accounted for about 5pc of the national area, but it dropped to only 2pc till ending 2020.

Water politics had also been playing havoc in Pakistan since its coming into being. The Tarbela and Mangla dams, the country's two major water reservoirs, reached their *'dead levels'* during last week of December 2020. The news had sparked a debate on social media over the inaction of authorities in the face of that crisis. The said two big reservoirs were able to save water only for 30 days. India can store water for 190 days whereas the US can do it for 900 days; the Indus River System Authority (IRSA) has all the figures about such facts; little details from its files are:

> *"Pakistan receives around 145 million acre feet of water every year but can only save 13.7 million acre feet. Pakistan needs 40 million acre feet of water but 29 million acre feet of* **our floodwater is wasted** *because we have few dams. New Delhi raised this issue with international*

bodies, arguing that it should be allowed to use the western rivers because Pakistan can't use them properly.

In 1960, the World Bank brokered the Indus Water Treaty (IWT) that gives Pakistan exclusive rights to use the region's western rivers — Indus, Jhelum and Chenab — while India has the authority over three eastern rivers. BUT New Delhi is building the Kishanganga hydroelectric plant in the north of Bandipore in India-administered Jammu and Kashmir region. Moreover, India violated the IWT by building the dam on a Jhelum River basin, which was against the terms of the said treaty."

The reality is that the Pakistani authorities could have stepped up efforts to overcome the water crisis much earlier - which is partly man-made. Pakistan's successive leaders and stakeholders could have taken ownership of this challenge and declare their intention to tackle it. *Simply blaming previous governments, or blaming India, for the crisis didn't solve the actual problem.* The governments were needed to institute a major paradigm shift that could promote more judicious use of water. *Unfortunately, no govt, military or civil, none of the PMLN, PPP or PTI leader, had ever seriously felt the need for remedy.*

TARBELA-5 INSTALLED BY PM KHAN:

On 12th August 2021: Prime Minister Imran Khan said his government had decided to construct 10 dams in as many years with a view to avert the looming threat of water scarcity in the country as well as protect the future generations. While addressing the ground-breaking ceremony of the Tarbela-5 (T5) expansion project, he said:

"We have decided to construct 10 dams including Dasu and Bhasha dams within 10 years. We may face water shortage in the future and would be unable to cope with the needs of people and farmers unless we have storage. With the financial assistance of the World Bank and Asian Infrastructure Investment Bank, the project costing $807 million would be completed within a three-year period."

The Tarbela-5 project was then aimed at protecting the Tarbela Dam against silting besides helping generate 1,530 MW of electricity and provide 1.34 billion units of power to the national grid. The construction of the said expansion project also intended to beget 3,000 jobs and enhance the power production capacity of the Tarbela Hydropower Project from 4,888 MW to 6,418 MW. It was planned to play an important role to cope with the country's needs of water, food, and energy – including the continuing water supply for irrigation purposes.

PM Khan told the gathering that the construction of the **Bhasha Dam** was decided in 1984 but was not constructed owing to a lack of long-term planning. The previous governments had signed exorbitant contracts making the country pay whether the electricity was consumed or not. The consumers including the industry had to bear the cost. Owing to the costly electricity, the industry could not compete with the world market until the government paid a subsidy - China made progress just because of the long-term planning.

The fact remains that Pakistan's rivers got 80% of water inflow within three to four months and the construction of reservoirs was extremely essential to store and supply water throughout the year. It was hoped that construction of the *Mohmand Dam* would be completed by 2025 and Bhasha dam till 2028 but *most things slipped into doldrums due to his departure in April 2022*. Till the departure of Imran Khan's government on 10th April, the projects those were in progress in terms of construction, planning and financial arrangements included Diamer-Bhasha Dam, Mohmand Dam, Dasu Hydropower Project, Sindh Barrage, Nai Gaj Dam, and K-IV Project. These large-scale hydropower developments were scheduled to be completed and made operational one by one – and mostly till year 2028; some of these had already been started during PM Shahid K Abbassi's PMLN government.

On 23rd July 2021: The PTI's government and the Asian Development Bank (ADB) got together and signed a $300 million agreement to finance the development of the **Balakot Hydropower Project**. The total cost of the project was estimated at $755 million. According to a statement by the ADB, the preparatory work on the dam had already been completed. The project was expected to create hundreds of jobs. The then Minister of Economic Affairs Omar Ayub Khan told that the construction of this hydroelectricity dam would take place on the Kunhar River; and the upcoming project would be able to generate around 300 MW of electric power.

The water crisis in Pakistan, as narrated in detail above, went worsened year by year, especially over the past decade. Many factors, including not getting enough rain sometimes, lack of planning, and the increase in population, got combined to make the daily life of the people living in

Pakistan an unusual challenge, to say the least. The shortage of water also played a significant role in the power shortage in the country. Thankfully, the last two successive governments of the PMLN and PTI had decided to start the construction of several new dams in the country to increase the overall water storage capacity and eliminate the deficiency of electricity in the country.

The population ratio of Pakistan witnessed a substantial increase over the past few years, which implied that the demand for water kept on increasing with every passing day; thus, the construction of new dams was vital to protect citizens, and the national occupation of the county – farming.

According to the records of the International Commission on Large Dams, the list of dams and reservoirs in Pakistan totals 150. Additionally, there are about ten major dam sites in the country including Tarbela Dam, Mangla Dam, Sukkur Barrage, Rawal Lake, Head Marala, Jhelum River, Margalla Hills – National Park, and Islam Headworks, out of which Tarbela Dam and Mangla Dam are the largest ones with the depth of 470 ft and 453 ft respectively. Also, the storage capacity of the aforementioned dams has been recorded at 13,690,000,000 m^3 and 7,251,811,000 m^3 respectively.

UNDER CONSTRUCTION DAMS IN PAKISTAN:

As per records of the Ministry of Water and Power, there has been already a scarcity of water in the country - which means that the governments remained in a race against time to achieve their target of developing new dams in Pakistan. Taking into account some under-construction dams, the *two main dams remained Mohmand and Diamer-Bhasha*, which we'll discuss in more detail separately. During Imran Khan's era, **Diamer-Bhasha Dam**, **Naulong Dam**, **Kurram Tangi Dam**, **Nai Gaj Dam**, and **Darawat Dam** were in the initial stages of development. These five dams combined had a storage capacity of around 7.747 million acre-feet, while, **Garuk Dam**, **Winder Dam**, **Papin Dam**, and **Pelar Dam** were four other dams which were all set to become functional in future. These four dams would have a water storage capacity of 0.142 million acre-feet. The PTI government was also planning to construct seven (more) dam-projects in Pakistan including **Hingol dam**, **Akhori dam**, **Shyok dam**, **Munda dam (Mohmand Dam)**, **Tank Zam dam** and **Chiniot dam**. These seven dams combined would add another 13.948 million acres of storage capacity to the already-existing water reservoirs in the country. Upon completion, the under-construction dams in Pakistan would collectively increase the water storage capacity of Pakistan by 21.837 million acre-feet.

MOHMAND DAM: The Government of Pakistan started the construction of Mohmand Dam <u>in July 2018 upon the directives of the Supreme Court of Pakistan</u>. The primary purpose of the dam was to resolve water shortage by storing water in the periods of surplus and releasing in the times of scarcity. Some secondary purposes served by the dam could include the production of hydropower and moderation of water flow in rivers. The moderation could result in flood mitigation and thousands of innocent lives being saved from natural disasters.

The new Mohmand Dam, also popularly known as the *Munda Dam* project due to its geographical location in Northern Pakistan was aimed to enhance the agricultural development at 16,737 acres – with 9, 017 acres on its left and 7,720 acres on its right sides. Built on Swat River and managed by WAPDA, it is situated approximately 5 km opposite to Munda Headworks in Mohmand Tribal District situated in Khyber PK. Originally launched in March 2019 by Imran Khan's government, Munda dam is a concrete faced rock-fill, and it is around 700 ft deep with a storage capacity of about 1.293 million acre-feet. Upon completion, the dam could have the capacity to generate 800 MW of hydro-electricity. Then the **estimate cost in PKR** was 309,558 million. The project was scheduled to be completed and made functional by July 2024 but the PTI govt was sent home in April 2022.

DIAMER-BHASHA DAM: More details have been separately dealt with in another scenario of this book.

Diamer-Bhasha Dam is one of the most crucial and state-of-the-art under construction dams in Pakistan. Considering the project's hype and reputation, it was justified to say that this dam would be a valuable addition to the assets of the country. Ideally situated on the Indus River, in the northern part of Pakistan, Bhasha Dam was originally estimated to cost around $14 billion.

The construction work on Diamer-Bhasha Dam was all set to begin in the second quarter of 2019; several consulting firms were invited to bid for the evaluation process of this Dam. The Government of Pakistan, the Supreme Court of Pakistan, and WAPDA worked together to expedite the development of this under-construction dam. *Although the project was proposed seven years back, the actual implementation and planning started in July 2018,* with the political will of Imran Khan and cogent assistance of the then CJP Saqib Nisar when he initiated an international donation drive for this dam's construction. Then the project was mostly sponsored through local resources, with an initial estimated cost of PKR 625 billion.

Moreover, Diamer-Bhasha Dam would be the highest roller-compacted concrete (RCC) dam in the world once it is completed boasting a water storage capacity of around 8.5 million acres feet. The reservoir is planned to serve irrigation and drinking purposes. Being a protection source of the 35-year-old Tarbela Dam, the multipurpose dam, when completed, would also be a source to control flood damages caused by the River Indus.

DASU DAM:

As per records of Pakistan's Ministry of Water & Power, the Dasu Dam's original inventory of March 2014 is here:

- Dasu Hydropower Project is a run off river project on Indus River located 7km upstream of Dasu Town, District Kohistan, Khyber PK. The site is 74 km downstream of Diamer Bhasha Dam site and 350 km from Islamabad.

- Dasu Hydropower Project was planned to have total installed capacity of 4320 MW with 12 generating units and was among the priority projects under the **National Power Policy 2013 and Vision 2025** of Government of Pakistan. Project's implementation was designed to be carried on in two Stages; each Stage with 6 units of capacity of 2160 MW. About 12 billion power-units could be generated annually on completion of Stage-I being in implementation stage. PC-I of the Project (Stage-I) for Rs:486,093 million was approved by the ECNEC promptly.

- Total land required for Project was 9917 acres; 2029 acres for Preparatory & Main Civil Work on priority basis and remaining land to be used as reservoir area to be acquired at later stage before impounding.

- Out of 2029 acres, 633.78 acres of land had been acquired during 2nd spill of PMLN government and possession handed over to Contractors. Remaining land was to be acquired by the end of January 2018. World Bank had extended the deadline till

20th November 2018 to utilize the funds allocated in IDA-1 Credit in respect of land acquisition payments.

- *Agreement between the Government of Pakistan, WAPDA and the World Bank for IDA-1 Credit of US$ 588.4 Million along with an IDA PCG of US$ 460 Million had already been signed on 25th August 2014 - Loan Agreement was made effective immediately and kept valid till 30th June 2022.*

WAPDA awarded five Contracts related to Relocation of Karakorum Highway (KKH), Access Roads and 132 KV Transmission Line. Contractors for three Contracts, KKH-01, RAR-01 & TL-01, were mobilized at Project Site; contracts of KKH-02 and RAR-02 signed and commencement launched. Bids for Project Colony & Dasu-RV (Resettlement Villages) were opened on 22nd November 2017. Three Contracts of Resettlement Sites were awarded and signed with Chinese firms; the contractors were asked to mobilize at Project immediately.

On 8th March 2017: Main Civil Works Contract - agreements were awarded to M/s CGGC, China. Just within three months, the contractors commenced the services and mobilized at Site (on 23rd June 2017 precisely). Construction activities on Access Roads (CR-1 & CR-2) to Diversion Tunnels Inlet started.

On 29th March 2017: Agreement with Local Commercial Banks led by M/s Habib Bank Limited (HBL) for financing up to Rs:144 billion was signed; 1st tranche of Rs:25 billion was released in May 2017.

On 29th June 2017: Agreement with M/s Credit Issue Bank for $350 million credit signed; next day, 1st tranche of $188 million was released by the bank.

On 9th August 2017; for Electro-Mechanical Works, the bidding Documents were issued to prequalified applicants; bid submission / opening date was extended till 10th January 2018.

A landmark moment took place at the Dasu Hydropower dam in February 2023 when Pakistan's largest river, the Indus, was successfully diverted from its course. In a country that is susceptible to severe flooding this achievement was no small success.

Although it was a project of WAPDA in pursuit of its ***Water Vision 2025***, Dasu Dam was financed by a number of funders. Besides the World

Bank's $588 million, as enumerative in above lines, local commercial financing from a consortium of local banks gave Rs:144 billion ($558 million), and foreign commercial financing from Credit Suisse Bank contributed another $350 million. WAPDA injected its equity equivalent to 15% of the project's base cost. Overall, it would reportedly cost an estimated $4.278 billion to construct the dam. The main civil works, undertaken by China's *Gezhouba Group Company Limited*, started in early 2018. Meanwhile, work on the water diversion tunnel was inaugurated in December 2018 by the PTI government.

Pakistan has been facing a serious water crisis since decades – that's due to the increasing population and declining water resources. Huge dams like Mangla and Tarbela helped in providing water to the population and crops. Since the construction of the Mangla Dam decades ago, the country's population has been rising and was estimated to go up to 280 million by 2025. With the increase in the population, not only demand for water for food crops would increase but also requirements for drinking water and electricity would also rise. Referring to **Sputnik** magazine of 17th February 2023:

> *"Hence, WAPDA's **Water Vision 2025** aimed to solve the water and energy crisis; Dasu Hydropower was a big step toward achieving that goal. In early 2023, stage 1 of the dam was under construction and was likely to start generating electricity in 2026; an annual energy generation of 12 billion units. The 2160 MW stage 2, when finished, would provide a further 9 billion units to the national grid. On completion of both stages, Dasu could become the project with the greatest annual energy generation in Pakistan at about 21 billion units per annum on average.*
>
> *For Pakistan, diverting **the Indus River** was of utmost importance because the river is the lifeline of country's economy; though can cause huge losses when it floods. **The great trans-Himalayan river of South Asia is one of the longest rivers in the world at 3,200 km.** The river's annual flow is about 241 cubic km, twice that of the Nile River and three times that of the Tigris and Euphrates rivers combined. Indus becomes much larger when it reaches Punjab because other rivers of the province combine into it and during the flood season (July to September) it becomes several miles wide."*

In Indo-Pak, modern irrigation engineering work started in 1850s and during the period of British administration, large canal systems were constructed. Thus, **the greatest system of canal irrigation in the world** was created and although embankments had been constructed along the

Indus River to prevent flooding, occasionally these give way and floods destroy large areas, demolishing crops and livestock in the country. The floods of 2022 had a devastating effect on Pakistan's economy as two-thirds of the country was underwater; more than 30 million people were displaced from their homes, over one thousand people died and thousands of livestock perished. Hence, it was vital for Pakistan to have a good network of dams such as Dasu with its diversion tunnels for controlling the river; so finally, it's there.

The diversion system of the **Dasu Hydropower Project** consists of two tunnels - tunnel A and B. Of these, tunnel B was completed in early 2023, which has the discharge capacity enough to divert water of River Indus during the lean flow season. Meanwhile, the 1.5 km long tunnel A, with 20-m width and 23-m height, was projected to be ready till ending 2023.

For the completion of the Dasu project, WAPDA signed a first Rs:52.5 billion ($200,000) contract with a Chinese joint-venture, regarding electro-mechanical works. This contract included design, supply and installation of the first stage's six 360 MW turbines, along with their generators, and transformers. Furthermore, WAPDA was spending Rs:17.34 billion ($66,000) on the schemes related to the resettlement, environmental management and social development in the project area; more than 3,700 jobs were created till then.

CHINIOT DAM:

On 26th January 2019: The interest expressed by Imran Khan's PTI government in building *five new dams*, including the Chiniot dam, was a positive sign to help overcome the impending water crisis in the country; the Faisalabad Chamber of Commerce & Industry had extended a proposal for constructing the Chiniot dam about a decade ago; the estimated cost was approximately Rs:146.3 million then – daily *The Express Tribune* dated 26th January 2019 is referred.

On 7th October 2021: During PM Imran Khan's governance, Pakistan Water and Power Development Authority (WAPDA) invited proposals by 21st October 2021 from qualified consultants to provide detailed engineering design, preparation of bidding documents and PC-I for the Chiniot Dam Project on the Chenab River.

The Chiniot Dam, 17m-high zoned earth-fill embankment dam, located near Chiniot in Punjab, was designed to store surplus flows from the

Chenab River to meet downstream irrigation water requirements as well as generate electricity for the national grid. The reservoir was to be bound by left and right sides dykes / embankments to create a gross storage capacity of 1110 million m3 (0.9 MAF) and a live storage capacity of 1048 million m3. The proposed barrage was designed to cater for the peak discharge of about 34000 m3/s at a level of 190 masl. Twenty-two radial type gates were proposed in the dam. A surface powerhouse was planned as part of the development comprising six 13.34 MW units with a combined installed capacity of 80 MW to generate average annual output of 275 GWh at a design discharge of 720 m3/s - comprising horizontal shaft bulb type turbines.

The objective of the consultancy services - to be financed by the Government of Pakistan, was to review the previous feasibility study, review and prepare the project planning report, detailed engineering design, preparation of bidding drawings / documents and PC-I Proforma of the project. The assignment was expected to be carried out in three phases over 18 months starting in March 2022:

- *An inception report to be completed three months after the start of the contract,*

- *A project planning report after 12 months and detailed engineering design report, preparation of bidding drawings / documents and PC-I by the 18th month of the assignment. Quality and cost-based selection method (QCBS-80:20) could be used following single stage, two envelope bidding procedure.*

- *Request for Proposals (RFP) documents, (containing all details, description of assignment and evaluation criteria) were made available along with the RFP documents.*

Referring to daily **THE EXPRESS TRIBUNE** dated 11th April 2022; during Khan's era, the Chiniot Dam located on the Chenab River was expected to be completed by December 2022. Located five kms from Chiniot city, the dam was projected to generate 80 megawatts of cheap and environment friendly electricity; additionally, the gross storage of Chiniot Dam was 0.9-million-acre feet (MAF). The project was near completion as the implementation agency WAPDA had expedited development work it. The PTI government provided Rs:50 million under the Public Sector Development Program (PSDP), whereas Rs:96.33 million was provided by WAPDA's own resources.

The feasibility study of the **Chiniot Dam Project** was carried out by WAPDA and had completed in 2019. The PC-II Proforma for Detailed Engineering Design was submitted to Ministry of Water Resources for consideration in forthcoming Departmental Development Working Party (DDWP) meeting which was duly approved. The project held a great deal significance, as it was meant to help generate a daily water supply for Chiniot city and help establish business opportunities for locals, such as fisheries and tourism.

CHAHAN DAM PROJECT:

Referring to daily **THE EXPRESS TRIBUNE** dated 8th April 2022, the cost of *Chahan Dam* water supply project surged to over Rs:8 billion after CM Usman Buzdar's Punjab government failed to release funds within given time; a revised project concept (PC-1) of the water supply project was sent to the Planning and Development (P&D) Department Punjab seeking the said amount of funds (Rs: 8.10 billion). In 2018, the original PC-1 had estimated the original cost of the project at Rs:5.50 billion.

The design of Chahan Dam was altered to ensure full pressure water supply to six densely populated union councils (UCs) falling within the jurisdiction of the Rawalpindi Cantonment Board (RCB). Under the new design, the route of distribution lines were changed to supply water at full pressure and prevent water theft and after the design alteration and the recent increase in the price of construction material, the original cost had increased to Rs:1 billion; with the completion of the project, 6 million gallons of water per day was to be supplied to the said densely populated areas; a grant of Rs:800 million had initially been released and the work on the project had to take start in May 2022 – but Imran Khan was no more there in saddles.

HINGOL DAM:

Hingol Dam is a small, low-head, Central Core Zone, hydroelectric power generation dam of 3.5-megawatt (MW) generation capacity, located in the Lasbela District across the Hingol River in the Balochistan province of Pakistan. It is located at a distance of 260 km northwest of Karachi and about 16 km north of bridge across the Hingol River on the Makran Coastal Highway and about 8 km north of Kund Malir where the river falls into the sea.

With the construction of the proposed Hingol Dam, flood waters of Hingol River were to be stored for irrigation. Gross storage of the reservoir was planned at 2.10 MAF of which an average of about 1.3 MAF water would be annually available for developing irrigated agriculture of 80,000 acres. This project was designed to produce 3.5 MW of power generation with annual energy of 4.4 GWh. Damming the flow of Hingol River would save the flood water for irrigated agriculture development, power generation and water supply for drinking etc. Maximum height of the Dam was worked out as 172 ft (52 m) while its length was proposed as 2,500 ft (760 m). The project was poised to uplift the local community of the area by consequently raising the living standard of the people and generating employment.

The project would greatly increase the development of fisheries in the area and provide employment opportunities to the residents. Estimated cost of the project was $311 million when conceived - $227 million for civil works and $28 million for electro-mechanical works.

Interestingly, feasibility studies for the dam were completed in 1992. However, due to various reasons including mainly the local opposition, *the dam is still not constructed. In 2008, members of the Balochistan Assembly opposed the construction of the dam.* The local Hindu community protested the construction of the dam as it could damage the historic Hindu temple Hinglaj Mata and would destroy the eco-system of the nearby situated Hingol National Park. The later proposed site was shifted 16 km upstream to facilitate the demands of local Hindu Community and to protect the temple; however, since then the progress on construction of the dam remained zero due to financial constraints.

The proposed plan to build that dam at the Hingol River close to the Shri Hinglaj Mata temple shrine was protested against because it was a major Hindu pilgrimage center in Pakistan. The dam could have flooded the accommodation roads to the temple and endangered the locality and its associated festivals. *Following protest from the Hindu community, the dam proposal was abandoned by the Balochistan Assembly.* However, the WAPDA initially suggested relocating three holy places to a higher elevation and guaranteed the construction of a new access road. This proposition was rejected by the Hinglaj Sheva Mandali, which argued that these sites were not like common temples and could not simply be relocated.

- *In 2008, the lawmakers in the Balochistan Assembly reacted to the concerns and protests of the Hindu community and asked the federal government to stop the project. In 2009, following a one-year of suspension, the WAPDA chose to continue with the controversial Hingol Dam construction plans. However, they decided to shift the site of the dam 16 kms north in order to protect the temple. This resolution was reached through a consensus among the Power Development Authority, the Balochistan Assembly, and the Hindu community. PC-I Proforma (New Site) was cleared by CDWP in its meeting held on 19th November 2009, and cleared for approval of ECNEC. Detailed Engineering Design and Tender Documents of the New Site were completed in January 2011. Construction bids were invited on 11th July 2011 but the project couldn't take start.*

PM Imran Khan had motivated the local politicians and Assembly members – and the time was announced to complete the said project till mid 2023 – but Khan was sent home in April 2022 – thus the project had to die its own death.

Scenario 253

DIAMER-BHASHA DAM DURING KHAN's TENURE

THE ORIGINAL CONCEPT:

Diamer Bhasha is a multi-purpose mega-dam project planned to be developed on the Indus River near Chilas, in the Khyber PK and Gilgit-Baltistan regions of Pakistan. It is the biggest ever dam project undertaken in Pakistan. Standing 272m-tall, Diamer Bhasha is also expected to be one of the tallest dams in the world. Construction on the project was originally planned to be started in 2020 with completion expected in 2029.

Diamer Bhasha Dam Location: The Diamer Bhasha Dam, with a huge reservoir, is located on the Indus River, in the Diamer district of Pakistan's Gilgit-Baltistan province, approximately 315km upstream of the Tarbela Dam and 40km downstream of the Chilas town. The two power-houses of the project were proposed to be developed in Kohistan, in the neighbouring Khyber PK province. The project area encompassed around 110km², extending 100km from the dam site up to the Raikot Bridge on the Karakoram Highway. <u>A total of 32,139 acres of land including 31,977 acres in Gilgit-Baltistan and 162 acres in Khyber Pakhtunkhwa was acquired as of January 2019,</u> which comprises approximately 86% of the total land required for the project.

Controversy over Diamer Bhasha Dam: The Diamer Bhasha Dam project had drawn controversy because of its location in Gilgit Baltistan, allegedly a disputed territory between India and Pakistan. (*India calls Gilgit Baltistan as the Pakistan-occupied Kashmir (PoK) and alleges that Pakistan is illegally holding this territory that originally belonged to its northernmost state Jammu and Kashmir. India has voiced concern with Pakistan as well as with China, US and global financial institutions requesting not to fund any infrastructure project in the PoK.*)

Situated near the Himalayan peak Nanga Parbat, the dam project was also alleged to be in a high seismic zone. It was apprehended to have ecological fallout such as landslides and floods that might affect the adjacent areas in Pakistan as well as in India. Bilateral territorial dispute and the seismicity of the project area had refrained the World Bank, the Asian Development Bank (ADB), as well as other international donor agencies from providing financial assistance to the said project.

The Diamer Bhasha project had also triggered significant local resistance, as it was estimated to displace more than 4,200 families in nearby areas and submerge a huge part of the Karakoram Highway to China. Moreover, since part of the project area comes in Khyber PK, it had led to a domestic dispute between two Pakistani provinces Gilgit Baltistan and KP with both contesting for claims over the royalty from the dam. The boundary issues between the two provinces remained unsettled till later.

The Diamer Bhasha dam project was conceived as part of the Water Vision 2025 presented by WAPDA in July 2001. It was the first and the biggest among the five multi-purpose dam projects to be undertaken as part of the North Indus River Cascade scheme announced by the Pakistani Government in January 2006; the project, however, remained in limbo for a long time due to non-availability of funds.

The initiative received fresh impetus with the inauguration of China's Belt and Road Initiative (BRI) in 2017, as China expressed its willingness to support the North Indus River Cascade projects under the Pakistan Economic Corridor (CPEC), a flagship framework under the BRI. *Pakistan, however, withdrew the Diamer Bhasha Dam from the CPEC projects list in 2018, due to China's strict monetary conditions as well as its ambition to hold ownership of the mega project.* Nevertheless, Pakistan was determined to proceed further.

The then Chief Justice of Pakistan, Saqib Nisar, initiated a crowd-funding campaign for the Diamer Bhasha Dam Project in October 2018. In August 2019, WAPDA received bids from two joint ventures, each comprising a Chinese and a local company, for constructing the dam. One joint venture included China Gezhouba Group Company and Pakistan's Ghulam Rasool & Company (GRC), while the other joint venture was between Power Construction Corporation of China and Pakistan's Frontier Works Organization (FWO).

Diamer Bhasha would be a roller compacted concrete (RCC) gravity dam with a crest length exceeding 1km and a maximum height of 272m. The RESERVOIR created by the dam would impound up to 7,500,000 acre-feet of water accounting for approximately 15% of the annual river flow. The GROSS STORAGE CAPACITY of the reservoir would be ten billion cubic metres (bcm), of which 7.9bcm would be the live storage capacity. SPILLWAYS of the dam would comprise of 14 radial gates, each measuring 16.25m-high and 11.5m-wide with maximum water discharge capacity of each gate being 18,128m³/s.

DAM's power plant: The Diamer Bhasha hydroelectric facility would consist of two underground power-houses on either bank of the Indus River, with an installed capacity of 2,250MW each. Each POWER HOUSE be equipped with six turbo-generator units of 375MW capacity each. The power intake structure for each powerhouse would include two surge tanks and two 15.3m-diameter headrace tunnels connected to three penstocks each. Each underground power-house would have separate transformer and switchgear caverns. Water from each power-house would be discharged back to the river through two 18.8m-diametre tailrace tunnels.

On 2nd April 2018; during the last days of PMLN government, a large chunk of land measuring 14,325 acres of the total 18357 acres of private land had been transferred finally to the Pakistan Water and Power Development Authority (WAPDA), paving way for the authorities to move forward for the execution of the 4,500MW Diamer Basha Dam project.

The dam's location is 40 km downstream of Chilas, the district headquarters of Diamer in Gilgit Baltistan. It displaced 30,350 people living in 4,266 households of 32 villages, situated above the dam site on both left and right banks of river Indus.

Total land required for the project was 37,419 acres which included 19,062 acres of state and 18,357 acres of private land under cultivation, barren and other uses. Wapda's one General Manager Shoaib Taqi told:

> "We can say that we have completed 85 per cent of the total land acquisition and nearly 95 per cent of the land required for the reservoir alone. And since it was the long-awaited requirement for the project, we consider this a major achievement of Wapda during the last one year."

The land acquisition for the two of the total three proposed model villages and the piece of land along the disputed boundary of Khyber PK and GB was a major bottleneck in the way of execution of the project. Among three proposed villages, land (687 acres) for *Harpan Das* had already been acquired where WAPDA developed community infrastructure and was ready for plots allotment to the affected people. The land at other two sites for proposed villages was yet to be acquired due to certain issues affecting the pace of the project in this context. Development through providing community infrastructure / social services as schools, health facilities, roads access, mosques, community centre and market places had been completed. Layout plan for approximately 1,350 residential plots had also been developed.

The affectees of Khan Bari, Thor, Hudar and Chilas comprising 2,937 households wanted to be resettled in Harpan Das that was beyond the capacity of this village with 1,350 residential plots only. The other available option was to link resettlement of Harpan Das with the completion of other two model villages—Thak Das and Sagachal Das. The location at Thak Das was identified jointly by the Diamer Basha Dam consultants, WAPDA and respective district administration in 2009. Land for model village at Thak Das, 1522 acre, was yet to be acquired. The inhabitants of Thak Das were not ready to surrender land for the establishment of model village.

The location of other model village--Sagachal Das-- was about 80km away from the Chilas town. The site was communal land of inhabitants of Goharabad. Area of Sagachal Das was 526 acres (4207 Kanls). As the locals of Goharabad had refused to allow the affectees of downstream of Chilas settle in Sagachal Das model village, thus (1,068 households) were to be resettled at this site under the plan requiring 1,820 kanal for the development of infrastructure. The authorities succeeded in acquiring a major chunk of land (both public and private), were then ready for the acquisition of remaining land (model villages, reservoir etc). Though the land acquisition was responsibility of the government, the dam authorities were equally contributing to efforts to complete the entire process.

> [**A side-note:** On 26th April 2018: *The ECNEC in its meeting approved Mohmand Dam Hydropower Project at a total cost of Rs: 309.558 billion including FEC component of Rs:71.548 billion. The Project's financing plan, according to which the cost of dam attributable to water sector and agricultural benefits was Rs:114,285 million which required funding from the Federal PSDP as a grant whereas the remaining amount of the project which was Rs:195.273 billion for power generation component had to be arranged in the form of WAPDA's equity, local and foreign commercial financing.*]

During the same month of April 2018, well before the 2018 elections, the Executive Committee of the National Economic Council (ECNEC) of the Government of Pakistan, approved £2.34bn (PKR474bn) for the preliminary dam construction phase.

The US Agency for International Development (USAID) had earlier approved $20m for conducting a feasibility study for the project in 2013. The USAID contracted Mott MacDonald to review the dam design in June 2015. Malcolm Dunstan & Associates (MD & A) served as the RCC specialist for Mott MacDonald. MWH Global, in consortium with National Engineering Services Pakistan (NESPAK) and Associated Consulting Engineers (ACE), completed environmental and social impact assessment (ESIA) for the project in August 2016, under a $17.9m contract awarded by the USAID.

- **On 1st September 2018:** the then Chief Justice Saqib Nisar ordered one of PTI's lawmakers from Sindh, Imran Ali Shah, to donate Rs:3 million for the construction of Diamer-Bhasha Dam as a fine; Shah had been involved in a controversy over the elections, when a video of him slapping and physically assaulting a man on the street during a heated argument surfaced online, sparking outrage on social media. Shah later apologised for his actions to the victim personally; his membership of PTI's Sindh chapter was suspended for a month, and he was also ordered by the party to pay Rs:500,000 in fines as well as bear the costs of medical treatment for 20 patients at an Edhi Foundation centre. The case was marked closed.

- **On 9th September 2018:** PM Khan called for public donations for *Prime Minister – Chief Justice fund for Diamer Basha and Mohmand Dam*. The funds details made open to the public were: Bank: State Bank of Pakistan; Account Name: SUPREME COURT OF PAKISTAN; with general Account Number and of IBAN ending 0014; it was the link for online donation.

- *For the Diamer-Bhasha project; a revised initial cost of PKR479.68bn was approved in Nov 2018 by PM Imran Khan.*

PM KHAN BOOSTED THE PROJECT's WORK:

On 26th June 2019: In an annual coordination session of the federal and provincial authorities held under Federal Flood Commission, Ministry of Water Resources reviewed preparedness for 2019-Monsoon Season. PTI's Federal Minister for Water Resources, Faisal Vawda, noted with concern that the encroachments in the river waterways besides major nullahs by the public masses in provinces had gone so frequent and in such magnitude that even the low floods create havoc in the communities. The case of 105,000 cusecs outflow from Jhelum River at Mangla was before them. He urged the provinces and federal line agencies for prompt approval of their respective Flood Plain Management Acts and their strict enforcement to prevent the encroachment in the waterways on permanent basis.

On 11th May 2020: Prime Minister Imran Khan chaired a briefing on National water security strategy and construction of dams to meet agricultural as well as energy requirements of the country. The Prime Minister was briefed in detail about the progress of resolution of all pending issues related to construction of Diamer Bhasha Dam. The Prime Minister was informed that all issues related to this critically important project, including settlement, detailed roadmap for mobilization of financial resources etc. had been resolved and the project was ready for commencement of physical work; the said project had remained stuck for decades due to various reasons.

The construction project of Diamer Bhasha Dam created 16500 jobs and was aimed to utilize huge quantity of cement and steel and give boost to Pakistani industry besides its main purposes of water storage of 6.4 MAF and producing 4500 MW of affordable electricity. The 6.4 MAF water storage capacity of the dam could reduce the then apprehended water shortage in the country of 12 MAF to 6.1 MAF. It was designed to add 35 years to the life of Tarbela dam by reducing sedimentation. It was informed that an amount of Rs:78.5 billion would be spent for social development of the area around Diamer Bhasha Dam as part of the project. It could also be a major source of flood mitigation and to save billions worth of damages caused by floods each year.

PM KHAN expressed satisfaction over the progress made and directed to immediately start construction activities of the dam; ensuring water security was the foremost priority of the PTI government. The Prime Minister directed that use of local material and expertise be accorded priority during the construction work. Chairman WAPDA briefed the meeting about progress of ongoing construction of *Mohmand Dam* that had started a little earlier.

The Prime Minister was, inter-alia, apprised of the progress on resolution of pending issues related to *Dasu Dam project.* He was briefed by WAPDA that funds had been arranged for *Naulong Dam, district Jhal-magsi* Balochistan and that the work could commence a year after.

The Prime Minister emphasized on starting Sindh Barrage as a priority project; it had huge benefits of addressing agriculture needs of the province. PM Khan also reiterated his emphasis on keeping a close watch on quality of work.

On 13th May 2020: WAPDA signed Contract Agreement for construction of Diamer Basha Dam Project with *Power China-FWO Joint Venture (JV)*. The worth of the agreement was Rs:442 billion then. The agreement included construction of diversion system, main dam, access bridge and 21 MW-Tangir Hydropower Project. Chief Executive Officer, Diamer Basha Dam Company, Mr Amir Bashir and Mr Yang Jiandu, representative of the JV signed the agreement on behalf of WAPDA and the JV respectively. Diamer Basha Dam Project, with a total financial outlay of about Rs:1406.5 billion, was scheduled to be completed in 2028. The total financial outlay included land acquisition, resettlement, confidence building measures for social uplift of the locals, construction of dam and power houses.

The Project had a storage capacity of 6.4-million-acre feet (MAF) and power generation capacity of 4500 MW power, with annual generation of 18.1 billion units of electricity per annum. It is pertinent to mention that WAPDA had already awarded contract of Rs:27.182 billion, for consultancy services of the project to Diamer Basha Consultants Group (DBCG). The consultancy agreement included construction design, construction supervision and contract administration of Diamer Basha Dam Project.

The JV DBCG comprised of 12 top-ranked national and international consulting firms including NESPAK (Pakistan), Associate Consulting Engineers(Pakistan), Mott MacDonald (Pakistan), Poyry (Switzerland), Montgomery Watson and Harza (MWH) International – Stantec (USA), Dolsar Engineering (Turkey), Mott McDonald International (England), China Water Resources Beifang Investigation, Design and Research Company (China), Mirza Associates Engineering Services (Pakistan), Al-Kasib Group of Engineering Services (Pakistan), Development Management Consultant (Pakistan) and MWH Pakistan (Pakistan) with NESPAK as the lead firm. These firms had a vast experience of providing consultancy services for mega water projects the world over.

On 13th July 2020: A Memorandum of Understanding (MOU) was signed on water resources management between Government of Pakistan and Govt. of Hungary. The purpose of the MOU was to establish a framework for cooperation between the parties in the field of water management on the basis of equality, reciprocity and mutual benefits. The salient features of the MOU, inter alia, included cooperation on integrated water resources management, waste water management and water related education research and development. Both countries pledged to strengthen their partnership in the water sector to undertake mutually beneficial projects.

The Hungarian Ambassador & Minister for Water Resources applauded the efforts of the government officials and exchanged views regarding opening new horizons of technical and economic cooperation at length after the signing ceremony.

On 15th July 2020: Prime Minister Imran Khan kicked off the construction work at Diamer-Bhasha Dam at River Indus near Chillas. The 272-metre-high dam, having storage capacity of 6.4-million-acre feet of water (MAF) was the country's third big dam after Tarbela and Mangla dams when completed. It was fan-fared as *'window of development and opportunities for the people of Gilgit-Baltistan'*. It envisaged a drastic change for locals and to bring immense development in the area - the PM said while addressing a public rally, after commencing the mega construction work of the dam.

PROJECT's BORDER DISPUTE RESOLVED:

On 11th January 2022; the long-standing dispute over the multibillion-dollar Diamer-Bhasha dam land site between two tribes of Khyber PK and Gilgit-Baltistan (GB) was finally resolved. The decision was announced by Thor-Herban grand jirga, entrusted with the task of resolving the festering dispute, in a ceremony. The 26-member grand jirga was constituted in 2019 to resolve the thorny issue of the boundary dispute between the two tribes and was fully facilitated by the civil administrations of GB, Khyber PK and WAPDA.

Soon after the announcement was made by the reconciliation committee, Prime Minister Imran Khan welcomed the settlement of the decades-old territorial dispute as a major development, saying it would allow smooth and timely completion of the dam. In line with the decisions made by the grand jirga, cheques worth about Rs:400 million were also distributed to the affectees of the 2014 clash that broke out between the two tribes, which claimed many lives, had inflicted damage to properties and to the cause of that giant economic project.

Pertinent to mention here that the disputed land was hampering the project's progress. The boundary dispute had deepened with the passage of time, with both tribes refusing to budge from their stance. Both tribes had claimed ownership of a piece of land spanning over eight kilometres in the Gandlo Nala area. Although a one-member commission was constituted to find a solution to the dispute in the past but both sides had rejected its findings. The former CJP, Saqib Nisar, had also taken notice of the land dispute when he took the initiative to raise funds for the project and asked the ruling PTI to try for an out-of-court settlement of the issue.

On 7th April 2023: The PDM government headed by Shahbaz Sharif approved the Diamer Basha power generation project at a cost of over Rs:1.2 trillion, showing an increase of Rs:302 billion against the original price. The Executive Committee of the National Economic Council (ECNEC), which approved the 4,500MW power generation project, considered all the 10 summaries. Majority of those came before the forum due to years of mismanagement requiring further cost escalation.

Headed by Finance Minister Ishaq Dar, the ECNEC approved the project at Rs:1.24 trillion against the original estimates of Rs:933.6 billion, with a noticeable increase of one-third or Rs:302 billion of the project costs within a few years. The ECNEC had also discussed the initial cost a year before but with no further action. The said cost included a foreign loan of Rs:409 billion - which component had then increased to Rs:598 billion at the average floating exchange rate of January 2023 – Rs:234.13 to a US dollar.

The Cabinet Committee on Energy had split the construction into two phases; the dam and power generation facilities. The ECNEC approved the dam in 2018. The National Transmission & Despatch Company (NTDC) was chosen to ensure that construction of the power evacuation infrastructure was synchronised with the commissioning date of the project and was tasked to explore financing from foreign lenders. _The projects were being approved at a time when there was acute scarcity of resources;_ **the government was drastically reducing development spending,** _except on schemes recommended by parliamentarians._

On 14th April 2023; just a year after IMRAN KHAN's departure, a resolution was tabled in the National Assembly, calling for **the amount collected in the Diamer-Bhasha dam fund to be deposited in the national treasury** - the resolution was presented by MNA Kesoo Mal Kheal Das. The resolution stated that:

> ".... former chief justice Saqib Nisar had violated judicial traditions and rules by collecting funds for the construction of new dams and water reservoirs, leading to the establishment of the Diamer-Bhasha and Mohmand Dams Fund."

The resolution also referenced to a news report stating a five-member bench headed by CJP Umar Atta Bandial was informed that as of January 2023, there were Rs:16.53 billion in the fund, with an expected increase to Rs:16.98 billion in the next quarter. The three-member bench directed the auditor general to review the entire record of the donations and capital disbursements together with the State Bank of Pakistan (SBP) and identify whether or not there were any irregularities in the documents.

- *State Bank officials informed the court that the dams fund currently had more than Rs:16 billion but so far neither any withdrawal had been made from the fund nor any expenditure incurred from that money.*

The court was informed that the money deposited in the fund was invested in government securities such as T-bills by the National Bank. Sitting on the bench, Justice Ijazul Ahsan said that the fund had Rs:10 billion which would become Rs:17 billion <u>on 26th January 2023</u>. The CJP said that the record of the donors of the dam-fund was available on the website of the Supreme Court; he stressed that the dams fund money would not be spent on repairing flood damage.

> [*On 10th July 2018; former CJP Nisar had established a Supreme Court of Pakistan Diamer-Bhasha and Mohmand Dams Funds to raise funds for the construction of both the dams. The State Bank of Pakistan website stated that the SC supervised the fund and its registrar directly operated its account. **Imran Khan had also thrown weight behind Justice (retd) Nisar's call for donations and had urged overseas Pakistanis to contribute to the effort to raise funds via voluntary donations.**]*

The resolution in the National Assembly stated that former chief justice Saqib Nisar had violated judicial traditions and rules by collecting funds for the construction of new dams and water reservoirs. <u>BUT the media and the civil society gurus both openly cursed the feudal lobby of parliamentarians which was always seen grinding axes against any good cause and its sponsors – just to create ill-will amongst the general masses.</u>

- *The Mohmand multipurpose dam project was approved to enhance water and food security, and improve the standard of living for the people of Khyber PK, where almost 80% of the population resides in rural areas, boosting the region's socioeconomic development by creating employment opportunities and reducing poverty levels. The project aligns with sustainable development goals of ensuring food security, clean water, and clean energy.*

11th December 2023: Water and Power Development Authority (WAPDA) Chairman Gen Sajjad Ghani visited the river diversion system, which had been operational for a week after partial diversion of the River Indus at the Diamer-Basha Dam Project site. The diversion system consisted of about one km - long diversion tunnel and two coffer (starter) dams - one at the upstream and other at the downstream of the main dam site.

A week earlier, WAPDA had succeeded in diverting the River Indus partially through the diversion system constructed for the purpose; the mighty River Indus was flowing mainly through diversion tunnel and diversion canal, while partly through its natural course. The Chairman was briefed about the test-run of the diversion system. The diversion tunnel and diversion canal were functioning on 13 sites simultaneously and satisfactorily.

The River Indus was successfully made flowing completely through the diversion system, bypassing the main dam site and re-joining its natural course after about a distance of 800 metres. The Diamer-Basha Dam was amongst 8 under-construction WAPDA projects, which were scheduled for completion from 2024 to 2028-29. These projects would add about 10,000 MW of environment-friendly electricity and store 9.7-million-acre feet of water.

On 13th December 2023: The Implementation Committee on Diamer Basha and Mohmand Dams (ICDBMD), constituted by the Supreme Court of Pakistan, convened to review the ongoing progress of both projects at its meeting in the ICDBMD Secretariat, Islamabad. Chaired by Chairman of Pakistan Water and Power Development Authority (WAPDA) and ICDBMD, Lt Gen Sajjad Ghani, the meeting brought together key stakeholders including the Chief Secretary of Gilgit Baltistan, Additional Secretary (Budget) from the Finance Division, and the Secretary / Senior Member Board of Revenue from Khyber PK and other officials.

Gen Ghani expressed satisfaction with the strides made by ICDBMD and its Sub Committees toward the expeditious execution of the Diamer Basha and Mohmand Dam Projects. In the meeting, Member (Finance) WAPDA presented an overview of the financial aspects of both projects. Detailed progress reports were also provided by the General Manager Land Acquisition & Resettlement, Chief Executive Officer of Diamer Basha Dam Company, and the General Manager of Mohmand Dam, outlining achievements and challenges encountered in the project development.

Updates highlighted substantial advancement in construction work for both projects. Till a week before, WAPDA accomplished partial diversion of River Indus at the Diamer Bhasha Dam Project, with plans to reach a crucial milestone in the coming days. Similarly, concerted efforts were underway to complete the diversion of River Swat for the Mohmand Dam during the current low-flow season. The Committee commended the progress made in land acquisition for both Diamer Basha and Mohmand Dams, lauding the collaborative efforts of WAPDA and district administrations. The meeting concluded with a positive outlook on the overall status of the projects, emphasising the collective commitment to their successful and timely completion.

26th December 2023: Pakistan was seen aggressively pursuing arrangements to secure $1 billion promptly to progress towards achieving financial closure for the strategic Diamer Basha Dam project; sources indicated the country needed approximately $3.5 billion for this purpose. During the visit of Caretaker PM Anwaarul Haq Kakar to Kuwait, Pakistan and the gulf state had signed an agreement to raise capital for the project. The project, in fact, was in its initial stages of construction and the said funding was required to achieve tangible progress, with a requirement of $1 billion immediately.

Pakistan had been struggling to raise funding for this strategic dam since long. Multilateral donors had refused to give financing for this project due to lobbying by India that the project was being developed in a disputed area. However, during the recent years, Pakistan had been actively working on the project. For decades, Pakistan had not been able to complete its mega water projects like Diamer Basha. In addition to raising capital for the dam, Pakistan was also working on some other projects as well.

A CRITICAL NOTE ON DIAMER-BHASHA DAM:

In August 2018, newly sworn in Prime Minister Imran Khan declared that building dams was the only way to tackle Pakistan's existential water problems. Fast forward a few years, the Water and Power Development Authority (WAPDA) had started construction on two major hydroelectric projects: Mohmand in Khyber PK and Diamer-Bhasha in Gilgit-Baltistan. The latter, a 272-meter behemoth, was billed as the highest roller compacted dam in the world - with a storage capacity of 8.1 million-acre-feet.

On the face of it, with reports warning that the country could *run dry by 2025*, an increase in storage capacity was imminently required, in theory, to increase the availability of freshwater during droughts. But experts disagreed – *'Nobody can deny this will increase storage but surface storage is the most inefficient kind and these dams don't increase year-on-year storage; they increase seasonal storage;'* **The DIPLOMAT** of 4th March 2021 is referred. It further argued:

> "Pakistan's two largest dams – Tarbela and Mangla – are seasonal regulators; they are filled during the monsoon season and drained during the dry winter months for crop production. This means that while Diamer-Bhasha may increase storage capacity in the Indus Basin seasonally, it won't create a perennial reserve of water to draw on during lean years.
>
> Then there is the price tag to consider. Pakistan has struggled to secure funds for the Diamer-Bhasha dam for years. The project was initially green-lit by President Pervez Musharraf's government in 2006, but both the World Bank and Asian Development Bank refused to finance it, citing the dam's location in disputed Kashmir. A well-intentioned attempt to crowdfund the dam in 2018 by the CJP Saqib Nisar of the Supreme Court also failed to raise enough money. Finally, in May 2020, China stepped in to bankroll part of the project."

But even at $14 billion, the estimated cost for Diamer-Bhasha might be too low. With inflation, debt servicing, and environmental externalities priced in, a dam could end up requiring twice its initial financial commitment with little chance of a return on investment. That meant that even if Diamer-Bhasha would be completed within the proposed nine-year timeframe, it would likely cost around 10% of Pakistan's GDP (in 2021).

Dam advertisements on WAPDA's official website ignored those nuances, perhaps because of the federal government's full-throated endorsement of Diamer-Bhasha and other hydroelectric projects. For Imran Khan in particular, a renewed commitment to massive infrastructure projects was a turn away from what the PM then described as *'a decade of darkness.'*

Imran Khan had made the comments at a screening ceremony for *'Pani ke Pankh'* (Water's Wings), a 30-minute, borderline video-script explaining how Pakistan had first beaten back terrorism and was then building dams. Domestic support for hydroelectric projects was further bolstered by India's resistance to that particular dam construction in Pakistan – *in fact the Diamer-Bhasha was a totally nationalist project.*

Growing support for dams reduced Pakistan's water challenges to a matter of scarcity and masking what experts sensed as the more acute problem of inefficient management – particularly in the agricultural sector. The western researchers held that *'the Indus Basin sits on a massive aquifer that was rapidly being depleted. This is because groundwater abstraction has been increasing in Pakistan since the 1960s.'* According to a 2021 World Bank Report, the number of reported tube-wells increased from around 98,000 in 1970 to over 1.3 million in 2017. The report estimated that groundwater was being pumped at a higher rate than could naturally be replenished through rain or seepage. Tracing it back to a colonial-era law known as the *Canal and Drainage Act of 1873,* still in vogue for water rights in Pakistan: 'The idea was to take available water and spread it as thinly as possible, as widely as possible; all that changed in the 1970s, when farmers began to use tube wells to increase their yields.'

The fact remains that *without an overhaul of the legal framework and farm level practices, dams like Diamer-Bhasha won't address Pakistan's food insecurity problems.* The upper Indus region already equipped to benefit from a vast network of link canals and dams, including Tarbela, which redirects river water southeast as it flows southwest toward the arid provinces of Sindh and Balochistan. According to the statistics, Punjab between 2011 and 2012 accounted for 83% of Pakistan's cotton, 63% of sugarcane, and 97% of aromatic rice – all major export crops. Thus, the political sloganeering that *'Dams are a Punjabi obsession - that water is going to sugarcane, rice, and cotton.'*

> After PTI government's practical support, the projects like Diamer-Bhasha and Mohmand kept developing during the next PDM and PMLN governments. They kept on moving as per availability of foreign funding despite India's desperate negative propaganda – AND the same are near completion now (in mid 2024).

Imran Khan's renewed emphasis on hydroelectric projects in Pakistan would continue to gain assent of the general populace – for all times to come.

Scenario 254

JUDICIARY's HI-VERDICTS (2018-22)

Glancing A Little Back ...

On 17th March 2009; on the conclusion of Barrister Aitzaz Ahsan's LAWYER MOVEMENT in early 2009, Justices Javaid Iqbal, Ijaz Ahmed, Ramday, and Fayaz Ahmad were restored to their position as of 2 November 2007 with Justice Iftikhar Chaudhry assuming the post of Chief Justice of Pakistan (CJP) on 22nd March 2009.

> [*The Fact remained that it was Gen Ashfaq Parvez Kayani, the then-army chief, who had played a vague role in intervening and encouraging a rapprochement between the government and the opposition. Neither side acknowledged it until lawyers' movement leader Aitzaz Ahsan publicly admitted later (in a rally at Gujranwala) about Gen Kayani's role. There were mass speculations that protestors and law enforcement agencies would have violently collided - had the Generals not intervened.*]

Immediately thereafter, the SC rendered its judgement declaring the appointments based upon PCO on 3rd November 2007 as null and void as well as declaring the NRO as null and void, that ultimately opened the investigations and cases against then-President Asif Ali Zardari and Prime Minister Gillani. But the media also flared up with hard facts that of the 14 justices that rendered a verdict related to taking an oath under the PCO, 12 had once taken the oath themselves under an earlier PCO including the CJP Iftikhar Chaudhry and his die-heart buddy Justice Ramday - they controversially did not apply the judgement to themselves.

On 31st July 2009; decision was handed down in the case of Constitutional Petitions 8 and 9 of 2009; two judges named Faqir M Khokhar and M Javed Buttar immediately resigned before their cases were referred to Supreme Judicial Council. In addition, about twelve more justices were removed from the SC on the ground that their appointments to the court was made without consultation with the *de jure* Chief Justice of Pakistan.

It was a controversial decision by all means as the SC summarily removed all justices of the higher judiciary who were not part of it as on 2nd November 2007. Their removal was ordered on the grounds that the *de jure* Chief Justice was not consulted or allowed to advise in those cases – and the *de jure* Chief Justice was J Iftikhar Chaudhry himself.

The SC bench that rendered the said decision <u>consisted entirely of justices who had taken oath under the PCO of 1999 themselves</u> - though had taken a constitutional oath later. The 1999 PCO and decisions made under it were given constitutional protection by 17th Constitutional Amendment. Thus, newly appointed judges who had never taken any sort of oath under any PCO were also removed while sitting judges who took an oath under the 2007 PCO were still acting as justices. Some sitting judges who were re-appointed and took oath under CJP Dogar were spared to act as justices with no action. More so, the judges who took oath under the PCO of 1999 were still functioning as justices of higher judiciary

The removed ad hoc judges of the Lahore High Court filed several petitions in the SC for review of its judgment, which sent 76 judges of Supreme Courts and High Courts immediately home. These judges argued that they were qualified to be appointed as judges of the High Court in accordance with the requirements of Article 193(2) of the 1973 Constitution and were offered to serve as ad hoc judges following the consultation required under the Constitution. They accepted the offer and took oath when the state of emergency was lifted. They never took oath under a PCO and continued performing the functions of judges of the High Court until the judgement of 31st July 2009 appeared against them.

These judges were appointed by Lahore High Court CJ Zahid Hussain, who was [strangely] still a justice of the SC and was not being tried before the Supreme Judicial Council. The petition also noted that none of the sacked judges were made parties to the decision against them, nor were they heard in person or collectively. Even the copy of the decision was not sent to the High Court or to the judges concerned – they got it through the media news.

Referring to the daily *'Times'* dated <u>9th November 2009</u>:

> *"..... the Supreme Court has applied its judgement retroactively, having effect from 3 November 2007. The 14-member Supreme Court bench has not, however, applied the sanction to judges who took oath under*

the 1999 PCO. Some of these are current justices, and some have not yet taken a constitutional oath.

It is inconsistent with the principles laid down in Malik Asad Ali's case where it was held that the Chief Justice was bound by the Court's judgement. Chief Justice Sajjad Ali Shah was removed from office based on this case.

Inconsistently with the decision, the present CJP Chaudhry has accepted the stance of the government that Justice Dogar was the Chief Justice until his retirement."

J SHAUKAT SIDDIQUI – A JUDGE ON TRIAL:

On 21st July 2018: Islamabad High Court [IHC] judge Shaukat Aziz Siddiqui made serious allegations against Pak-Army's security agency in a speech delivered before the Rawalpindi District Bar Association. He said:

"In today's era, the ISI is fully involved in manipulating judicial proceedings; their personnel get benches formed at their will."

The remarks made by Justice Siddiqui were strong and unusual coming from a senior judge; he did not mention particular cases for ISI's interference in the judiciary except that:

"....the agency approached the IHC CJ M Anwar Khan Kasi urging that ....We [ISI] do not want to let Nawaz Sharif and his daughter come out [of the prison] until elections, [also that] do not include Shaukat Aziz Siddiqui on the bench [hearing Sharifs' appeals].

I know who takes whose messages to the Supreme Court. Why was the administrative control of the accountability court taken away from the Islamabad High Court? The judiciary's freedom has been divested and that it is now in control of 'those with guns'. I was told that 'if you assure us of decisions in our favour, we will end references against you'; and [I shall] be made chief justice of the high court by September (2018)."

At that time, two references against Justice Siddiqui were pending at the SJC. The first reference was of a corruption case filed against him by an employee of the Capital Development Authority [CDA]. In the second reference, the SJC questioned his critical comments regarding the role of the Army during last year's Faizabad sit-in.

Likewise, a similar Show Cause Notice was issued to Justice Siddiqui under Article 209 (5)(6) of the Constitution by the SJC on a reference moved by Advocate Kulsum Khaliq on behalf of former member of the National Assembly Jamshed Dasti alleging that the high court judge J Siddiqui had, during one of the hearings on a case relating to the 20-day Faizabad sit-in, objected to a compromise between the federal government and the protesting TLP. The compromise was facilitated by the armed forces.

The SJC held an inquiry against Justice Siddiqui with regard to the above-mentioned references. After scrutinising the reference, a meeting of the SJC held on 6th Feb had observed that the judge was guilty of misconduct and should be issued a show-cause notice in this regard.

However, Justice Siddiqui re-affirmed his earlier words that the Big Spy-Agency people were (and had been) manipulating judicial proceedings in the country; adding that he would resign if the bar found that he had been involved in corruption; making remarks that: *'50 per cent of responsibility of the country's current situation lies with the judiciary while other institutions are responsible for the rest'.*

On 11th October 2018: President Arif Alvi **removed Justice Shaukat Aziz Siddiqui**, a judge of the Islamabad High Court [IHC] after the Supreme Judicial Council [SJC] recommended his removal. The council, comprising five Supreme Court judges, said it found Justice Siddiqui guilty of misconduct over a speech he delivered in July earlier that year before the Rawalpindi District Bar Association. The SJC was unanimously of the opinion that '*in the matter of making his speech before the District Bar Association, Rawalpindi on [21st July] Mr. Justice Shaukat Aziz Siddiqui had displayed conduct unbecoming of a judge of a high court and was, thus, guilty of misconduct and he is, therefore, liable to be removed from his office under Article 209(6) of the Constitution.*'

Later, in a statement issued in response to the SJC's recommendation of his removal, Justice Siddiqui said:

> "The decision was **not unexpected** for him. When nothing came out of a baseless reference started in the name of alleged refurbishment of [my] official residence about three years ago. Despite full effort, my address to a bar association, every word of which was based on truth, was used as the justification [to dismiss me].
>
> This reference was not heard in open court despite my demand and clear verdict of the Supreme Court, and neither was a commission formed to examine the facts described in my speech.

> *I am completely satisfied with the requisites of my conscience, my nation and my rank; he will present his detailed stance before the public very soon. I will also reveal the facts which I had presented before the Supreme Judicial Council in my written statement and state the actual reasons behind the dismissal of a high court judge."*

Much later….

In daily the **DAWN** dated 28th September 2023, *Usama Khawar* wrote:

> *"Unlike previous cases where judgements against military generals came after they were removed from power, this verdict [penned down by Justice Faez Esa] targeted the current dispensation of the military establishment.*
>
> *Previous cases, such as the declaration against Gen Yahya Khan in the Asma Jillani case, the judgment for Gen Aslam Baig in the Air Marshal Asghar Khan case, and the direction for initiating a treason trial against Gen Musharraf in the PCO Judges Case, had all been heard after the military officials' respective tenures.*
>
> *In contrast, this decision was delivered while the military had become an even more dominant force in Pakistan's political landscape, and the Generals had been promoted, marking a significant departure from established norms of holding generals accountable only after their removal from office."*

The most striking aspects of the judgement was its unflinching examination of the roles played by the armed forces and intelligence agencies, including the ISI and Military Intelligence (MI). **Justice Isa questioned the role of state agencies, particularly the ISI, in failing to counter the threat of violent extremism posed by groups like the TLP and others.** He expressed disappointment in the alleged interference of ISI in matters of political significance, highlighting that *military agency should never be seen as supporting any particular political party.*

Additionally, the judgement provided specific directions for initiating action against members of the armed forces who had violated their oaths and ventured into political activities. It also called for bringing intelligence agencies under legal frameworks. It also aimed to shield other state institutions and the media from undue influence by intelligence agencies.

The judgement took a stance against religious extremism and bigotry propagated by groups like the TLP. It did not mince words and issued strong directives to counter religious extremism. This resolute approach highlighted the judiciary's commitment to curbing radicalism and preserving social harmony in the country.

The Faizabad Dharna Case and its subsequent developments had far-reaching consequences for Pakistan's judicial, political, and broader landscape. However, Justice Isa and his family went through a tough time on that count. Even the then Prime Minister Imran Khan had eventually admitted that the reference regarding his family-properties against Justice Isa was a mistake pushed by the establishment's agenda. The subsequent erosion of the court's authority and the impact on civil liberties painted a vivid picture of how the Faizabad Dharna Case left its mark on Pakistan's legal and political scene.

On 22nd March 2024: The Supreme Court of Pakistan (SCP) set aside the dismissal of former Islamabad High Court (IHC) senior judge Shaukat Aziz Siddiqui, declaring he should be entitled to all the perks and benefits as a retired judge of the high court. The 23-page verdict compiled by CJP Justice Qazi Faez Isa stated that Siddiqui should be declared as a retired high court judge and would also get the perks and benefits of retirement.

A five-member bench led by Chief Justice of Pakistan (CJP) Qazi Faez Isa, including Justice Aminuddin Khan, Justice Jamal Khan Mandokhail, Justice Hasan Azhar Rizvi, and Justice Irfan Saadat, on 23rd January 2024, had reserved its verdict on Siddiqui's plea against his removal. The proceedings of the case were broadcast live on the apex court's website. In his petition, the former judge had challenged a decision of the Supreme Judicial Council (SJC) about his dismissal from service.

The former judge had challenged the Supreme Judicial Council (SJC) about his removal from service after a speech he had delivered at Rawalpindi Bar Association. Lawyer Hamid Khan represented the former IHC judge in the case, while Kh Haris appeared before the apex court to represent former DG ISI Lt Gen (retd) Faiz Hameed and Brig (retd) Irfan Ramay. The proceedings were broadcast live on the apex court's website and as on YouTube channel.

At the start of the hearing, J Siddiqui's lawyer urged the court to conduct a fair inquiry of the matter, arguing that under Article 209(6) of the Constitution, the SJC could not present a report to the country's president without conducting an inquiry. Chief Justice of Pakistan Qazi Faez Isa said the problem was not the speech but its text; if a judge was removed for giving a speech, then half of the judiciary would go home.

It is pertinent to mention here that the then President of Pakistan Dr Arif Alvi had removed Islamabad High Court (IHC) judge Shaukat Aziz Siddiqui from his post in the light of a recommendation by the Supreme Judicial Council (SJC); the SJC's opinion about Siddiqui's dismissal and the subsequent notification issued in October 2018 were SET ASIDE. Also, that:

> *"A 'delay that occurred in hearing and deciding these petitions meant that in the interregnum, Justice Siddiqui attained the age of 62 years, at which age a judge of the high court retires. Therefore, Justice Siddiqui cannot be restored to the position of judge. Consequently, Justice Siddiqui shall be deemed to have retired as a judge of the IHC and he will be entitled to receive all the benefits and privileges due to a retired judge, by allowing these petitions in the above term.*
>
> *…..that a failure to abide by the fundamental right of due process resulted in Justice Siddiqui being treated unfairly and it was conjecturally assumed that he was making false allegations. The action, as it was taken, against Justice Siddiqui constituted mala fide and the SJC had acted coram non judice."*

The judgment also said the SJC had determined J Siddiqui as guilty of misconduct *'without ascertaining the veracity of allegations and without conducting an inquiry and merely because he had taken the matter public. If all that Justice Siddiqui alleged was true then it would be unjust and unfair to punish him for highlighting wrongdoing at the highest level. But, if on the other hand what he had alleged was found to be false then he would be guilty of misconduct.'*

It stressed the need to ascertain the veracity of the allegations against the former judge, noting that *'the then-army chief and the government had explicitly requested the same.'*

The bench determined that the SJC did not state what particular misconduct Justice Siddiqui was guilty of. The SJC felt shocked because J Siddiqui had made serious allegations and had done so publicly; without appreciating that these were not generalised allegations with regard to the ISI as a whole but against certain officers within its ranks, and specific allegations against his own Chief Justice – not so serious deliberation it was.

GEN MUSHARRAF SENTENCED:

On 17th December 2019; a special court in Islamabad declared Gen Musharraf guilty of high treason and handed him a death sentence under Article 6 of the Constitution. It was short order while the detailed judgement was to be released later.

> [Article 6 of Pakistan's Constitution: Any person who abrogates or subverts or suspends or hold in abeyance, or attempts or conspires to abrogate or subvert or suspend or hold in abeyance the Constitution by use of force or show of force or by any other unconstitutional means shall be guilty of high treason.]

On 19th December 2019; the Special Court released the written judgment in Gen Musharraf's hi-treason case for which a 4-liner short order was read out two days earlier. It comprised of 169 pages. The special court in its detailed verdict of death penalty given to former Pakistan Army Chief and ex-president - **ordered to hang the convict [Gen Musharraf] by neck till his actual death.** The detailed verdict issued in the said treason case shocked the people especially the armed forces of Pakistan. The orders penned down in the verdict were traumatizing; it contained:

> "As a necessary corollary to what has been observed we find the accused guilty as per charge. The convict be hanged by his neck till he dies on each count as per charge."

> "We direct the law enforcement agencies to strive their level best to apprehend the fugitive / convict [Gen Musharraf] and to ensure that the punishment is inflicted as per law **and if found dead, his corpse be dragged to the D-Chowk, Islamabad, Pakistan and be hanged for 03 days.**"

[D-Chowk was named to as Democracy Chowk (crossing); a large square located at the junction of Jinnah Avenue and Constitution Avenue in Islamabad and is notoriously famous place for rallies and protests.]

> "It would be in the interest of justice that all those involved (if any) in facilitation of the escape of the fugitive accused may also be brought in the net of due course of law and their criminal acts (if any) may be investigated and tried in accordance with law."

Dismissing criticism of a trial conducted 'in haste', the Special Court said:

> ".....that Gen Musharraf had been afforded more than his due share of fair trial and given every opportunity to defend himself."

> "....that the facts of the case are well documented and clearly demonstrate guilt on part of the accused".

> "The trial of high treason is the requirement of the Constitution against those individuals who undermine or attempt to undermine the Constitution by any means."

> "This Court after the presentation of undeniable, irrefutable and unimpeachable evidence by the prosecution against the accused reaches to the conclusion that indeed accused [Gen Musharraf] is guilty and deserves exemplary punishment."

The court sentenced Gen Musharraf to death for imposing a state of emergency on 3rd November 2007, adding that it had found him guilty of high treason in accordance with Article 6 of the Constitution of Pakistan. The case was heard by a bench comprising Justice Waqar Ahmad Seth of the Peshawar High Court, Justice Shahid Karim of the Lahore High Court and Justice Nazar Akbar of the Sindh High Court. The unprecedented judgment read:

> "We, with the majority of 2 as to 1, allow the complaint and hold the accused guilty of high treason as defined at Article 6 of the Constitution and pass punishment under section 2 High Treason (Punishment) Act, 1973 - the convict be hanged by his neck till he is dead."

> "The then Corps Commanders Committee, in addition to all uniformed officers who were guarding him [Gen Musharraf] each and every time, with boots on, are equally and fully involved in the act and deeds of the accused person."

> "Each and every member of the Armed Forces, as per their oath under the 3rd schedule to the Constitution in pursuance to Article 244 is bound to bear true faith and allegiance to Pakistan and uphold the constitution which embodies the will of the people. They have also sworn not to engage themselves in any political activities....."

The judge noted that Gen Musharraf's aiders and abettors were not made part of the complaint when it was filed by the federal government. However, the verdict said: **"...that does not absolve the government from investigating these officers and filing a complaint against them".**

The 169-page verdict was written by *Justice Seth*, who along with Justice Shahid Karim said that the evidence presented had proved that Gen Musharraf committed a crime. However, the third judge, J Nazar Akbar wrote a dissenting note saying:

> *"I have respectfully gone through the proposed judgement wrote by my brother Waqar Ahmad Seth J [...] with my humble comprehension of law and justice, I happened to dissent with majority view of my learnt brothers."*

After release of the detailed verdict against Gen Musharraf, members of the legal fraternity began weighing it on the severity of paragraph 66 of the judgment which called for *'the former president's body to be dragged to D-Chowk in Islamabad and hanged for three days'*. It was authored by Peshawar High Court Chief Justice Waqar Ahmad Seth; however, J Shahid Karim of the Lahore High Court [LHC] and J Nazar Akbar of the Sindh High Court [SHC] disagreed with such a method of execution prescribed by their fellow judge.

Invariably all the senior lawyers, though belonging to different schools of politics in Pakistan, termed Justice Seth's judgment as *"condemnable and unlawful"* and found Justice Karim's opinion balanced overall. All were of the view that there were multiple grounds for appeal available there. One senior Barrister reminded everyone that the country had fought against the menace that had derived pleasure from exactly this kind of corpse-dragging. *"No sentence in law provides for a three-day lynching and no crime in this country attracts it. Justice is never for the mob."*

The high treason trial of Gen Musharraf was raised purely on ill-will, pay-back retaliation and revenge by two persons who were at the helm of the affairs in the country then; the CJP Iftikhar Chaudhry and the Prime Minister Nawaz Sharif. The charge was of clamping the state of emergency on 3rd November 2007 as a result of which Gen Musharraf had put certain judges including the CJP under house arrests.

Gen Musharraf was forced to resign from the Presidential assignment in Pakistan in August 2008. He left the country but kept on visiting his former republic regularly till ending 2013 when the two narrow minded and vindictive souls determined to take revenge from Gen Musharraf for their rough dealings – so this case of hi-treason was developed.

It was the first time in Pakistan's history that a former army chief and ruler of the country was sentenced to death. Gen Musharraf, who was sentenced in absentia, was out of the country since 2016, when by the same courts he was allowed to leave on bail to seek medical treatment abroad. The former military chief was then lying in Dubai's hospital following deterioration of his health since earlier that year. In a video statement from his hospital bed, he called the treason case 'absolutely baseless' while adding that:

> "I have served my country for 10 years. I have fought for my country. This [treason] is the case in which I have not been heard and I have been victimized."

Gen Musharraf was booked in the treason case in December 2013 and indicted on 31st March 2014. The prosecution had tabled its evidence before the special court in September the same year however, due to various legal lacunas, his trial lingered on and he left Pakistan in March 2016 to seek medical treatment. The military as an institution remained silent over the courts' proceedings – but the members of the Pak-Army had taken it at their hearts.

Gen Musharraf graduated from Pakistan Military Academy [PMA] Kakul in 1964 and was then commissioned in the Pakistan Army. His first battlefield experience came during the 1965 Indo-Pak war and he served in the elite Special Services Group [SSG] from 1966-1972. During the 1971 war with India, Gen Musharraf was a company commander of an SSG commando battalion. After 1971, he continued to excel in several military assignments and gained regular promotions within the army.

In October 1998, he was appointed as chief of army staff by the then Prime Minister Nawaz Sharif. <u>On 12th October 1999,</u> troops had to take over the Prime Minister House after Nawaz prevented Gen Musharraf from landing at Karachi airport upon his journey back from Sri Lanka. He was in a normal plane in which other 200 civilian passengers were flying. In fact, the hijacking had catalysed the take-over then when Gen Musharraf and other 200 passengers' lives were endangered.

It was a hairline escape from a major disaster. Pak Army's Lt Gen Usmani, the then Corps Commander Karachi, immediately took over the control of the airport and when the plane landed it had exhausted all its fuel while waiting in air. Gen Musharraf had to undertake power and he declared a state of emergency, suspended the Constitution and assumed the role of Chief Executive. There were no protests against the coup within Pakistan whatsoever. In June 2001, Gen Musharraf declared himself as the President of Pakistan – as had been the tradition in the country's history.

Coming back to the TRIAL: A 3-member special court comprising Chief Justice of the Peshawar High Court [PHC] Waqar Seth, Justice Nazar Akbar of the Sindh High Court [SHC] and Justice Shahid Karim of the Lahore High Court [LHC] was made to hear the case. On behalf of the PTI government, the prosecution team, led by Advocate Ali Zia Bajwa, argued before the court to amend the indictment against the former military ruler. He contended to frame charges against former PM Shaukat Aziz, former CJP Abdul Hamid Dogar, and the then Federal Minister Zahid Hamid arguing that *"... it is imperative for all accused to be tried simultaneously. The aiders and abettors should be tried as well"* – but the court didn't respond.

It was a majority verdict, with three of the two judges giving the decision against Gen Musharraf. It is pertinent to mention here the special court on 19th November 2019 had said the verdict in the case would be announced on 28th November but the Islamabad High Court [IHC] barred it from doing so due to numerous legal lacunas. However, in utter disregard of the IHC's orders, the Special Court announced the short verdict that day flouting two basic legal requirements:

- Firstly; the defense statement of the accused was never recorded by the court.

- Secondly: it was the first case in the legal history of Pakistan when the accused was given death penalty when he was not present in the court.

The intelligentsia held that the special Court victimised Gen Musharraf in haste, allegedly, to please the out-going CJP Asif Saeed Khosa who was retiring on 21st December 2019. The prejudice and bias had no parallels in Pakistani judiciary. Just a week earlier, CJP Asif Khosa had declared his intent when he mockingly raised his hands sarcastically and cynically copying *'Gen Musharraf - the beloved leader'*. The judiciary was, perhaps, desperately trying to recover its lost prestige but that highly controversial Judgment affixed another black mark on the so-called sane judges of the country.

This was absolute injustice.

Even the members of the high legal fraternity, former attorney general Irfan Qadir and Barrister Ali Zafar were the first to come out and speak that the higher judiciary had purposefully attacked the solidarity of Pakistan because the decision had no merits at all. The General was victimized by the former CJP Iftikhar Chaudhry, who had been in cahoots with the former PM Nawaz Sharif; cases were on record to prove it. Nearly whole of Pakistan mourned the injustice and tyranny of the judiciary that day.

The verdict in the treason case against Gen Musharraf marked an unprecedented shift in Pakistan's history. It was far inconceivable that any military ruler of this country could be convicted of high treason. The trial lasted nearly six years, four times the judges of the special court were changed on one pretext or the other till this last bench declared the former army chief guilty of the offence; Gen Musharraf had suspended the Constitution <u>on 3rd November 2007</u>, when he imposed emergency in the country in consultation with the then Prime Minister Shaukat Aziz and his cabinet members.

Some might see this as the wheel having come full circle. Judicial independence cuts both ways, depending on where one is standing. There were legal remedies available to him as part of his constitutionally protected right to due process. His lawyers, and the PTI government, daring announced they would appeal the special court's decision.

Fighting for one's country does not preclude the commission of treachery. Two senior uniformed officials, as high as of Lt Gen rank while the other was Brigadier, were court-martialed and convicted on charges of espionage earlier that year of 2019.

The moment news about Gen Musharraf's conviction appeared in media, Maj Gen Asif Ghafoor, DG ISPR, in an official statement said '<u>the decision given by special court has been received with lot of pain and anguish by rank and file of Pakistan Armed Forces</u>'. The statement by the Director General of Inter-Services Public Relations [ISPR] came after a meeting of the top military leadership was held at the Army General Headquarters [GHQ] in Rawalpindi where the said judgement was discussed. The statement said:

> "*An ex-Army Chief, Chairman Joint Chief of Staff Committee and President of Pakistan, who has served the country for over 40 years, fought wars for the defense of the country can surely never be a traitor.* **The due legal process seems to have been ignored including the constitution of special court, denial of fundamental right of self-defense,** *undertaking individual specific proceedings and concluding the case in haste.*

> *Armed Forces of Pakistan expect that justice will be dispensed in line with Constitution of Islamic Republic of Pakistan. (For him) it was a dark day, when an Ex-Commando General who had fought valiantly three wars for Pakistan, who defended his country silencing the most formidable and aggressive journalists with his eloquence when his country was fighting the worst war on international media, who in his heart and mind was the one of the biggest patriots his country had produced was given death penalty on charges of treason.* (<u>Gen Asif dared to question the so called honourable Chief Justice</u>) ....*it was shame for all the members of judiciary – and he [the CJP] was retiring with utter disgrace just four days after.*
>
> *Nawaz Sharif has been allowed to go abroad with his entire family. Shahid Khaqan Abbasi was the Chairman PIA and one of the accomplices. There are many more."*

See the media posts on the count:

> *"This verdict against Gen Musharraf is as per the* **'sweet will of CJ'** *---he had already barred his teeth and announced in Public that Gen Musharraf will be punished. Although IHC has stopped any further action on this case and LHC has also approved to form a new Bench,* <u>but someone at the helm of affairs was in hurry - passing the judgment just TWO DAYS before his retirement</u>.*"*

.... Another media comments in that regard:

> *"What a farce our judicial system is.* <u>Those who have been convicted for embezzling tons of public money have been given relief</u>. *If this is not treason what else can be. An army chief, when he takes over the reins of government by abrogating the constitution, does not act on his own. It is an institutional intervention and is necessitated by compelling circumstances and absolute intellectually corrupt practices allowed by some family-ridden politicians in power. Today's judicial decision has created further fissures......*
>
> *These Judges might be lured like Judge Arshad Malik for delivering the verdict in a hurry. The Hon CJ of IHC has (already) raised objections about the constitution of the charge-sheet itself. There is also a second application pending about the validity and powers of this Hon court to decide this case.* **The verdict which has been delivered in such a hurry is worth throwing in dust bin.** *The matter is NOT repeat NOT going to end here. A long way to go."*

BBC's NOTE ON JUSTICE SETH:

On 13th November 2020: The judge, who wrote the judgment awarding the said derogatory sentence in Gen Musharraf's trial, named J Waqar Seth, died after contracting coronavirus. He was an outspoken judge of a kind rarely seen in Pakistan and an unlikely source of opposition to the powerful hi-officials of the country. Tributes described him as bold, fearless and independent; he was 59.

As chief justice (CJ) of Peshawar High Court (PHC), J Seth passed judgments that angered both the military and the government - including the above paragraphed death sentence on exiled former ruler Gen Musharraf that had made headlines around the world. He had been critical on human rights abuses in striking down a law under which the military ran secret internment centres and acquitting dozens of people convicted under anti-terrorism laws for lack of evidence.

Justice Seth's death was seen as a major loss in country's judiciary where the unknown forces had been expanding its influence again in years after the rogue 9/11 episode. Waqar Seth became chief justice of the Peshawar High Court in 2018 but was not promoted to the Supreme Court; his goal remained to struggle for judiciary's independence in Pakistan's quasi democracy. Justice Seth represented the tradition of conscientious and fearless judges... who unfortunately always remained in minority in the country's judicial canvas. A tweet said that Justice Seth's stature was raised not just by the list of his remarkable judgments, *'but also the oppressive conditions that required courage for writing such judgments.'*

Supreme Court Bar Association president Abdul Latif Afridi described him as "a courageous and uncompromising" person who didn't shy away from a fight with the high-ups whether from executive or military; and he paid a personal price for it - that the CJ Peshawar had been denied elevation to the Supreme Court three times despite his seniority.

Justice Seth made history when the three-member special court he headed sentenced Gen Musharraf to death a year earlier in absentia. The General had been found guilty of treason for suspending the constitution and imposing emergency rule in 2007. News of Gen Musharraf's sentence in December 2019 had sparked widespread protests in Pakistan. However, it was the first time the treason clause in the constitution been applied to anyone by a civil court in a country where the military had controlled political decision-making during the said General's tenure from 1999 till 2007. *The penalty was unlikely to be carried out* because Gen Musharraf had been allowed to leave Pakistan for Dubai in 2016 on medical grounds where he died later.

Due to his unprecedented and blatantly odd judgment in Gen Musharraf's Case, there was outrage, with the government seeking to disbar Justice Seth for being unfit for office, and legal experts calling the instructions unconstitutional. The Pak-military had to issue a rare statement saying the verdict was *'received with a lot of pain and anguish by the rank and file of the armed forces and that Gen Musharraf can surely never be a traitor.'*

Justice Seth was never liked rather immensely hated by the general populace of the country when soon after taking charge as chief justice PHC in June 2018, he acquitted key-butchers convicted in trial by the military court that had been constituted following the 16th December 2014 massacre by the Pakistan Taliban at Peshawar's Army Public School in which 143 children and 11 lady teachers were axed and butchered mercilessly. The whole world media had narrated that mourning episode for days and weeks; the Pak-Army had done great efforts for locating them in Afghanistan and their repatriation to Pakistan and had done a military trial. Justice Seth applied his rogue mind and cited *a lack of evidence and malice in facts and law as grounds for those acquittals.*

Waqar Ahmad Seth was born on 16 March 1961 into a middle class family in the city of Dera Ismail Khan, Khyber PK. He received most of his education in Peshawar, graduating in law and political science in 1985. The same year he enrolled as a practicing attorney. Lawyers who knew him said he was a socialist at heart; was active in the student wing of the left-leaning Pakistan People's Party (PPP) and later hung portraits of Karl Marx, Vladimir Lenin and Leon Trotsky in his private law office. Given his habit of shunning the grand security protocols other senior officials crave, the lawyers' fraternity often feared he was putting his life in danger. *He always used his personal car to drive to work and back, and could often be seen in the market doing shopping with his family, or sipping tea at a cafe with an old friend, just like a common man.*

The International Court of Justice (ICJ) in its briefing paper on Pakistan's military courts, released in January 2019, admitted this much when it mentioned that while petitions of people convicted by military courts had been rejected by the Pakistani Supreme Court in 2016 for lack of jurisdiction, the outcome was different when the same petitioners approached Justice Seth's high court in 2018. Many thought he might further rock the Pakistan's national cause by acquitting on appeal the *'Bin Laden doctor', Shakil Afridi,* who had helped the US find Bin Laden in Abbottabad. Dr Afridi was accused of treason as per Pakistani law in vogue and there was sufficient evidence availalable on record.

IHC RELEASED CONVICTED PRISONERS:

On 20th March 2020; the Islamabad High Court [IHC] ordered the issuance of bail for prisoners who were facing trial for minor crimes in order to prevent the spread of the covid-19. IHC Chief Justice Athar Minullah made the decision after hearing a case regarding 1,362 prisoners being incarcerated in overcrowded jails.

Deputy Commissioner Islamabad Hamza Shafqaat assured the court that no prisoner held at Adiala Jail had been infected with the virus. However, Justice Minallah worried that the corona virus outbreak had worsened in China after it spread among prisoners. The court was seen inclined that relief would also apply to prisoners facing NAB trial considering the phenomenon as *unnecessary arrests*. The court also ordered the release of suspects then in police custody.

Within a week, a writ petition against the IHC judgment for release of 400 under-trial prisoners from Adiala jail was filed before the Supreme Court. A five-member larger bench of the apex court headed by Chief Justice of Pakistan Justice Gulzar Ahmed heard the appeal against the said order. The petition contained that release of 400 criminals was unprecedented and unconstitutional. The Superintendent, Central Prison, Rawalpindi, had submitted a report in the IHC that the authorized occupancy of the Central Prison Rawalpindi was 2,174 while the number of its present inmates was 5,001 that day. The number of under-trial prisoners whose cases were pending before the courts was 1,362. Majority of the prisoners were alleged to have committed offences falling within the ambit of the non-prohibitory clause; and several convicted prisoners were above the age of 55 years while some suffering from serious illnesses. The fact remained that the IHC CJ while in chamber exercised his sole jurisdiction and converted the report into a petition under Section 561 A of the Criminal Procedure Code [CrPC] on the ground that a national calamity had been declared by the federal government in the wake of corona-virus threat and that the situation in the over-crowded Adiala Jail was alarming.

The IHC was not vested with jurisdiction to exercise such *suo moto* powers, thus the impugned judgment dated 20th March 2020 was illegal, without any jurisdiction and was liable to be set aside. The remedy under Section 561-A CrPC was not an alternate and substitute for an express remedy as provided under the law. The petitioner urged that in the instant case '*the provincial government is empowered under the Pakistan Prison Rules, 1978 read with Section 401 of CrPC to suspend the sentence*'. The Islamabad Capital Territory [ICT] administration didn't find it expedient to come forward and invoke the said provisions. The petition was admitted for hearing.

On 30th March 2020; a five-judge bench, comprising CJP Gulzar Ahmed, Justice Umar Ata Bandial, Justice MAK Miankhel, Justice Sajjad Ali Shah and Justice Qazi M Amin, heard the said petition. The CJP remarked:

> "…..how the high courts could have ordered the release of under-trial prisoners. Corona-virus is a grave matter and a serious issue but we cannot allow the release of the prisoners involved in heinous crimes. We're well aware about the country's situation but we'll have to see under what authority the IHC had ordered the release of the said prisoners."

The SC's larger bench thus **threw away the judgment of the IHC** and also suspended all the directives of the other courts regarding release of prisoners. The provincial home secretaries, IG Prisons, Prosecutor General NAB and ANF were also notified not to release any prisoner until the apex court makes a ruling on it.

ATIF ZAREEF CASE OF 2021:

On 4th January 2021; a Supreme Court bench headed by Justice Mansoor Ali Shah gave remarkable verdict in two cases titled as Crl Appeal No.251/2020 & Crl Petition No.667/2020. The two cases were against the judgment of Lahore High Court, Rawalpindi Bench, dated 09.06.2016, passed in Crl. A. No.393/2013, and Capital Sentence Reference No.14-T/2013 and against the Order dated 09.06.2020 of that Court declining suspension of sentence in Crl. Misc 822/M of 2020. **Barrister Rida Tahir,** *a distinguished human rights activist*, analysed the judgement of the Supreme Court of Pakistan in the said case and the re-victimisation faced by female survivors of sexual violence in the criminal justice system of Pakistan. She wrote:

"Across Pakistan, the conviction rate in sexual violence (SV) cases stands <u>at less than 3 per cent</u> (a Research Paper of 2021 at www.las.org.pk/wp-content...is referred), despite their high level of prevalence. Rape is a <u>severely under-reported crime</u> in Pakistan and there are no reliable statistics due to under-reporting and <u>no centralised data collection</u>. An <u>analysis</u> reveals that the causes of the under-reporting of SV crimes and a large number of acquittals by the courts is due to, among other things, **the re-victimisation of female survivors of SV by the criminal justice system.**

This includes the use of the <u>two-finger test (TFT)</u> and the impeachment of the chastity and morality of female survivors by questioning their prior sexual activity and maligning their character in their cross-examination by the defence."

[**Two Finger Test (TFT)**; also known as the virginity and hymen test is an <u>old practice</u> and has <u>long been a routine part</u> of criminal proceedings in Pakistan. It is conducted on female survivors / victims of rape and SV in Pakistan. It is a <u>practice whereby two fingers are inserted inside</u> the female genitalia by a medico-legal officer to check its size and elasticity. The TFT is based on the <u>unscientific</u> and misogynist assumption that a woman who engages in sexual intercourse is less likely to have been raped hence she lacks the moral authority to make an accusation of rape or SV.]

The Supreme Court of Pakistan (SCP)'s landmark judgement in the said cited case, which held that *recording the sexual history of the survivor by carrying out the TFT and questioning the survivor on her sexual history or character in order to discredit her credibility is unconstitutional and illegal.*

Art. 14 of the <u>Constitution of Pakistan</u> (Constitution) grants the right to dignity. In *Atif Zareef v. The State*, the SC held that reporting and recording the sexual history of a survivor by conducting the TFT was contrary to Art. 14 as it amounted to degrading her human worth by discrediting her independence, identity, autonomy and free choice. It was also held that the TFT had no scientific value. The TFT was previously held unconstitutional and illegal by the Lahore High Court (LHC) in *Sadaf Aziz v. Federation of Pakistan;* however, the LHC's judgement <u>only (practically) applied to the province of Punjab</u> whereas the SC's judgement, through that verdict of 2021, made it a binding precedent across the whole country.

Moreover, Art. 4(2) (a) of the Constitution stipulates that, *"...no action detrimental to the life, liberty, body, reputation...of any person shall be taken..."* The SC held that mentioning the sexual history of a survivor by making observations about her body, such as, *'the vagina admits two fingers easily'* was contrary to the reputation and honour of the survivor and (thus) violated Art. 4(2) (a) of the Constitution. Whereas, the TFT was based on the unscientific and misogynist assumption that *'a woman who engages in sexual intercourse is less likely to have been raped hence she lacks the moral authority to make an accusation of rape or SV'.*

During SV trials, the accused was often defended on the basis that the survivor / victim had a unrestrained background and that she was a woman of immoral character and on that basis, she might had consented to the alleged act of rape or her testimony was less worthy of belief. Art.151 (4) of the **Qanun-e-Shahadat Order** 1984 (QSO) stipulated that, *'when a man is prosecuted for rape... it may be shown that the victim was of generally immoral character to impeach her credibility.'* It was omitted by the Criminal Law (Amendment) (Offences Relating to Rape) Act 2016. However, the practice of questioning survivors on their sexual history and chastity continued. The SC referred to *Mukhtar Ahmad v. Govt. of Pakistan,* wherein a full bench of the Federal Shariat Court (FSC) had earlier declared that the provisions of Art. 151(4) of the QSO was repugnant to the Injunctions of Islam.

The SC stated at paragraph 14 of the judgement that: *'evidence relating to sexual history should not be admitted in order to draw inferences supporting the 'twin myths', namely, that by reason of that sexual history, it is more likely that the complainant may have consented or become less worthy of belief.'* It was also held that the omission of Art. 151(4) of the QSO left no doubt in discovering and ascertaining the intention of the Legislature that in a rape case, the survivor was not to be questioned about her alleged general immoral character. Further, the SC held that the declaration of the FSC of Pakistan as to the provisions of Article 151(4) of the QSO, since omitted, also barred such questions.

Often, expression such as, habituated to sex, woman of easy virtue, woman of loose moral character, and non-virgin are used to describe survivors of SV in Pakistan. The SC held that *'... **such expressions are unconstitutional and illegal. The courts should discontinue the use of inappropriate expressions even if the charge of rape is not proved.'***

The judgment in Atif Zareef v. The State was widely celebrated across Pakistan. However, in order to cease the re-victimisation of SV survivors in courts, meaningful transformations in the CJS's response to SV was needed to be made; gender sensitisation trainings could have been provided to judges, lawyers, prosecutors, medico-legal officers, police officers and all responders to SV crimes in the system. Secondly, lawyers and prosecutors could be provided with ethical training on advocacy and education on the existing laws on SV along with specialised sexual and gender-based violence mechanisms.

Lastly, the government could provide Standard Operating Procedures (SOPs) for prevention and response to SV based on international good practices, such as, the framework issued by the World Health Organization (WHO) and UN Women on preventing violence against women and girls. The government and civil society organizations could have acted in harmony and devise appropriate strategies in order to bring reforms to the CJS and female's dignity in the society.

SC BANS EXECUTIONS OF MENTALLY-DISABLED PRISONERS:

On 10th February 2021; the Supreme Court of Pakistan (SC), while commuting the death sentences of Imdad Ali and Kanizan Bibi, placed a ban on the death penalty being applied to those with mental disabilities. Amnesty International said:

> *"This landmark judgment from Pakistan's Supreme Court marks an important development not only for the death penalty, but also for mental health. Imdad Ali and Kanizan Bibi should have been taken off death row the moment their history of severe mental disabilities was brought to the fore. This historic precedent puts a stop to the execution of other prisoners with similar conditions, many of whom have yet to be diagnosed."*

Imdad Ali and Kanizan Bibi, who were on death row since 1991 and 2002 respectively, had been repeatedly diagnosed with schizophrenia. Both had multiple execution warrants issued for them before securing stays on the basis of their mental disabilities. Both Imdad and Kanizan were convicted of murder. On 10th February 2021, the Supreme Court passed a historic order commuting their death sentences, stating: *'After considering the material discussed herein above, we hold that if a condemned prisoner, due to mental illness, is found to be unable to comprehend the rationale and reason behind his / her punishment, then carrying out the death sentence will not meet the ends of justice.'*

NCM - DETAILED JUDGMENT OF 7th APRIL 2022:

On 13th July 2022; the Supreme Court of Pakistan (SCP) published a judgment detailing the reasons for issuing its landmark unanimous short order dated 7th April 2022 which order had declared the ruling of the deputy speaker of the National Assembly (NA) dismissing the resolution of no confidence (RNC) motion against the country's PM Imran Khan *'to be contrary to the Constitution and the law and of no legal effect.'*

The judgment held that the ruling and the subsequent acts of the PM and the President dissolving the NA were a nullity in the eye of the law.

Background to the Judgment was that on 3rd April 2022, PM Imran Khan was set to face a no-confidence resolution vote under Article 95 (*Vote of No-Confidence Against Prime Minister*) of the Pakistan's Constitution, after the opposition said it had the simple majority numbers needed to remove him. However, NA Deputy Speaker Qasim Khan Suri dismissed the motion, ruling that it was in breach of Article 5 of the Constitution (*Loyalty to State and Obedience to Constitution and Law*) because the opposition was alleged to be complicit in a *'collusion with a foreign state'* purportedly evidenced by a diplomatic cypher. The foreign state and a few members of the National Assembly were said to be using the RNC process to oust the PM. Although it was not mentioned in the ruling, short order, or judgment, the alleged foreign state was widely identified in media reports as the United States.

On the same day, PM Khan advised the country's president Arif Alvi to dissolve the NA under Article 58 (*Dissolution of National Assembly*) of the Constitution and prepare for new national elections.

On its own motion, the apex court (SC) took notice of the matter. On 7th April 2022, it issued a short order unanimously setting aside the deputy speaker's ruling on the no-trust motion. The court said: '... *the ruling was contrary to the Constitution and the law and of no legal effect.'* It restored the NA by declaring that the advice given by the PM and the order of the president were unconstitutional and null. The court declared that the NA was in existence at all times and would continue to remain so. (Short Order 5). The order also stated that detailed reasons for the order would be recorded later.

The detailed judgment was authored by Chief Justice Umar Ata Bandial, with concurring judgments by Justice Mazhar Alam Miankhel and Justice Jamal Khan Mandokhel. Preliminarily, the court said it had original constitutional jurisdiction under article 184(3) of Pakistan's Constitution, as '*it relates to the enforcement of a fundamental right or the concerns of the public at large.*' The court found that the ruling and subsequent actions of PM Imran Khan and president Arif Alvi *prima facie* infringed the fundamental rights of the Opposition Parties and the public at large. Namely, '*the Deputy Speaker's ruling and the actions of the PM and the President defeated the right of the Opposition Parties to test their voting strength in support of the RNC and if successful, to form the next Government in exercise of their fundamental right under Article 17(2) of the Constitution.*'

Regarding the invocation of **Article 5 and national security** in the deputy speaker's ruling, the court said that:

> ".... although courts should exercise caution and restraint in matters of national security, judicial review is permissible on narrow grounds. When national security is taken as a defence to sustain a decision by the Government that is prima facie unconstitutional then the Government is under an obligation to substantiate the bona fides of its defence. To do so the Government must produce evidence to demonstrate the defence in order to escape legal scrutiny of its impugned action.
>
> (Because the contents of the cipher were not produced and other evidence detailing those members of the national assembly were involved in the conspiracy was not provided) ... The Court cannot accept the Respondents defence that the alleged contravention of Article 95 of the Constitution by the Deputy Speaker is protected from judicial scrutiny on the claim of national security."

The court also found that the deputy speaker's ruling was not protected by the immunity provided by Article 69(1), which could bar the courts from inquiring into proceedings in Parliament **to the extent that the same suffer from an irregularity of procedure.** Further, the apex court held:

> "*The ruling fails to qualify for protection as part of the internal proceedings of Parliament, (as the ruling was not) the outcome of a vote in the NA but instead, it was a unilateral decision taken by the Deputy Speaker at the behest of the Law Minister....*
>
> *The current Constitution empowers the superior courts to examine and adjudicate the validity of proceedings in Parliament if these contravene the substantive or procedural provisions of the Constitution. Although courts will ordinarily exercise restraint and not enter into the domains*

of the Legislature and the Executive, they will intervene when either of these branches overstep their constitutionally prescribed limits.

(Because the deputy speaker's ruling is unconstitutional).... **the RNC against the PM stands revived.** *Furthermore, in light of the Explanation to Article 58(1) of the Constitution, a PM against whom notice of an RNC has been given cannot advise the president to dissolve the NA, and thus, the president's order also loses constitutional legitimacy. These findings accord with a settled principle of law that when the basic order is without lawful authority and <u>void ab initio</u>, then the entire super-structure raised thereon falls to the ground automatically.* ***Therefore, the NA stands restored with immediate effect, and in fact, it is deemed to have been in existence at all times.***"

Scenario 255

100 DAYS (PERFORMANCE) OF PM KHAN-I

ANALYSIS OF PM KHAN's (51) PROMISES:

The *announcements & re-assertion of promises* continued even during the first 100 days and beyond BUT the PTI couldn't deliver much due to Covid-19 AND paucity of funds and most projects were *left un-finished* when the Parliament passed No Vote Confidence against them in April 2022.

Talking about details of 51 promises of Imran Khan, done by him and his key-team members, immediately before the elections of July 2018 and during the first 100 days of the PTI government after taking over the office of the premiership, the intelligentsia and larger sections of Pakistani media held that the PTI manifestly fell short living up to its promises. In fact, some of those promises were so flimsy, light and fragile that shouldn't have been labelled as PROMISES in political sense - *were simply a step forward towards change of personal traits – delicate wishes or bahaviroal pattern – which had nothing to do with the national economy or people welfare or tax-reliefs or industrial or infrastructural expansions etc.*

For example, Imran Khan had promised in his inaugural speech that he would answer parliamentarians' queries twice a month in a session that was to be known as the *'PM's Question Hour'*. However, the initiative never really took off despite some attempts to amend the National Assembly's rules to make it tangible - but couldn't make it happen. BUT what was the loss to the nation or public exchequer on that count – nothing in real terms.

Seven broad promises out of total 51 were meant to address a very diverse range of issues. More promises that could not be delivered on despite some efforts to make things happen included a promise to establish juvenile detention centres and prisons for women [PTI's FINAL MANIFESTO uploaded on insaf.pk on 9th July 2018 is referred], where some progress appeared to have happened only in Khyber PK, and a promise to make *Pakistan Television* and *the Radio Pakistan* totally independent like BBC or EU Channels was never fulfilled - it remained completely under the government's control even if there were improvements in their operations.

- *BUT, at the same time, if such promises couldn't be implemented effectively, the opposition cannot label the party (PTI) of gross failure or extending irrepairable loss to the state.*

Two broken promises were related with Karachi's water anguishes, where the PTI had promised to set up a ***desalination plant in the city*** (it never really took off) and a ***crackdown against Karachi's water mafia***, which continued to operate with impunity during PTI tenure though their dens were seldom raided by the agencies and law enforcement people – but the menace remained there with full force and like in previous regimes.

- *The truthful analysis comes up that the 1st promise could have been fulfilled as it was related with general public welfare – irrespective of the fact that it was a 'PURE PROVINCIAL' matter after famous 18th Amendment in vogue. However, the 2nd promise was purly of local administrative domain – NOT even of provincial govt level. Khan had just floated it as promise – for nothing beyond fun sake.*

Two promises were left completely unattended, with little being done to even get the ball rolling. Those were the proposal to give ***parliament the power to ratify international treaties*** and an ***'adoption of madrassah scheme'*** which could make the students better citizen, curb multi-polar sectarian trends, lessen fear of terror-threats and offer apprenticeships, especially in IT fields, in return for tax benefits.

- *For the 1st proposal, only an executive or administrative order was needed for all the federal secretaries, nothing beyond. It could be ill-intentions of the PM's Principal Secretary showing corrupt loyalties with rogue bureaucracy in Pakistan. Even parliament could do it as its own – no permission or approval was required of any sort.*

- *For the 2nd proposal, in fact badly required since much earlier in the country, was a GOLDEN promise for the shining prospects of future generations. Imran Khan had done his work – got sufficient success by converting about 5300 madrisas (out of 30,000 then on record) into regular schools. It was, in fact, like running against the wind because the religious leadership as well as Ministry of Education – both were not willing to do the job whole-heartedly.*

Let us dissect the Deliverance ....

FIRSTLY, one can find a promise that could be considered to have been fulfilled; PTI's promise to *build a special task force to recover looted national wealth*, can be marked as technically completed, even though the task force's performance and ability to deliver on its mandate left a lot to be discussed. Mr Khan, uptill his last day, had known that this task-force had worked hard to recover the looted money but for their own personal gains – not for the state; the big fish were openly sold; court cases were flouted and media was fed with wrong information. In short, NOT A SINGLE RUPEE WAS BROUGHT IN THE STATE EXCHEQUER while millions were spent on the upkeep and moving activities of the said Task Force.

Secondly, Like the previous two big political parties, PTI completed its promises where more jobs were done happily which involved CASH-DISTRIBUTION amongst the masses. These included its promise to *substantially expand the Benazir Income Support Program (BISP)*, which the PTI office-holders fulfilled exceptionally with much enthusiasm and labour.

> [*In fact, Pakistan is known for its beggars' mentality; from a street beggar to the parliamentary beggars. The ministers and the members of national & provincial assemblies virtually fight each other to grasp positions & postings in BISP, BAIT ul MAAL, ZAKAT FOUNDATIONS, FLOOD RELIEFS, UTILITY STORES etc just with a psyche of 'feeling honour in CASH DISTRIBUTION' – the major source of state-sponsored corruption for BUREAUCRACY & some politicians.*]

Since 2008, every ruling party continued with this lucrative program [BISP] and with increase of multiplied amounts every year. Enormous increase in multi billion rupees each year in all governments straightaway proved that the number of (so-called) poor people increased in Pakistan thus the program should have been discontinued much earlier – but all the leaders and their governments opted to continue. Perhaps, it was because the distribution secretariat had to add names & numbers of fake recipients only, revise their computerized lists only and amounts were claimed through so many accounts or cash spending. The amounts remained so meagre (Rs:2000 pm in PPP & PMLN regimes; Rs:3000 pm in PTI era) that even the actual recipients would get only two day's food from that support money – BUT the political leaders involved and bureaucrats got tens of billions each year.

Imran Khan redirected the **BISP grants to his EHSAS Program** which was run by one Sania Nishter. However, the people were expecting these grants to build new primary schools, reinstate and run some closed, old or depleted schools, use the village mosques as properly regulated schools and give villagers the needed funds / grants, establishing professionally sound vocational schools for boys and girls. This could create enormous spaces for employments and was the best way to address the poverty issues by raising national literacy rate, producing lots of skilled workers – which was also Imran Khan's core objective given in PTI's manifesto.

> [*On another count;* **Ehsaas** *deserves a special commendation for the key role it played in getting critical monetary aid to the most vulnerable social segments during early days of Covid-19 pandemic when businesses were shut and many daily wagers had no opportunity to put bread on their table. The breadth of initiatives launched under the Ehsaas program — like homeless shelters, subsidized ration programs, soup kitchens, and nutrition programs — was commendable because it showed that the govt was serious about going the extra mile to protect country's most vulnerable communities.*]

Thirdly, the PTI government made good on its commitment to *__developing financial instruments to attract investment from overseas Pakistanis__*, with the Roshan Digital Accounts (RDAs) standing out as its biggest achievement in Pakistan's economy. On a positive note, RDAs facilitated the inflow of remittances and acted as major support for Pakistan's foreign exchange reserves. Through RDAs, overseas workers were (*and still have been*) able to invest in Naya Pakistan Certificates, real estate and the Pakistan Stock Exchange, significantly increasing their contribution to domestic economy.

PROMISES LEFT IN PIPELINES:

There were **10 other promises on which implementation was at an advanced stage** at the time the PTI government was sent home in April 2022. People would recall and recognize at least half of these promises, as they featured prominently in news headlines, political discussions and media talk-shows. The first: __launching of the billion Tree Tsunami program__ for reforestation, of which 44pc of the target had been achieved by March 2022. The program garnered praise from the UN Environment Program, the World Economic Forum and global leaders and was a commendable initiative to address one of the most pressing empirical crises of modern times.

The second was about **VOTING RIGHTS FOR OVERSEAS PAKISTANIS**, which the PTI was successful in doing by getting approved the relevant laws through the Supreme Court of Pakistan and the ECP in 2018.

On 17th August 2018; a day before Imran Khan took oath as premier, the Supreme Court of Pakistan [SCP] ruled a landmark decision *allowing overseas Pakistanis the right to vote* via an internet system. The court had been hearing a petition filed by Mr Khan who had long sought voting rights for Pakistanis abroad, with his party enjoying a large following amongst the diaspora. Overseas Pakistanis were able to avail this right during the by-elections scheduled on 14th October 2018 for 37 constituencies.

Following orders of the SCP, the ECP issued necessary notifications and made viable arrangements for overseas voters so that they could be able to cast their votes in the supplementary elections of 14th October 2018. However, the overseas voters were not found serious at all even they could have cast their votes on ECP's internet facility while sitting at their homes from all over the world. See the ECP's figures released to media on 18th September 2018:

> "The campaign to register overseas Pakistanis for internet-voting in the upcoming by-polls evoked a lukewarm response, with only 7,419 expatriates out of the total 632,000 registering to avail the facility offered to them for the first time in the country's electoral history. The process of registration of overseas Pakistanis from the 37 constituencies where by-elections are to be held on Oct 14 had started on Sept 1 and came to a close on 17th September 2018 at 9am. The website for the overseas voters remained functional 24/7 throughout the registration process and did not face any technical problems.
>
> This way, as many as 632,000 overseas Pakistanis from the 37 constituencies settled in 177 countries of the world were eligible to vote through the internet — which is 84 per cent of the total overseas Pakistanis from the given constituencies.
>
> Under the plan, over 7,400 registered voters were sent voter pass (password) between Oct 10 and Oct 14 on the email address mentioned in their online application for registration, through which they were able to cast their votes on election day. On polling day, the voter could log in to the website using his username and password and enter the voter pass emailed to him earlier. This was to direct the voter to his

registered national and provincial assembly constituencies to enable him to cast the vote.

A designated list of candidates of the selected constituency was displayed by the system and the voter had to select the election symbol of the candidate to cast his vote. Upon successful submission of the vote, a **confirmation message** was to be displayed on the screen.

The ECP had already uploaded on its website separate video tutorials in Urdu and English languages as well as step-by-step help materials to guide voters through the registration and voting process. An advertisement campaign was launched through media to create awareness about the facility of internet voting made available for the overseas Pakistanis and the embassies and consulates of Pakistan had also been involved in the campaign."

Later, Mr Khan took this reform through the parliament in November 2021 but the fate of the law was unclear as the ECP remained unsure that overseas voters would get to vote in the next general election in 2023 due to resources and time constraints. The relevant facility which the ECP had given to overseas Pakistanis (casting their vote via internet – as is prevailing in many developed countries) was also *bulldozed through parliamentary controversial discussions – with no tangible results till today.*

The Third was the *implementation of a policy framework* **TO BUILD FIVE MILLION HOUSES,** called as the Naya Pakistan Housing Program and various sub-initiatives were taken under it. It is worth pointing out here that the government itself had not committed to build five million houses, but to act as an *'enabler and facilitator'* only. A number of housing projects catering to middle and low-income households were launched during the PTI government under the said initiative, attempting to make ownership of a home possible for workers and labourers – *but at the end it was a total failure.*

PTI govt tried to invite and convince certain builders and construction companies but ALL were there to play loot-game. One contractor was especially brought from Manchester UK, he made some watering announcements to invest his own money and build low-cost homes; he was made an Advisor to Mr Khan on Housing, too; but after having certain photo-sessions and enjoying official dinners, he fizzled away with his plans & investment and never showed his face again. *Most contractors were after the pieces of precious lands and huge bank-loans* on concessionary rates – NOT at all serious for the noble cause of Mr Khan; thus, the program failed.

The Fourth promise: Let the people recall the PTI promise of **CREATING 10 MILLION JOBS** over five years, but PTI govt was seen partially committed. If the results of the relevant Labour Force Survey released by the Pakistan Bureau of Statistics are to be believed, the government was successful in adding 5.5m jobs in its first three years of power before it was dismissed; *Dawn.com* survey dated 25th April 2022 is referred.

It is worth mentioning here that job creation didn't literally mean the PTI govt itself created 5.5m jobs out of thin air: these jobs got created indirectly as a result of government policies regarding various sectors of the economy, especially agriculture, industries and construction.

The Fifth Promise: Mr Khan's dearest and recognizable promise had to do with the **SEHAT INSAF CARD**. It can be marked partially complete as the PTI had promised to roll it out to all of Pakistan, which it was able to do partially. Former PM Khan launched the said scheme of *Sehat Insaf Card* through Dr Zafar Mirza. It had expanded its coverage to Punjab, providing Rs:1 million cover to each family. Baluchistan approved the card towards the end of the PTI regime, but Sindh insisted on not signing it.

Intelligentsia gurus and some columnists, however, commented that through the said scheme of *Sehat Card*, the private hospitals and the clinical labs remained the actual beneficiaries rather than the poor patients. Fake prescriptions and fictitious medical & test reports had mostly been used for minting moneys from the state exchequer. In other words, *new flood-gates of corruption got opened for private hospitals and medical specialists. However, Mr Khan's scheme was marvelous but corruption in Pakistani society in known to all.*

The Sixth one: Onto the lesser recognized promises - these included the facilitation of **PUBLIC OUTREACH TO POLICE**, which noticeably improved through various IT related initiatives like apps, websites and hotlines launched by the police forces of KP, Punjab and ICT, where the PTI govt had direct control. However, a lot more work needed to be done to make access to police services easier for citizens. The facts went overlooked by the PTI and Mr Khan that the Pakistani police on the whole has gone more lethargic and more corrupt because still the organization works under the provisions of Police Act of 1861 and Police Rules of 1934.

Patch-work in the shape of Police Order 2000 & 2002 was done but basically it is the responsibility and obligation of the Parliament to make out new legislation as per ever-changing circumstances. For 75 years Pakistanis are being treated like animals and traitors of the British rule.

Pakistan's successive parliamentarians and the ruling parties have been so irresponsible, negligent and sluggish that they couldn't feel the necessity of formulating new Act, laws & rules to improve the quality of policing for their people. All politicians themselves have been suffering due to these old colonial police system, and still suffering (Mr Zardari, Sharifs and later Mr Khan himself are typical examples) but they never opted to get the new police order during their respective tenures of statesmanship – so, *tey pher bhugto*…. (…means continue to suffer it).

The Seventh one: The PTI had promised to create a **NATIONAL COMMISSION OF MINORITIES**, which it did, but it wasn't really able to resource and empower it like it was envisioned. It couldn't be rolled out in the provinces as well. No activity has been heard under this Commission, no media news, no mention of achievement heard ever. If the body was to be ignored with zero activity, then why the PTI spent public money on its formation and running it. The people and media were often found worried if the Commission's Secretariat was in place and / or if the body had its members – enjoying perks & numerations etc for nothing doing.

The Eighth Promise: The PTI was also able to enact legislation to create **SPECIAL COURTS FOR GENDER-BASED VIOLENCE** but was never seen them fully functional before its time ran out; in fact, Khan's useless team couldn't apprehend their leader's vision – thus no work was done on this promising undertaking. Some media people had also pointed out that the issue didn't merit TO BE A PROMISE. Developing new courts was an extra burden on state exchequer. Instead, the parliamentarians could have worked out to adopt new procedures like in other welfare states – the existing number of courts and judges could do better.

The Nineth One: The PTI also started a program to provide **STIPENDS TO SCHOOL GIRLS** under the *Ehsaas Taleemi Wazaif* banner but the people were unable to see it rolled out on the scale that it had envisioned. The program was launched by PM Khan himself under Ehsaas Education Stipends program on 1st September 2021. The program got started too late and nearly 40 days after the PTI govt got landing in troubles; the event concerning Gen Faiz Hamid (ISI Chief)'s transfer had started shaking the PTI govt's foundations; after a short while, the military & PDM made PTI to go home.

The Tenth Promise: the PTI had pledged to take up the **KASHMIR ISSUE** and resolve it *within the parameters of UNSC resolutions.* While the issue remained unresolved (*as it remained so during previous govts for 75 years*), the PTI did successfully mobilize the OIC and the UNSC to take up the issue on multiple occasions. It kept referring Indian atrocities and excesses to the UNSC and using the platform of the OIC to develop broad support for its position in the dispute. PM Khan stated on multiple occasions that Pakistan desired to improve its relations with India, but there needed to be progress on Kashmir before things would move forward. India gave deaf ears to this issue like before.

- *The media broadly held that PTI was unable to complete some of its promises; **most pledges were left at intermediary or early stages at the time the party was removed from power.** The pending promises were a mix of well-recognized commitments as well as lesser-known ones.*

The 11th Promise: the pledge to turn **PM HOUSE INTO A UNIVERSITY** remained in the memories of learned and scholarly people; work on this pledge started, but was never materialized. The latest on this was that just *in early 2022, the Senate Committee had rejected a bill seeking to establish a university at PM House,* recommending that existing universities be strengthened instead. Some columnists opined that this move was maneuvered from the PTI members from inside.

The 12th Promise: It was announced that the PTI would **OPEN ALL GOVT GUEST HOUSES FOR PUBLIC.** Work on this promise was partially done, with the Khyber KP government leading the way in converting its properties to public facilities. However, other provinces were unwilling to follow the suit barring some in Punjab. AJK, Gilgit, Sindh and Baluchistan were not seen convinced with the idea and the PTI federal govt could not get the scheme implemented in the later mentioned territories.

- *Basically, it was a provincial domain and PM Imran Khan's wish could be taken as a noble suggestion which the provincial bureaucracies didn't like because of their own vested interests.*

The 13th Promise: Within its three years' rule, the PTI delivered to a considerable extent on its commitments to **EXPEDITE CONSTRUCTION**

OF DIAMER-BHASHA DAM and got prepared feasibility studies for other dams too; while also building many small dams for water conservation purposes. These were critical initiatives considering Pakistan was facing the threat of severe water shortages. These projects can be marked as *in progress* because although the paperwork for many dams was completed and initial construction activity kicked off, many projects were yet to be completed when the PTI left. PM Khan had personally kicked off construction work at the Diamer-Bhasha dam project on 15th July 2020. For dams in Mr Khan's era, see a separate chapter in this book.

The 14th Promise: The PTI's efforts to replicate its reforms in other provinces and **APPOINTING PROFESSIONAL IGPs,** were never accepted by the provinces; the idea couldn't take off, with Punjab representing the worst example of government interference in the institution. Though efforts were initially made to give the police force some degree of independence, both Islamabad and Punjab were plagued by frequent transfers of senior officials that really disrupted their functioning. None of the IGP performed up to his capacity due to fear and distress that whether he would see the next dawn in uniform. The opposition parties had the opinion that the IGs in Pakistan were being remotely controlled by the FIRST LADY & her sons – *giving weight to the fact that CM Buzdar had no acumen to take required results from his officers in uniform and others in field postings.*

> [*On 28th February 2021:* The federal government transferred 15 senior police officers under the new rotation policy 2020 approved by PM Khan in order to rotate the officials after completion of 10-year period in a province or region. The DIG-ranked officers, serving in grade-20, were reshuffled from the provinces and the federal govt institutes. The main feature was that the federal government slapped a ban of two years for officers on their postings in the geographical limits of the station from where they were transferred. It was named as the rotation policy.
>
> The reshuffle of selective officers somehow shocked the PSP community as it believed that only 20 per cent of the total officials falling under this policy in the same grade were transferred, *due to likes and dislikes.* Most of the officers who had completed their more than 10-year tenure or even for more than 20-year period were yet serving in Punjab and Sindh; it was taken as victimisation.]

The 15th Promise: PM Khan had a plan to **MAKE PEMRA INDEPENDENT;** but then abandoned it as the PTI got diverted its focus on creating a new media regulatory body. It was PTI Minister Fawad

Hassan Ch's brain-child; working was complete and implementation strategy was also finalized to make new media body called PMRA to keep an eye / control over all types of media, including print, digital, broadcast and online. However, the idea became controversial within the PTI ranks and the promise died at its own.

The 16th – the most important Promise: Mr Khan's well-known promise to create **NATIONAL CONSENSUS ON SOUTH-PUNJAB PROVINCE** was also left incomplete, with the government being shown the door before it could have a legislative bill seeking the creation of South Punjab passed by parliament. PTI had gone too late in fact. To its credit, the PTI remained committed to the cause, with many developments reported on the executive and administrative end of making the promise a reality as well. See more details elsewhere in this book ....

In addition, the promises done during first 100 days of PM Khan's government - amongst the lesser-known commitments, most made for the **betterment of DISABLED persons** did not get the sustained attention they needed. Considerable work was done, no doubt, for *special assistance programs* for them, but the PTI government couldn't consolidate its efforts together under a single umbrella to create a uniform program for persons with special needs – moreover, it was not an issue to be solved at federal level.

> [The PTI, in its manifesto, said that as part of its expansion of the social safety net, it would *'launch special assistance programmes for differently-abled persons'* for their better integration into mainstream society. On 29th February 2022; the Punjab cabinet's standing committee on legislative business approved the draft of *Empowerment of Persons with Disabilities Act 2021*. The said eye-wash legislation was NOT enough as it was never implemented; whereas other provinces never seen convinced in this regard.]

Likewise, **DISABILITY RESOURCE CENTRES** were supposed to be set up in every district of the country, but work done on this promise was very limited. The government had also promised a **2pc JOB QUOTA FOR DISABLED PERSONS**, but the PTI govt could never get around for enforcing it in a uniform manner. A point to appreciate that the Sindh Empowerment of Persons with Disabilities Act, 2018 appeared to be the most progressive legislation, which asks for *'care-giver allowance to PWDs with high support needs'* to ensure their right of adequate living standards & social protection. However, no report with media is thre to judge the implementation level.

Till the ending year 2018, Punjab and Khyber PK provinces increased their quota for disable persons from 2pc to 3pc and some districts like Rawalpindi had sincerely implemented it. The departments were conveyed the federal instructions for implementation; the provinces, during the 1st week of January 2019, started asking the ways and means to implement the said instructions – especially for issuing driving licences to the people with hearing loss as per international practices; providing free wheelchairs to persons with physically handicaps; and white canes to the visually impaired and giving health cards to all the special persons. Serious exercises got started all over Pakistan then.

The letter from the federal government said the employment quota would be calculated against the posts being advertised / fixed at a particular point of time. As this practice was leading to negligible appointments against the quota, there was a need to work out the quota against the total posts of every department – in short, more serious home work was needed.

On 21st June 2019: The Supreme Court sought a comprehensive report from the federal as well as provincial governments on appointments of disabled persons. A 3-member bench, headed by Justice Sheikh Azmat Saeed, heard a case concerning fake recruitments made allegedly on the quota of disable persons. Nearly 4,712 fake persons had been appointed on the basis of disabled persons' quota; and the private sector had (till then) provided Rs:50 million for the disabled persons BUT there were no details as to how the said fund was utilised. Khyber PK govt informed the court that they had made 427 appointments on the disabled persons' quotas; also, that the National Council for Disabled People was being restored in that province.

On 16th May 2020: The SECP declared that *'Section 459 has been omitted to remove ambiguity and avoid conflict of laws and to ensure that the quota of disabled persons provided in the Disabled Persons (Employment and Rehabilitation) (Amendment) Act 2015 and other related legislations is given effect and implemented in letter and spirit'*.

On promises for women, the PTI remained unable to roll out a **NATIONWIDE MATERNAL HEALTH PROGRAM,** even though it did launch several initiatives around it that would have supported its goals.

[In order to promote gender parity, the PTI, in its manifesto, stated that "...*it will establish a large scale national Maternal Health Program to provide assisted births along with family health and planning information to women*". The PTI also vowed to "*double the size of the LHW programme to ensure each woman has access to complete package of Lady Health Worker (LHW) services*".]

CONCLUSION:

The fact remains that the bulk of the PTI's work remained undone at the time it was pushed out of office in April 2022. Mostly it was because the PROMISES were mainly of good wishes about the *'personal human problems'* sometimes addressing with minute issues concerning with gender specifics – ***not at all related with major issues of development at the national level*** or concerning with majority-sections of the society. For example, see 'another promise of PTI': Provision of **HOUSING TO DISABLED PERSONS** – which could never get implemented at the level it was promised; probably nowhere in the country the work could be started on it.

- *It doesn't mean that Imran Khan did wrong by thinking over the above issues or problems – it was all human and it, in fact, reflected the inner-good of Mr Khan as a leader – BUT in Pakistan like poor countries, the leadership could also think about BIGGER ISSUES to address majority of population and improve their quality of life.*

- *In PTI era, about 50% population was living BELOW THE POVERTY LINE; leaders should think and decide –*

    o Should govt feed BREAD & BUTTER directly to those 50% for living OR

    o Should govt provide SKILLS & TECHNIQUES to many of those 50% to earn their own Bread & Butter.

While the PTI was able to deliver in some areas, it faced quite steep challenges in others. Of course, the Covid-19 pandemic and global economic conditions in its aftermath do explain why the PTI government seemed to struggle so much during its time in power. Another reason cited was the PTI's razor-thin majority in the National Assembly, which didn't really give it much room to quickly execute its legislative agenda.

On the other hand, intelligentsia pointed to the Imran Khan-led government's inexperience and its apparent ineffectiveness. The musical chairs of key ministers and senior officials and frequent U-turns on key policies gave weight to the later argument that the way the country was being managed was quite chaotic and therefore things were doomed to collapse. Had there be a good team with him, things could have been better given their honesty an edge.

One media tracker found [up till 18ᵗʰ August 2021] that the PTI-led government had to launch 51 projects as per their manifesto and promises done with the nation during its first 100 days of rule and also set in place the instruments required for the fulfillment of some of its promises at the national, and in some cases, even provincial levels. Progress on some promises was still stuck in its initial stages or had been marred with delays beyond comprehension. However, the record till the 3 years after remained: that **Out of 51 PROMISES, 7 were still pending to take start.**

Scenario 256

100 DAYS OF PM IMRAN KHAN-II

ON WOMEN EMPOWERMENT IN PTI ERA:

The PTI, in its manifesto, stated that: *'It will increase* **FEMALE PARTICIPATION IN PUBLIC SECTOR** *by establishing significant quotas for women in local government and boards of public bodies'*. No doubt, the PTI was able to put adequate efforts for filling of <u>quotas for women in public bodies</u> and substantially increase their participation in the govt departments – but might be missing rosy picture of complete success or their input due to Covid-19 and insufficient tenure of stay in government.

On 19th April 2019: The Khyber PK cabinet approved an amended version of the Local Government Act 2013 wherein, inter-alia, the village and neighbourhood councils were asked to have 33pc quota for women, five per cent for youth, while that of minorities was kept intact in the amended law. Whereas, in media headlines of <u>30th June 2019</u> had held that <u>'...the new Punjab Local Government Act of 2019 offers little to women for their political participation and their reserved seats have decreased'</u>. Therefore, the Punjab government was supposed to amend the PLGA of 2019 to enhance ratio of women representation to at least 33pc through reserved seats – *but CM Buzdar was unable to do it.*

In a conference titled *'The new Local Govt Law and Women Representation'*, organised by the <u>'Women in Struggle for Empowerment'</u> (WISE), the councillors held:

> "Though women are 49% of the population, the ratio of their representation at different tiers like metropolitan, municipal corporation and tehsil council etc is not more than 16pc. This gradual decrease negated the government commitments under sustainable development goals, national policies and action plans devised for the political empowerment of women."

According to a media report, titled as *'The Punjab Local Govt Act 2019'*, launched <u>on 26th July 2020</u>; the representation of women was seen much reduced, from 33pc cent in 2001 to less than 10 per cent in the successive local governments. This was highlighted therein that women, peasants and labourers representation ratio had considerably lowered over the time. The report was issued by the Women in Struggle for Empowerment (Wise) in Lahore – and the PTI govt took it as challenge to move forward.

The PTI govt's commitments were very clear so as the PM's promise, its national policies and its action plans devised for the political empowerment of women. Refusing special representation for peasants / labours in the neighbourhood councils by previous govts had led to further marginalization of the vulnerable sections of society. Irony remained that in the history of local governance in Pakistan, not many genuine efforts were made to protect the political and electoral interests of such sections including women.

On 6th August 2020: In *CASE NO. 29-RH-2019* the PUNJAB PUBLIC SERVICE COMMISSION announced that *'the under mentioned candidates have been recommended to the Provincial Government for appointment to the posts of DEPUTY DISTRICT ATTORNEY (BS-18+RS.17,500 - AS SPECIAL ALLOWANCE) IN THE PUNJAB LAW AND PARLIAMENTARY AFFAIRS DEPARTMENT'.* (Thereafter, 8 male names were given as selectees) Then the following NOTE:

> Note: - i) Two (02 including 01 post reserved for women quota and 01 post reserved for special persons' quota) posts remained vacant due to non-availability of candidate.
> ii) No more Female candidate is available for the above said post. Therefore, as per notification No. SOR-IV(S&GAD)15-1/2012(3) dated 21-05-2012, one (01) post reserved for women quota shall be treated as unreserved and filled on merit.   (SECRETARY)

On 24th March 2021: PTI's Federal Minister Shireen Mazari said the crisis emanating from the coronavirus pandemic had created an important opportunity to take stock of the progress made globally in advancing the protection and promotion of the rights of women. In her statement during the 65th Session of *the Commission on Status of Women* held from 15-26 March in New York, she said it was a time to reflect on the challenges that continue to stand in the way of women's rights and equal participation in decision making in all facets of public life. She said that *'The protection and promotion of the rights of women are one of the key pillars of Pakistan's development paradigm'* – but practically the process was under progress till then.

The protection of women was one of the key priority areas of PTI's Action Plan on Human Rights. Women Protection Centres were established all over the country to address grievances. A National Helpline (1099) also provided (still it's in place) free legal advice and a robust redressal and referral mechanism. The Ehsaas Program's **Social Protection Program** was designed to provide social assistance to women and improve financial inclusion and economic empowerment of women. In order to encourage women's employment, the PTI Govt had announced a minimum of 10% quota for women in public sector employment. To facilitate working women, women hostels and day-care facilities were being provided at public and private offices.

On 8th March 2022: Radio Pakistan presented an analytical report on Women development and its allied fields. The theme of that year's International Women's Day was: *'Gender equality today for a sustainable tomorrow';* the PTI govt asked the people to raise their voices against violation of women rights. The right of women specified a share of inheritance and entitlement to own and possess property, as enshrined in the Quranic edicts and duly regulated by State legislation.

Ehsaas program launched by the PTI government and run under the control of **Dr Sania Nishtar** was aimed to support the women especially. Initially, 50% quota was allocated to the females in the program but after three years of its implementation, *the quota was increased to almost 98%.* In Ehsaas program, the girls were getting more stipend-amount as compared to the boys. Moreover, as per the policy, the girls were getting 50% of total scholarships provided by the government.

In PTI regime, Pakistan did well regarding women empowerment. The state had first time a 3-star female General in the Pak-Army. Justice Ayesha A. Malik became the first female judge of the Supreme Court in the history of Pakistan. It was good development that the PTI govt ensured representation of women in every field and majority of women parliamentarians from the PTI were also in the congregation to show women empowerment. However, there was a big challenge of increased violence against women not only in Pakistan but across the globe. The Constitution of Pakistan also guaranteed safeguards in that respect.

> [*However, the fact remained that the real powers were concentrated with the provincial governments instead of local governments, which negated the real spirit of Article 140-A and Article 32 of the Pakistan's Constitution. In Pakistani society it has been the practice since decades but little disappointments cropped up because the populace was*

expecting cogent results of NAYA Pakistan – forgetting that ROME WAS NOT BUILT IN A DAY.]

The PTI did make much better progress on a core promise for women; the establishment of **WOMEN POLICE STATIONS** in each district of the country. The PTI had high hopes to reform police in Pakistan, an institution the party termed *'ill-equipped, poorly trained, deeply politicised, and chronically corrupt'*, in its manifesto, adding that *'Police reforms have been neglected by successive governments to continue using the force as a political tool'*. One part of the reforms promised was the establishment of women police stations and desks *'at all levels to facilitate female empowerment'*.

On 27th November 2018: Khyber PK police established 22 model police stations in various parts of the province to provide easy justice and access to the high echelon of power. **Women desks** were also established in these model police stations for redressal of their confronting problems and grievances; ladies' police were deployed on duty in that regard. Besides, two lady doctors were also performing duty on these desks to provide first aid to the injured persons of any incident.

On 30th April 2019: Balochistan's first women police station was seen by media members under construction at a cost of Rs:50 million. *'Due to traditional and tribal taboos women cannot visit common police stations to lodge their complaints. With the opening of the first women police station, most legal and social issues of women will be resolved. The completion of a police station for women will also provide jobs for females.'* The IGP Baluchistan told the media.

On 13th May 2020: City Police Officer (CPO) Rawalpindi constituted women police unit in Rawalpindi police, in accordance of which lady police officers and lady police constables were to be deputed in 12 police stations of Rawalpindi. The said Unit was equipped to address and resolve complaints and issues of women in relating cases of women in police stations. Later, these women police officials were deployed as Additional SHOs in 12 police stations of Rawalpindi. During September till December 2021, many exclusive 'women only' police stations and special desks were opened nearly in all provinces including AJK; some districts were Jhelum, Swabi, Peshawar, Swat and Rawalakot [AJK].

On 5th March 2022: The first police station for women in Baluchistan opened its doors; the facility in Quetta was inaugurated by Inspector General Police (IGP) Baluchistan. The police station dedicated to serve women in Baluchistan came into existence *28 years after the first such facility* was set up else where in the country. Pakistan's first women police station was inaugurated by late PM Benazir Bhutto in Islamabad on 25th January 1994.

PTI PROMISES ON EDUCATION:

PM Khan's other promise: In order to promote gender parity, the PTI, in its manifesto had stated that it 'will prioritise establishment and **UPGRADATION OF GIRLS SCHOOLS**. Much was done during 3 year's short span; but more work still left to be done.

On 13th April 2019; Gilgit-Baltistan CM Hafiz Hafeez told the media that his Govt would set up ten model schools in the region every year to impart quality education. At the inaugural ceremony of Begum Waqar-un Nisa Higher Secondary School in Kashrote area of Gilgit, he said 282 middle schools were established in Gilgit Baltistan during the previous four years. On 24th June 2019: Special Secretary Khyber KP Education Department told that work on construction of 70 girls' schools was in full swing. On 1st October 2019, buildings of two new degree colleges for girls in Orakzai and Wana, South Waziristan were okayed for construction.

On 18th August 2021: *ONE Girls high school* was re-opened in newly constructed building after 8 years; around 200 girl students attended the classes on the very first day. The school had been destroyed in a blast eight years ago and since then it was closed. The students were sent to Colony High School then, located at some distance from Miranshah city.

On 15th March 2022: Elementary and Secondary Education Foundation [ESEF] announced to establish 1,000 more girls' community schools in the upcoming academic year to enroll out of school children in the targeted areas of Khyber PK. The said schools were to be set up in those localities where there was no government school at a distance of 500 meters in hilly areas and one km in the plan areas. Though the schools were for girls, yet in many of such schools the foundation had enrolled boys also because of the non-availability of schools for them in the near vicinity. Other ESEF schools were to be upgraded to middle and high levels in two years

The ESEF produced exemplary results during one year on job; a total of 2,219 community schools were operating in 26 districts of the province and the number could cross the figure of 3,000 with the establishment of some more such schools. 500 community schools were set up in year 2021. 154,650 students were enrolled in the community schools where 3,172 teachers were imparting education to them.

Complete digitalization of ESEF was another milestone achievement of the foundation to ensure transparency. Digital profiling of 3,000 teachers and 145,000 students was complete (till then) while online attendance of 130,000 students were ensured on daily basis. *ESEF was set up to enroll out of school children in areas where formal government schools were not available.* The foundation was the brain-child of the PTI govt; more than Rs:2200 million budget was released by the provincial educational admin.

> [*One can seriously ponder upon the speed and level of interest the PTI govt had been showing during their 3+ years tenure. Target was settled at 100% literacy rate in NAYA PAKISTAN; the PTI govt did their best in Northern Areas & Khyber PK but in Punjab, the CM Buzdar went lethargic in the education field too.*]

'On a similar count, the establishment of five universities during the first two years of the PTI government was a matchless achievement while work on three more universities was underway in Punjab'; media news, both print and electronic of 17th December 2020 is referred.

More so, 1500 lecturers were also being recruited through the Punjab Public service Commission (PPSC) to overcome staff shortage in colleges. Academic activities at the University of Mianwali, Women University Rawalpindi, University of Chakwal and Kohsar University Murree, had started while Baba Guru Nanak University in Nankana Saheb was under construction. Work got started on the establishment of Thal University in Bhakar; the foundation of the University of Hafizabad was laid down by PM Khan himself while Sialkot University of Applied Engineering & Technology worth Rs:14 billion had been set on working.

Government College University Faisalabad, Government College Women University Sialkot, Women University Bahawalpur, Nawaz Sharif University of Technology, University of Sahiwal and University of Jhang were being uplifted because those were in poor condition since many years.

Additionally, the statutes of certain universities were not established by the previous governments. The PTI govt managed to organise the statutes of 18 universities and the summaries were (then) moved for approval.

During the PTI regime, the higher education department launched e-transfers of their teaching staff. The e-transfer mechanism not only closed windows of red-tape but also established a corruption-free merit system in the department. Moreover, Rs:28 billion were allocated for the Annual Development Plan of the higher education sector but it had to be cut down after the Covid-19 pandemic.

REVAMPING OF MADRASSAHS:

The PTI, in its manifesto, had stated that '*it will map out and register all seminaries across Pakistan and introduce science and mathematics teaching as formal subjects within the Madrassah curriculum*'. Let us take it up under a broad heading: **REGISTRATION OF MADRASSAHS**; while revamping of their curriculum was their main objective.

On 3rd October 2018: A delegation comprising five heads of major *madrassah* boards held a meeting with PM Imran Khan and discussed the government's agenda on *madrassah reforms;* the delegation was headed by Mufti Muneebur Rehman. Accompanied with Education Minister Shafqat Mehmood, the premier informed the delegation that *mainstreaming education standards of religious seminaries was among the top priorities of the government.* PM Khan wanted to eradicate the class-based education system and introduce uniform syllabi and curriculum in the education sector, which included the seminaries.

On 7th December 2018: PM Khan reiterated his resolve through a joint communique (*Usman Dar's meeting with Minister for Religious Affair is referred*) to include all young students who study in seminaries into the framework of his *Naya Pakistan Youth Program.* On 6th May 2019: Education Minister Shafqat Mahmood told the nation through a media conference that education ministry *had completed its initial work to register all seminaries* and none would be allowed to promote hatred and sectarianism. The heads of religious boards / seminaries – had also agreed and finalised with consensus an agreement for *registration of all 30,000 seminaries operating in the country,* subsequently the number raised to 35,000.

The education ministry was ready to set up 10 regional centres in various parts of the country for registration of seminaries; those seminaries which would not acquire registration were to be closed. All registered seminaries were instructed to have an account in schedule banks. Registered seminaries were allowed to enrol foreign students (*which practice has already been there in most madrissahs BUT without permission or even knowledge of the respective governments*). The foreign students, mostly from Afghanistan, were to continue for NINE years and the education ministry could help those students in their visa and settling down processes.

For Technical and Vocational Education, the seminaries were to be facilitated in getting registered with vocational training institutions. After holding discussion, **all decisions were made with consensus, and the religious scholars signed the document,** detailing all decisions made that day. PTI government was to provide all necessary patronage to seminaries so that their students could also get maximum chances to excel. They were promised for chances to get contemporary education besides religious education.

Next day, the federal cabinet approved a uniform curriculum for all education institutions in the country, including 30,000 madrassahs.

However, just after about 3 months, on 10th August 2019; in a very odd move, *Ittehad Tanzeemat-i-Madaris Pakistan* [ITMP] **declined to share data of religious seminaries** with personnel of any law enforcement agency and warned to announce a protest movement in case the process of data collection was not stopped forthwith. Sharing details of the agreement signed between the ITMP and PTI government dated 6th May 2019, they accused the federal government of failing to set up regional centres for registration of the religious seminaries with ministry of federal education and professional training.

The fact remained that Shafqat Mahmood's federal ministry had done nothing for registration of 30,000 madrassahs nor any centre was established as per agreement, nor any arrangement to facilitate the seminaries in getting registered with vocational training institutions was done.

> *Instead, various law enforcement agencies had started collecting details regarding the students and teachers; also, that govt personnel had started visiting the female seminaries and that too at night – (might be an allegation or exaggeration BUT the matter could have been investigated in detail and seriously) - intolerable for ITMP – NO investigation done into those odd events whatsoever.*

On 19th December 2019: A Directorate established in Religious Affairs ministry for registration of over 35,000 seminaries, operating across the country. The seminaries had, in principle, agreed with the govt's initiative for bringing their students in the mainstream in order to ensure a uniform education system in the country. *"The religious seminaries had affirmed that their students would appear in middle, secondary and intermediate (O & A level) examination of Federal Board like other public or private schools."*

> IN FACT, IT WAS AN UPHILL TASK WHICH THE PTI GOVT DARED TO START AND HANDLE – BECAUSE THE RELIGIOUS MADRASSAHS HAD ALLEGEDLY EARNED THE REPUTATION OF BEING CENTRES OF HATRED & SECTARIAL VOILENCE. MOSTLY, THEIR SOURCES OF INCOME ARE UNKNOWN AND NO ACCOUNT-BOOKS OF THEIR EXPENDITURES ARE ON PUBLIC-RECORD.

The PTI government had established **National Curriculum Council [NCC]** under which the new curriculum from class one to five was being prepared AND to be introduced by March 2020. All stakeholders including public and private sector schools, *Madrassas*, concerned departments were taken on board while preparing new curriculum. The public, private schools and religious seminaries were made bound to adopt *One National Curriculum*.

Then the news appeared in media on 31st December 2019 that the federal government had planned the registration of the country's all religious schools by the end of its five-year constitutional term in 2023 - **PTI was doing the right job BUT the process was going slow because of federal education ministry's lethargic and sluggish attitude; it was not taken as MISSION.** New govt directive was:

> *"We've around 35,000 seminaries across the country, which all will be registered in the next four years as part of our efforts to bring them into the mainstream. Our registration exercise will target 2,000-3,000 religious' schools in the first year and the rest in the next three years."*

Federal Education ministry had established a directorate and 16 countrywide offices for seminary registration. Every seminary had to appoint two teachers of its own choice to impart contemporary formal education to students with the federal government paying each of them Rs:17,000 stipend a month. It was a serious effort for mainstreaming of seminary-class and to ensure their contribution of seminaries in the national development. However, statistics about achievements in this regard were not placed before media.

Education continued to be a provincial subject as guaranteed in the 18th Constitutional Amendment. Federation and provinces were jointly working on education reforms, especially uniform curriculum, so decisions and moves in that respect were acceptable to all – it was an indication of national spirit. Look the apathy of Imran Khan's chosen team here:

> *"Under an initiative of the education ministry,* **0.2 million (only?) children are being provided with technical education.** *We're also going to launch a comprehensive programme with the $450 million assistance of the World Bank to improve the quality of education in schools;"* – progress either remained NIL or it was blatant lie by the rogue management members of the PTI; Imran Khan was helpless, many had the opinion.

Till 20th February 2020 at least, the registration process had not taken shape; however, by 9th May 2021, 5,000 seminaries were got registered across the country. On 25th March 2022, 9000 plus religious seminaries were existing on the federal ministry's roll – PTI had given a guideline at least.

The Single National Curriculum (SNC) and model textbooks were to be adopted across the Punjab province for grade pre-1 to 5 in the academic session beginning August 2021, according to a notification issued on 1st January 2021 by the provincial curriculum and textbook board - public, private and religious seminaries all were adopting it – but no statistics on record.

The Punjab government on 25th March 2022 distributed Single National Curriculum (SNC) textbooks for primary grades to students and administrations of 500 *madaris* at a ceremony. National Curriculum Council (NCC) told the media that: *"…36,500 seminary children would benefit from these books. For the first time in the history of the country, children in madaris will be taught science, mathematics and English like other school children."*

PTI ON TECHNICAL EDUCATION:

Imran Khan's PTI, in its manifesto, stated that '*PTI will establish at least 10 technical universities in Pakistan to provide skills to our youth*' – but **couldn't find time to establish the first NEW one even.**

On 23rd November 2018: Punjab cabinet validated establishment of Punjab University of Technology campus in Mandi Bahauddin. On 7th March 2019: The Punjab Assembly passed a Bill for the establishment of first state of the art university of technology in Dera Ghazi Khan division. The Rs:2.3 billion project was meant to promote research for producing quality technical human resource. The PC-1 of the project had been prepared in advance.

The said technology university was spread over 288 kanal land. 14 colleges of technology were imparting technical education to students in DG Khan division. The project of Mir Chakar Rind University of Technology was included in the annual development programme of 2019-20. Four technology subjects were to be taught in the university at the initial stage, including electrical, mechanical & civil engineering [*manifestly the old beaten subjects – producing another junk-lot of useless engineers*] and computer technology. Since DG Khan was situated on the western route of China Pakistan Economic Corridor (CPEC), it was beneficial project for youth.

On 6th December 2019: Peshawar's Technical Education and Training Authority [TEVTA] approved the execution of an Annual Development Programme (ADP) scheme regarding the establishment of a *Government Polytechnic Institute* (GPI) in the Mathra neighbourhood of Peshawar through a budgetary allocation of Rs:17.24 million.

The TEVTA board approved a revised budget for the fiscal years 2018-19 & 2019-20 worth Rs:3.99 billion also. The board also approved the Project Concept-I (PC-I) for the establishment of GTVC at Bakhshali with a sub-campus in the Sawal Dher Industrial estate in Mardan at a cost of Rs:120.04 million, purchasing 10 kanals of land for setting up the GPI and the GTVC in Matta, approving the PC-I for the establishment of GTVC at Pind Cargo Khan in Abbottabad at a cost of Rs:159.88m and six months mandatory training curricula for TEVTA teaching staff. The board also provisionally approved a PC-I for establishing a GTVC for boys in Bannu for Rs:146.998 million.

On 16th December 2019: Baluchistan's Finance Minister Mir Buledi laid the foundation stone of a 150-bed hospital and a Pak-China Friendship Technical and Vocational Training Institute at Gwadar. China provided a grant of 240 million RMB (Chinese currency) for the construction of the hospital and 87 million RMB for the construction of the institute. The two projects were to be completed within two years. Till ending PTI govt in April 2022, Technical & Vocational institute was nearly ready to welcome students.

On 8th **March 2020:** The Technical and Vocational Training Authority [Tevta] started handing over assets of four of its colleges to three newly-established technology universities including Punjab Tianjin University of Technology (PTUT) Lahore, Punjab University of Technology Rasul (PUTR) Mandi Bahauddin and The Mir Chakar Khan Rind University of Technology Dera Ghazi Khan. The said 3-universities were established by the Punjab Industries, Commerce, Investment and Skills Development Department (PICISD). Under the relevant Act of 2018, the Punjab government had to transfer all the assets & liabilities to the pertinent specified universities. Mostly the employees, regular or contractual, serving these colleges were transferred to the universities concerned.

Tevta started upgrading the colleges to universities under the quota of 80pc students of DAE *{Each polytechnic runs its own* **Direct Admissions Exercise *(DAE) for students with local or international qualifications who are not eligible to apply for courses under other admissions exercises.}*** to get admission there; earlier there was only 2pc quota for DAE students in technology universities of the country. The said colleges were constituent colleges of the university and all their courses could continue as such. Tevta was having 44 technology colleges in the province and four of them were upgraded. Tevta adjusted those employees because the department was facing shortage of around 6,000 teachers then – *a remarkable contribution of Imran Khan* towards the national cause.

On 17th January 2021: The Khyber PK govt approved a plan for *establishment of Swat University of Engineering and Technology* [SUET] within three years at a cost of Rs:8 billion. The varsity was being set up to produce market-oriented graduates. The state-run universities in Khyber PK province were financially dependent on the govt but the new university in Swat was planned to be self-sustainable, being the 1st of its kind in Khyber PK. A *triple helix model* was worked out for this university by connecting government, industry and academic with each other. Dr Najeebullah, the project manager of the proposed Swat University, told the media:

> *"The new university would offer degree programs that were benchmarked against international standards and by implementing international practices for curricula design and teaching. From day one the university would explore all auxiliary enterprises for its self-sustainability. We will focus on building technical, management and outreach capacity of SUET and strengthening its coordination with Higher Education Commission, industry and government stakeholders besides international partners.*

Market-driven curricular programmes are planned for all the disciplines to be taught in the university; curricula and extra-curricular programs would be developed with the support of international partners and public and private sector stakeholders. The university would also develop teaching and research laboratories as per national and international needs."

In this regard, SUET had planned to enter into technical cooperation **partnership with the University of Utah USA**, which was expected to facilitate building its connections with other reputable international engineering universities, research institutions and policy think tanks; also, to pursue efforts to introduce dual / joint degree programmes with such universities.

Initially six disciplines including electrical and civil engineering, institute of materials, mining and metallurgy, computer engineering, bio-medical engineering and institute of manufacturing were to be introduced in the university. The loud thinking was that '...*it will not be another engineering university - rather focused has been made on international linkages and students exchange with the best universities of the world*'.

On 12th March 2021: PM Khan himself inaugurated **AL-QADIR UNIVERSITY** at Sohawa near Jhelum. He had plans to transform the system of Al Qadir University similar to that of Egypt's Al Azhar University, a prestigious institution of the world. Besides taking inspiration from the West in technological development, the Prime Minister held, '...*there are several aspects of their culture such as truth and honesty that merited replication*'. Al Qadir University was scheduled to be completed by September 2021.

On 5th July 2021: The federal and Punjab govts pledged to jointly provide funds for establishment of the **University of Applied Engineering and Emerging Technologies (UAEET) in Sialkot**. The Punjab govt provided a free-of-cost 500 acres piece of land near Sambrial for the project whose total estimated cost was Rs:16.8bn. The federal and Punjab govts planned to provide half of the amount each for the project scheduled to be completed by 2027. The university was being established in collaboration with Austrian and Chinese technology universities and Dr Attaur Rehman, vice chairman of PM's taskforce on knowledge-economy, was already working on it.

As per the project's plan, at least five major bachelor's and master's degree programmes would be launched at the university, such as industrial engineering, manufacturing and mechatronics, chemical and materials engineering, information technology, artificial intelligence, agricultural engineering, industrial biotechnology and business management & entrepreneurship. The UAEET would also offer dual degrees of the foreign partner institutions to its graduates. Ultimately, the university would become a knowledge city, having a technology park, which will have the incubators for start-ups and shell units for small and medium size companies.

At least five academic blocks and one admin block with central library and three hostels (one for girls and two for boys), housing colony for faculty, furnished family suites for foreign faculty, activity centre, guesthouse, mosque, school, sport complex and other related facilities would be a part of project.

On 1st October 2021: The first Pakistan-China technical vocational institute, launched under the China-Pakistan Economic Corridor (CPEC), was inaugurated in Gwadar. Nong Rong, China's Ambassador to Pakistan, attended the inauguration ceremony through video link and told that the institute, which *had been completed at a cost of $10 million in only 20 months*, was a sign of 70 years of Pak-China friendship.

The institute had been equipped with the state-of-the-art machinery for imparting the best technical education and skills to the youths of Baluchistan, especially of Gwadar. The students would be not only provided free accommodation but also scholarships during training in the institute. Zhang Baosheng, Chairman of the China Overseas Port Holding Company, said that:

> 'Technical institutes play an important role in industrial development and the trained youths would have golden opportunities to get employment in Gwadar Port, Free Zone Industry and other projects of the CPEC'.

The PTI, in its manifesto, had stated that *'it will launch a **nationwide literacy programme** to engage its 50,000 youth volunteers to teach literacy in exchange for university credits'*.

PTI PROMISES ON HUMAN DEVELOPMENT:

On 21st November 2018: The National Health Services [NHS] decided to start work on the **FIRST NURSING UNIVERSITY IN PAKISTAN**;

a longstanding issue of the unavailability of land was addressed by National Health Institute [NIH] Executive Director because the project was facing delays on account of possession of their lands so he decided to hand over NIH's 237 *kanal* land to the university.

> [King Hamad of Bahrain had in 2014 announced that he would provide funding for the university as a gift for the people of Pakistan. It was decided that the Pakistani government would arrange the land and utility services for the university while Bahrain would fund the construction work.
>
> The King Hamad University of Nursing and Associated Medical Sciences was to be established on Park Road, Chak Shahzad. The university had to cater to 2,000 students with 500 annual admissions. Residences were also to be provided to 1,000 female students at the campus as well.]

In July 2016, a delegation from Bahrain led by Dr Sheikha Rana bint Isa bin Daij Al-Khalifa visited Islamabad to finalise the project. On 6th January 2017; the then PM Nawaz Sharif laid the foundation stone of the university on the site. However, possession of the land could not be secured as 700 people had filed applications with the Capital Development Authority [CDA] that they didn't want to give their lands despite they were paid their price. In mid-November 2018, PTI decided to construct the university; the project was promised to be built on turn-key basis.

On 19th September 2018: During its first 100-days of PTI's rule, the **NATIONAL COMMISSION FOR HUMAN DEVELOPMENT [NCHD]** formulated the **NATIONAL ACTION PLAN** under the Federal Ministry of Education and Technical Training *to ensure 90pc literacy rate in the country.* The said NAP envisaged that the provincial authorities would use the plans to transform policy decisions into action at the ground level.

A National Training Institute was also established to ensure quality education in its feeder schools and **ADULT LITERACY PROGRAM** along with other projects. That institute was to build capacity of professionals working in the field of literacy and non-formal education. It would also prepare Accelerated Learning Modules and condensed syllabus to provide a second chance to the interested ones to take part in educational activities. The core theme remained that education was the best remedy to all problems prevailing in the form of extremism, poverty, inequality and social injustice in the society.

In Pakistan, ironically, one fourth or 22.6 million children of 5-9 age groups were still out of school and 40pc of adult population were illiterate and thus, hampering national development and progress. It was held that providing an equal education opportunity in the remote areas was the basic right of all the citizens of the country.

> [*The NCHD adopted a two-pronged approach to address the issues of illiteracy in the country, adult literacy for age group 14 and above and primary education both formal education for age group 5-9 and non-Formal education for age group 10-14 to achieve 90pc literacy rate in the country.*]

The NCHD made 3.96 million people literates since its inception and providing education to 335,164 children in 5,949 feeder schools in the remote areas to the marginalised group. The organization had exercised a number of innovative approaches to reach the marginalized group. Its chair-person told the media that:

> "We are working in jails with the aim to provide education to the convicts and make them useful citizens. We've approached learners in seminaries with reforms and introduced primary education along with religious education in order to bring them in the mainstream of higher education."

During those days, the NCHD was successfully working in 100 Seminaries of former Federally Administered Tribal Areas [FATA], Azad Jammu and Kashmir, Gilgit Baltistan and Islamabad Capital Territory. In collaboration with Japan International Cooperation Agency [JICA], the commission had launched a model of non-formal school system where 20 schools were functional for children of age 10-14 who could be admitted neither to the primary school nor to adult literacy centres.

To bring the disliked and **hated transgender people** at par with the rest of the society, the PTI government got set up two literacy centres in Rawalpindi; they had started operations on 3rd December 2018.

On 7th December 2018: The Punjab govt unveiled its five-year program, titled **'THE NEW DEAL 2023'**, to transform school education with a focus on learning, access and equity and governance. A comprehensive plan was finalized to achieve the goals set by the leadership. Under the 2023 plan, they would introduce short-, mid- and long-term strategies to reform state schools; especially, that reforms in public schools were required in learning, access, equity and governance. To re-educate more than 70pc students who left schools after their primary education and didn't enter middle classes: *'We are working towards starting afternoon classes in 20 districts in March (2019) to provide access to children to middle and high-level classes'.*

The Integrated Management Information System (IMIS) was launched to foster data-driven decision making and devising data-based performance management system; its PC-1 was ready. The IMIS could connect 450,000 teachers with the department for getting promotions online. Education in primary schools could be imparted in Urdu and English taught as additional subject. Compulsory sports could be introduced and the program to provide bicycles to students in 20 districts were extended to other districts too.

Besides, construction of girls-friendly toilets was to be completed on priority. Similarly, a compulsory health-check program was launched in 1,700 selected schools. Weak school structures were also being restored in flood-affected areas of the province.

Drafts of **_Punjab Educational Professionals Standards Council Bill 2018_**, **_Punjab Private Education Reform Bill 2018_** and **_Punjab School Truancy and Compulsory Admission Bill 2018_** were prepared with the objective to regulate and improve the schooling system. Work was also being done on a performance management framework for education managers at tehsil, district and provincial levels. The govt was adopting rationalization to address the shortage of teachers also.

PTI's educationist and some professionals had opined that *Daanish School System was not a viable project* as Rs:18,000 per month (then) was being spent on one child, while millions of other students had no access to even basic facilities in public schools. Good schooling, of whatever kind, is the basic need of the country to improve literacy rate – thus PTI govt did nice that Daanish Schools were allowed to continue as such.

On 22nd February 2022: CM Khyber PK announced **FREE TECHNICAL EDUCATION FOR 4000 MEN & WOMEN** of the newly merged tribal districts of the province. The announcement was made during a ceremony held in collaboration between Technical Education and Vocational Training Authority and Germany's Patrip Foundation developing a centre of renewable energy at Hayatabad, Peshawar. The Tevta also signed an MOU with Skilled Women Service Centre and KP EZDMC. The CM asked traders and industrialists to contact Tevta for skilled manpower – a commendable job in fact.

Germany's Patrip Foundation okayed to provide funding and technical assistance for the initiative, while the **Wish International** played a key role in the promotion of training. It was rightly held that CPEC and Rashakai Economic Zone necessitated the production of skilled manpower to guide the future of the province. Also, the PTI government had a vision for the poverty reduction and economic stability, and opening new avenues of employment to the skilled manpower; 4000 youths were to begin getting training then. The Women Vocational Training Centre was expanded enabling youths to get a place in the market matching their skills.

LITERACY CENTRES IN MOSQUES:

On 3rd October 2019: PTI planned to launch **LITERACY CENTRES IN MOSQUES** under the administrative control of provincial *Auqaf* Department across Punjab. *Auqaf* Department was taken on board and educated *Imams* of the mosques were engaged for teaching; to teach Mathematics, English and Urdu besides the religious teachings in vogue; *Auqaf* Department started preparing the lists of their Imams.

For such programs, the **Japan International Cooperation Agency [JICA]** had agreed to provide support and grant for the literacy and non-formal basic education after three years break; it pledged to provide support for teachers training and curriculum development as well. Japan govt's confidence was reviving after the PTI govt's transparent policy on projects while 220 institutes of the departments were revamped with the support of UNICEF during the one year.

238 new literacy centres were set up in jails since the PTI govt came to power. Also, that first time in the history of Punjab province, three centres were made for the transgender and 15 institutes for gypsies while 22,000 new students were enrolled. 1300 literacy centres in total were set up by the literacy department in various backward areas of the province; over 400,000 deserving male and female children (till then) were getting primary as well as technical education in those centres.

As per media reports dated 28th December 2019, The National Commission for Human Development [NCHD] had established 2,000 literacy centres in all provinces including Gilgit-Baltistan and Azad Jammu & Kashmir [AJK] to increase literacy rate in the country. To mainstream seminaries in line with the modern curriculum, 100 schools were also established with 100 teachers which enrolled 3,142 students, recognizing the fact that adult literacy was the key to improve standard of living.

The NCHD had set up these adult literacy centres in local communities providing basic literacy skills to the individuals (especially women) between the age group of 11-45, who were either never enrolled before or dropped out. The syllabus and textbooks of those centres were designed for easy learning and functionality, while communities were mobilised to provide space and appointed educated youth of the area particularly women to join those centres.

On 31st December 2019: A new model of ***non-formal education*** that combines literacy & labour and market skills for illiterate children and youth was developed and launched as pilot project in selected districts of Punjab and Sindh provinces with the World Bank [WB] assistance. WB had agreed to provide $2.73 million for the pilot project, which was expected to be implemented in partnership with the Sanjh Preet Organisation [SPO] — a Lahore-based non-governmental organisation [NGO] — which had, till then, implemented 34 different projects nationwide in partnership with public, non-public, academic and international agencies and organisations, including Japan International Cooperation Agency [JICA], UNICEF and USAID.

> [*The project was designed to deliver two core services to the beneficiaries:* <u>*accelerated learning programs for out-of-school children of primary and secondary school age*</u>*, and* <u>*integrated literacy and skills program for illiterate adolescents and young adults*</u>*.*
>
> *These programs were to be delivered through* **Community Learning Centres** *[CLCs] with direct involvement of communities; offering various programs to beneficiaries in different age groups based on the community's needs and decisions – to provide support functions to the beneficiaries, including counselling and moral support to them and day-care services for beneficiaries with young children.*]

However, such facilities were open to the risks of kidnapping, abuse and accidents, thus additional security requirements of a requisite standard were required: advised the WB.

Punjab had lower rate of poverty and the highest human development index (HDI) in Pakistan. Social and economic deprivation, as reflected in the health and education outcomes and household income, was highest in the southern Punjab districts. Sindh was the second-largest province in terms of population and the second-largest economy due to Karachi, it had the second-highest HDI in Pakistan. In Sindh the social and economic deprivation in terms of health and education outcomes and household income was quite high; mostly because the PPP in power there since 15 years had given zero attention towards the RURAL Sindh, even LARKANA couldn't get face.

On 6th March 2020: The media reports divulged that the PTI govt could ensure free education and health for the people of the province in 10 years if subsidy being given to Metro Bus and amount spent on Orange Line Train projects were withdrawn. Without subsidy the Orange Line Train ticket would be of Rs:287 as per its calculations. The said media reports were based on launching of the *Punjab Literacy and Non-Formal Basic Education (NFBE) policy 2019* in Lahore.

The new policy aimed to provide access to education in remote and far-flung areas; the PTI govt was determined *to achieve 100pc literacy rate in the province by 2030* to fulfil the constitutional commitments under articles 37B and 25A. The main purpose of the policy was to ensure the alignment and integration with provincial and national constitutional and legal obligations and international commitments for better service. PTI was proud to launch the **first-ever** literacy and non-formal education policy 2019.

TELE-SCHOOL — A DEDICATED TV CHANNEL:

On 14th April 2020: PM Imran Khan inaugurated a national broadcast education channel to mitigate the loss faced by the students due to the closure of educational institutions (till 31st May then) in the wake of Covid-19.

Tele-school — the dedicated TV channel — was aired through a beam provided by Pakistan Television [PTV] the next day across the country from 8am to 6pm for online education from class one to 12. The tele-school was able to help students learn during the closure of schools; including students of far-flung and remote areas, which didn't have access to education facilities and infrastructure otherwise. Pakistan had a large number of out-of-school children (OOSC), the initiative helped the govt to help them. The project was highly productive in the given circumstances because no one could predict when Covid-19 would be eliminated; it could take many months to go.

PM Khan was of the opinion that this project should continue even after the pandemic was over and reopening of schools; it would help promote education in remote areas of the country. Adult literacy could also be promoted through this project. The education ministry was also mulling to develop an app to benefit over 20 million out-of-school children and promote adult literacy. Pakistan had just 60pc literacy rate then thus the education ministry was trying to link education with technology so that adults who wanted to learn had access to education through mobile phones.

> "The literacy rate is higher in urban areas (74pc) than in rural areas (51pc). Province-wise analysis suggests that Punjab has the highest literacy rate with 64pc followed by Sindh and Khyber PK (minus ex-FATA areas) with 57pc, Khyber PK (including merged areas) with 55pc and Baluchistan with 40pc" – **Pakistan govt's Social Survey for 2018-19** at daily **DAWN** dated 14th June 2020 is referred.

The dedicated TV channel, *Tele-school*, was available on satellite, terrestrial and cable networks so that it would be accessible to most parts of the country, including hard-to-reach remote areas, ensuring equity in learning; the ministry initially inked an agreement with PTV for three months, but the PM expressed his desire for the project's continuation beyond that.

During that process, online content was developed in accordance with country's curriculum and it was made attractive for students. '<u>The credit of making that project possible in less than a month goes to unsung heroes: content developers, teachers and staff of Federal Directorate of Education, editors, technicians and producers of Allama Iqbal Open University and PTV</u> - HATS OFF TO ALL OF THEM FOR THEIR NATIONALIST APPROACH.'

On 9th January 2021: The Punjab Literacy Department launched **'ADOPT A SCHOOL PROGRAM'** under its initiative of '<u>Friends of Literacy and Non-Formal Schools</u>' in 36 districts of the province. As the initiative had been planned keeping in view the Covid-19 scenario, it also included provision of face masks, hand sanitizers, soaps, besides free stationary to the students, mainly belonging to the poor segments of society. It was designed to make up the funds-shortage being faced by the literacy department that didn't have additional financial resources for provision of such facilities to the students and teachers of non-formal schools across the province.

> [*Till then, as per official figures, 428,000 students had been enrolled in around 13,519 non-formal schools in Punjab, with each school having one teacher, functioning under the literacy department. The Punjab government had allocated around Rs:515 million annual budget for the department to be mainly spent on the teacher's (then) monthly Rs:7,000 stipend, and the school's utility bills.*]

As per approved plan of the initiative's implementation, sponsors were to be engaged for adoption of those schools. A sponsor / donor, approved by the District Education Officer (DEO-literacy), could adopt a school in his / her native district by contributing at least Rs:2,500 to 3,000 per month for stationary and Covid protection items, besides a one-time donation of Rs:33,000 to Rs:35,000 for the provision of bags, clothes and stationery for the students to a school; under a written agreement for a year at least.

Directions were issued to all the DEOs across the province to launch a campaign for the plan, whereas the Deputy Commissioners concerned were asked to patronise it by engaging local philanthropists for the initiative; International Non-Government Organisations (INGOs) or local NGOs were also allowed to adopt such non-formal schools after getting a no-objection certificate (NOC) from the home department.

On 23rd January 2021: The Punjab's Ministry for literacy confirmed that:

> '*...the govt has provided all necessary resources to achieve 100pc literacy rate in the province. In addition, transgender individuals have also been provided facilities for education for the first time as part of the adult literacy program. Purposeful efforts to increase literacy rates are being made with education as well as remedial training being imparted to citizens serving sentences for various crimes in prisons."*

The PTI govt seemed to be committed to play a practical role in the process of national reconstruction by giving the *first-ever literacy policy*. The literacy department was made fully functional while reviewing the progress on adult education facilities and other projects in informal schools, jails and social welfare centres in various cities of Punjab province.

On 14th June 2021: The *Punjab govt allocated Rs:442 billion for education* in the financial year 2021-22 with an increase of 13pc from the previous year; while proposing Rs:54.22bn for development expenditure and Rs:388bn for current expenses making spending on education - 17pc of the total Punjab budget. Out of Rs:54.22bn development outlay, Rs:33bn were set aside for school education, Rs:15.065bn for higher education, Rs:755 million for special education; Rs:2.9bn for literacy & non-formal education.

To achieve maximum literacy rate, **INSAF SCHOOL-UPGRADE PROGRAM** was also launched and during the year 25pc of primary schools (8,360) were being given the status of elementary schools and around 40pc of those schools were situated in south Punjab.

> On 10th November 2021: In Punjab, Minister for Literacy and Non-formal Basic Education Raja Rashid Hafeez inaugurated *NFE Curriculum Punjab 2021 Accelerated Learning Program – Primary-scale;* the primary literacy program was to be conducted in formal schools in two and a half years only. The said accelerated program was especially designed for the education and training of the youth who had been deprived of education for any reason and they had not been admitted to a school due to their overage. The program was formulated on a very comprehensive, complete and concise pattern under single national curriculum so that they could complete it in less time. Skills such as citizenship, tolerance, peace and harmony were included in syllabus; and new textbooks, training system, examination and certification system was to be developed according to the accelerated curriculum.

On 25th January 2022: In Khyber PK, the **EARLY AGE PROGRAM** was kicked off to impart digital literacy education to students in the province. In the first phase - 336 schools, in the second phase - 510, and in the third phase - 324 schools were selected to start the **DIGITAL LITERACY PROGRAM**. Class 6 were to be taught subjects like basic digital literacy, problem solving and algorithms and class 7 were to be taught: MS office, web literacy, MIT scratch & Mobirise, while class 8 were to be taught app inverter, social media ethics, monetization & land commercialization – what a wonderfull change it was launched – highly appreciable move it was.

The Minister for Literacy said that it was the vision of KP government to provide maximum IT training to students and the project was initiated at school level. Khyber PK's Information Technology Board and Elementary & Secondary Education Department extended the project to maximum schools across the province. The said programming was to prepare students for coming times; it was fascinating to see the children of public sector schools learning how to invent apps and code from an early age.

PTI ON HEALTH & HOSPITALS:

PM Imran Khan and its PTI, in its manifesto, had stated that '*...it will build state-of-the-art hospitals in major urban centres to ensure the best healthcare facilities for the poor*'.

On 28th October 2018: while following the above pursuit, Federal Health Minister reiterated that PTI govt was taking revolutionary steps for promoting health sector; FOUR new hospitals being established in Islamabad. On 22nd November 2018: A new hospital was to be established in Rawalpindi. On 26th November 2018, PTI's Dr Yasmeen Rashid announced to open three childcare hospitals in south Punjab; next day, PTI announced to build and open Rehab hospital in Peshawar for ice addicts. On 12th December 2018, the PTI government decided to establish the first state-of-the-art cancer hospital in Islamabad. On 29th December 2018, a free kidney dialysis unit was inaugurated in Islamabad. On 12th January, 2019: the federal minister announced that the Federal Government Hospital in Chak Shahzad would be upgraded into a modern facility with the cutting-edge equipment.

In an expansion mode of **HEALTH INSURANCE SCHEME** first launched by the KP government, PM Khan's government expanded the *Sehat Sahulat Program* at the national level and on 4th February 2019, Prime Minister himself launched the nationwide **Sehat Insaf Card**, which was to provide free medical treatment to approximately 80 million people.

The project was successfully launched in Punjab province; Khyber PK province was already enjoying it but Sindh provincial govt didn't consider it suitable for its populace. Perhaps the biggest highlight of the project came when the prime minister, on 28th October 2020, said UNIVERSAL HEALTH COVERAGE would be offered to everyone in Punjab and KP within a year. Khyber KP, meanwhile, had already offered health cards to every citizen; within three months Punjab followed the suit; in Dec 2020, the health card facility was also launched *for 1.2m families in Azad Jammu and Kashmir.*

On 11th May 2019: Construction of Mother and Child Hospital in Rawalpindi resumed; this 400 beds Child Hospital had been under construction on the Asghar Mall Road since last decade. Work on the hospital worth Rs:2.5 billion was inaugurated by former PM Shaukat Aziz in 2006 but the project was halted after the PMLN formed the government in Punjab in 2008. A nursing school was also to be established as well as a Chest Disease Centre for TB and breast cancer patients under that scheme.

On 9th July 2019: Work started on an eye hospital in Gujrat; on 20th July 2019, foundation stone was laid for a hospital in Nowshera, Khyber PK; on 21st July 2019, announcement was made to set up a cardiology hospital in Quetta with the help of UAE government for which negotiations were on at state leve. On 25th July 2019: Khyber PK govt announced to spend Rs100 million on the Oghi Tehsil HQ Hospital in Mansehra. On 17th October 2019, the CM Punjab announced that 200-bed Jinnah Institute of Cardiology would be established in Lahore; on 30th October 2019, Punjab Health Minister Dr Yasmin Rashid said that a 500-bed teaching hospital would be constructed in Sialkot.

> [**On 27th May 2022:** *The Cardialogy Hospital, later titled as* Sheikh Muhammad Bin Zayed *Al Nehan Institute of Cardiology at Quetta became operational with the support of the United Arab Emirates (UAE).* **Work on this Cardiac hospital had started in 2019 during PM Imran Khan's regime.** *In a short span of two years, the construction of this state-of-the-art hospital was completed. This 132-bed hospital provides the people of Balochistan with the best treatment facilities for all heart diseases at their doorstep.*]

On 1st February 2021, the premier Mr Khan congratulated Khyber KP province for becoming the first province to provide universal health coverage to all its residents. The *Sehat Insaf Card* was also announced in Islamabad, Gilgit Baltistan, tribal districts of KP and Sindh's Tharparkar district. The Tharparkar centres of the facility, however, were closed due to financial constraints of the Sindh government.

Over the PTI's three years+ tenure, the government awarded extension of coverage of the health card to journalists, Islamabad police, the transgender community, overseas labourers and persons with disabilities. Initially some part of Punjab and the whole of Balochistan couldn't be covered by this scheme. Despite PTI govt's best and perpetual efforts, that *promise of Imran Khan remained in progress till his departure in April 2022 because of the project's enormous volume – BUT it was definitely a positive step towards the perfect socio-economic system for a poor country like Pakistan.*

Scenario 257

100 DAYS OF PM KHAN's (PERFORMANCE)-III

Prime Minister Imran Khan announced, while in Karachi <u>on 2nd February 2019</u>, that a university would be built in Hyderabad and reverse osmosis plants would be installed in areas of Tharparkar; he had already announced a health package for Sindh, under which as many as 112,000 families were listed to get *Insaf Health Cards* – what was the final fate of those announcements, but Sindh govt didn't agree to the scheme.

'We want to make Karachi the urban jewel of Pakistan,' the PTI stated in its manifesto, while announcing a number of steps towards transforming the metropolis. Among the party's commitments was to improve the capacity of <u>Karachi's mass transit system</u>, <u>develop a desalination plant</u>, <u>provide clean drinking water</u> and <u>crackdown against the city's water mafia</u>. During a visit to Karachi <u>on 30th March 2019</u>, PM Imran announced a Rs:162bn development project for the city. Of the 18 proposed projects, 10 were related to the development of the public transport network in Karachi and seven to the water and sewerage infrastructure.

On 5th September 2020; the premier Imran Khan unveiled a Rs:1.1 trillion package for Karachi's transformation. He visited the metropolis a week earlier and reviewed progress on five of those projects, which were a part of the Karachi Transformation Plan. *But despite all the rhetoric, the PTI government, which won a sizeable mandate from the port city, had yet to deliver on many of its promises that they had campaigned before coming into power.* <u>Mr Khan was often seen upset due to ineffectiveness, ineptitude and incompetence of PTI's team at Karachi</u>. See below….

On 28th September 2019; the schemes and system were so corrupt that when one PTI Minister Zaidi took the initiative of cleaning six major nullahs of the city it came to his knowledge that most of the *'kachra kundis were sold'* and it was a big business. But the most startling disclosure made by the minister was related to the cost of removing garbage from city areas to earth-filled site. When he awarded contract of cleaning major city nullahs to the FWO (Frontier Works Organisation), the per tonne cost was $6.5 only. Behria Town Karachi, when contacted to give quotation for garbage removal, also quoted price at $6.5 per tonne.....

> *However, according to Fed Minister Zaidi, had the garbage first removed to garbage transit stations for drying purpose and then to earth-filled site the cost was $10 per tonne. But the Sindh government's cost for removing garbage stood as high as $28 per tonne – so massive corruption there was.*

The federal minister had observed that out of two weighing machines at the earth-filled site only one was working and each truck on an average carried a load of 35-40 tonnes of garbage. He further said that one truck at the earth-filled site was recorded for four trips a day and it was how public moneys were being burgleed and looted, allegedly by PPP & bureaucracy.

MASS-TRANSIT SYSTEM (MAS) IN KARACHI:

For Karachi, the PTI, in its manifesto, said that '...*it will transform and massively enhance the capacity of Karachi's mass transit system by leveraging on public and private financing* at the earliest possible time.

The fancy story of Karachi in the PTI era starts from 6th October 2018 when Sindh Governor Imran Ismail said local train and circular railway would soon be launched in the city; Railway Minister Sh Rashid made announcement [for these schemes] on 16th October instant in Karachi - the governor was addressing the Karachi Chamber of Commerce and Industry [KCCI]. The local rail service could be operated on the main line from Landhi to Cantonment station; tenders had been issued for the procurement of fire engines; a water desalination plant was be set up at Karachi Port..... **then there was a series of PROMISES from various organs of the PTI** – people were anxious to know when the projects get start.

On 11th February 2019: PM Khan was set to announce package for Karachi; President assured CM Sindh of early completion of federal projects in the province; on 26th March 2019: PM Khan was scheduled to launch mostly Centre-funded projects in the city till September (2019); **but the progress remained confined to the briefings & meetings only.**

In between, on 30th March 2019, PM Imran Khan announced a Rs:162 billion development packages for Karachi, which included grants for 18 projects focusing on *priority areas like transportation and water provision*. Out of the 18 proposed projects, 10 were related to the development of the public transport network in the city. Seven other projects were related to the water and sewerage infrastructure. The premier also said that while a master plan for Karachi was essential, an interim plan for the city would be put in place to address the pressing challenges that the metropolis was facing. Also, that further horizontal expansion of the city must be stopped and the slum areas of the city would be developed.

On 27th August 2019: PTI's federal govt cleared six more development projects worth Rs:*218.5 billion, including two **Karachi-based mass transit projects*** funded by international creditors. The Central Development Working Party [CDWP] approved two projects worth Rs:3.33 billion and recommended four schemes costing Rs:215.2 billion to the Executive Committee of National Economic Council (ECNEC) for approval. (*The CDWP had deferred approval for six projects, mostly belonging to other provinces, including a Gwadar project.*) The authority **had taken up two mass transit schemes of Karachi for the second time in the past four months.** It recommended the Asian Development Bank-funded Bus Rapid Transit - Red Line - to ECNEC for approval at a cost of Rs:78.6 billion. However, the World Bank-funded Karachi Urban Mobility project - *Yellow Line* - was conditionally referred to ECNEC at a cost of Rs:61.5 billion.

> The PTI govt had also set up the **NATIONAL DEVELOPMENT COUNCIL**, *which was parallel to NEC, but it didn't possess constitutional cover – thus as exercise in futile*. No one knows who was the mastermind ADVISOR or bureaucrat behind it.

Cost of the *Red Line project* increased nearly double due to currency depreciation; originally it had been estimated at Rs:65.6 billion. When it actually started in year 2021, the total Project cost re-calculated was USD 503.2 million and co-financed by ADB (USD 235 million), AFD (USD 71.8 million), GCF (USD 49 million), GoS (USD 75.6 million) and AIIB (USD 71.8 million). The loan became effective on 13th April 2021 and the Project was still progressing – till May 2022 at least, when PM Imran Khan left the reins.

The project was originally expected to facilitate 300,000 commuters every day. However, with further additions and re-routing, the *Karachi*

Bus Rapid Transit Red Line project could provide a 26.6km corridor and associated facilities benefiting 1.5 million people (10% of Karachi's population) who lived within a kilometre of a Red Line station.

The World Bank had approved $382 million for construction of a **21km long yellow corridor** in Karachi. ***Karachi Yellow Line project*** needed Rs:1.7 billion annual operational subsidies. In May 2019, the CDWP had also considered the Yellow Line project for approval; however, recommended the project subject to the condition that its cost and scope should be rationalised.

The CDWP had also given directives for operationalising the ***Green Line Karachi project*** and integrating all mass transit schemes in the city under one mass transit authority for operation and maintenance purposes but the government of Sindh did not give response to those observations. However, on 28th September 2019, just four weeks after the announcement of PM Khan's Karachi-Package worth Rs:162 billion, PTI's one Federal Minister Syed Ali Zaidi, while speaking at a seminar organised by the FPCCI, said that:

> "...funds from the Karachi package of Rs:162 billion recently announced by Prime Minister Imran Khan would only be released after adopting a financial discipline and monitoring policy."

On 7th October 2019: PTI's govt at Islamabad earmarked 1st bundle of Rs:16 billion for 44 ongoing and new development projects executed through the federal Public Sector Development Program [PSDP] for metropolitan city of Karachi for the on-going fiscal year 2019-20. It was titled as Prime Minister Package but development of the city remained neglected from so many years owing to political cum administrative lapses. That Karachi package included five projects with estimated cost of Rs:35.206 billion out of which the required funding of Rs:9.369 billion was to complete the ongoing projects.

> [On 29th November 2019; ONE MORE HIGHLIGHT FROM PTI appeared - the Asian Development Bank [ADB]-funded ***Red Line Bus Rapid Transit*** [BRT] project (a 26.6 km corridor joining Model Colony and Numaish), **was the <u>world's first zero-emission</u> mass transit service.**]

The mentionable project, in fact, was ***Green Line Bus Rapid Transit System*** [BRTS] but it couldn't get the needed priority – thus only meagre funding as there were four new projects under the said package with estimated cost of Rs:11.898 billion. The official data showed that total number of ongoing and new development projects for Karachi stood at 44, including 29 ongoing project and 15 new projects with estimated cost of Rs:106 billion; till then, the expenditures incurred on ongoing 29 projects stood at Rs:56 billion and the PTI govt could allocate Rs:16 billion only due to non-availability of funds in the national kitty. Another reason for neglecting BRTS remained that its cost then stood at Rs:24.604 billion out of which the system had already utilized Rs:21.166 billion; thus, the Federal Govt allocated Rs:2 billion only in that on-going fiscal year – but then *held it non-functional for dubious reasons* – then again revived it on 22nd January 2020.

PTI govt, the fact remains, decided to revive the $2b for *Karachi Circular Railway* [KCR] *project* and directed EAD, then headed by Asad Umar, for implementation mechanism and framework agreement under CPEC. The meeting, comprising of federal secretaries of relevant ministries, discussed various issues hampering the implementation of KCR project as indicated by the government of Sindh. That day, Federal Minister Asad Umar was given a detailed briefing on the project; that PC-I of KCR project was approved in October 2017 by the ECNEC at the total cost of $1,971 million; however, no progress could be made because no lender had agreed to feed the said project neither in PMLN regime nor in the PTI govt. He confirmed that the federal govt was fully committed to support the KCR project for its expeditious implementation in consultation with the Chinese side. The minister directed Planning Division and EAD to immediately initiate work for finalising the implementation mechanism with the Chinese side.

Referring to daily **The Nation** dated 23rd January 2020:

> *"...that since the project of Karachi Circular Railway (KCR) was delayed for almost two and a half years therefore the existing feasibility need to be revisited. Feasibility of Karachi Circular Railways was completed in May 2017 and it needs to be updated. Similarly, the cost of the scheme also requires re-evaluation. The provincial government of Sindh will re-submit an updated feasibility study of the project."*

Later, the 7th Joint Cooperation Committee (JCC) of the CPEC had agreed in principle for inclusion of *Mass Transit System Karachi* as part of CPEC component and tasked Transport Working Group to work on the projects. *However, no implementation mechanism could be finalized during past two and a half years for the execution of KCR project.*

Once more, the matter went into pending phase for re-negotiations with China for final approval.

> [*The key-point was that KCR's total length was made around 50 km and it included the revival and transformation of the old Karachi Circular Railway (KCR) into a mass transit system.*]

On 19th June 2020: The Asian Development Bank [ADB] inked $235 million loan agreement with the federal govt for the development of **_Bus Rapid Transit (BRT) system_** in Karachi; the loan was initially approved by the bank in July 2019. The project, developed in partnership with the Transport and Mass-Transit Department of the Sindh govt, was all set for fast-track implementation with the start of procurement activities for civil works. Little details from the accord:

> [*The Project will restructure the entire width of the Red Line BRT corridor, including the construction of 29 stations and dedicated lanes along the 26.6km stretch; improvement of the mixed-traffic roadway with up to six lanes in each direction; inclusion of on-street parking and landscaped green areas in various locations; improvement of the drainage system to make the corridor climate-proof; and installation of bicycle lanes, improved sidewalks, and energy-efficient street lights.*
>
> *In addition, the ADB will also administer a $100 million loan from the Asian Infrastructure Investment Bank (AIIB), a $100 million loan from Agence Francaise de Development (AFD), a $37.2 million loan and a $49 million grant from the Green Climate Fund (GCF) to finance climate change adaptation and mitigation measures.*
>
> *Meanwhile, the PTI govt brought another promise for the nation to introduce **electric buses in Karachi & Islamabad**.*]

(Press conference of Federal Minister Fawad Chaudhry dated 4th October 2020 at Karachi is referred.)

KARACHI CIRCULAR RAILWAY:

On 19th November 2020: Karachi Circular Railway [KCR] **_started partial operations_** on a 14km cleared stretch of around 55km route of the old KCR; it was on Karachi City-Orangi-Karachi City route and the rail-pass was made available for Rs:750 (then).

[*Opened in 1964, the route of the old KCR started from Drigh Road and ended in downtown Karachi. It ceased operations in 1999 after suffering huge losses for years.*]

In the first phase four trains were to run daily from Pipri to City Station. It was a success because there was a huge land mafia on the KCR tracks and the Sindh government knew it. Railway's Federal Minister Sh Rashid held:

"In 25 years, the land mafia has taken over the KCR tracks. We are making efforts ... We are fully cooperating with the Sindh government. They have started work on sewerage lines; they have [issued tenders] for over-bridges. As more bridges keep coming, we will increase the KCR [tracks]. We are going to do lots of work in railways and will completely modernise [the KCR] within a year.

About the cost of the project: One coach cost Rs:9 million and 40 coaches have been refurbished. Around Rs:1.8 billion has been allocated of which Rs:17m has been spent so far."

Earlier, on 25th September 2020, the Supreme Court of Pakistan [SCP] had cautioned the Sindh govt as well as the Pakistan Railways *not to exceed the timeline prescribed by it for revival of the Karachi Circular Railway* (KCR). When a 3-judge SCP bench, headed by Chief Justice Gulzar Ahmed, took up a *suo motu* case, it was informed that the Frontier Works Organisation [FWO] had proposed the construction of underpasses and overhead bridges for smooth running of trains on KCR route.

The SCP had proposed in February 2020 that work on revival of the KCR should commence within six months. The SCP was informed that survey for the construction of 11 underpasses had been completed by the FWO while the remaining 13 would be completed soon. Planning had been done while designing work was in progress, the court was informed. During the hearing, the Railways Secretary assured the court that no impediment had been created by the Sindh government and work was in progress day and night to start running trains on the route within the timeline agreed upon. The Sindh government had also taken a number of steps to remove the encroachments on both sides of railway track.

On 14th February 2021: Federal Minister for Planning & Development Asad Umar was seen still in promising mode while assuring Karachiites that the Green Line bus project would kick off operations by August

(2021) and a prototype bus for the purpose would soon be ready. He criticised the provincial government for '*not empowering the civic bodies as it should*'.

As per PTI's claims, the federation was working beyond its responsibility to give Karachi its due rights; also, that work was underway to implement the *Karachi Transformation Plan though couldn't see the dawn during the PTI regime at least.* The ruling govt had given another deadline for opening of the *Green Line Bus Rapid Transit System* (BRTS) project in July-August (2021)– it proved to be a distant dream for Karachiites who were waiting for the project's completion ever since its ground breaking was performed by former PM Nawaz Sharif on 16th February 2016.

However, shifting deadlines were not new for the people of Karachi who badly needed a proper mass transit system in their city; originally the said project was to be completed by the end of 2017. When it was inaugurated in Feb 2016, the estimated cost was Rs:16.85 billion. Later, the project was extended by another 10 kms as initially sought by the Sindh government and the estimated cost jumped to Rs:24bn. The Transport Crisis, a media report highlighted the sorry state of the public transport sector of the country's largest city, which was (and still it is) on the verge of collapse due to its history of failure, negligence, inefficiency and lack of follow-through in both government and public-private partnership projects.

Once more, the PTI's federal minister [Mr Asad Umar], on 22nd March 2021, set deadlines to put into operation two mega transport projects in Karachi — the Rs:300 billion **Karachi Circular Railway** [KCR] and Rs:25bn **Green Line Bus Rapid Transport** — later that year. The Planning ministry in a statement said that:

> '...*the deadline for signing of first package (A) of the Integrated Transport System (ITS) contract has been set as 26th March, followed by package B contract signing on April 2. The deadline for award of operational and maintenance contract for the project would be given by May this year (2021)*'.

While presiding over a meeting of the stakeholders —the federal minister Railways confirmed that the prototype buses would be ready for testing and commissioning by *25th April (2021)*. It was mutually agreed that the projects would be initiated in Public Private Partnership / Build-Operate and Transfer [BOT] modes. Mr Umar directed that the Green Line BRT should be operational by August 2021. A ray of hope, however, emerged on 18th September 2021 for the Karachiites when the first consignment of 40 buses for the Green Line bus rapid transit system (BRTS) reached the city; and the PTI felt little satisfied *'terming it another milestone'*. The second consignment of 40 more buses was expected to reach Karachi within next month then.

Federal minister Asad Umar said at the Green Line fleet arrival ceremony that a comprehensive Command and Control Centre had been established for transport projects including Green Line, Orange Line, and others. A bus depot was built for 80 buses, while 22 bus stations were constructed as part of the project. Finally, the service line was inaugurated on 10th December 2021 by PM Imran Khan himself – and the Karachi-residents were able to see the plans of 2017 coming true in ending 2021.

On 25th January 2022: PTI government approved the transaction structure and project proposal for the construction and operation of *Karachi Circular Railway* (KCR) on public-private mode at an estimated cost of about Rs:220bn. Under the transaction structure approved by the board of Public-Private Partnership Authority (PPPA), the private sector could finance, develop and run the project on commercial lines; the meeting was presided over by Minister Asad Umar.

The project cost was initially estimated at Rs:201bn excluding Rs:20.7bn worth of loop section to avoid 22 crossings already under implementation. The board also decided that based on revised cost estimates, the federal govt would finance 40pc that would work out at about Rs:80-90bn and provide this financing to the concessionaire at the outset (first three years) to help operationalise the project. Also, that the railway board would be asked to lease out for 99 years 13 properties en-route the KCR project to meet the initial financing. In the project, the private sector was made responsible to finance the construction of the civil works, electrical & mechanical (E&M) component including procurement of rolling stock and operations & maintenance (O&M) of the project from its own resources.

AND **on 10th February 2022:** The Central Development Working Party [CDWP] cleared all the three development projects with a cumulative estimated cost of about Rs:280 billion, including the *Karachi Circular Railway* (KCR). The Planning Commission had finalised the projects at Rs:273.071bn the cost of KCR as a modern urban railway project and requested the Executive Committee of the National Economic Council (ECNEC) to approve its implementation by the Public-Private Partnership

Authority (PPPA) on a build-operate-transfer [BOT] basis. The 43-km dual track of the *Urban Rail Mass Transit System* was going to be constructed in a period of three years on PPP basis. The plan expected to deploy the use of electric trains and keeping them operational round the week. The project involved 30 stations along the corridor covering the most densely populated areas of Karachi.

WATER FOR KARACHI...   *blame game and delays

On 16th September 2018: While paying first visit to Karachi after winning elections of 25th July 2018, Prime Minister Imran had announced the installation of a desalination plant for Karachi on his maiden visit. On 21st October 2019, the premier again urged the contracted firm to expedite work. The PTI had also vowed to crackdown against the water mafia in the city. Meanwhile, the federal government started working on the Greater Karachi Water Supply Scheme (K-IV), which had plans to supply 260 million gallons per day of water to Karachi in phase one. The said project was originally being handled by the Sindh government.

On 7th October 2019: For the above mentioned Water Supply Scheme (K-IV), the total cost was standing at Rs:12.755 billion out of which the incurred expenditures stood at Rs:9.598 billion till 30th June 2019. The federal government then allocated Rs:800 million afresh for that fiscal year in the PSDP against throw forward of Rs:3.157 billion. Under an arrangement with the provincial government, the federal government took up the implementation of the project as part of the prime minister's package for Karachi and directed the Water & Power Development Authority to take over the implementation responsibilities of the scheme. In June 2020, the Centre blamed the PPP-led provincial government for delays with the project.

On 5th September 2020: PM Imran Khan re-affirmed his promises over which no mentionable achievement was seen till then and the *Karachiites* were going furious. He unveiled a historic financial package worth Rs:1.1 trillion for Karachi's transformation that was to address the chronic municipal and infrastructure issues of the country's financial hub. The *city's drainage and sewerage issues* were brought into national focus a month earlier after record-breaking monsoon rains caused widespread devastation and left dozens of dead.

The premier told media that the federal and Sindh governments had decided to deal with Karachi's problems together; both were contributing to the Rs:1100 billion package. In a statement, the PPP chairperson Bilawal Zardari told that out of the Rs1.1 trillion, the federal government had allocated Rs:300 billion while the Sindh government committed more than Rs:800 billion. The transformation plan was to be implemented through the Provincial Coordination Implementation Committee (PCIC) under the chief minister Sindh AND with the active help of the Pak-army.

The first problem the plan could address was identified as the Greater Karachi Water Supply Scheme - called K-IV. The second problem was of encroachments on nullahs on which the National Disaster Management Authority (NDMA) had already started work. The third and fourth issues that the plan was to be focused on were the city's sewerage system and solid waste disposal. PTI's Minister for Planning, Development and Special Initiatives Asad Umar said K-IV, the modern Karachi Circular Railway (KCR) and freight corridor projects' construction would start within the same fiscal year. That fiscal year had ended and yet, the citizens of Karachi were found waiting for the promises to materialize.

> *Work on promises to end Karachi's water mafia and the development of a desalination plant in the metropolis for clean drinking water had NEVER STARTED, in fact – neither by PPP's 15 years governance on Sindh nor by the PTI's central command for about THREE years.*

FOCUS ON OVERSEAS PAKISTANIS:

PM Imran Khan, during his election campaign, had vowed to ensure a greater stake for overseas Pakistanis. Among a number of goals set to achieve this promise was ensuring voting rights for overseas Pakistanis and developing financial instruments that could create attractive investment opportunities for them in their native homeland.

On 17th August 2018; a day before Imran Khan took oath as premier, the Supreme Court of Pakistan [SCP] ruled a landmark decision allowing *overseas Pakistanis the right to vote* via an internet system. The court had been hearing a petition filed by Mr Khan who had long sought voting rights for Pakistanis abroad, with his party enjoying a large following amongst the diaspora. Overseas Pakistanis were able to avail this right during the by-elections scheduled on 14th October 2018 for 37 constituencies.

Just after a month, the formal notifications were in place; overseas Pakistanis were given the opportunity to vote for the first time in

Pakistan's electoral history. This was duly regulated by the Election Commission of Pakistan [ECP] on the basis of the SCP's order. The ruling party PTI, meanwhile, was also pushing for the use of Electronic Voting Machines [EVMs]. However, PM Khan was disappointed due to traditional lethargic attitudes of the overseas Pakistani community. Here are the details:

> "...the campaign to register overseas Pakistanis for internet-voting in the upcoming by-polls evoked a lukewarm response, with only 7,419 expatriates out of the total 632,000 registered to avail the facility offered to them - first time in the country's electoral history."

The process of registration of overseas Pakistanis from the 37 constituencies where by-elections were to be held on 14th October 2018 had started on 1st September and came to a close after 30 days. As per press statement released by the Election Commission of Pakistan [ECP], the website for the overseas voters remained functional 24/7 throughout the registration process and did not face any technical problems.

The ECP said only voters holding national identity card for overseas Pakistanis (NICOP) or machine-readable passports [MRPs] were able to register to vote. This way, as many as 632,000 overseas Pakistanis from the 37 constituencies settled in 177 countries of the world were eligible to vote through the internet. Under the plan, over 7,400 registered voters were sent voter pass (password) between 10th Oct and 14th Oct on the email address mentioned in their online application for registration, through which they were able to cast their votes on election day. Casting one's vote was quite simple as they usually do in their respective foreign countries. Upon successful submission of the vote, a confirmation message was displayed on the screen.

The ECP had also uploaded on its website separate video tutorials in Urdu and English languages as well as step-by-step help materials to guide voters through the registration and voting process. An advertisement campaign had also been launched through media to create awareness about the facility of internet voting made available for the overseas Pakistanis; the embassies and consulates of Pakistan had also been involved in the campaign.

The complete procedure had been defined by the ECP after being ordered by the Supreme Court to provide internet voting facility to the overseas Pakistanis for the upcoming by-polls. After two major opposition parties criticised ECP for what they called a hasty move but the ECP was satisfied with its progressive adoption. The ECP had advised the said political parties to hail the initiative which was a landmark innovation in Pakistan's voting system.

On 31st January 2019; the premier launched the **Pakistan Banao Certificate** — a dollar-denominated diaspora bond aimed at attracting investment from overseas Pakistanis to help strengthen the national economy. The State Bank of Pakistan (SBP) had also launched the **Roshan Digital Account** (RDA) for non-resident Pakistanis to enable them to remotely open bank accounts in the country through online digital branches without physically visiting banks. By the end of July 2021, the inflows through RDA had reached $1.87billion (*during July 2021 the remittances reached $1869 million*) – very encouraging it was; **daily DAWN** dated 6th August 2021 is referred for more details.

In November 2020, the SBP launched a savings scheme — the **Naya Pakistan Certificate** — offering significantly higher interest rates compared to those prevailing in most of the developed and developing economies. Facilitating overseas Pakistanis, PM Imran's government also provided incentives such as tax exemptions and simplified biometric verification. Investments in property, tourism and the construction sector were also encouraged. *This makes it one of the significant promises that were completed by the government.*

On 10th June 2021; the Elections (Amendment) Bill 2020 was passed by the National Assembly amid the opposition's outcry. It was then tabled in the upper house on 16th Oct that year wherein PM Khan's party emphasized the need to grant overseas Pakistanis the right to vote before next elections in 2023. In order to attract investment from overseas Pakistanis, the PTI introduced a number of projects that focused specifically on the promise of attracting overseas investments.

10bn TREE TSUNAMI – CLIMATE CHANGE:

Addressing a tree plantation ceremony on 27th May 2021 at Haripur, Khyber PK, Prime Minister Imran Khan held that Pakistan was unfortunately among the 10 countries worst hit by climate change and global warming would play harmful impact on coming generations if the current trends were not reversed. *'The PTI government is, however, utilising its best efforts to slow down and reverse the harmful impacts of climate change,'* he said. This was in line with the documented commitments of the PTI, which promised to **'tackle climate change and champion green growth'**.

One of the hallmark projects of the PTI government during three years tenure had been the **10 BILLION TREE TSUNAMI** drive, which was expanded from the Billion Tree Tsunami project launched in KP in 2015. Under that program, seasonal plantation drives were held in various parts of the country, with the target to plant 10 billion saplings before 2023's elections. On 17th June 2020, the premier told the nation that under the program, **30 million trees** had been planted and new nurseries were working at top speed to increase the number to one billion by June 2021.

On 9th August 2021; the premier launched the world's biggest **MIYAWAKI URBAN FOREST** in Lahore. Falling under the 10 Billion Tree Tsunami project, various projects including 20 Plants, 20 Numbers, Billion Tree Honey Initiative and olive tree plantations were inaugurated. The *Green Stimulus Package* was launched in April 2021 to extend green cover and provide employments for the youth, particularly in the wake of Covid-19.

Alongside the 10 Billion Tree Tsunami, the government also initiated the **Clean Green Pakistan** drive to tackle the challenges of rising pollution and global warming. On 25th November 2019, the Clean Green Pakistan Index was launched, under which 19 cities were to compete on certain issues of public interest in the initial stage. With considerable work done to launch the program in many parts of the country, the said promise was PARTIALLY COMPLETE because just after five months Mr Khan was no more in saddles.

The PTI had vowed to **INCREASE PROTECTED AREAS** from one per cent to 10pc of the coastline. This promise had seen little progress; the climate change ministry in June 2021 said the promise would be fulfilled by 2023. On 21st March 2021, the premier had asked for *Charna Island* to be turned into a marine protected area.

On 31st August 2020, President Arif Alvi promulgated the *Pakistan Islands Development Authority (PIDA) Ordinance* 2020, to facilitate the federal govt to take control of *Bundal and Buddo islands* in Sindh. This ordinance, however, lapsed, amid backlash from the Sindh government. The said project was NOT in the list of PM Khan's promises whatsoever.

EHSAAS — WELFARE PROGRAM:

Poverty Alleviation: The PTI had planned to initiate a poverty alleviation drive across the poorest districts of Pakistan. In order to do so, it promised to launch special drives to improve access to sanitation and potable water; besides increasing funding for the most impoverished districts through poverty alleviation plans, provided *Sehat Insaf Cards* to residents and augmented the existing Benazir Income Support Program (BISP).

In April 2019, the federal cabinet approved the formation of the <u>Social Protection and Poverty Alleviation Division</u> to overcome poverty in the country, adding that the then incumbent BISP chairperson Sania Nishtar would head the new division as well. Then in June 2020, it decided to <u>increase</u> the monthly stipend given to poor families registered with the BISP from Rs:2000 to Rs:3000. Nishtar also worked on the removal of beneficiaries from the BISP database who were either ghosts or UNDESERVING.

A move to change the name of BISP was met with the opposition's resistance, and was subsequently abandoned. The party instead placed it under the umbrella of **Ehsaas — the PTI's flagship social safety program.** Alongside the BISP, the federal government worked on various other projects under the Ehsaas program, which the premier Imran Khan thought about turning Pakistan into an ISLAMIC WELFARE STATE.

In the World Bank's report, it had <u>listed</u> the **Ehsaas Emergency Cash Program** among the top four social protection interventions globally in terms of the number of people covered. <u>The program distributed cash among 15 million under-privileged families after they suffered financially due to Covid-19 related lockdowns.</u> Therefore, the promise to augment the existing BISP program was nearly complete.

Coming to providing **CLEAN DRINKING WATER**, to about 250 million population, the PTI's performance was most noticeable in Punjab. A month after the passage of the *Punjab Aab-e-Pak Authority Bill 2019* by the provincial assembly in March 2019, the Punjab Aab-e-Pak Authority was <u>established</u>. Nearly two years later, <u>on 11th January 2021</u>, the first water project under the authority was <u>launched</u> in Chak Jhumra, Punjab. PTI govt held that <u>water filtration plants were being installed in jails, hospitals, educational institutions and police lines under the Sarwar Foundation to provide clean drinking water to the people</u>. Till <u>10th August 2021,</u> 1,500 projects of the authority were to be completed that year and seven million people in Punjab could be provided with clean drinking water daily. On the whole, a perfect intiative and noble thought on the part of PTI it was.

Many of the PTI's commitments to education were connected to their promises for youth development. A key example of this was the **KAMYAB JAWAN PROGRAM** (KJP) launched in October 2019. It was an aggressive small-and-medium-enterprise lending scheme, aimed at stimulating job creation and economically empowering the youth. As of July 2021, the government had disbursed soft loans amounting to Rs:17 billion among more than 14,000 entrepreneurs via the Youth Entrepreneurship Scheme of KJP.

- *NO FEEDBACK THEREOF: No one can comment that Rs:17bn had created how many compnies, business concerns, how much employments created, what kind of businesses done with that money, how much were Tax Registered and how much successful – OR SIMPLY THE MONEY WENT WASTE with no results on record.*

Another project launched by the PTI government was the **HUNARMAND JAWAN PROGRAM** aimed at the economic emancipation of the youth by providing them quality training. Launching the project on 9th January 2020, the premier Imran Khan had expected that the project would see the training of 500,000 youth; the first 70 skill centres were to be set up in madrassahs and in the next phase, 300 smart training centres were to be raised in various parts of the country.

- *NO FEEDBACK ON RECORD: Again no one can comment that where those 70 Skill-Centres were located, where those 300 Training-Centres were opened; how many youths got certificates / diplomas from those centres; what skills they got and where they were absorbed and how much successful – OR SIMPLY THE MONEY WENT WASTE with no results on record.*

However, in Pakistan all such WELFARE PROJECTS and plans are always available in tailor-made form with all the bureaucrats who keep enough experience to 'put the new political party and new ministers' on such new tracks of HUMAN INVESTMENTS. No one has the statistics of any such program started and carried on in Gen Musharraf's regime, PPP, PMLN or PTI's respective eras. ALL THERE WILL BE FUDGE FIGURES ON FILES. THUS PEOPLE BELIEVE THAT ALL SUCH SOFT LOANS, HELPS, CASH INVESTMENTS ETC ARE EATEN UP

BY BUREAUCRATIC HANDS IN COLLABORATION WITH THEIR ASSOCIATE POLITICAL WORKERS.

Had they been truthful, there should have been no poverty in Pakistan; whereas the practical situation is that each year about 10% people are moved to BELOW POVERTY LINE. See UNDP 2021's report here.

UNDP REPORT 2021:

Referring to **UNDP's Report on Humanity** released in first week of April 2021 as appeared in world media, including **AL-JAZEERA** on 13th April 2021: 'Economic privileges accorded to Pakistan's elite groups, including the corporate sector, feudal landlords, the political class and the country's powerful military, add up to an estimated $17.4bn, or roughly 6 percent of the country's economy.'

The UNDP report used the prism of *'Power, People and Policy'* to examine the stark income and economic opportunity disparities in the developing country – named Pakistan. Powerful groups use their privilege to capture more than their fair share, people perpetuate structural discrimination through prejudice against others based on social characteristics, and policies are often unsuccessful at addressing the resulting inequity, or may even contribute to it. The regional chief of the UNDP had been on a two-week tour of Pakistan to discuss the report's findings; also, holding talks with the then PM Imran Khan and other top members of his cabinet, including the ministers of foreign affairs and planning. Ultimately she wrote:

> "[In our remarks in meetings] we focused right in on where […] the shadows are, and what is it that actually diverts from a reform agenda in a country. My hope is that there is strong intent to review things like the current tax and subsidy policies, to look at land and capital access."

The biggest beneficiary of the privileges – which may take the form of tax breaks, cheap input prices, higher output prices or preferential access to capital, land and services – was found to be the **country's corporate sector**, which accrued an estimated $4.7bn in privileges.

The second and third-highest recipients of privileges were found to be:

- the country's richest 1 percent, who collectively own 9 percent of the country's overall income,

- the feudal land-owning class, which constitutes 1.1 percent of the population but owns 22 percent of all arable farmland.

- The country's military is found to receive $1.7bn in privileges, mainly in the form of preferential access to land, capital and infrastructure, as well as tax exemptions.

All above classes have strong representation in the Pakistani Parliament, with most major political parties' candidates' drawn from either the feudal landowning class or the country's business-owning elite. This creates a paradox where those responsible for doling out the privileges were also those who were receiving them. *'If with one hand you are providing a gain that benefits yourself, and taking the gain with the other hand, then what we have lost is that sense of separation of powers and oversight.'*

The report noted, however, that:

> "Pakistan's military is also the largest conglomerate of business entities in Pakistan, besides being the country's biggest urban real estate developer and manager, with wide-ranging involvement in the construction of public projects.
>
> These things are not neatly separate entities. You do see some of… these are overlapping so you almost get a double privilege by the military. The minute in a country the military is a part of big business, it obviously doubles the issue and the problem."

In a country like Pakistan, a movement may erupt any moment to displace structures of power that are so entrenched and deep-rooted. It's a tough …. power politics (here in Pakistan) and it would be naïve or childish of anyone to expect or to recommend to leaders on what to do in this respect.

It's very clear from the analytics, …. and then it is up to the country, both the state and the people to say: *'Enough, here is how we need to take break up these strongly-held power groups and dynamics in this country.'*

Aliona Niculita, deputy resident representative of the UNDP in Pakistan, added in the report:

> "The wide-ranging NHDR provides detailed data on deep-rooted inequality in Pakistan's economy. While the richest 1 percent held 9 percent of the country's income of $314.4bn in 2018-19, the report found that the poorest 1 percent held just 0.15 percent.

> *Overall, the richest 20 percent of Pakistanis hold 49.6 percent of the national income, compared with the poorest 20 percent, who hold just 7 percent.*
>
> *The poorest and richest Pakistanis effectively live in completely different countries, with literacy levels, health outcomes, and living standards that are poles apart."*

Of further concern to Pakistani policymakers is a shrinking of the middle-class, with the UNDP's data showing middle-income earners fell from 42 percent of the population in 2009 to 36 percent in 2019. The data highlights regional inequalities in service delivery and shows how higher-income areas also see higher rates of public expenditure. The report said further:

> *"The NHDR 2020 reveals that Pakistan's people do not benefit equally from public expenditure. The overall share is 14.2 percent for the poorest income [category], compared with 37.2 percent for the richest [category].*
>
> *Pakistan ranks second-to-last in South Asia based on HDI, outperforming Afghanistan but lagging behind all six of its other regional neighbours.*
>
> *Is there a glass ceiling to human development and why, and what is needed to crack it?"*

The UNDP recommended policies that focus on removing privileges and targeting spending on outcomes that provide both structural support for the country's poor and on the infrastructure – such as education and healthcare – that would provide them further economic opportunities. Look at another tragedy:

> *"Pakistan ranks 153 out of 156 countries on the World Economic Forum's Global Gender Gap Index, with 32 percent of primary-school-aged girls out of school – matter of shame on all country managers. The evidence across the world on one of the biggest returns on investment comes from educating all of our children and getting them and keeping them in school.*
>
> *But a huge return is that all of those missing girls from school and missing women from the workplace – bring them back in streams."*

No doubt, Pakistan is still moving back into the stone-age.

Scenario 258

IMRAN KHAN: CAUSES OF DOWNFALL

What were the reasons for fall of Pakistan's PM Imran Khan?

IMRAN KHAN was good as a cricketer in the 1990s; his rise started with his personality trait as a cricketer. He came into politics in 1996 where he also founded his own political party named *Pakistan Tehreek e Insaf* [PTI]. He saw himself as Hercules who appeared to save the nation from decay; the scapegoat was Nawaz Sharif who was called corrupt and global beggar.

Imran Khan supported the military coup of October 1999 and was later offered by Gen Musharraf to hold PM's office in 2002 but he refused; he became known as a professional politician when he had lost to Nawaz Sharif of Pakistan Muslim League (Nawaz) [PMLN] in 2013's general elections. In year 2014, he and his supporters besieged the capital Islamabad.

HIGH SLOGANS OF NAYA PAKISTAN (?)

(Naya Pakistan here means New Pakistan, a slogan given by PM Imran Khan during his election bid in 2018)

For 2018 elections, Mr Khan knew that he would not win either, so he allegedly contacted the Pak-Army to help him – OR the Generals contacted him – both were keen to help each other for some settled motives.

The PMLN in Punjab and the Awami National Party [ANP] in Khyber PK were then ousted by the army in favour of the PTI. Basically, it's said that Imran Khan didn't win the elections; in fact, the Pak-military had carried out a coup d'état. However, the finger-pointing started when he, being new in practical politics, miss-handled the governance affairs which were mainly in favour of the satus-quo in the country. He made noble but ideal promises, many of them were unrealistic in that time's Pakistan - thus could not keep them up and hence labelled as *'Mr. U-Turn'* by some rogue political opponents.

As a politician, Mr Khan was successful in Khyber PK province with more than two Governments in succession; however, as a member of National Assembly of Pakistan, his contribution was found as *'below the mark'*. As prime minister, he allegedly dragged Pakistan in to some precarious confrontations with friendly countries like China, Saudi Arabia, Malaysia, Iran, the US, the EU and others. Being a leader, he was expected to lead his country out of its falls and down turns. Pak-Army mainly remained un-concerned about the economic agenda of the country whatsoever so pulling the string from the back didn't help Mr Khan either. When Imran Khan succeeded in 2018's general elections with the backing of the Pak-Army, he could achieve certain fantastic and far-reaching goals for his nation with the help of the same tall military personnel at his back had his team done the proper home work.

Mr Khan as PM, with the proper planning and utilisation of Pak-Army's skills and team-spirit, *could have achieved the 100% literacy rate for the nation through its Education Corp, the best road infrastructure of roads & bridges through its Engineering Corp, the best public health facilities through its Medical Corp, the best rail-network, development of harbours through its Naval skills, re-establishing the doomed Airlines PIA like through its Air expertise and numerous industrial projects.* The list is endless......

But Mr Khan remained tied with his own philosophy of calling for huge gatherings at various places and speaking out his venomous mantras of *'Corruption of Political Opponents'* – practically did nothing to tie them up through effective amendments in respective laws through the parliament. He had the mistaken belief that the bureaucracy would follow what he wished or said – but practically it didn't happen so. He got misguided due to his inexperience – bureaucracy always follow rules and policies what the political masters coin through parliament or temporarily via presidential ordinances AND give them for implementation. Khan's team was mostly lethargic, inexpert and ill-educated for governance.

Despite achieving an un-precedented GDP growth of 6% in his last year of rule, the country's economy, poverty and unemployment remained at level where its so-called rival India had been in before 1970s. The reason, every successive ruler of the country, more vigorously the PM Imran Khan, continuously kept their people illiterate; and leaving them in their religious and sectarian cages shouting at each other instead of contributing towards development – thus leaving the average citizen in doldrums, hungry, unemployed, shelter-less and unskilled.

Imran Khan, in 2018, rose with the aspirations of the people that within FIRST 100 DAYS the foundations for a developed state would be laid down; 200 years old laws, regulations and policies would be changed; industrial estates would be inaugurated; one-window infrastructures would be effectively run and monitored for each venue of investment; Revenue Collection would be made simplified – BUT nothing happened - he didn't have the proper team to study and import or follow any good system from the UK where he and his close cabinet members had spent youth in studying, playing and sensing the fruits of developed, vibrant, industrious, business-oriented and self-sustained welfare society – nor the state provided them required infrastructure to move forward. Critics held that like the previous regimes, Khan also made (bad) choice of serving his friends' circles around.

In October 2019; an open media discussion was held online in the West and America on the topic '*Why is Pakistani PM Imran Khan crying?*'; the response was great but certain pit-falls were also pointed out; see the salient points in the following lines.

"**Imran Khan is not foolish but over smart.**

- *Pakistan claimed backing of enough members in 47 member UNHRC but failed to get support of 16 members to table a resolution against India.*

- *Imran Khan seems to be more concerned about India than Pakistan. He is very worried for Indians because (in his words) India is being run by a Hitler type leader Modi and Nazi type party BJP. But the whole world including some of his best friends (China, Saudi Arabia, UAE etc.) has no issue in dealing with so called 'Hitler'. Even Modi was able to organize a rally of 50,000 people in United States and Trump attended that rally.*

- *One day he said that ISI helped CIA to locate Osama Bin Laden; on another day he said that Americans were listening to conversation of the Pak PM and Army Chief during Osama raid. Again, one fine day he admitted that Pakistan was training Al-Qaeda and Taliban right up to 9/11 attack.*

- *When he returned from his previous US trip then he said that he felt like returning to Pakistan after winning a World Cup. In a month, India rocked his boat by removing Article 370 and his (so called) good friend Trump had virtually accepted Indian move.*

- *He used to tell that as PM of Pakistan he will never ask for loans but when he became PM, he travelled to so many countries for getting loans including the IMF."*

See another media comment:

"Well... Imran Khan (in his early political career in 90s) started criticising on big two Monopoly of Pakistan (PPP and PMLN). He won a seat in Elections of 2002, President Gen Musharraf offered him Premiership but Imran Khan refused saying 'he doesn't want to be a dummy Prime Minister and PM under a dictator'. Gen Musharraf got annoyed and put him in jail.

Imran Khan continued his struggle and boycotted Election 2008. Till then, he was getting popular day by day but he got media attention in his largest jalsa (gathering) of 300k-400k people in Lahore.

Later, many popular politicians joined Imran Khan. His party Pakistan Tehreek-e-Insaf (PTI), despite finishing third in terms of seats, received the second largest number of votes in the general elections. **PTI polled 7.7 million votes to win 28 National Assembly seats,** *whereas the PPP, which led the outgoing government, took 32 seats with only 6.9 million ballots. in Election 2013. It was only Imran Khan who in true meaning exposed Nawaz Sharif.*

Imran Khan continued exposing Nawaz Sharif and Zardari's corruption. Meanwhile Panama Leaks happened so Nawaz got disqualified and later got sentenced 10 years of imprisonment on corruption charges from the competent court in Pakistan.

It was (and still it is) Pakistani folks which backed behind Imran Khan from day one. You can see still 100k-300k+ people in his every jalsa in every city, so he is getting more popular day by day."

Imran Khan, as the Prime Minister of Pakistan was at top of his popularity having a huge following in KP, urban Punjab and Karachi. He had availed his government with help of the Pak-Army but he paid back the favour by granting an extension to Gen Bajwa. During the first six months, PM Khan's government was perceived differently; people and observers in other countries were impressed *'that how Pakistanis rejected status quo....'* but much was to be done by his team. The impact of electing a new face instead of recycling rogue & tested family politicians of PPP or PMLN was evident and brought renewed faith in the country's state institutions.

Instead of admitting his failures and adopt corrective measures, he blamed the previous governments of the PMLN and the Pakistan Peoples Party [PPP] for the odd criticism on his governance results. Thus, certain high analytical world forums had started propagating about his possible failures right from his early periods in saddles; for more details see **S Hussein Shah**'s essay dated **4th July 2020** on western media.

Many of the opponents, belonging to the PPP and PMLN in fact, termed PM Khan as the 'Selected PM' to get the public believe that Imran Khan was shoed-in by the Establishment & didn't win the elections fair & square. Khan himself never denied it. Interestingly, the PMLN had tried to get him out of the politics / elections by filing 32 cases against him during its tenure in power; they failed. The PPP had threatened for his life and tried under-hand deals to get him out; however, they also got botched.

The general populace, however, welcomed *Mr Khan's 'NAYA (new) Pakistan'* - the original Pakistan of Muhammad Ali Jinnah.

During PM Khan's years 2019-20, **Corona** remained a real bad issue for all. List of few **big problems** included that Pakistan was once declared as the new epic centre of Corona virus / Covid 19. Most importantly the people were not supporting the government. They reopened the mosques and religious institutions under pressure from religious scholars; a gross mistake they made.

Pakistan neither had resources to fight against corona nor they had money to feed its poor populace; 45% of them were daily wage earners so they were deprived of their meagre earnings. Increased criticism of the world-media brought direct effect on Pakistan; the EU and China reduced their assistance to Pakistan government and thus the people. The country was not in a position to show a transparent picture of Corona cases to the world. However, *PM Khan pulled over those hard days in a befitting manner – in a way made the whole world speechless.*

PM Imran Khan was blamed for being an army-puppet; his opponents lodged this propaganda but he snatched enough seats of PMLN, PPP and ANP with the back of Pak-Army. Imran Khan's slogans were mostly against corruption BUT he could not manage even a single LAW AMENDED to eradicate the same, though it needed simple majority in the parliament – ultimately caught in the same *'trap of alleged corruption'* later during 2022-23.

No doubt, Imran Khan remained one of the two dynamic prime ministers in the 75 years of history of Pakistan. He demonstrated his ability successfully to improve country's economy but couldn't reduce corruption. His team couldn't show improvement in the tax & revenue collection, couldn't improve law & order situations especially in Baluchistan and on western borders, left negative indicators in the field of mass-education AND showed compromised attitudes towards CPEC – ultimately making the whole lot of on-going development projects stand and still.

Imran Khan started two new hydropower projects in four years; good job done but couldn't finish because the power projects and dams normally take decades to complete and his tenure lasted for 3+ years only. Khan couldn't significantly improve foreign and internal investments; constructions of road network especially the motorways and inter-city links were ignored so the PMLN's image couldn't be beaten in that field. No infrastructure, industrial zones or factory areas were developed for the medium sized manufacturing.

Mr Khan's Islamic ideology of *'Madina State'* didn't pay him much – rather remained a laughing stock for his critics. His efforts towards Kartarpur corridor at Indian Border went supreme, unforgettable and praised by all walks of life across the world.

In the field of Pakistan's foreign policy, his first year in power was remarkable but thereafter the odd compromises made him virtually alone amongst international community. His self-pride was closely observed and negatively analysed at home and abroad when he engaged himself with America regarding regional issues. He became a first-line leader among the Islamic world by publicly exposing America for its hypocrisy against Pakistan during two decades of Afghan War after Nine Eleven of 2001. Though the US manifestly disliked him, but its entire political establishment knew that he was an honest man contrary to the previous lot of Pakistani leaders.

PAKISTAN's DEPRIVED ECONOMY:

Pakistan's Economy has always been this way, bubbles of unequal growth, followed by high inflation and recession, and net decline. A few Pakistanis get richer, most go worse off.

In the field of its economy and development, Pakistan has over the years made itself heavily dependent upon foreign aid and assistance from foreign institutions and countries for its annual budgetary finances. During Imran Khan's regime, the country's debt-to-GDP ratio was 92.7% with a fall in per capita income from $1625 to $1325, accompanied by rapid inflation with an average of 10.9%. Speaking of export-imports, its trade deficit increased to 32.9% for the outgoing fiscal year of 2021 and a dollar-cost 170+ Pakistani rupee. The country became the net importer of food grains (*for decades it remained the net exporter*) – one could think how many hardships a common Pakistani had faced.

During the same PTI regime, Oil and gas prices had skyrocketed and forced the government to ration gas-supplies in major cities. Load-shedding and long power-cuts of more than 10 hours had become normal then which also impacted its financial capital Karachi. The appalling state of health and education sector resulted in a lack of skill development and human capital formation. Piling debt and practically no revenue, the govt had no money for repair works on many big public projects. Many pieces of major infrastructures like airports, motorways, and public parks had to be mortgaged later. The proposed new project for Port Qasim Karachi under CPEC was then heading for the same fate as was failed Gwader.

But despite all of those historic and present challenges, the said hybrid democratic setup continued with visible faults as had been alive for 74 years! Gen Bajwa said in the Islamabad Security Dialogue, back in March (2021) that:

> '.... (for) his country's prospects in the realms of geo-economics - the world knows that we are geo-strategically placed, to be a bridge between civilizations and connecting conduit between the regional economies. We are a nation of significance due to our large and enterprising demography, fertile soil and adequate logistical infrastructure. We intend to leverage our vital geostrategic location for ours own, regional and global benefit;"
>
> Full Text of Gen Bajwa's Speech dated <u>18th March 2021</u> on media pages is referred.

<u>{Indeed, for years since its inception, Pakistan's geostrategic location has got important significance in global politics. It is surrounded by China in the north, Afghanistan, and Iran in the west, and India in the east. As Iran remains a skeptic player among the western think tanks, the only gateway to Afghanistan and Central Asia is through Pakistan. Also, Pakistan is a country with a dominating coastline as it is just close to the Strait of Hormuz and the Gulf of Oman alongside the Arabian Sea giving Pakistan</u>

the close access to the 35% of the world's seaborne oil shipments and 20% of oil traded worldwide. Pakistan's location connects very important Asian Civilizations and Economies that are of interest to everyone.

Why a fragile hybrid setup eludes western powers towards Pakistan is because it gives them the flexibility to trade terms due to its location. For long, it has been used by Pakistan's rulers and the establishment as a bargaining chip to maximize their multiple strategic objectives and with the added benefit of the nuclear umbrella after 1998, it has pacified the matters in favour of Pakistan.}

However, after the Afghanistan's freedom on 15th August 2021, the hybrid democracy setup of Pakistan contrasted to the commitments that it had sworn to honor. The rising radicalism **'Naya Pakistan was attractive' but it also threatened the regional BALANCE OF POWER in South-East Asia.** The world in those uncertain times of post-pandemic order was not able to afford another Afghanistan with nuclear capabilities boasted proudly as the 'Islamic Bomb'. Thus, a consistent pressure with fair accountability was in demand so that the said imminent disaster could be averted.

PM Khan was blamed for being no better, and likely worse in certain ways, than the economic managers who preceded him. PMLN under Nawaz Sharif did nothing to resolve the country's perennial tax deficiency either, nor the overstuffed state expenditures. *Pakistan remained like a child trying to grow with a millstone round its neck; no matter how much nutrition or exercise it was given, the stone ensured the child should never reach full potential.* Pakistan's prime institutions and top bureaucracy always benefited from this millstone directly, made sure the nation wouldn't progress towards resolution; **UNDP's Report for year 2021** is referred.

The Pakistani nation expected that Imran Khan would BREAK THAT MILLSTONE and the child would grow through Naya Pakistan's glittering beams – but this leader also left the country at STATUS QUO position in the hands of the same rogue bureaucracy. Now new scheme, policy, pattern, plan or structure like Mohatir Mohammad of Malysia, Hasina Wajid of Bangladesh, Modi of India or Tayyab Ardgan of Turkey could be introduced.

A country, like a business or a household, needs to earn more than its expenses, to stay afloat. Imran Khan inherited a country with a lot more expenditure than income, with its import bill at $60 billion plus, three times its exports at just over $20 billion. Even with the foreign workers' remittances of around $20 billion, there was a gap of $20 billion and only $8 billion Reserves were with state exchequer in mid-2018. To make matters worse, Imran Khan's government had more than two years' global Pandemic and high oil prices in international market to deal with.

- *Despite all this, Imran Khan's government boasted more than $30 billion Exports earnings; the foreign Remittances had also risen to more than $30 billion. All other fundamentals were moving in the right direction too; the country posted a growth rate of 5.37 %, Covid-19 notwithstanding – though on* **NEW DEVELOPMENT PLANS** *like counts he failed.*

In Pakistan, like most poor countries, the inflation remained on rise, especially under food indices. During 2018-19, this menace had its roots internationally. Pakistan never had any control over oil prices, freight and cooking oil and other food commodity prices; the same remained true with PM Khan. These factors and *the burgeoning population indeed posed serious problems.* The hope was that with the continuing economic growth and industrial & agricultural uplift, the country could have moved into higher wage era; but the PTI govt couldn't gain much.

Even then realistically, for Pakistan and for its tattered and shattered economy – PM Khan did better than anyone else in the past regimes; at least *he had not allowed the economy to completely collapse.* He kept things tied together and showed the guts to leave the US Umbrella aside and presented an independent path to the nation for survival. Till ending 2019, PM Khan was quite popular within Pakistan; then it started declining; several reasons can be cited for that. The PTI couldn't actually deliver on the promises about **planned economic development and growth**; the people madly wanted to see an **INDUSTRIAL REVOLUTION** as had been assured before 2018's elections. Add to this the problem of mis-governance and rising inflation; keeping the Covid pandemic aside.

Most people were getting actually fed up with him constantly blaming previous governments for everything – NOT guiding them what PTI govt was doing for them. Also, PM Khan and his 52-members team could have exhibited high-performance in basic fields and shown the true directions of progressing Pakistan. People were less willing to accept excuses [*and deflections towards the previous governments*] year after year till early 2022.

- *PM Khan was still popular enough within Pakistan and amongst foreign patriots; he could have maintained his alliance with the military establishment like in 2018 till the country's poverty turned into 'developing phase'; especially when there was no real opposition in the parliament and outside.*

More generally, Mr Khan had the best intentions but failed to build strong managers' teams unlike in cricket. He was expected to prioritize the two or three fundamental national issues, and to first work out a practical plan for solution. It's called management and Imran had never done it before – **but had also no intention to seek guidance from academicians due to HIS EGO.** From his first speech to the nation, right after being sworn in [2018], listing over 50 separate challenges his government was going to take on – the intelligentsia and serious nationalists got indication that he was going to fail ultimately while opening so many sectors simultaneously.

As a cricket player, supreme self-confidence and refusal to surrender served Imran Khan well. However, unfortunately for Pakistan, *he couldn't demonstrate genuine political intellect, or an ability to show qualities which any reformer or true leader must have in order to navigate the treacherous tides of the nation's politics – even when the establishment was available there to help him.*

Referring to FAHD HUSSAIN's essay titled as '*.... a dream gone sour*' published on media pages on 2nd April 2022; the most important factor remained:

> "**Mismanaging the Establishment:** *This was the easiest relationship to nurture because it formed the genesis of the PTI that was reborn, revamped and refuelled somewhere around 2011.* PTI's path to power was red-carpeted by the establishment without much care for nuance or subtlety. *Imran Khan began his stint as the prime minister with one hundred per cent support from the establishment, a luxury few leaders had enjoyed before. And yet, event by event, issue by issue, and policy by policy, the PTI leadership began to rack up completely avoidable irritants with the establishment that finally exploded into an open controversy…*"
>
> See its details in the daily **DAWN** dated 22nd August 2022;

DIRECT ALLEGATIONS ON 'NEUTRALS':

Former prime minister Imran Khan levelled a series of allegations against the *'neutrals'* — a term he used to allude to the military establishment — saying as per the *'information he received from insiders'* they were the ones who were allegedly responsible for the (then) ongoing crackdown on the PTI.

Addressing a political gathering at Rawalpindi's Liaquat Bagh on 21st August 2022, the PTI Chairman said that with this gathering he had started the journey to achieve *real freedom* for the country and he would not rest until he achieved his goal. Further he said:

> 'On 25th May 2022, *when the police used violence against us, I was told by insiders that the police were ordered from above, which means that neutrals pressurized them to give PTI workers a thrashing,'* Mr Khan said and questioned *whether the neutrals were really neutral.*

Speaking about the **disqualification case** against him in the Election Commission of Pakistan (ECP), the PTI chairman alleged:

> "*The Chief Election Commission[er] is giving every decision against us … I got information from the inside that he [the CEC] was not doing anything on his own but there was pressure from above.*"

PTI leaders condemned *'disruption of YouTube service'* during Imran's speech on that day (25th May 2022). Mr Khan further alleged:

> "*The police said that they were not responsible for the torture of his aide Shahbaz Gill - …. it happened **after orders from behind**. They [police] are also pointing fingers towards you… whenever anything wrong happens in Pakistan, you (The Army) are blamed for it.*"

> "*I want to ask whether you are **neutral or not**. If you stand with these people [PDM government], will the nation stop thinking of them as thieves. A certain Mr Y has come to Islamabad…I know what their plan is; the government wanted to get rid of him (Mr khan) by putting him in jail and sideline the PTI.*

> *PTI was, and still is, the **biggest party at the federal level** and any attempts to break the party would hurt the country. Political parties are the glue that keeps the country together.*"

The former premier spent the first half of his speech on why he was ousted from power. He claimed that he was removed because he wanted to bring independent foreign policy. Mr Khan further accused the authorities of harassing visitors to Banigala, his residence in Islamabad, and said the people who came to meet him *'received calls from the intelligence agencies'*.

The *YouTube Services* in parts of the country faced disruptions during Imran Khan's speech; but it was also a fact that his live addresses were banned on TV channels on that night by the PEMRA, the electronic media regulator in Pakistan, in light of his controversial remarks about judges, Generals and police officials. The PTI had noted that *'coincidentally, YouTube was back to being fully operational as soon as our historic rally finished. Freedom of expression is completely finished in Pakistan.'*

In a late-night development, a heavy contingent of police reached outside the *Banigala* residence of Imran Khan and erected barricades to stop PTI workers from proceeding to his house. After the conclusion of his Liaquat Bagh rally there was a possibility that he could be arrested under a non-bailable case already registered against him at Margalla police station Islamabad – but Mr Khan did not return to his hilltop house after the public meeting and stayed at an undisclosed location.

The other mentionable events in Military-Khan relations remained.

Firstly, **DIRECT CLASH FOR DG-ISI**: In fact, the DOWNFALL of Mr Khan started from here. Every sane person in the PTI knew that if there was one relationship that could be said responsible for sustaining the PTI in power till its end, it was the ISI. And yet the PTI leadership blew up this very connection through sentimental statements. There was then plenty of time with the party high-ups to review the series of odd decisions that went into wrecking this serious patronage, and figure out who had advised Mr Khan to make such blunders, and why to satisfy one's ego.

Imran Khan faced consequences that every party and its leader had once faced in the past by taking a stand against the Military. The refusal or delay of PM Khan to sign the orders of Lt-Gen Nadeem Anjum's appointment as new DG-ISI did raise eyebrows in GHQ Rawalpindi. The drama of twist and turns unfolded when Gen Bajwa visited ISI Headquarters on 18th October 2021 after the approval over the summary that had not come back from the PM Office. That was not a pre-scheduled or planned visit, it came after a press brief on 12th October 2021 by I&B Minister Fawad Chaudhary stating that *'legal procedure will be followed in the appointment of DG ISI'*.

- As the issue was aggravated, both sides bombarded each other down the line by mounting pressure on each other. While Military leadership showed maturity and acumen to meet its ends while on the other side, Mr Khan and his ilk struggled to keep its flock together.

- Rumors and tapes of the parliamentary group meeting called by PM on this issue surfaced in the media where PM Khan's desperation to keep the then DG ISI, Lt-Gen Faiz Hameed to his position further led to speculation of some understanding between Gen Faiz and Imran Khan - Khan could appoint him as next Chief of Army Staff (COAS) and in turn, Gen Faiz had to help him in the 2023 general elections.

- Though some may regard this as mere speculation, but this lingering fact had haunted Imran Khan and Gen Faiz since 2017 when Gen Faiz (was then Major General) was the deputy chief of this spy organization.

Secondly, **its continued reluctance to build a working relationship with the opposition**: see Mr Imran Khan's views in *his address to scholars and writers* at the inauguration of 'Hall of Fame' at Pakistan Academy of Letters (PAL) in Islamabad:

> [**On 5th November 2021**: PM Imran Khan said he had no personal enmity with former prime minister Nawaz Sharif and ex-president Asif Ali Zardari but he intentionally avoided meeting the opposition leaders facing corruption charges; saying:
>
> "People ask me that I do not shake hands with the opposition leader. He [opposition leader] is facing corruption cases of billions of rupees. If I shake hands, I make it [the crime] acceptable in society. A nation dies when it loses the ability to differentiate between good and bad [...]. When you see something wrong and don't call it out, that means that your decline has begun. ...... In United Kingdom, a parliamentarian who was facing corruption allegations was neither invited to TV programmes nor allowed to enter parliament until he was cleared of the charges."]

In PTI government, however, the party needed to change gears. A basic working relationship with the opposition could have kept the political temperature down and enabled a smoother running of the affairs of the state. *This would have also helped the government focus more on delivery as its primary agenda.* The PTI, however, took its eye off the ball of governance and started chasing the wrong targets.

THIRDLY, **The Buzdar Blunder**: It was a blunder since the very first day; he could not deliver as the Chief Minister of Punjab. And yet, *it was (only) Imran Khan's ego that perpetuated the error instead of correcting it.* As time went by, the blunder gave rise to multiple crises:

(i) It became the first source of friction with the establishment (*it was contrary to Gen Bajwa's sane advice*) and kept on getting worse over the years

(ii) It led to worsening governance in the province in sharp contrast to the Shahbaz Sharif years, and began to cement the perception of incompetence for the party (PTI)

(iii) It resulted in poor political management among the elected members of the party leading to factionalism, groupings and ultimately *breakaway of members* fed up with not having their issues resolved by the weak leadership of the party.

The Buzdar blunder was an avoidable one. When *it was not avoided, it became one of the leading factors for the PTI's failure.*

FOURTHLY, **The Choice of WRONG Team**: The gap between what the PTI promised and the people it selected to deliver on was wider than anyone could have imagined. The PTI's cabinet team was probably the weakest in the living memory — and this explained why the PM had to reshuffle it so often. There were of course some exceptions like Shah M Qureshi, Dr Sania Nishtar and Dr Faisal Sultan, but the overwhelming majority was ill-suited for the tasks at hand – thus the failure for sure. In short:

- *The team had no specific central vision; had zero concept of a welfare state; they depended on odd schemes and projects conjured up by bureaucrats.*

- *Critical ministries like finance, energy and information saw constant change of hands thereby keeping key-areas in constant state of flux.*

- *There was disastrous performance in ministries and divisions like aviation, human rights, accountability which saw little or no change thereby reinforcing the governance crisis.*

- *Collateral damage was exacerbated by poor and negative communication by an array of spokespersons who remained more busy trying to demolish the opposition than to build up their own government's perception, plans & deliverance.*

FIFTHLY, <u>the arrogance exhibited by PTI's leadership</u> including Imran Khan himself: This misplaced sense of egoism, entitlement and self-righteousness became one of the key factors for PTI's failure. This attitude of contempt towards everyone else, laced as it was with mocking and sneering in press conferences and statements, injected a deadly dose of toxicity, antipathy and revulsion when what the PTI really needed to do was to inspire hope, inclusivity and a feel-good factor. *Ego & arrogance became second nature of the PTI as a political party, it turned off entire segment of intelligentsia, think-tanks and nationalist well-wishers.* The PTI had hurt itself - thus got a humiliating ouster from power.

> *Students of politics would judge the PTI's capacity to learn from its mistakes — <u>stop blaming the world and look inwards to find the reason for the disaster</u> that has befallen on it. Shallow mantras of Madina-like-state, Langar & Serai Schemes and all-time narrations of corruption stories of opponents didn't work at all in comparison with trying to achieve goals of 100% literacy rate, effective measures for population growth, building up stadiums, massive industrialization, curbing religious extremism & polarization, revamping the tax-collection laws and machinery, prioritizing expansion of mid-order technical institutions and revisiting 150 years old laws, legal procedures and criminal justice system – to say the least....*

CRITICAL ANALYSIS OF PTI FAILURES:

The *Pakistan Tehreek-i-Insaf* [PTI]'s spell (August 2018-April 2022] in power came to a callous end on <u>10th April 2022</u>, putting the brakes on a boisterous power-journey that had started with high hopes but ended in bitterness. Over the course of that period, the party had emerged as, still continues to be, the strongest challenge to Pakistan's Sharif and Bhutto family dynasties.

Struggling with the intricacies of wielding power over a nation of 240 million, PTI's main difficulty was due to the fact that *this was party's first time in government thus its lack of experience.* Throughout its tenure, the PTI could never display its capacity to command the executive to its will, nor was its lack of understanding for parliamentary procedures and the art of practical politics helpful when it desperately needed bipartisan support to help implement its vision for **NAYA Pakistan.**

The premiership tenure of PM Imran Khan was unique for many reasons. His journey from the container to the corridors of power was predetermined; his mission was to deliver a economically developed state, an efficient administration, corruption-free society and self-sustained social set-up. PM Imran Khan had won Cricket World Cup in 1992 and so the popular vote of the country two years earlier so could lead the country like the best nations. A coalition of dissimilar and disparate political groups was *raised* to provide him enough support in parliament – thus he was in saddles.

Next came the real test for PM Khan to prove his courage and spirit as a leader. *He struggled but couldn't sail through the sticky mud. It was not only about his inexperience but also his team of power-thirsty trainees that he fielded which brought disaster;* understanding of statecraft was totally missing – of course, some sincere, honest and nationalist but experienced hands were needed. There was the captain whose honesty was supposed to be the big PTI edge and key to rapid progress. However, his honesty couldn't compensate for his own incompetence and the apparent dishonesty and ineptitude of many within his cabinet and party. The project had to go a long way, means beyond five years' term as per expectations of the general populace and the PM Khan too.

> *"In the PTI, many key positions belong to recently inducted electables or unelected advisers who lack party loyalty, e.g. interior, finance, law. Pervez Khattak, Asad Umar and Shah Mahmood are exceptions. But here too there are issues of party strife as all three are seen as strong contenders in any minus-one move. The large numbers of inept unelected advisers have helped nix the myth - that unelected ministers will be more competent."*
> 　　　　　*[Ref:* **Dr Niaz Murtaza**'s *analysis*
> dated 28th July 2020 on media pages.]

It's not surprising that the government survived despite a very thin majority that was breathing on the support of a few manifestly dodgy, doubtful and saleable political figures; sufficiently selfish and cheap commodity in Pakistan. This situation was seen to reinforce hybrid rule. Many saw the imprint of the establishment all over. That provided the PTI government an impression of stability yet the duality of power had its own hazards coupled with hidden threats. It caused more confusion and affected the real essence of good governance. That was what happened over the first two years of PTI rule as was seen by the intelligentsia – and also by history-writers.

For the PTI government, the situation was not at all encouraging; *good governance remained the major problem area.* PM Khan had promised the nation to bring new talent to build a *NAYA Pakistan,* but an ill-tended and disgruntled cabinet was completely opposite to the promise of delivering worldly smart things; PM Khan's collection of *'talents'* only provided amusing speeches, press-conferences and media interviews in times of crisis. Borrowing words from **Zahid Hussain's** essay spread on media pages dated 19th August 2020:

> *"The much-touted reform agenda is lost somewhere in the chaos.*
>
> *Two years on, there is no sign yet of the PTI government having developed the capability to take rational decisions on critical domestic and foreign policy issues. The government's increasing dependence on the security establishment for survival has further undermined its ability to improve and course correct. Consequently, the establishment's extending shadow can be discerned in all dimensions of the state. It seems that the perpetual state of confrontation among political forces has allowed the establishment to play arbiter of political power in the country."*

The quality of regime's governance depends on the quality of its strategies which in turn hinges on its team quality; it relates to citizen welfare via the *five power functions of ongoing service delivery, projects, policies, legislation and institutional reform.* Two years could be taken a little short period to judge PM Khan's assignment in terms of citizen welfare or even the five functions. But at least, the weak quality of his team was evident to predict that it would fail not only to achieve its promises but even match the last two civilian regimes widely linked with family-nepotism, corruption, dishonesty and incompetence.

The selective application of NAB laws further exposed the PTI government; *allegations of a political witch-hunt appeared open in media.* Many opined that PM Khan's anti-corruption drive against political opponents was, in fact, a cover for his team's incompetence; claims of a clean government were becoming questionable in all media discussions and most live-TV programs. Till the two years' end, there was no visible evidence of NAYA PAKISTAN beyond the official rhetoric. In short, for some, it was beginning of the end of the PTI sloganeering era.

Inexperience was only half the explanation for the PTI's first term troubles: the other half was due to its own inability to marshal and retain enough well-rounded experts to manage government; especially the economy, CPEC, Industrial Development and Foreign Policy. The fact remains that well before the opposition parties formally tabled a motion of no-confidence against PM Khan in March 2022, his government had been floundering due to its inability to handle inflation (*though it was manyfold multiplied during next two years of PDM rule*) while it was a global commodity price-hike cycle.

Imran Khan's exit was seen by all but he quite shrewdly saw an opportunity to divert his electorate's attention from his party's failings during its years in power. He seized on the narrative that he had been ousted as part of an international conspiracy and completely reframed his politics as an **independence struggle** against what he described as an 'imported government'. If the crowds at his *jalsas* — both on-ground and virtual — were any indication, this new narrative could prove to be his ticket to a triumphant return to power – but the political scenario suddenly changed during next few months; his and other PTI members' sufferings increased manyfold.

In short, PM Khan and the PTI failed to solve any of the real on-ground problems Pakistan was facing in terms of social development, economic imbalances and public service management.

KHAN's AUTHORITARIAN POLITICS:

Extracted from person-to-person interview of Imran Khan conducted by **PROSPECT magazine**'s Atika Rehman at his family home in Lahore in November 2022, it concluded that: '*As the bullets were going over my head, I … was smiling…*'

The said words were referring to an anti-government roadshow on 3rd November 2022 when a gunman shot him four times. He said: '*The bullet missed my main artery by a fraction of a millimeter….. (Long poise – coffee sips in between) ….*'

However, it was remarkable how popular Khan had become out of office, although the performance was better than all other governments, only the local media was against him. Fact remained that a Pakistani would never name his child after Nawaz Sharif or Asif Ali Zardari, but would feel pride giving him Imran Khan's name.

After his departure in April 2022, the PDM government of Shahbaz Sharif and later the then care-taker setup of Kakar remained nervous about Khan's popularity — his party PTI had triumphed in 27 of 36 byelections held since his removal. Out of favour with the army and hated by his opponents, Khan faced a slew of court cases and (possible) disqualification from the electoral process altogether.

For Pakistan's shaky and precarious democracy, Mr Khan's surging popularity was not all good news. *He wanted to rule with an iron fist and visualized about a China-style political system.* As prime minister, during a state visit to Beijing he said that: '*... in western democracies, it is difficult to bring change as you are bound by rules and regulations. Democracies of today plan only for the next five years. The Chinese Communist Party achieved better without democracy.*'

In office, Mr Khan refused to negotiate with the opposition even on crucial reforms of national importance. He didn't seem to care much for press freedom, either: Reporters Without Borders listed him as one of the world's 37 worst rulers in 2021. But he remained unfazed. *'Had we been so powerful, there would have been no criticism of us,'* Khan told Atika.

Atif Mian, a respected economist and professor at Princeton University, who was chosen as a member of Khan's Economic Advisory Council but later was ditched for being a member of the Ahmadi faith, once commented:

> "*Mr Khan was a new face in power, and as such many hoped he would bring about some positive change. But effective change requires a vision that spells out the new direction for the country, and that vision must be backed up with political courage to take difficult decisions. Unfortunately, neither vision nor courage was there during PTI's tenure. And so, the country finds itself back in usual troubles, except now the hole is even bigger.*"

After the 2013-elections, Imran Khan's politics went on high pitch; his narrative became a symbol of success for the media channels, and he enjoyed the full support of powerful sections of the state. Like an agitator, he reduced all of Pakistan's problems to a single issue — NO MORE CORRUPTION — and presented himself as the solution. In the form of *'Naya Pakistan'* he promised a utopian model that was both moral (think — Madina) and material (think Scandinavian states).

His narrative of change had a logical explanation of how Pakistan would change under his command. As per his calculations, a bunch of politicians were responsible for the rot in Pakistani state and society, and it was their greed and corruption that was pulling the country down and backwards. For such cleaning operation, the nation needed an incorruptible leader at the top. Once the system is cleared of corruption, Pakistan would start making tremendous progress. HOWEVER, *under Khan's rule, the promised change did not happen....* The promised change - end of corruption - failed to materialize as Pakistan's position on the Transparency International's Corruption Perception Index constantly declined during the PTI's governance. Pakistan's economy that was in a boom-bust cycle for decades, also remained stagnant as no stabilizing policy could be worked out. No way was left, even within the first year of PTI's govt, except to approach the IMF for bail-out.

- *Failing to deliver on his earlier promises of 100-days fame, Khan started looking for a new narrative. He opted to go with short or condensed versions of his earlier promises, **focusing only on corruption of other politicians, for whom he didn't legislate afresh and couldn't guide his team to bring summary procedures on the Chinese or Scandinavian lines. How could 200 years old PPC, CrPC and Evidence Acts eradicate corrupt practices of 2018-21.***

Since the time a no-confidence motion was launched against him, Khan came up with yet another narrative that linked the democratic opposition against him with a conspiracy hatched by the US government to overthrow him. In his new narrative, only those who supported him were patriotic while everyone who opposed him was a traitor. PTI used this narrative to subvert the constitution by killing the no-confidence motion in the parliament – but failed due to Supreme Court's intervention.

It was a tragic end of Mr Khan's first stint at least.

In the name of **AUTHORITARIAN POLITICS** Mr Khan was often compared with President Donald Trump, whose supporters had stormed the Capitol Building in Washington DC on 6th January 2021, the day Congress was meeting to confirm Joe Biden's election victory. Celebrity journalist and author Ben Judah, in an interview published in *The Sunday Times* had compared Khan with Trump on a number of issues. Similar observations were made by many Pakistani analysts and political scientists as well. What had put the two in the same league was *'authoritarian populism'*; often associated with a strongman ruling a country. Mr Khan was a suitable example for that term.

In short, 'like his European counterparts, Khan attacked democracy from the inside'; quoting on media analyst Zaigham Khan. The critics held that *he subverted the democratic development that happened during 2008-18 turning it into democratic decay, without delivering anything in return.* With his resolute will, charisma and determination, Khan was a larger-than-life figure, however, many of his qualities that served him well in sports turned into liabilities in politics and he failed to leave a positive legacy in the country's highest political office. For his failure he may blame his opportunism wrapped in moral garb, his self-love, his single-minded pursuit of personal ambitions, his burning desire for vendetta, his flaws of intellect and lack of experience.

Like his earlier narratives, Mr Khan had borrowed the new stance from past military dictators and civilianized it BUT he had sucked both the media and the opposition into the discourse. At the end, it's the help from his core followers loyal to him, which would be taking him out through the sticky dirty waters of Pakistani-brand politics. Refusal to build a working relationship with the opposition: The PTI's ingrained divisiveness in its worldview worked well when the party was in the opposition. While in government, however, Imran Khan and his PTI as party needed to change gears.

Though, as prime minister, Khan addressed a balance of payments crisis with bailouts from the IMF; he presided over a shrinking current account deficit; limited defence spending to curtail the fiscal deficit and also gave lead to some general economic growth – but the people expected a lot more 'expanded economic development' from him.

IMRAN KHAN's TEAM ISSUES:

A golden maxim for good governance is the quality of outcomes a regime achieves depends on the quality of its strategies which in turn depends on its team quality. The main outcomes a regime achieves relate to citizen welfare via the five governance functions of ongoing service delivery, projects, policies, legislation and institutional reform; as said earlier.

100 days-period was too short a period for Imran Khan and its PTI to judge its work in terms of citizen welfare or even the five functions.

One could easily find the weak quality of its team then to predict that it would fail to not only achieve its promises but even match the last two civilian regimes widely linked with malpractice, dishonesty and ineptitude. The time proved that the fears stood validated. The PTI team continued to suffer from infighting and ineptitude and cases of negligence, corruption, untruthfulness and mismanagement emerged frequently.

PTI's 52-member cabinet resembled not a cohesive national team but a disjointed and weak Pakistani Cricket team. The PPP and PMLN had team issues too but at least most of their key cabinet nominees were party devotees. In the PTI, many key positions went to freshly inducted electables or unelected advisers who lacked party loyalty. The large numbers of incompetent unelected advisers and certain regular ministers like Farogh Naseem were inducted due to 'coalition pressure' where the main flag-holder (PM or CM) had to accommodate junior partners and independents under compulsion – otherwise threats of slip-out were there – which ultimately happened; MQM, BNP and Saraiki Mahaz had left Khan at the time of No Confidence Motion in March 2022. In PTI's goverments, parties like JI, MQM, PMLQ, PML-Awami (Sh Rashid's party) and BNP all got their share without contributing anything in nation-building process.

The PTI's record was just as bad as that of its fore-runners. There was an influx of non-civilians in key positions even beyond the cabinet. Some presented that *hybrid command and control governance* as a possible future way but others recalled how such influxes earlier led to takeovers. Given their training and ethos, non-civilians were unsuited for civilian tasks. The influx reflected desperate attempts by alleged selectors to shore up a weak team. Finally, there was Imran Khan, whose honesty was supposed to be the big PTI edge and key to rapid progress. *However, his honesty couldn't compensate for his own incompetence and the apparent deceit and incompetence of many within the PTI.*

With such huge team issues, achievements went naturally poor albeit it was still unfair to judge the PTI on proxy public welfare indicators like jobs and growth rates since these were dented first by the slowdown phase started under the PMLN and later by Covid-19. So, one could only review its work on their contributions and governance they delivered in their specific field. Institutional reform in the shape of NAYA PAKISTAN was the big hope from the PTI and its cabinet but the PTI went utterly failed to change the colours & tones of the FBR, bureaucratic-control, the *police & thana* culture, judiciary and jails - it failed as badly as the previous govts. In fact, it created more instability amongst various institutions by making frequent transfers in many top postings in FBR and Police in two provinces.

Imran Khan and the PTI passed some legislation but none had been as crucial as like 18th Amendment and FATA merger bills passed by the PPP and PMLN respectively. It couldn't even manage to get through the most required bill concerning with Saraiki // Southern Punjab province. In fact, PTI was bent upon rolling back the 18th Amendment – but couldn't succeed.

In the area of projects, the Peshawar BRT project remained a constant blot while work had apparently slowed down on CPEC projects. The PTI failed to unveil out-of the-box economic policies for increasing tax and export revenues and <u>revitalising industry; not a single mentionable project could be installed</u>. Also, there was little improvement in daily service delivery in critical areas like <u>school education and technical training polytechnics were totally ignored – not a single new school / institution could be made open</u>.

Thus, in most aspects of governance, PTI's record remained as bad as or worse than those of the PPP, PMLN and the army-rule during last three decades. *The PPP had clear capacities in legislation work and the PMLN in project work – however, with the PTI, it was hard to identify even one area of competence.* In fact, the nation went in reverse gear compared to the 2008-18 era where at least clear political progress occurred with the 18th Amendment, free polls, and less victimization of the media. The selected cabinet strength was largely weak; even more influx of unelected civilians and non-civilians couldn't bring fruits.

Imran Khan's inefficiencies didn't just reflect the failures of a party (PTI) but the disappointments of the impatient worldviews of a large chunk of the middle class, which kept constantly demeaning democratic processes and looking for unrealistic shortcuts to rapid progress. It also reflected the failures of political engineering by forces averse to democratic processes; the middle class went crushed amongst PTI's new experiments with zero inputs, in fact; *Berkeley fellow Niaz Murtaza's* dissertation on media pages dated <u>28th July 2020</u> is also referred for more cogent analysis.

See a voter's dilemma after about 3.5 year's PTI rule. Then next elections were one+ year away and the parties were simply re-organizing their barracks and barrels for the next move. A big fight was ahead and it was going to be tough and emotionally taxing much for voters and political leaders; most lots were double minded then. An intellectual and perceptive (inner) fight between two competing narratives had started cropping up - PTI on one hand and all others on the other. Essentially, for PTI likers, *it was a swing of corruption and incompetence with high slogans, speeches and stories structured around honesty vs effectiveness.*

The PTI, despite having gone up 16 points on the recent (for ref: **TRANSPARENCY INTERNATIONAL**'s index of 15th February 2022) TI's corruption index from 124 to 140, kept using the corruption narrative as its most lethal weapon against its two arch rivals — PMLN and PPP. Corruption, the PTI claimed, had done irreparable damage to the economy, democracy and public institutions. PM Imran Khan didn't miss an opportunity to call leadership of the other two parties by name and attribute every structural and cultural problem to elite capture. Wealth, in Pakistan, remained the source of power and vice versa. A tiny rich class, IK asserted, had an inherent advantage over the bulk of population created by the British-designed apartheid education system which propelled it to find place in all the power structures like legislature, bureaucracy, judiciary, military and media.

Most people, particularly the urban-educated-middle class, were convinced that IK's failure, to deliver on his promises, had to do more with the powerful mafia, which had hindered him from reforming the system of governance, than his competence and commitment. BUT he also made compromises on his principles, calling it strategic adjustment, just to cling to power. He was surrounded by ministers and advisers who were once the blue-eyed of someone else and shared the DNA with those who IK had promised to fight.

Contrary to IK's sympathizers, a significant segment of population did buy the 'incompetence' narrative developed and promoted by the opposition. It is now widely believed that IK, having no political background, had no deep insight into the complex interplay between institutions, Centre and provinces, mass education, judicial gimmicks and international relations. He had a grand vision (or delusion) of making Pakistan an economic powerhouse with ethical foundations of the state of Madina but had no plans to realize it. He tried to run the country on trial-and-error basis and most often offered simplistic solutions to complex problems – but the things didn't work.

Instead of fixing the system of governance, Imran Khan deluded himself and his followers through quick fixes of making reshuffles in bureaucracy and in the cabinet. Luckily, the narrative of incompetence, though appealing to reason and substantiated by what the common man experiences on a daily basis, didn't give political edge to the opposition. Their own dismal performance over the years both at the Centre and in provinces and absence of democracy within their ranks, they (PMLN, PPP, JUI) couldn't allure voters to try them again. And here was the dilemma seen! People lost faith in democracy which was evident from some surveys that pointed out an attitude of indifference (& cursing all parties) creeping into the masses.

Democracy should promote accountability, transparency and rule of law but let it truly represent the people and let the people own it. Elections, manipulated or poorly participated, hardly make any difference to the integrity and prosperity of a country. There was ample time with both the government and the opposition to come out with a *'charter of governance'* to restore the lost confidence of people in democracy – but every leader lost it; democracy would a lost concept very soon in Pakistan.

Imran Khan's DOWNFALL starts as PM: The US withdrawal from Afghanistan pulled out the last leverage the PTI government enjoyed since its inception; commented *Jan Achakzai* in daily **'the News'** of Pakistan dated 7th March 2022. The PTI government had been increasingly promoting a narrative that the international establishment, presumably and notably the US, was behind the Opposition's move i.e., *no-confidence motion (NCM)*. The question; did the US attain such capability of affecting regime change in Pakistan? Some events below contextualised why PTI supporters were promoting that narrative.

In fact, the PTI government failed to break the ice with the then US Admin since President Biden's election campaign when the then MOFA, a former Pakistani ambassador in Washington and certain Pakistani community leaders were openly campaigning for President Trump's re-election. *It was a tactical mistake by the PTI govt setting a stage for the Biden Admin to look at Mr Khan through a negative prism.*

An expected courtesy-call in ending 2021 was not made to PM Khan by President Biden which left the PTI government bitter towards the US Admin. The PTI government boycotted the *'Democracy Conference'* called in and presided over by the Biden Admin. The PTI government also failed to put forth any cogent reason for the boycott except linking the move with ostensibly balancing Chinese concerns.

In mid-August 2021, the US withdrawal from Afghanistan bolstered the feeling in Washington that the Biden Admin no longer needed the active support of the PTI government in Pakistan. **In February 2022;** Prime Minister Khan undertook a much earlier scheduled visit to Russia. The timing inadvertently became highly controversial; hard luck for PM Khan.

> [*It was perceived as visibly anti-US no matter how hard the PM tried to balance it. When the whole world, particularly the US and Europe, were against the Russian invasion of Ukraine, the PM Imran was in Moscow – though on no-fault on the part of PM Khan.*]

The PTI government tried to balance by not joining condemnation of Russia and abstained in UNGA while making statements that implicitly disapproved invasion. It made the government appear on the wrong side of the US Admin-led international consensus. The perception of hard lean on Russia was the last thing the PTI government wanted - the PTI government became an unwitting victim in the resurgent Cold War against Russia.

Additionally, the usual bridge between the PM and the Trump Admin, was not available this time. Thus, despite good ties of Pakistan's Military Generals with the US establishment, including the Pentagon and the CIA, it failed to prevail over frostiness between the PM Imran and President Biden. **On the other hand,** the PMLN supremo Nawaz Sharif kept good ties with President Biden which had developed over the years. President Biden, being a veteran politician, also had a good liaison with the then President Asif Ali Zardari. He was seen being lobbied hard for Bilawal Zardari as the next PM. The new US Ambassador to Pakistan, Donald Blome, an old Pakistani hand in Islamabad for the US, was a friend of Bilawal Zardari, it was known to many.

Against the said backdrop, the relations of PTI government with the Biden Admin could not thrive. Nor it publically proved the conspiracy theory that the Biden Admin was after Imran Khan's removal. ***Thus, the proposed no-confidence motion by the PDM was mainly an outcome of new domestic political associations.*** The PTI government's foreign policy and economic policies were not the main reason galvanising Opposition and the dissidents of PTI - the PM's radical political policies caused a backlash within the PTI. <u>The Opposition feared for its political survival; NAB's alleged accountability witch hunt; nightmare prospect *if PM gets another five-year term;* escalating inflation and misgovernance, especially in Punjab and Khyber PK, were also the cogent factors.</u>

On another count, the ***PM Khan's proud-behaviour treating every PTI member as a dispensable commodity*** led to defection and groupings within the party. Since the empowering factor behind the PDM's **No**

Confidence Motion (NCM) was not the number of the Opposition MNAs, but the number of PTI dissidents which encouraged the PDM to launch the said NCM. The narrative of the US being behind the NCM was systematically promoted to make the PM a *'political martyr for defying the US'* but the main factors behind the NCM were domestic.

The tragedy remained that tabling the NCM in the assembly was opposition's constitutional right, but it was odd on the PTI government's part to neutralise it through public meetings. *How the PTI government could compete with opposition in holding rallies; long march from Karachi to Islamabad was a blunder producing zero results.* Many critics held that the government could only cool down the political temperature; it was not a way to show loyalty – PTI harmed herself.

STANCES OF KHAN's ODD-BEHAVIOUR:

Referring to THE SUGAR REPORT of 2020, the PTI govt picked up **EIGHT sugar mills** for penal action and the millers included leaders of the PTI itself and the opposition leader, Shahbaz Sharif. All got the clean chit except ONE person - Jahangir Tareen. **Ishaq Khaqwani**, a stalwart leader of the PTI from Southern Punjab pointed out the reasons of PM Khan's DOWNFALL, on 7th March 2022, in an interview with **Saleem Safi at GEO TV:**

- *"PTI govt could have proceeded judiciously like others. The PM House cannot interfere in the Jahangir case. Many people like me hold the opinion that harm is being done with Jahangir Tareen.*

- *Imran Khan had no acquaintance with Usman Buzdar before the elections; neither he nor Jahangir Tareen proposed Usman Buzdar.*

- *Mr Khan changed four finance ministers but failed in conducting privatisation process……did nothing on the accountability matters during three-and-a-half-years; PM's 'ehtesaab team' was provenly ineffective.*

- *The Foreign Minister uttered words against Saudi Arabia on a TV channel.*

- *PECA Ordinance was not needed in the present situation.*

- *Cricket and government are two different fields. In politics, you have to talk with your opponents."*

Referring to **Cyril Almeida**'s analysis published in Pakistani media dated 10th April 2022: Imran Khan's tumultuous term as prime minister of Pakistan ended, following weeks of high political drama and days of constitutional chaos. The Supreme Court's landmark verdict restored a parliament that Mr Khan had sought to disperse – the move to dissolve parliament was declared illegal and ordered the house be restored. The decision came after four days of hearings by the top court. Khan had to face a no-confidence vote by lawmakers that he had tried to sidestep.

Mr Khan was effectively left with ONLY ONE choice: *resign or be voted out of office.* The former prime minister's political demise was rooted in twin new realities.

- *Inside the parliament, Mr Khan's PTI had lost the support of coalition allies, denying him the majority he needed to defeat the vote of no confidence.*

- *Outside parliament, Mr Khan appeared to lose the support of Pakistan's powerful military, which the opposition alleged helped him win the 2018 general election, and had recently publicly fallen out with the prime minister over senior military appointments and policy decisions starting from October 2021.*

During those days, as the principal opposition parties, the PPP and PMLN, ramped up their efforts to dislodge PM Khan, coalition allies became vocal in their dissatisfaction with him.

"As far as governance was concerned, the government had totally failed," said Senator Anwaar ul Haq Kakar of the Balochistan Awami Party (BAP), a coalition ally that withdrew support for Khan in late March 2022. There was disgruntlement for the past two years. The BAP was not happy about its share in the federal government and the ministerial portfolio it was allocated. Nadeem Afzal Chan, a special assistant to the PM also resigned his position and rejoined the opposition PPP in early March (2022). Chan said:

> *"I was impressed by Khan's anti-corruption platform and was tired of the status quo. But then I saw: while Khan publicly talked about the poor, privately he surrounded himself with wealthy investors."*

Economic agony: A deepening economic crisis contributed to dissatisfaction with PM Khan's strategies while double-digit inflation was dodging much of his term. In February 2022, as opposition momentum against Khan was being built, the PM announced a cut in domestic fuel and electricity prices despite a global rise, pledging to freeze prices until the end of the fiscal year in June. This step piled further pressure on Pakistan's chronic fiscal deficit and balance-of-payment troubles.

That week, the rupee fell to historic lows (then) against the US dollar and the State Bank of Pakistan (SBP) sharply increased interest rates in an emergency meeting. Although, part of it was the situation they inherited from the previous government and part of it was of course COVID but the government fell quickly into firefighting and reforms were brushed aside. Inflation, fertilizer shortages, Buzdar government in Punjab, rogue policing, it had all got too much. The two biggest economic challenges facing Pakistan at that moment were high inflation and fast depleting foreign exchange reserves.

Inside parliament, the loss of the allies' support reversed the numbers for Mr Khan. BAP, the *Muttahida Qaumi Movement* (MQM) and Pakistan Muslim League – Quaid (PMLQ) account for fewer than five percent of the seats in the 342-member National Assembly. But by pledging to support the no-confidence vote against Mr Khan, the coalition allies effectively ended his three-and-a-half-year spell as prime minister. The opposition parties also claimed to have the support of a number of dissident PTI parliamentarians.

Military's role: With Mr Khan's exit confirmed, former allies were increasingly candid about the third rail of Pakistani politics: civil-military relations. The prime minister's parliamentary support began to dissolve *when the military signaled it would not side with Mr Khan against the opposition, a policy of so-called neutrality.* Senator Kakar of BAP said: '*When the establishment became neutral, the allies saw that the government wouldn't survive. Once the view was entrenched that he can't stay, it was only a matter of time.*'

Khan was the latest in a long line of Pakistani prime ministers who had fallen out with the military over key appointments and foreign policy. In October 2021, simmering civil-military tensions exploded in public view when Mr Khan tried to retain Lt Gen Faiz Hameed as the military spy chief, rejecting the nominee of army chief Gen Qamar Bajwa. Gen Bajwa's nominee, Lt Gen Nadeem Anjum, was eventually appointed as the new DG ISI, but the weeks-long standoff was bruising and ominous.

Gen Bajwa's second term as army chief was ending in November 2021, with Gen Hameed one of the senior-most Generals eligible to replace him. Extraordinary too, was Khan's *neutral foreign policy* and travelling to Russia on 24th February 2022 played their own role. ***Though the Pakistani military had formally backed Khan's Moscow trip but Khan's public rally in Islamabad on 27th March 2022 with a wavering letter in hand altogether changed the shades of Mr Khan's gloomy politics.***

Maj Gen ® Athar Abbas, a former military spokesperson and Pakistan's Ambassador to Ukraine from 2015 to 2018, described a number of differences between Mr Khan and the military leadership that had hoarded over Khan's time in office, including poor political and economic management of PTI that was acting as a drag on the military's public image. On Mr Khan's opposition to military operations inside Pakistan and US-led wars internationally since the 9 / 11 attacks, the army lot was seen much worried. On policy matters, Mr Khan could be mercurial; there was no predictability or stability in his person. Imran Khan was a populist, that was his vulnerability too.

.... MISTAKES ADMITTED AT LAST:

On 5th April 2022: Interim Prime Minister Imran Khan [*He was interim PM for a week from 3rd – 10th April 2022 under Presidential order.*] acknowledged that mistakes were made by the PTI in the past for which *'it paid a high price'* - adding that the party had now wisened up and would prioritize its ideological workers. While addressing a ceremony at Punjab Governor House in Lahore, Mr Khan instructed the PTI workers to get prepared for elections, saying that this time the party would give tickets to those who were aligned with the party's political philosophy. He said:

> *"There were mistakes [committed] by us in the past for which we had to pay a high price. So now after learning from our mistakes, our first decision is to give tickets after a great deliberation. Tickets would be given to all the MPs in attendance who still supported and continued to support the party (PTI)* **during difficult times"**.

The interim prime minister reiterated his rhetoric claim that a ***vast foreign conspiracy*** was hatched against his government, referring to the opposition's no-confidence resolution against him. He alleged that there was a plan made abroad for a regime change in Pakistan in which *'traitors here (opposition) joined with them (conspiracy planners).'* Also, that most of the people who supported this 'conspiracy' had done so inadvertently with only those at the top being in the know.

Mr Khan warned that in the upcoming elections they wouldn't only lose but *'their political graves will be made forever.'* Referring to disgruntled PTI MPAs staying at a private hotel in Lahore, he said this spectacle was laid bare in front of the whole nation to see where people who were elected on PTI tickets and reserved seats, had sold their conscience. The PTI had approached the Supreme Court against those traitors and opined that apart from lifetime bans, they should also be imprisoned.

"Today is a decisive and defining moment in our country," Mr Khan said. He called on the people to wage peaceful protests daily, saying that to do so was their duty along with defeating the alleged conspiracy against his government. The purpose of the demonstrations (he explained) was to send a message to the US and its alleged collaborators here that *'this is a living nation and it won't allow any scheme [against it] to be successful.'* Mr Khan told his supporters to stage a demonstration at Islamabad's F9 Park that night after *Isha* prayers.

Scenario 259

PM's DOWNFALL – 'OTHER' KEY FACTORS

CM USMAN BUZDAR FACTOR:

On 17th August 2018; a day before Imran Khan was sworn in as Pakistan's prime minister, he made an announcement that left his followers stunned, deepening the factionalism in his *Pakistan Tehreek-i-Insaf* (PTI). Mr Khan announced that he had picked his candidate for the office of chief minister of Punjab — the most politically important province of the country. Mr Khan told the rationale for the selection saying:

> "I have nominated Sardar Usman as Punjab chief minister and I want to tell you the reason for doing so......
>
> He belongs to an area of Punjab that is the most backward. People there have no water or electricity or hospital. The special thing about Sardar Usman is that he is well acquainted with how people live in those areas and secondly, he is aware of how the poor lead their lives. When he will assume the office of the chief minister he will know the nature of the plight that faces the under-privileged people of Pakistan....."
>
> [**Barthi in Jhandi Tribal Area,** Buzdar's remote town on the outskirts of *Taunsa Sharif* along Punjab's border with Baluchistan, had no access to basic civic facilities; health facilities were so poor that most local women suffered from night blindness due to malnutrition and in the early '80s, leprosy was diagnosed amongst record residents there.]

Nominated CM Usman Buzdar — the son of a three-time former MPA - had triumphed in the 2018 general elections from PP-286 [Dera Ghazi Khan (DGK)-II] by securing 26,897 votes. He was a *tehsil nazim* of a mountainous tribal area of DGK during president Gen Musharraf's era.

Designated CM Buzdar was a member of the Pakistan Muslim League-Quaid (PMLQ) from 2002 to 2011. Later, he left the party to join the PMLN. In 2013, he ran for provincial assembly seat on PMLN ticket but was defeated by a PPP contestant. Before the 2018 general elections,

Buzdar joined the *Janoobi Punjab Suba Mahaz*, which then merged with the PTI, thus making him a member of Khan's party. Buzdar has a bachelor's degree in law and master's degree in political science.

Curiously, Mr Khan was going to nominate Usman Buzdar, but his choice clearly did not sit well with many in the party — especially those who had financed PTI's campaigns for years and were expecting some experienced head in Punjab. The skepticism over Buzdar's selection was so rampant within the party that Imran Khan had to take to Twitter the morning after taking his oath; while defending his decision, saying:

> "I want to make it clear [that] I stand by our nominee Usman Buzdar for Chief Minister Punjab. I have done my due diligence over the past two weeks and have found him to be an honest man. He has integrity and stands by my vision and <u>ideology of Naya Pakistan</u>."

But the tweet did little to appease party stalwarts from the province, as well as its newly elected members of the provincial assembly, who were still in disbelief. Many believed that '***Usman Buzdar was picked up on the instructions of his new wife Bushra Bibi who had got some spiritual guidance from......***'. PTI's elected MsPA did not know anything about Buzdar, except what Imran Khan had told them in a video message and later through his tweets. Few, if any, believed that Buzdar could effectively run the government in the stronghold of the Sharifs, which they had just snatched from them — with much difficulty and might be 'accidently'.

Imran Khan's reasons for handpicking Buzdar from anonymity were simply discarded by the PTI voters, at least on the face of it that Mr Buzdar was from one of the most backward areas of Punjab — and that Buzdar was the only member of the Punjab assembly who did not have electricity at home. Mr Khan repeatedly assured his party members saying he fully backed Buzdar all the way. Since the first day of his office as the CM Punjab, Usman Buzdar had been firefighting rumours of his early departure. Despite growing unease within the PTI's ranks about his effectiveness, he continued to bank on the support of PM Imran Khan.

When Buzdar's critics painted him as a failure with nothing tangible to show, PM Khan predictably turned to cricket comparisons. '*He will prove to be Wasim Akram Plus,*' the PTI leader said on multiple occasions. PTI's most members ridiculed at the idea that Imran Khan selected Buzdar for the position solely because he was from an underdeveloped region having no electricity, water and a hospital. One PTI MPA often pointed out that the region did not have these facilities *'in spite of the fact that Buzdar's father had been in active politics since the early 1980s and was thrice returned to the provincial assembly between 1985 and 2002.'* One could imagine what was the capability, acumen and wisdom of his father / family.

See one Lahorite MPA's arguable comments:

> *"The man we were ordered to elect as the Leader of the House had made it to the provincial assembly for the first time and had no prior administrative experience to handle the Punjab's bureaucracy. Who would entrust such a man with such a huge responsibility of running the country's most populous and politically most important province? He may be a good man but he was NOT THE RIGHT PERSON FOR THIS JOB he had been given. Time has proved us right."*

The cynicism about Buzdar's ability to match his restless predecessor, PMLN's Shahbaz Sharif's abilities wasn't the only factor that caused an outrage among the PTI old guard. Buzdar was not only an unknown commodity in the political arena but his ties with the party were also rather recent. He had contested and lost the 2013 election for a provincial seat on PMLN's ticket, a party he had joined after quitting PMLQ. He quit PMLN only a couple of months before the 2018 elections to join the ***Junoobi Punjab Sooba Mahaz*** (The Southern Punjab Province Front), which was formed by PMLN 'dissidents' led by Makhdum Khusro Bakhtiar, who was later the PTI's federal Minister for National Food Security. The *Mahaz* opted to merge with PTI after dissolution of the previous assemblies (2013-18); so Buzdar was there.

The fact remains that Buzdar was chosen for the same reasons that made him ineffective; unlike his other major rivals for his job, he lacked an independent power base and that made it easier for **PM Khan to control Buzdar and rule the Punjab province indirectly from** *Bani Gala*.

Buzdar was also aware that his opposition from within the PTI, especially from Lahore through MPA Aleem Khan and from Multan via Shah Mahmood Qureshi, would prove to be major challenges for him during his tenure. Hence, when he rose from his seat after his election as the chief executive of the province, to thank the House, he decided to first shut up his detractors — not from the opposition benches, but from the treasury benches of his own PTI; how pity it was. *"I proposed someone else instead of Usman Buzdar for Punjab CMship: Jahangir Tareen"*; **Daily Pakistan Global** dated 23rd October 2018 is referred.

PTI's inner circles knew that Buzdar's background was not the only reason for his elevation to CM's office; his wife was close to Mr Khan's isolated spouse, Bushra Bibi. Others, such as well-known TV journalist **Sohail Warraich**, contended that the premier was told by his wife to pick a man whose name begins with the Urdu letter *aen*; further explaining:

> "There were only two people elected to the provincial assembly in 2018 whose name started with that letter. One of them died, leaving Usman Buzdar as the only choice for Imran."

Hasan Javid, an associate professor at the Lahore University of Management Science (LUMS), argued that PM Khan had also been trying to balance the factional conflict within the PTI by choosing a 'neutral' candidate. PM Khan was also operating under the [mistaken] belief that he himself would be able to ensure effective governance in Punjab through Buzdar. *But it was not the first time a party leader tried to control Punjab remotely.* In the 1970s, Zulfikar Ali Bhutto had changed four chief ministers — Mustafa Khar, Hanif Ramay, Sadiq Hussain Qureshi and Meraj Khalid — in Punjab. Mr Bhutto kept changing his CMs in Punjab so that none of them could grow ambitions to challenge his authority.

On 18th November 2019: Chief Minister Usman Buzdar faced a volley of criticisms from party MPAs at a PTI parliamentary party meeting as they expressed dissatisfaction over the performance of the Punjab government during the past 15 months; *TV news* of that day are referred.

The parliamentary party meeting, called ahead of the Punjab Assembly session, was meant to take party MPAs into confidence with regard to plans for holding the local government elections in March 2020. In the meeting the MPAs complained that the bureaucracy was not cooperating with them and even their genuine issues were not being resolved. Unbridled price hikes and unemployment or facing salary cuts were also discussed; thus, PTI's popularity had hit an all-time low.

> [*In Pakistan, the parliamentary party meetings are usually called to allow the party MPAs to vent their anger in a closed-door meeting instead of expressing resentment in the assembly session and bring embarrassment for the government.*]

Referring to an essay in the **daily 'DAWN'** dated 9th February 2020:

> "Apparently, PTI party leaders fear similarly that the success of their proxies in governing Punjab efficiently could eclipse their own performance and create a threat to them.
>
> Even Nawaz Sharif never trusted anyone except his younger brother for this office. The only time he agreed to give the job to someone outside the family was in 1990, when he selected Ghulam Haider Wyne. But that was meant to keep Pervaiz Elahi out — a step that sowed the seeds of an unbridgeable rift between the Sharifs and the Chaudhrys from Gujrat."

CM Buzdar was seen as an unassuming, modest and quiet person; was often felt knowledgeless and ineffective in comparison with his predecessor Shahbaz Sharif of the PMLN. Buzdar had always been at the center of media speculations about his looming departure. A senior Lahore-based journalist pointed out that PM Khan had intentionally not groomed anyone from his party for the Punjab CM's slot.

> "His party [PTI] didn't promote any specific candidate who could replace Shahbaz during its campaign for power in 2013 and 2018. In my view, Imran Khan realized that the day he announced his candidate for the post of Punjab's chief minister, the party would lose all its popular momentum and might as well break up. Thus, he deliberately kept his options open until his ascension to power."

'*The Blunders of 'Kaptaan*' in **Newsweek Pakistan** dated 14th March 2022 is referred here for the following script:

> "Under Buzdar's watch as the Chief Minister, five Inspector Generals of the Punjab Police were changed. He was largely and consistently criticized for his incompetence during his time as chief minister, and one of the worst appointments Khan made during his tenure. It was later revealed that several PTI members including Jehangir Tareen and Asad Umar were against Buzdar's appointment as Chief Minister, and it was one of the major points of disagreement among Khan and other party members."

In fact, none of the PTI leaders such as Aleem Khan, Shah Mahmood Qureshi and Aslam Iqbal — who were often discussed by the media as potential candidates for the coveted position — were ever given any signal by Imran Khan; they were mostly wild guesses by the media.

Buzdar represented a new experiment in Punjab. It was after almost 45 years that Punjab had a chief minister hailing from South Punjab and the first who didn't have any links with the urban industrial business community and the middle class from central Punjab. Also, he was the first chief minister who was not groomed politically under military rulers.

BUZDAR – WHY SO DESPARATELY NEEDED?

PM Khan's relentless support for CM Buzdar notwithstanding, he remained under clouds ever since his election as the 26th chief executive of the province. One TV anchor after another and one columnist after another predicted Buzdar's imminent downfall. His own PTI colleagues were not happy with him and considered him an ineffective manager, ill-equipped to handle the Punjab's tedious affairs. He had not only survived this onslaught of speculative attacks but also managed to throw out key-people like his media adviser Shahbaz Gill (Mr Gill had tried to exercise PM Khan's executive powers).

CM Buzdar kept rival Aleem Khan, who could prove a threat to him, out of his cabinet; of course, it could be a direction from the top boss, PM Khan. *A number of PTI leaders believed that CM Buzdar would be the main factor if the party's popularity declined in Punjab - an eventual downfall.* Governor Punjab Ch Sarwar had been often accused of supporting efforts to oust Buzdar, or at least bring him under his wing. Allegedly, Aleem Khan was nursing a grudge against Buzdar for refusing to re-induct him in the cabinet. After all, Aleem Khan had generously financed the party's campaign for power in the province and he could have been in Buzdar's place, but the National Accountability Bureau (NAB) cases against him were the main hinderance.

Some of Buzdar's cabinet ministers also kept on nurturing hopes of one day replacing him; yet he was there despite all the loud media speculations, which peaked in ending year 2019 when 20 PTI MPAs from south and central Punjab formed a pressure group to secure development funds for their constituencies. Some reports suggested that the group was created at Buzdar's own behest to thwart his opponents campaigning with PM Khan for *'odd changes in Punjab scenario'*.

During CM Buzdar's times, most political analysts agreed that the then *'political crisis in Punjab'* was mainly linked to factional fighting within the PTI government as well as to the popular perceptions about **Buzdar's**

incompetence. It was clear that Buzdar's appointment had always been an issue for the PTI governing figures. From the beginning, the Punjab government had to deal with competing centers of power; thinking about Jahangir Tareen, Pervaiz Elahi and, to a lesser extent, Aleem Khan and even Shah Mahmood Qureshi — initially all were vying for the [Buzdar's] position, of course with their own agendas.

The attacks repeatedly mounted against Buzdar by his detractors who always focused on underscoring poor governance and ineffective administration under CM Buzdar. No one ever accused him of corruption, apart from giving a few jobs to his relatives and friends and diverting huge development funds to his home constituency. One of his critics asked from his own PTI:

> "Who needs corruption charges to bring him down? His incompetence and poor governance are enough to topple him whenever his opponents get the signal from the right quarters."

Throughout CM Buzdar's governance, there had been signs of visible decline across the province: stalled infrastructure projects, erosion of projects, such as dengue control and garbage collection in Lahore, that were previously seen to work well. All of this, coupled with the wheat flour shortages and delayed actions to fight smog in the cities had harmed his image. On top of that, the federal government's own problems with the economy, growing inflation and bureaucratic slowdown in fear of NAB cases, had reinforced the idea that the Punjab government remained weak and ineffective for the period CM Buzdar incumbered. A compromised CM, Buzdar had always been perceived as weak and, thus, an easy target for his critics, precisely because he lacked a credible base of his own.

In a context where the Punjab government was existing with a razor-thin majority, it was not difficult to see how PMLQ, the main ally of PTI in the province, for example, could tighten the screws in the hopes of gaining more concessions and control at a given time. This was where the governance issues popped in. Under PMLQ and PMLN since 2002, Punjab was governed by strongmen — Pervaiz Elahi and Shahbaz Sharif — who, despite their many failings, had delivered in tangible ways. See a media comment here:

> "A lot is made of how a disproportionate amount of attention was paid to Lahore and, it was seen when comparing Lahore's infrastructure with any other Pakistani city. Both PMLQ and PMLN had invested

> *heavily in developing the entire province's road network, upgrading sanitation and, less successfully, uplifting schools and hospitals.*
>
> *Traditional patronage politics also continued under them, but visible signs of improved service delivery like roads and sewers supplemented the <u>thana-kuchehri</u> [police station and court] politics as a basis for the support enjoyed by their governments. **Under PTI, there is less visible evidence of service delivery.** While the government talks about health insurance, etc., the effects of such initiatives are too diffused to be seen by the electorate."*

In later months of the PTI rule, there were signs of visible decline across the province in various organizations. Sohail Warraich, a top journalist and widely respected person, broadly agreed with the analysis but said the uproar over Buzdar's ineffectiveness was never the objective of the so-called pressure group of PTI MPAs to blackmail him or get him replaced. Further he commented that:

> *"They had come together to support the chief minister and help him take back some administrative powers over the bureaucracy and the police from **Imran Khan, who has been directly and remotely controlling the province from Islamabad.** The federal interference in the province's administration increased to a new high after wholesome changes in the provincial bureaucracy and police with both the new Chief Secretary and Inspector General of Police directly reporting to the prime minister."*

The fact remained that even PMLQ didn't want Buzdar to go. It didn't suit their interests, they wanted Buzdar to be a strong chief executive so that they could share power in the province with him in exchange for their support in the assembly. This was a (hidden) major bone of contention between Imran Khan and the Chaudhrys of Gujrat, in fact.

There had been strong indications that CM Buzdar's poor governance was also a concern for the establishment, as Punjab was the key to governing Pakistan and anything that could undermine PTI's credibility in Punjab would weaken their backers as well. Many times, there were disturbing posts on social media that *the first line of difference amongst PM Imran Khan and Gen Bajwa [the then Army Chief of Pakistan], drawn during ending 2018, was about the removal of an ineffective administrator named CM Usman Buzdar which suggestion was turned down by PM Khan very cold bloodedly and without any discussion on merits of the advice.* An Islamabad-based political analyst and a think tank said:

> "The establishment is a major stakeholder in the new political system that has emerged in Pakistan after the 2018 elections. But I don't think it is involved in day-to-day politicking. ...... [though] they will not mind using the allegations of poor governance in Punjab as an excuse to control or replace PTI, [if and when] they need."

Federal Railways Minister Sh Rasheed contended that the real target of the campaign against Buzdar was his leader, Imran Khan, and not the chief minister himself. According to him: '*.... once Buzdar is shown the door, Imran Khan's opponents will come after him*'.

Journalists community and the electronic media affirmed that:

> "There is a lot of truth in Sh Rasheed's claim. Those who are pursuing Buzdar are actually after the prime minister, there is no doubt about it. But it is true to the extent of opposition parties and not for those who aren't in any way linked to the PTI-led coalition in the province or in Islamabad."

For PMLN and other opponents, weakness in Punjab — particularly in terms of governance — created the opportunity to attack the government and build support. At a time when there were rumours of an understanding being reached between the establishment and Shahbaz Sharif, a change in Punjab was in fact a cogent precursor to bigger changes in Islamabad. The establishment always wanted to keep civilians off-balance by not allowing any single party to consolidate its support. They cut PMLN down to size and did the same with PTI in April 2022; No Confidence Move is referred.

Many still believe that the establishment had correctly managed to avert the crisis of legitimacy that had initially emerged from the persisted crisis of governance in Punjab. Instead of getting a change in Punjab, they got the whole table turned in Islamabad, PM Khan sent home; it was done through creation of forward blocs in PTI and the resurgence of PMLQ and PMLN.

PMLN played its own game. It wanted the cracks in the coalition and within PTI to bring down the governments in Punjab and then in the Centre - while watching the game from the sidelines. The infighting ultimately pulled down the PTI-led administration in Punjab through its bureaucracy – and then they aspired to jump in higher stakes. PMLN came in a good position to capitalise on PTI's weakness in next elections. The rumours of a rapprochement between the establishment and

Shahbaz Sharif came true and the political scenario started changing in March 2022 with full fervor, passion and eagerness.

It was extremely unlikely that Buzdar's removal could lead to the fall of the PTI government in Punjab at that time. But the PMLN succeeded in creating a small forward bloc defecting from PTI in the Punjab and National Assemblies both. History tells us it was not a difficult task — with the right signals from Rawalpindi — so it was dramatically launched in early 2022 to pack the luggage of PTI and also for PM Khan.

Despite all odds, CM Buzdar was indeed a lucky man; his future was closely tied to the first lady Bushra Bibi and in turn with PM Imran Khan because his dismissal could be taken as a big defeat for the prime minister, who kept on refusing to relent in the face of pressure from his party. Ultimately, Buzdar's incompetence dragged his leader, PM Khan, with him.

SARAIKI SUBA (PROVINCE):

The Punjab game, in fact, had slipped out of PMLN's hand on 21st April 2018 when *Junoobi Punjab Sooba Mahaz* [JPSM] president Makhdoom Khusro Bakhtayar had urged all the political parties to support their demand of SEPARATE PROVINCE and added that it would only be possible with consensus of all the political parties. Terming the JPSM a voice of over 35m people of south Punjab, Mr Bakhtiar said:

> *"If someone cannot contribute to resolve their problems, they should not create hurdles – ours is a one-point agenda of the creation of south Punjab province for the political and financial well-being of the people of the region. In the past all political parties made commitments to us - but were never fulfilled.*
>
> *It is regretted that the budget for the Orange Line Metro Train Lahore was over Rs:240bn [then] whereas the budget for the whole south Punjab region stood at Rs:206bn."*

On 8th May 2018; the negotiations between *Pakistan Tehreek-e-Insaf* [PTI] and JPSM concluded while general elections were ahead. The JPSM group, which comprised of more than 21 sitting and former elected representatives of the PMLN, made its merger official after meeting PTI Chairman Imran Khan there and then.

In fact, the PMLN had not fulfilled its promise of *declaring the Southern Punjab a province* during its full tenure of five years – thus the reaction was evident. Next day, during the joint media conference, Mr Bakhtiar explained his agenda that *'new provincial demarcations are the need of the time. The demarcation of new provinces will ensure that funds allocated for Rajanpur are not given to Multan.'*

During the interim government period, they were ready for dialogue with any party. But the PTI had backed the JPSM's demand for a separate province - not for linguistic reasons but on administrative grounds to mitigate the miseries being faced by some 35 million people living in Bahawalpur, Multan and Dera Ghazi Khan Divisions. *As per their written and signed contract, the PTI had agreed to include the formation of southern Punjab province in the PTI's agenda for the first 100 days – if they came in power.* Contrarily, PMLN's Federal Minister Maryam Aurangzeb had claimed that 'those lawmakers' had already been planning to quit the party, and termed them a bunch of opportunists.

Later, the said estranged PMLN lawmakers making JPSM officially merged into the PTI to contest the 2018 general elections under the PTI banner. Mr Bakhtiar again highlighted that the PMLN had been ruling Punjab for the last 30-35 years kept south Punjab with itself not for the sake of federation but just to keep on ruling. PTI's Imran Khan had assured the JPSM leaders that agreeing to the formation of a new province was not a political decision but [his] conviction.

SARAIKI SUBA: WHAT PROGRESS IN PTI ERA:

Making a new province in the Southern Punjab was the main and written promise of Imran Khan in their original manifesto before the general election of 25th July 2018. When his party Pakistan Tehreek e Insaf [PTI] got majority vote in the elections and Mr Khan took the office of the premiership, he reiterated his promise again through his 100-days agenda. The people of the region had high hopes that the PTI government would make their dream come true but the initial serious work for constitutional amendment couldn't be taken up till the last day of that year. No preliminary practical measures were taken in this regard whatsoever.

Earlier, the Pakistan Muslim League Nawaz [PMLN] and Pakistan Peoples Party [PPP] had promised to establish South Punjab province during their respective tenures but both parties failed to implement their resolve. One Tahir Bashir Cheema had also established his separate *South Punjab Province Mahaz* [SPPM] and ran the campaign before 2018-elections. During that campaign, Imran Khan had announced that the province of South Punjab would be established within the **first 100 days** of his government. After the aforesaid written agreement, the SPPM also merged with PTI and participated in the elections on PTI ticket calling a sweeping victory in their respective areas of influence – all for the PTI chief, Imran Khan.

After the polls, PTI won more than 50 provincial and 29 National Assembly seats in Southern Punjab and became a representative majority party of the region. *But despite completing 100 days, the ruling PTI failed to present a Constitutional draft in the National Assembly for the formation of South Punjab province; instead, PM Khan formed an Executive Council for the said purpose.* An office had also been provided at chief minister's secretariat in Lahore. Five meetings were held by that Executive committee / council members over the matter; every time discussions were held but no practical measures could be taken to make out the required 'constitutional draft'. It was an uphill but an essential task; meetings were held amongst the secretaries of related departments, including revenue, finance, water resources, education and legal departments, *however, no fruitful results seen.*

On 17th November 2018; Punjab Chief Minister Usman Bazdar, during his visit to Dera Ghazi Khan had once more repeated that the prime minister would soon announce establishment of a separate South Punjab province. However, the PTI remained confined to negotiations with 'other' stakeholders on different issues for the creation of a separate province and PM Khan couldn't succeed in fulfilling his promises. One local MPA Owais Leghari said before the press that:

> "PTI is a U-turn party and they can step back from its promises. Hundred days have been completed yet so far their ministers did not raise the issue of South Punjab province in any assembly."

Khawaja Ghulam Farid, head of another but similar *Saraikistan Qaumi Ittehad*, said that:

> "...the present government (of the PTI) has completed its hundred days so they should fulfill their promise. Balanced federation is a symbol of strong Pakistan. The leadership of the SPPM is also (asking for) stability in the country; now the **province of Siraikistan** should be established."

Recalling back; PTI's one of the promises before forming the government was to *'spearhead the creation of a South Punjab province on administrative lines'*. Punjab Chief Minister Usman Buzdar, in October 2018, had said that *'the dream would come true during PTI's tenure'*. In late 2018, the party had started off on an active footing, setting up the Executive Council on Creation of South Punjab province and forming a committee to develop political consensus over the creation of the new province.

Over the 3+years PTI's stay in power, however, much of the progress towards creating the said new province remained focused on setting up the *South Punjab Secretariat*, described by the PTI as the first step towards establishing the new federating unit. However, *differences emerged over whether the sub-secretariat would be set up in Bahawalpur or Multan,* with PTI stalwart Jahangir Tareen admitting that there were divergent opinions within the party over the location. PTI's Foreign Minister Shah Mahmood Qureshi had announced that the prime minister would make the final decision on the location of the secretariat after meeting representatives from the areas.

On 28th January 2019; the PMLN took lead on the said old issue and submitted in the National Assembly a constitutional amendment bill for creation of the Bahawalpur and South Punjab provinces. *PTI's job was actually done by its opposition in parliament and PM Khan could have taken it as blessing and welcome the bill* <u>FOR THE SAKE OF STRONGER PAKISTAN</u>. The bill demanded that Article 1 of the Constitution be amended to create the Bahawalpur and South Punjab provinces. The Bahawalpur province would consist of the then administrative Division, while the Divisions of Dera Ghazi Khan and Multan would fall into the South Punjab province.

The bill also called for amending Article 51, over-seeing the changes in allocation of seats in the National Assembly, making way for representation of the two new provinces in parliament. Once the amendment was done, Bahawalpur would have 15 general and 3 women-seats, bringing the total count of seats to 18. The bill also called for the allocation of 38 seats to the South Punjab province. After the amendment, the total number of seats on the NA floor would be 326; 266 general seats + 60 as women-specific seats.

The amendment also called for relevant changes to be made in Article 59 of the Constitution; it was regarding the seats for non-Muslims.

The amendment called for 39 seats of the Punjab provincial assembly to be allocated for Bahawalpur; 31 general seats + 8 for women. According to the bill, 80 seats were to be allocated for the South Punjab province; 64 general seats + 14 for women and 2 were to be allocated for minorities. The bill also called for an amendment in Article 154 of the Constitution, through which a <u>National Commission for the Creation of New Provinces</u> was to be constituted to deal with the area and other such specifications of the new provinces. The bill also said that Article 175(a) of the Constitution should be amended to create respective seats of the Supreme Court and the high court in new provinces. *The bill pointed out that <u>on 9th May 2012</u> the Punjab Assembly had already approved the creation of these provinces.*

Speaking to the media regarding this development, PMLN leaders Shahid Khaqan Abbasi, Marriyum Aurangzeb and Ahsan Iqbal announced that *the PMLN would support the PTI government unconditionally* to create the two promised provinces.

However, the PTI and its leadership didn't take interest in obliging their own signed contract for the Southern Province. In fact, after three years, the PTI and Imran Khan both paid much heavy price for it – Khusro Bakhtiar of the JPSM, though was holding a portfolio as federal minister for Food then, was the first parliamentarian to quit the PTI's coalition govt along with his companion-MsNA in early 2022 – thus carving path for NO CONFIDENCE MOVE in March 2022 – which sent the PTI home <u>on 10th April 2022</u>.

On 30th June 2020; the Additional Chief Secretary (ACS) and Additional Inspector General of Police were formally appointed. The secretariat was to cover the Divisions of Multan, Bahawalpur and Dera Ghazi Khan and the civil servants were to be divided between Multan and Bahawalpur – but the **CONSTITUTIONAL AMENDMENT WAS THE BASIC REQUIREMENT** for which the PTI had missed the train in early 2019.

Calling it a major milestone in the establishment of the South Punjab province, Mr Qureshi, <u>on 1st September 2020</u>, announced the posting of high-level bureaucrats to South Punjab for a fully functional secretariat. Six months later, Prime Minister Imran Khan laid the foundation stone of the secretariat in Multan.

SARAIKI SUBA: FINALLY IN OFFING?

On 9th April 2021: Apart from the establishment of secretariats, PM Imran Khan approved a plan for the development of South Punjab as a separate administrative zone. He also gave consent to amend the Punjab Civil Servants Act of 1974 and to carry out necessary legislation to dedicate 32 per cent job quota for South Punjab — proportionate to the region's population percentage in the province. *In June, however, the Punjab Cabinet Committee on Legislative business deferred the proposal for the job quota.*

PM Khan had given signal to a plan envisaging development of the South Punjab in ending 2020 - as a *'separate administrative zone'* within the Punjab province with an all-powerful secretariat to tackle issues ranging from lack of resources to under-representation of the region's populace in public sector jobs especially in Education and Health sectors.

However, the South Punjab secretariat comprising *15 departments* remained under criticism since their inception in September 2020 as *the Punjab govt had failed to give any changeover plan to transfer the due administrative powers to the new administrative secretaries posted there.* The plan came under wider public scanner when the PTI government withdrew two notifications, issued on 29-30th March, regarding rollback of these establishments. *While the rules of business had been formulated in December 2020, they were never notified.* Eventually, Punjab CM Usman Buzdar had to himself appear before the media to claim that *'the issuance of the notifications was a technical mistake and human error'* – BUT there was no compensation or re-issuance of the same.

The issuance and withdrawal of 'erroneous notfications', however, provided enough time to the Punjab govt for captivating all necessary measures it had been reluctant to take for the past seven months. The plan that got the PM's approval was prepared by Punjab Finance's ministerial committee after marking all the possible and practical hurdles that, till then, had been delaying vital decisions and measures. It was placed before the Prime Minister Khan during his next visit to Lahore.

The prime minister was informed that poverty rate in South Punjab was twice as much as in rest of the province as the region had been given only 17 pc of the development share despite having 32pc of the population of the province. During his presentation, the PM was told that the PTI government had allocated a minimum guaranteed annual development program (ADP) share of 33 pc and ring-fenced the allocation by the provincial cabinet. Also, that a separate ADP book would be published for the south Punjab region in the upcoming budget.

It was also suggested that amendments would be needed in the Punjab's Civil Servant Act 1974 (Act VIII of 1974) to allocate a quota for the region in the public sector jobs and the same would be possible through provincial legislation, as all the provinces except Punjab had the powers to allocate jobs on zonal / regional basis; Balochistan had seven zones, Khyber PK five and Sindh had two zones. Thus, the south Punjab region was entitled for 32pc job quota in line with its population base.

A PC-I had to be developed to offer technical assistance to all the departments being moved to South Punjab secretariats to ensure a smooth transition and meet operational challenges. However, the power thirsty Lahorite-bureaucrats suggested that the devolved departments such as *finance, planning and development, law, services and general administration (S & GAD) as well as home department be reverted back to Lahore* to be run at the central level and their devolution could be reconsidered in a second phase by the ministerial committee.

Besides the above said five departments that might be moved back to Lahore, and send the *livestock and dairy development, agriculture, health, education, wildlife and fisheries, irrigation, housing, urban development and public health engineering (HUD & PHE), board of revenue (BoR), communication and works, local government and community development* to the South Punjab's new secretariat at Mulatn. The Punjab government also had plans to initiate work for the construction of new buildings for the secretariats in Multan and Bahawalpur on immediate basis during that fiscal year.

Shah M Qureshi also called on PPP and PMLN politicians from South Punjab to help the government establish the new province and form political consensus in this regard. Days earlier, the foreign minister had announced that a bill for the creation of the new province would be tabled in the National Assembly but that day never saw dawn during PTI's government. With a lot of work yet to be done, the PTI was sent home in April 2022 – the setting up the new Saraiki Suba was no more on the cards of new incumbents.

The end-story was: the controversy that surrounded the Punjab government's plans regarding the future of an administratively and financially autonomous south Punjab was not likely to move ahead with the withdrawal of notifications that reportedly rolled back the powers to be devolved to the people of this area. Once CM Buzdar said that *'human error'* was responsible for those notifications. One notification had *'erroneously taken back'* the order issued in September (2020) to administratively separate the province's three divisions — Multan, Bahawalpur and D.G. Khan — with split secretariats at the divisional headquarters of Multan and Bahawalpur.

The other notification amended the rules of business for south Punjab, limiting the authority of officers appointed in the South Punjab secretariat. The CM announced the formation of a ministerial committee that was supposed to come up with recommendations for reinforcing the separate administrative set-ups for the southern districts and devolving more functions and departments to improve governance and resolve problems at the local level.

The PTI had won the majority of seats in the national and provincial legislatures from south Punjab in the 2018 elections on the promise of creating a new *Janoobi Punjab province*. Although it ring-fenced the share of the southern districts in the provincial development budget in accordance with their population, the administration continued to delay bringing the issue of the new province to the legislature for Punjab's division into more parts.

Not only did it take CM Buzdar administration two years to set up a separate secretariat for the region, the officers working there had limited powers to take administrative or financial decisions in their jurisdiction. This led to frustration even within the ranks of the ruling party. Indeed, the division of a province was never easy and required much political give and take and several changes in the country's constitutional and legal framework. But a fully functional and independent south Punjab secretariat equipped with complete administrative and financial powers could have been the first effective step BUT the intentions were NOT honest.

Much later....

On 3rd August 2021: A well-attended procession reminded PM Khan and the ruling PTI of its electoral promise to establish a *Seraiki province* in its first 100 days of the government in Layyah's Kot Sultan town. The rally was organised by the *Seraiki Sooba Saang Committee* in which a large number of people—women, students, intellectuals, journalists and local political activists—were present. The rally was supported by the *Seraiki Lok Saanjh, Seraiki Students Council, Seraiki Wasaib Movement, Bazam-i-Farid, Seraiki Action Committee, Sindhu Bachai Tarla and Seraiki Tareemat Saanjh* - small local groups of the areas around.

[Point to Ponder: *if there were so diverging groups in one small district, not joining hands under one banner or putting support for SPPM, one can understand how serious the Seraiki people were for their cause; may be it that was why they all failed to get separate province for them – as a collective cause.*]

The issue of the Seraiki province had been hovering for many years. Initially, the PPP passed a bill in 2012 in the upper house of parliament to carve out a *Seraiki* province. Not Just that, the PPP tabled another bill in the Senate in May 2019 in order to accelerate the efforts to make the province but it remained a fruitless exercise. The PTI also came up with a south Punjab secretariat, the future of which was equally uncertain. *It was all a story of the false promises of the province – and for vested interests of many from within the Saraiki political gurus.*

Had the PTI wished to survive and sustain its vote bank in this part of Punjab, it could work to fulfil the said promise; *all political parties had empty slogans in their bags.*

In fact, the *Seraiki* Sooba could serve as a corrective measure to the past injustices inflicted upon the *Seraikis;* one speaker in the procession opined.

> 'Our leadership is silent over the matter as they had been awarded ministries. If the prime minister wants political stability in the region – Seraiki Province is the answer.'

IK DITCHED HIS (INVESTOR) FRIENDS: FAMOUS SUGAR REPORT (2020)

[*In Pakistan,* **Sugar cane** *support price was Rs.180 per kg in December 2019. Industrial standard says that from 400kg sugar cane, 56kg Sugar is refined; means that each kg sugar costs Rs:32.14 as per sugar cane price. 15% (Rs:4.82) was the industry running cost - bringing the sugar's final price at about Rs:37 per kg. Adding 17% Taxes on sugar, bringing its price for the consumer at Rs:43.29.*

But in 2019, sugar was being sold at Rs:60 [*on 8th December 2019 for reference*]*, while the Government of Pakistan used to pay additional subsidy to sugar industry; the industry also cheat the farmers every year by creating delays in buying sugar cane.*

> *If the sugar cane is left lying in the sun for some days after harvest, it loses weight by losing water content and this factor nets less cash for the farmer. The sugar industry shows a lower production, selling more than 35% sugar production as undeclared - by declaring a low conversion %age in Industry calculations. In Pakistan, the sugar industry easily avoids taxes on this undeclared sugar production.*
>
> *It is also on media record that some sugar mills had not delivered Sugar stock on contract to the Government of Pakistan for more than a year and availed stay orders from the courts to avoid punishment or paying of taxes. Thus, it was logical for the Government to take strict action against the sugar mafia that was cheating the entire Pakistani nation. However, <u>the successive Governments in Pakistan were never seen willing to take action against the cheating sugar industry as most of the industry was (and still) owned by first tier politicians, government bureaucrats and policy makers</u>.]*

On 22nd February 2020; Prime Minister Imran Khan constituted a three-member committee headed by Director General FIA as convener to conduct an inquiry into an abnormal hike in sugar prices during past two months. The other two members of the committee included a senior officer of the Intelligence Bureau [IB] and the Director General Anti-Corruption, Punjab. The convener was allowed to co-opt for any other member for the completion of given assignment.

The Terms of Reference [TOR] included to identify and fix responsibility, if any, on any individual, officer or organisation or any purported benefit to a private party, besides suggesting a way forward for future course of action. The committee was asked to look into the matter from various angles, keeping in view mainly 14 questions, which included: was the then export of sugar justified? Any subsidy was given on its export and its impact, with potential beneficiaries within or outside government.

The other questions for the committee were: <u>whether the production this year was low as compared to past years. Was minimum support price sufficient? Did the mills purchase sugarcane at exorbitantly higher prices than minimum support price</u>; if yes, reasons thereof? Reasons for the mills not purchasing sugarcane, for a limited period of a few weeks from farmers and its impact, if any, on sugar price? <u>Basis for determination of ex-mill price and reasons for increase in ex-mill price? Market manipulation / cartelisation by sugar mills? Impact of tax increase on sugar price at ex-mill / retail level? Hoarding at wholesale or retail level and within sugar mills</u>, vis-à-vis <u>stocks of last year</u> etc etc.

On 4th **April 2020:** GEO TV News told that, as per report of the Federal Investigation Agency (FIA), some top PTI members were among those who gained from the the then sugar crisis in the country. The more influential were Jahangir Khan Tareen [JKT] and a brother of Minister for National Food Security Khusro Bakhtiar.

The report also claimed that the companies belonging to Moonis Elahi — a PMLQ's MNA and son of the then sitting Speaker Punjab Assembly — profited from the sugar crisis. The document didn't mention under whose influence Punjab government had issued subsidies amounting to Rs:3 billion to sugar mills or why the Economic Coordination Council [ECC] approved the decision to export sugar. Tareen, PTI's former General Secretary, said that out of the Rs:3bn subsidy to the sugar mills, Rs:2.5bn were given in the PMLN's government. A tweet from JKT said:

Some points to note on sugar inquiry report:

@JahangirKTareen
1. My companies exported 12.28% while my market share is 20% so less than I could have.

2. Export was on First come First serve basis.

3. Of the total Rs:3 bn subsidy rec'd Rs:2.5 Bn came when N was in power and I was in opposition.

The PM was also sent the investigation report on the wheat crisis, compiled by a three-member bench headed by DG FIA Wajid Zia. As per report, the crisis originated due to poor planning by the centre and provincial governments. The Punjab Food Department was unable to control flour mills and started collecting wheat after a delay of 20-22 days. The food department failed to come up with a process for the demand and supply of the crop and products; they did not take decisions as the situation was deteriorating.

Former Secretary Food Naseem Sadiq and ex-food Director Zafar Iqbal were blamed in the report for failing to handle the wheat crisis. Furthermore, the Punjab food minister Samiullah Chaudhry did not take the measures necessitated by the situation. *"No single individual can be held responsible for procuring inadequate wheat from Sindh,"* the report said.

In fact, the Sindh government had not taken any decision on the summary for wheat procurement; thus, responsibility of buying wheat in low stock couldn't be placed on any single person. Khyber PK Food Secretary Akbar Khan and Food Director Sadaat Khan were also held responsible for not procuring wheat in accordance with the government's target and plans.

Amid the growing public anger, instead of firing Khusro Bakhtiar from his ministry and immediately ordering an inquiry against him, PM Khan made him minister for Economic Affairs instead, while Samiullah Chaudry resigned as Punjab's food minister.

Now details of the **FIA Committee's Report:** In its 32-page report, the committee on sugar price hike termed *Pakistan Tehreek e Insaf* [PTI] government's decision to allow export of sugar unjustified as it caused a 30% increase in its price. The report said:

> *"The exporters of sugar gained benefit in two ways: first they were able to gain subsidy and secondly, they made profit from the increasing sugar prices in the local market.*
>
> *Sugar mill owners who availed maximum subsidy had political clout and influence in decision making and they tried to gain maximum benefit in a very limited time."*

The committee report revealed that PTI's former Secretary General JKT and Federal Minister for National Food Security Makhdoom Khusro Bakhtiar were among the main beneficiaries. Both these stalwarts went away with Rs:1.03 billion subsidy on the export of sugar, paid out from the taxpayers money, which was equal to 41% of the total subsidy the government of Punjab paid to sugar barons.

On the recommendations of the Inquiry Committee, an inquiry commission was instituted by PM Khan under the Commission of Inquiry Act of 2017, showing his determination to fix the culprits. Nine teams were doing forensic audit, including the sugar mills owned by JK Tareen. The Commission was given 40 days to complete its work.

It transpired that respective government's decision to allow export of sugar led to increase in the retail price. Before the decision the per kilo sugar price was Rs:55 in December 2018 that jumped to Rs:71.44 per kg in June 2019 – an increase of Rs:16.47 per kg or 30%, according to the findings. Moreover, despite the clear calculations of the stock position after deducting the strategic reserves, Sugar Advisory Board in its meeting of June 2019 did not ban the export of sugar.

There were signs of *"cartelization and manipulation"* by sugar mills and the ex-mill sugar price determination formula was also *"unfair"*, according to the findings. For concrete evidence, the inquiry committee recommended forensic audit of the mills. Very few top heads controlled the industry in fact; six groups were in control of 51% of the production of sugar in Pakistan.

> *[JDW Group of Jahanghir Khan Tareen controlled 19.97% production; RYK Group of Khusro Bakhtiar controlled 12.24%; Al-Moiz Group controlled 6.8%, Tandlianwala Group 4.9%, Omni Group 1.7% and the Sharif family owned 4.5% of the production]*

The FIA's inquiry noted that many policies were conveyed to the sugar mills from the platform of the Pakistan Sugar Mills Association [PSMA]. The strike call that the sugar mills once gave to bring sugarcane prices down was observed by the mills owned by JK Tareen, Sharif family and Khusro Bakhtiar sugar mills initially.

The increase in the sales tax rate from 8% for filers and 11% for non-filers to 17% did not contribute much to the ex-mill price increase, which was largely made before the budget. The agony was that neither the provincial nor the federal government had any clue how the ex-factory prices of the sugar was calculated by them collectively. In fact the ex-mill pricing formula was manipulated jugglery; it was *"faulty and unfair"*. The assumptions to set that ex-mill price were wrong. The federal government had allowed to include the GST into the ex-mill price which was not right; the report urged. The report said:

> *"The calculation of the ex-mill price provided by the PSMA cannot be relied upon unless full audit of all determinants of ex-mill price are calculated in a financial audit."*

The Punjab government also gave Rs:3 billion subsidy on export of sugar at Rs:5.35 per kg to the millers. The sugar mills owned by JK Tareen availed Rs:561 million subsidy, which was equal to 22% of the total allocated amount. The sugar mills owned by Food Minister Makhdom Khusro Bakhtyar availed Rs:452.3 million subsidy, which was 18.3% of the whole chunk. Astonishingly; the Punjab government was giving out the subsidy for export of sugar at a time when the price of sugar was increasing in the domestic market; the Chief Minister Punjab should have been caught by neck in such situations. The report said:

> *"The committee is of the considered opinion based on documentary evidence that the export of sugar was not justified as the sugarcane production was expected to be low in the upcoming harvesting season…..that despite 2.7% reduction in the cultivation area this year the sugarcane production increased 1% till 25th of February. The crushing season continued in March as well."*

The committee underlined that the sugar millers purchased off-the-books sugarcane and its production was also kept off-the-books to evade the General Sales Tax [GST]. It was the responsibility of the Cane Commissioner to record full sugarcane production while the FBR was responsible for recording the sugar production.

The fact remained that quantity of sugar produced was sufficient for annual national consumption. The retail price increase from Rs:55 in December 2018 to Rs:74.64 per kg in January 2020 was not at all justified while major increase was enforced much before the start of the new crushing season.

The committee also found that the Rs:190 per 40 kg sugarcane support price was sufficient but this price increase [in sugarcane] was delayed, depriving the farmers from making an informed decision. Also that the sugarcane was purchased at about 15% higher than the support price [of Rs:190 per 40kg] but it observed that the mill owners were also **"larger growers of sugarcane"**, which could *"potentially be a reason for higher than the support price buying of sugarcane"*.

That's why recommendations were made for proper forensic audit to examine the possibility of a grower-cum-miller buying the commodity at higher price. The inquiry report rejected the PSMA's claim that it closed mills operations for few weeks due to the less availability of the sugarcane; in fact the mills were closed to bring prices of the key input down.

It was also revealed that the provincial governments had not maintained any record of stocking the sugar despite it was required under the law. There was likelihood of further increase in sugar prices before Ramadhan [April-May 2020] so hard crackdown against the major players was needed.

As apparently evident from above, two reports on the sugar and wheat crises in the country were made public, exposing ruling PTI's bigwig Tareen, Khusro Bakhtiar, PMLQ's Monis Elahi and their relatives as being involved in the scam and benefiting from export subsidies at a time when the commodity was short in the country. Prime Minister Imran Khan was waiting for a detailed forensic report on the matter before taking action against anyone. The PM Khan vowed that no powerful lobby would be able to gain undue profit and create an artificial shortage of essential items in the future.

Next day, in a surprise move, the prime minister reshuffled his cabinet for a third time since forming his government in August 2018, removing among others the minister for national food security, Bakhtiar, who was also named as a beneficiary in the FIA reports, instead assigning him the portfolio of economic affairs which news was in offing.

On 6th April 2020: PTI stalwart Jahangir Tareen acknowledged he was no longer as close to Prime Minister Imran Khan as he used to be but maintained that the premier was still his friend and that he would continue to stand by the PM's cause. Tareen was talking exclusively to **Dawn News TV's** Meher Bokhari in her show *NewsEye* after a Federal Investigation Agency (FIA) team released reports on the sugar and wheat crises and beneficiaries of subsidies obtained by the industry's bigwigs and just hours after news began circulating that Tareen had been sacked as the *Chairman of the Agriculture Task Force* in the light of those findings.

Rejecting that he was fired from any position *'because he was never appointed in the first place'*, There had been media talks that *PM Khan and members of the FIA inquiry commission had been threatened with dire consequences if the reports were made public.* The sugar cartel had also threatened the committee that if the report was issued, the commodity would be vanished from the market. But the FIA reports were made public on the directives of the prime minister who, according to Special Assistant on Accountability Mirza Shahzad Akbar, had ordered stern action against those found involved in the crises *irrespective of their status and party affiliation'*.

Mr Tareen had no issues with Imran Khan; however, he acknowledged that:

> *".... he has a long-running conflict with Azam Khan, the Principal Secretary of Imran Khan. When we came into power, I had a different vision on how to govern the country. He (Azam Khan) has a different one. I had told Mr Khan that the government's job was not to enact incremental change but to transform the entire country.... I have always been against bureaucratic hurdles."*

The sugar baron also revealed that a vast majority, about 70%, of the prime minister's cabinet agreed with his vision for the country. But the prime minister fully trusted Azam Khan thus the anti-JKT lobby had become dominant. Tareen also criticized the inquiry reports on sugar and wheat crises, calling it a report without context; 'The weakness of this report is that it has no flesh, it consists of bare bones,' Tareen said. He also said there was no correlation between sugar exports and the rise in the commodity's price because there had been no shortage of sugar in the country; adding that: *'Sugar prices rose only because sugarcane's price increased - 80 per cent of sugar's cost of production is the price of sugarcane'*.

Tareen rubbished opposition leader Shahbaz Sharif's claim that he (Tareen) had been given a *'gift of Rs:18 billion'* by Prime Minister Imran through subsidies, saying no player in the industry received direct transfers.

See a media comment on media pages (FB) sent by one Sohail Anwer **on that day of 6th April 2021:**

> "Jahangir Tareen was Khan's best friend. He helped Khan in most tough times. He even helped Khan become the PM. Did JKT cheat Imran Khan? Did he refuse something IK wanted for himself? None of that.
>
> So, what happened? What went wrong? Pakistaniat happened. IK's love for Pakistan happened.
>
> JKT's name along with others came in a report exposing those who harmed Pakistan's treasury and tax payer money. That was enough for Imran Khan to break his own friendship. He himself published the report exposing the name of his friend among those of other parties. Why? Just for Pakistan. Just so poor tax-payer money is saved.
> And guess what. No one mentioned other names. Multiple names from all parties were exposed in the same report."

On 5th May 2022: Former prime minister and PTI Chairman Imran Khan revealed the reason behind his differences with former aides Aleem Khan and Jahangir Tareen and said that both were seeking *'illegal benefits from him'*. Speaking during a podcast (*a program made available in digital format for download over the Internet*) with GEO TV that day, the former premier revealed that differences with both estranged leaders developed when he, as PM, refused to entertain their requests; *'Aleem Khan expected me to legalize his 300-acre land near Ravi - from then onwards, I developed differences with him.'*

Talking **about Jehangir Tareen**, the PTI chairman stated that:

> "...*his problem was the Sugar Mill Scandal on which a commission was also formed. Tareen stood with those who are the biggest dacoits in the country. When I ordered a probe into the matter, differences developed with Tareen.*"

Mr Khan said that even if PTI lose the election, they would not give tickets to those who enter politics for personal gain. *'Our system is such that money is spent in Senate elections. But Yousuf Raza Gilani's son was spared after he was caught bribing lawmakers.'*

On the other count, just next day on 6th May 2022; Aleem Khan challenged Imran Khan to have a live debate with him and Jahangir Tareen regarding the allegations levelled against them; he was addressing a press conference. The separated PTI member revealed that the land Imran Khan was talking about was his property since 2010.

> "*I was with Imran Khan in the Opposition from 2010 to 2018 and I own the property since 2010; the PTI chairman also visited the property when his father died. Did I know 10 years ago that Imran Khan will become the prime minister in 2018?*" he questioned.

> (*Correcting the figures, he said) that he owns 3,000 acres of land and not just 300 acres, mentioning that he did not acquire lands but instead bought them from private landlords. This land is now with Ravi Urban Development Authority (RUDA) — which was formed by Imran Khan – (but) how RUDA sold this land to private developers when it bought the land at the govt price. An investigation should be done regarding the developers who were given the land.*"

Aleem Khan also revealed that the land was given to favoured private developers. *"If your [Imran Khan] golf course can be constructed under RUDA then why not my housing society?"* Aleem Khan questioned. He said if Imran Khan wanted to unveil the truth, then he should sit with him and Tareen to hold talks.

Scenario 260

PM KHAN – ARMY RELATIONSHIP

PRO-ARMY STALWARTS LOST IN ELECTION-2018:

Allegations of rigging in Elections-2018 were generally raised by the opposition parties as per routine with fingers pointed in all directions, including the security forces. However, the results of elections 2018 suggested that major politicians who were supposed to be the *'pawns of the establishment'* suffered a defeat while the so-called army critics won their seats. The results surprisingly suggested that two major politicians linked to the **Pashtun Tahafuz Movement (PTM)**, Ali Wazir and Mohsin Dawar, won elections from NA-50 South Waziristan and NA-48 North Waziristan, respectively.

Two of the biggest critics of the army within the PMLN, former defence minister Khawaja Asif and Rana Sanaullah, won elections from NA-73 Sialkot and NA-106 Faisalabad respectively. On the other hand, Elections-2018 proved to be a nightmare for most of the politicians who had leaning towards the military openly or covertly. Almost all candidates of *Pak-Sarzameen Party* (PSP), being viewed as pawn of the establishment to dislodge *Muttahida Qaumi Movement-Pakistan* [MQM-P] from urban Sindh, lost their seats. Chairman PSP Mustafa Kamal also lost the elections from both his National Assembly seats in Karachi; another, Raza Haroon met the same fate.

PMLN's ex-interior minister Ch Nisar Ali Khan, a political bigwig with pro-military views, suffered defeat at the hands of PTI's Ghulam Sarwar Khan from both NA-59 and NA-63 Rawalpindi. Also, chief of Balochistan Awami Party [BAP] faced defeat in NA-272, though known for being near the top army brass. Another pro-establishment politician Lt Gen Qadir Baloch lost in NA-268 Chaghai; he was a federal minister in PMLN government. Pro-army politician Amir Muqam lost to PTI's little-known politicians from two National Assembly constituencies; NA-2 Swat and NA-29 Peshawar. Ijazul Haq, son of Gen Ziaul Haq and another so-called pro-establishment politician, suffered defeat in Bahawalnagar though he had been winning from here since three decades.

In Sindh; total number of 26.99 million voters were registered of which about 17 million were male and 9.95 million were female voters who elected their representatives contesting elections on 61 National Assembly and 160 Provincial Assembly seats in the 11th general polls of the country. Amidst strict security measures, with personnel of both the police and military deployed, polling began at 8 am and, without any break, concluded at 6 pm across 17,758 polling stations of the province, out of which 2,716 had been declared highly sensitive whereas 10,864 were declared as sensitive.

Referring to daily **'Pakistan Today'** dated **26th July 2018:**

> "......results are pouring in from various constituencies after successful and peaceful holding of general elections 2018 in the country, the dwellers of Karachi have largely disappointed 'bigwigs' of known major political parties by defeating Pakistan People's Party (PPP) Chairman Bilawal Zardari and Mutthida Qaumi Movement-Pakistan (MQM-P)'s Dr Farooq Sattar."

The PPP had ruled Sindh over the past three decades but could not save its own Chairman Bilawal Zardari in NA-246 Lyari, once the stronghold of PPP while MQM-P's Dr Farooq Sattar was in the run for NA-245 and NA-247 of Karachi South and East but lost at both his parental constituencies. Interestingly, Dr Farooq Sattar lost NA-245 constituency while securing only 35,247 votes against his competitor Dr Aamir Liaquat of PTI who got 56,615 votes. Dr Sattar also lost NA-247 seat against PTI's Dr Arif Alvi.

PPP's Shehla Raza and MQM-P's Ali Raza Abidi lost NA-243 constituency against PTI Chairman Imran Khan who got 91,358 votes. MQM-H's leader Afaq Ahmed who was contesting elections from NA-240 and PSP's Asif Hasnain also lost against MQM-P's Iqbal Muhammad Ali Khan. PSP leader and former mayor Mustafa Kamal was contesting elections on various constituencies including NA-253, PS-124 and PS-127, but could not win either seat. *Muttahida Majlis Amal* [MMA]'s Asadullah Bhutto and PMLN's former federal finance minister Miftah Ismail lost NA-244 against PTI's Ali Haider Zaidi. Most interestingly, Irfanullah Marwat of Grand Democratic Alliance [GDA] also lost PS-104 against PPP's Saeed Ghani.

In short, PTI surprisingly emerged as a major political party in Karachi; it was ahead on 12 National Assembly [NA] seats out of 21. 2018's general elections produced surprise results in the metropolis for the first time in almost 30 years as Karachi's most popular party MQM-P could get six NA seats only. The Karachites turned down the election boycott call of MQM's London based Altaf Hussain, made on 23rd July 2018 via video message; the peaceful citizens of Karachi city had rejected his call and voted for change.

With Nawaz Sharif and his daughter Maryam in prison and the PMLN headed by Shehbaz Sharif, and with several legal cases hanging over the heads of the PPP's leadership most notably Asif Ali Zardari and his sister Faryal Talpur, street agitation was neither likely nor anticipated. But even if complete calm were to prevail at home, the PTI government could still face challenges in the foreign policy field. It was clear that Pakistan's turbulent politics was not likely to set sail through calmer waters.

The new PTI government was required to ensure China stay committed to its planned $62bn investment in the China-Pakistan Economic Corridor [CPEC] which was expected to develop direly needed infrastructure for the 240 million people of Pakistan.

IMRAN KHAN - GEN BAJWA - TLP:

How Gen Bajwa was selected in 2016: - Gen Qamar Javed Bajwa was a firm opponent of extremism and terrorism. He was expected to come more forceful in the fight against terrorism than his predecessor, who was credited with launching Operation Zarb e Azb, which helped lower the frequency of terrorist attacks – and Gen Bajwa continued with the same force. In Feb 2017, Gen Bajwa himself started another *Operation Raddul Fisaad* (2017) to end the terrorism from the country.

During the last week of November 2016, Gen Qamar Javed Bajwa's pro-democracy credentials and his low-profile influenced Pakistan's then Prime Minister Nawaz Sharif to appoint him to the post of COAS, the army chief of Pakistan forces, superseding four top Generals. He had succeeded Gen Raheel Sharif who had completed his normal tenure then. With his elevation as army chief, Gen Bajwa had superseded Lt Gen Syed Wajid Hussain (Chairman of Heavy Industries Taxila), Lt Gen Najibullah Khan (DG Joint Staff HQ), Lt Gen Ishfaq Nadeem (Corps Commander Multan) and Lt Gen Javed Iqbal Ramday (Corps Commander Bahawalpur). Media had frequently mentioned then that Nawaz Sharif picked Gen Bajwa because of his low-key style - the fourth oldest COAS in Pak-Army.

It was prime minister's discretion to appoint anyone among the four candidates. The PM Sharif wanted to appoint an army chief who should be military expert as well as backing democracy in the country. All the four Generals being considered for the post of COAS were passed out from Pak Military Academy on the same day, but Gen Bajwa had an experience more diversified than all others. Gen Bajwa's calibre, credentials, experience and holding the biggest core also helped him to be appointed the Chief of Army Staff. Gen Bajwa's relatively more moderate view of the relationship with the civilian government proved to be the decisive factor in PM's decision.

Gen Bajwa, an infantry officer, had commanded the famed 10 Corps, the army's largest, which is responsible for guarding the area along the Line of Control with India. But here, the PM Sharif made sure that the fight against terrorism would take preference. Gen Bajwa, his colleagues said, was a firm opponent of extremism and terrorism – and he proved it as such. He rather proved even more forceful in the fight against terrorism than his predecessor, who was credited with launching *Operation Zarb e Azb*.

It was the first time when, during Gen Bajwa's original tenure, a video surfaced at Pakistani media channels where the then Maj Gen Azhar Naveed, DG Pakistan Rangers was spotted distributing envelopes containing Rs:1000 each to the demonstrators of *Tehreek-e-Labbaik* (TLP) after Nov-2017's dharna (sit-in) in Islamabad. PMLN leader Nawaz Sharif claimed later that the protest of this barelvi obscurantist set was planted by the ISI to remove him from his office and help Imran Khan in his election bid. Other opposition leaders and parties had repeatedly claimed the same stance – and also that the ISI was involved in the meddling of 2018's polls. Those accusations held some merit as Maj Gen Azhar Naveed had become one of the deputies in ISI when Lt Gen Faiz Hameed took over the wing on 16th June 2019.

> {Allegedly, the TLP, was the organization that gave momentum to Mr Khan back in ending 2017 against Nawaz Sharif's PMLN, but later twisted the PTI to succumb to its demand over the then ongoing protests over the expulsion of French ambassador for publication of caricatures depicting the Prophet Mohammad (PBUH) in a French satirical magazine and incident of Samuel Paty. Though the movement calmed after it suddenly re-energized when Mr Khan was having differences with the Army Chief over new DG ISI's posting.
>
> In the past, TLP's former leader Khadim Hussain Rizvi was on record to state how his organization was used by some institutions to fulfill

> their designs. *In the past, Gen Zia's doctrine to promote religious fringe groups in political discourse as the instrument of state policy was something used by the Pakistani deep state for a long time to meet its strategic objectives.*}

The TLP's activity and the standoff with the military started at the beginning of October 2021 and ended as soon as indications came that a compromise had been achieved. Through shuttle diplomacy of Minister Fawad Chaudhary and Sh Rasheed, Gen Bajwa agreed to a face-saving measure to allow Lt-Gen Hameed to continue till <u>19th November 2021</u> and PM Khan gave approval for Lt Gen Nadeem Anjum. During the same time, Govt of Pakistan engaged with TLP leadership, and a compromise there too was achieved. No surprise, in this meeting which concerned civilian issues, Gen Bajwa graced the occasion and played a crucial role in this process. In a hybrid setup, this is what one gets, a confrontation spinning into a cold war – and the sudden compromise in the given situations.

> However, during Mr Khan's era of 2018-22, <u>the socio-political problems in Pakistan **were NOT engineered by the establishment,** as was widely alleged then; BUT most of those were the consequence of PTI cabinet's own mis-governance. The matters concerning administration had deteriorated from worse to worst due to visible poor performance of the whole team and PM Khan's appalling leadership. PTI had failed miserably on many core issues of foreign affairs, infrastructure, industrilization and religious extremism.</u>

The blame didn't stop here, the list was going long and exhaustive. With each passing day, Mr Khan's problems doubled down – because, allegedly, Gen Bajwa had started patronizing PM Khan's political opponents like Shahbaz Sharif with whom some mutual intimate meetings were also extensively reported in electronic media of the country.

GEN BAJWA's EXTENSION CASE IN SCP:

On 19th August 2019; Prime Minister Imran Khan approved an extension in the tenure of COAS Gen Bajwa for another three years. <u>On 26th November 2019</u>, the chief justice of Pakistan (CJP) took up a withdrawal application of a petition filed by The Jurists Foundation challenging the extension in Gen Bajwa's tenure. The top judge, however, rejected the application to withdraw the petition, saying it fell into the domain of public interest under Article 184 (3) of the Constitution; thus, the case was converted into a *suo motu* notice.

The CJP Asif Saeed Khan Khosa questioned the rationale behind the extending a new term for the COAS; the court suspended the earlier government decision, saying a *'detailed examination of the matter of extension / re-appointment of Gen Bajwa, the COAS* was needed. Referring to daily **'the Telegraph'** of UK dated 26<u>th November 2019</u>:

> *"Pakistan's top court blocked an extended term for the country's powerful army chief, potentially setting the judiciary on a collision course with the powerful military and a key ally of Imran Khan. The supreme court suspended a government decision to give Gen Bajwa a fresh three-year-term in office and ordered a detailed investigation into his extension.*
>
> *The court's surprise questioning of a decision, previously seen as a formality, threatened to trigger a confrontation between the country's powerful military and its civilian institutions."*

The supreme court's three-judge panel was worried about the legal basis for the extension. PTI government's spokesman Shafqat Mahmood told: *"It is the prime minister's discretion to decide whether there is a need to grant an extension to a services chief in unusual circumstances."*

Farogh Naseem, the federal law minister, resigned that day to appear before the supreme court as Gen Bajwa's lawyer. The court was still likely to award the extension to Gen Bajwa, but its resistance had weakened a key safeguard of Mr Khan's government. Gen Bajwa's military had been seen as close to Mr Khan's government, with few of the disagreements which marred relations with PMLN leader Nawaz Sharif under the prior PMLN government. There had been speculation that *Gen Bajwa's extension had been unpopular with his subordinates in the military, who feared for their own promotion prospects if he seized prolonged control.*

The CJP Asif Saeed Khosa, called on the PTI government to *'step back and assess what it is doing and not to do something like this,'* also pointing out that the *'regional security situation justification for the extension was quite vague.'* He even gently questioned its validity: *'If at all there is any regional security threat then it is the gallant armed forces as an institution that are to meet the said threat and an individual's role in that regard may be minimal.'*

During the court proceedings, Justice Khosa mostly ended up castigating the law ministry for its errors that were causing disrespect to the army chief. Media and legal analysts were trying to predict what would happen on 28th November, warning of the instability that could follow a potential court decision that struck down the army chief's extension altogether. The power an extension grants to the army chief, and the blow that would follow from it being revoked; it was not lost on anyone. In the end, the court saved face all around: *'It gave the army chief a six-month extension and directed the federal government to have parliament legislate on such extensions and their duration.'*

> [Later, it transpired, that seven Generals of the Pakistan Army had joined hands with the CJP Asif Saeed Khosa to block the PTI government's move to grant three-year extension to the COAS Gen Bajwa. The list of disgruntled Generals included Corps Commander Multan Lt Gen Sarfraz Sattar who was on top of the seniority list for appointment as the Chief of Army Staff; Lt Gen Nadeem Raza, Lt Gen Humayun Aziz, Lt Gen Naeem Ashraf, Lt Gen Sher Afghan and Lt Gen Qazi Ikraam. Chief of General Staff Lt Gen Bilal Akbar stood at the seventh place on the seniority list to succeed Bajwa.
>
> Lt Gen Sattar (senior-most after Gen Bajwa) had finally resigned after being superseded; also, said to have had a row with Bajwa a few weeks ago, having accused him of ruining the army's image. The fact remained that Gen (retd) Raheel Sharif, before his retirement as Chief of Army Chief, had suggested Sattar's name as one of the options for the top post for continuation of his policies.
>
> Two indicators of differences in the army: First, the antecedents of the petitioner show that he has been filing cases that serve the army's interest. So, the only explanation of his filing the case against Bajwa's extension was to be that some strong lobby in the army had put him up to it. Second, **a three-year extension meant to have retired about 24 Lt Generals in the row.**
>
> If Bajwa would get an extension for three years, the most senior Generals will not remain eligible for the post of Army Chief. Chief justice Khosa, who himself was retiring next month (20th December 2019), was part of the game. By extending Bajwa's term for 6 months, he had provided the ones-in-line an opportunity to manipulate the legislation process.]

There was a real question as to whether parliament would consider such legislation or whether it would seriously debate it. PM Khan had a majority in the lower house, but the opposition had control of the senate, and the polarization between Khan and the opposition parties had guts to stall the legislative process. There was also the question of what prompted the CJP to take notice of the petition challenging the army chief's extension at the last minute (intriguingly, after the petitioner tried to withdraw it). The last extension to be granted, Gen Kayani's, had also been challenged in the Islamabad High Court in 2010, but that petition was struck down. Some speculated that rival officers to Gen Bajwa prompted this case; others considered the recent back-and-forth between Khan and the judiciary over the cases of former leaders Nawaz Sharif and Gen Musharraf had provoked it.

Whatever be the hurry, the whole affair — and its clash of egos and a tug-of-war over power — revealed two things: In Pakistan, *PM Khan's government was beholden to COAS Gen Bajwa, at least; and opposition parties were either unwilling, or unable, to take it on.*

Nawaz Sharif's PMLN was the one which had tried to take on the military in recent years; in 2016, it tried to assert some semblance of civilian supremacy over security policy, and many attributed Mr Sharif's downfall *'for that arrogance'* coupled with corruption. Nawaz Sharif was in UK then for medical treatment, so PMLN preferred to go silenced into passivity vis-à-vis the army. The PTI government also showed its weakness for the judiciary: It was left awkward and panicked by the last-minute hearing, unable to successfully defend itself, or its constitutional prerogative to appoint (*and presumably re-appoint*) the army chief, in court while the justices criticized it.

It was a new front opening between the judiciary and the military. In the past, the judiciary had mostly unconditionally supported the military at the expense of civilian governments, rubber-stamping military coups via the *doctrine of necessity* and disqualifying prime ministers, including Nawaz Sharif. That new judiciary-military tension forced the country to think about a practice - it took for granted that effectively strengthened the military at the expense of civilian institutions.

However, the softness of PTI's civilian government vis-à-vis both the army and the judiciary were clear: *The judiciary had, through Gen Bajwa's case, assumed the role and the power (whether legally or not) to force Pakistan's politicians to fully define its institutions.* That whole episode explained the saga of what kind of democracy Pakistan would have, and how its politicians would shape its institutions — whether to the strength of its civilian government, or to its disadvantage.

Let us see it in more details: This case was unprecedented — no such hearing over an extension for an army chief has ever been held in Pakistan, despite a history of army chiefs' tenures being extended. The case also has wider, significant implications about the state of civil-military-judiciary relations in Pakistan. On 19th August 2019, Gen Bajwa's three-year term was set to end, PM Khan's government — citing an emergency in the *regional security situation* — issued him a three-year extension beyond November (2019). The regional security issues at play were India's revocation of Kashmir's autonomy and Pakistan's ongoing help in the US-Afghan peace process. But many argued at the time that by granting Gen Bajwa an extension, Khan was ensuring smooth sailing for his own government for another three years — given the ways in which the army, under Gen Bajwa, had primed, the path for Mr Khan to become prime minister in 2018.

During the last week of November 2019, the CJP Khosa took the federal government and its Attorney General to task, pushing the decision down to the wire: the day the army chief was set to retire (28th November 2019). The court argued that the government had botched the bureaucratic process for Gen Bajwa's extension (alternately referring to it also as his re-appointment, or the limiting of retirement), but *it also emerged during the proceedings that there was no legal basis — not in the constitution, nor in the army rules — for this extension, and certainly nothing specified that the duration needed to be three years.*

In Gen Bajwa's case, it appeared the PTI government had simply followed previous practice: Army chiefs either granted themselves extensions when they were in power, or civilian leaders did so. Most recently this occurred in 2010, when President Zardari extended the term of the then-army chief Gen Ashfaq Kayani.

ON THE SAME PAGE *MANTRA*:

On 27th August 2018: Pakistan Army chief Qamar Javed Bajwa extended his congratulations to PM Khan on being elected as premier; the two held their first meeting at Khan's office. Three days later, Khan paid his first visit to GHQ in Rawalpindi; and the iconic claim of *'civil-military leadership on one page'* appeared on the new government's agenda. Mr Khan's meeting at the GHQ lasted eight hours, during which he received briefings on highly sensitive and confidential security matters from the military establishment.

Next day, PM Khan said his foreign policy would prioritise the nation's interests above all else, that Pakistan would *'not become part of a war of any other country in future'*. He also ruled out the frequently discussed *'civil-military'* dynamics as a myth, stating:

> "There is no such thing as a civil-military tug of war... Our goals are same, that is to make Pakistan as one of the greatest countries of the world."

The Pak-Army supported Imran Khan and his party PTI before he formed his government, leading the opposition to claim that the PTI owed its victory in the 2018 elections to the army-generals. After Khan took power, he enjoyed nearly free rein in the domestic domain while the military high command retained control of sensitive foreign and security policy files. PM Khan and his cabinet ministers were often keen to emphasise that the PTI government and the military leadership were *'on the same page'*. However, despite all the adversaries, see below the Pak-Army's cooperation with the PTI government. Referring to __Drazen Jorgic__'s analysis reported by **REUTERS**.com dated 5th June 2019:

> "Pakistan's powerful military has agreed in a rare move to cut its hefty budget for a year to help ease the South Asian **country's critical financial situation.**
>
> Pakistan has struck an agreement in principle with the International Monetary Fund (IMF) for a $6 billion loan but Islamabad is expected to put in place measures to rein in a ballooning fiscal and current account deficits to get access to the funds. The IMF (wished that) the primary budget deficit should be trimmed by the equivalent of $5 billion, but previous civilian rulers have rarely dared to trim defence spending for fear of stoking tension with the military."

Same day PM Khan tweeted that he appreciated the military's *'unprecedented voluntary initiative of stringent cuts in their defence expenditures for next financial year because of the country's critical financial situation'*. This allowed extra money to be spent on the development of the tribal regions bordering Afghanistan, (still) recovering from more than a decade-long Islamist insurgency, and violence-wracked Baluchistan province. The previous governments hiked military spending by 20pc to 1.1 billion, but, for PM Khan, the military had overshot that figure.

Unlike some other civilian leaders in Pakistan's fragile democracy, PM Khan had good relations with the Generals. Under Pakistan's devolved system, reshaped after passing 18th Amendment in the constitution during PPP's last stint (2008-13) the federal government must hand over more than half its budget to the provinces, and the remainder had been mostly eaten up by debt servicing and the military's vast budget.

> [*Pakistan has one of the world's largest armies but critics say the military's spending is unnecessary and holds the country back in key areas such as health and education. More than 40 percent of the population is illiterate*]

However, the relationship became increasingly strained between the military and PM Khan when later encroached on the military's institutional autonomy. In October 2021, Khan refused to speedily sign off on the military's nominee for the crucial post of Inter-Services Intelligence Chief. He backed down in the end, abandoning efforts to retain his preferred candidate Lt Gen Faiz Hameed on the grounds that he was best placed to deal with the crisis next door in Afghanistan, and approving the high command's choice, Lt Gen Nadeem Anjum. But the damage had already been occurred – it was irreparable. With the second extension stint for the COAS Gen Bajwa, the senior-most military officer, due to finally retire in November 2022, the Generals thought that Khan would once again try to keep him as the next chief.

ANTI-WEST FOREIGN POLICY:

PM Khan's hardline anti-West foreign policy also likely played a role in the military's decision to distance itself from him. The prime minister's visit to Moscow in Feb 2022 had taken place ignoring Washington's calls to cancel the trip. PM Khan also got offensive at an open letter (dated 1st March 2022) from 22 Islamabad-based diplomats, including envoys of all the major European Union states, asking Pakistan to condemn Russia's aggression in Ukraine at the UN General Assembly. Imran Khan vowed in a public meeting, while saying:

> *"Are we your slaves?"*

The EU remained Pakistan's largest trading partner and a source of much-needed assistance for its faltering economy, particularly through the provision of GSP+ status. PM Khan's hostility toward the EU came at a time when the military high command was attempting – including through a mid-February visit by Gen Bajwa to Brussels – to ease tensions with EU institutions [*…some analysts opine the said trip was to buy the*

Pak-Army over differing approaches toward Taliban-controlled Afghanistan].

On 30th March 2022; at last-minute, PM Khan approached Gen Bajwa and his intelligence director and discussed **three (given) options with the prime minister: resign, call for new elections or face the vote of no-confidence.** PM Khan opted for new elections, but the joint opposition insisted that he should either resign or face the no-trust vote. The Supreme Court's intervention would decide the fate of the prime minister and his government. Yet the army high command's decision to keep Mr Khan stay out of the political fray could bear implications for the country's future.

On 31st March 2022: Differences between PM Khan and Gen Bajwa grew even wider after the PM said in the high command National Security Council meeting that Pak-Army backed the opposition in connivance with the US to remove him from the chair [details of the Cypher Case are referred]. In fact, it was a stinking note for Washington for its policy of *'blatant interference in Pakistan's internal affairs'*. As the PTI government continued to insist that the military was on its side, a day before the opposition's no-trust vote against Khan, the army chief issued what appeared to be a public rebuke of the prime minister's anti-Western and seemingly pro-Russian agenda – PAK-ARMY WENT NEUTRAL.

On 1st April 2022: PM Imran Khan revealed that the 'establishment' had given him three options: *'resignation, no-confidence [vote] or elections'*, following the filing of a no-confidence motion against him in the National Assembly; an interview aired on *ARY News TV* on 1st April 2022 is referred. He further said: *"We said elections is the best option, I cannot even think about resigning and as far as the no-confidence vote is concerned, I believe in fighting till the end. It will be better for Pakistan if we hold elections again. If we win [in] this [no-confidence] vote, it is a very good idea to go for early elections."*

The premier Khan also said in his interview on live TV that:

> *"…there is a threat to my life; those conspiring to topple my government are scared knowing that even if he is ousted, the public will continue to support him. I am saying this openly that there is a threat to my life.*
>
> *They, all those who have colluded [against me], know that I will not sit silently. What do they think? They will spend Rs:20 billion, Rs:25*

billion and topple my government and I will watch silently? (...*they want to kill me*) because I don't suit those involved in the conspiracy as well as people like Shahbaz Sharif, who polishes boots and are slaves to money".

PM Imran Khan added that they (?) would try their best through local collaborators, the three stooges — a term he occasionally used to refer to Shahbaz, PPP co-chair Asif Ali Zardari and Pakistan Democratic Movement [PDM] Chief Fazlur Rehman. During that week, one PTI leader Faisal Vawda had made similar claims, stating that a conspiracy was being hatched to assassinate the prime minister Khan '*over his refusal to sell the country*'. Vawda had made the remarks on **ARY News** show 'Off the Record' in response to a question about a letter PM Imran waved at the PTI's 27th March 2022 public address in Islamabad.

Earlier in that interview, PM Khan revealed that he was aware of the conspiracy being hatched to oust his government since August 2021; that planning was ongoing in London. He had reports from agencies in this regard; also named PMLN supremo heading the conspiracy. [*Nawaz Sharif had meetings with the people like Hussain Haqqani (of Memogate repute) whom he had met on 3rd March 2022*...]. Also, that people who had colluded in this purported conspiracy were also against the Pakistan Army. Prime Minister Khan categorically stressed that:

> "**Pakistan has been surviving because of its army. And Nawaz Sharif and his daughter have openly railed against the army.** *The joint opposition was making efforts to oust his government in order to get an NRO (amnesty). But I will never give them an NRO. Moreover,* **external powers needed robbers and thugs** *... and the corrupt who become their slaves to save their corruption*".

During that media interview, PM Khan, inter-alia, said in response to a question about civil-military relations with respect to '*an appointment in October (2021)*' — which was an apparent reference to the appointment of a new Inter-Services Intelligence director general (DG ISI) — "*We were all on one page. We had no differences.*" He further elaborated that he had no issues with the military leadership unlike past leaders, who were scared of the army because of their corruption. When the anchorperson specifically named the former ISI chief, Lt Gen Faiz Hameed, asking whether the premier wanted him to continue as the spymaster because he was his favourite, PM Imran said he had worked with Lt Gen Faiz for three years and he knew that the winter of 2021 would the most difficult time for us.

Citing economic difficulties and the situation in Afghanistan after the US exit, *'I was insisting on him (Lt Gen Faiz) continuing till winter as he was experienced. They had their own view, which was that there was a system in the army. They had their own perspective and I had mine. But I wasn't thinking about who will be the new army chief.'* PM Imran Khan also denied reports that he intended to de-notify Gen Qamar Javed Bajwa as the army chief and said *'it was the PMLN's disinformation campaign.'*

Further, speaking at an event in Islamabad on 2<u>nd April 2022</u>, Gen Bajwa strongly condemned Russia's invasion of Ukraine and also emphasized that Pakistan had a *'long and excellent strategic relationship with the US, which remains our largest export market.'*

On 10th April 2022: Following Imran Khan's ouster as Prime Minister, supporters of Khan's party PTI called for Gen Bajwa's resignation as army chief on Twitter, and Twitter trends denouncing the General as a 'traitor' reached over a million tweets. The supporters claimed that Gen Bajwa conspired to remove Khan from office along with the country's opposition parties.

After Gen Bajwa's retirement, the mother of slain journalist Arshad Sharif requested the Chief Justice of Pakistan to formally charge Gen Bajwa, among other military officers, for the '<u>targeted, premeditated, planned and calculated murder' of her son</u>, claiming members of the military's Public Relations division began threatening Sharif after he emerged as a critic when vote-of-no-confidence was instituted against Imran Khan. Particularly when a program called *'Woh Kon Tha'* got aired **on ARY News,** in which Sharif insinuated Gen Bajwa had a hand in ousting an elected PM Imran Khan.

KHAN & MILITARY – HOW FELL APART:

Imran Khan used to admire aspects of the military's influence; see his words – referring to an interview of November 2022 (about seven months after his departure) done by **ATIKA REHMAN** of a magazine titled **PROSPECT:**

> *"… it's **pragmatic** to work with the Generals - the idea of removing them from politics altogether is **idealistic**. He respects the military's power and organizational skills, (and believes) he would allow it to work to some extent outside of its constitutional mandate if that served his purpose."*

An extensive discussion was there during the said interview. <u>Notable gaps between what he had promised and what he delivered was enormous</u>. For diehard Khan loyalists none of that mattered. Khan worked 12 hours a day, didn't take a single day off. The most attentive statement from Khan was:

> "<u>Pakistan is run by Generals</u>. *As well as commanding one of the world's largest armies, a handful of them play politics, install governments and manipulate elections. They dictate Pakistan's nuclear and foreign policy and much of what happens at home too. Elected prime ministers have one task that supersedes all others: keep the army happy. Politicians in general, with their lust for political success and the riches that come with office, are often ready to cut the deals that keep them in power—an unsettling but chronic flaw in a system that is ostensibly democratic.*"

> "*... that the army defied him when he was prime minister. I could not push them to take action against the corruption of the elite. The outgoing army chief Gen Bajwa all but dictated political appointments in Punjab, the country's most populous province where electoral victory paves the way for power in the center. The military thwarted his efforts to introduce electronic voting machines — he (Gen Bajwa) suspects the technology would have made it harder for the army to manipulate election results.*"

Atika Rehman held that it was fascinating to see him (Mr Khan) hurl those allegations. Not because they were untrue — but because in Pakistan it was widely believed that it was the army that had put him in power in the first place. However, Cyril Almeida had the opinion that:

> "*For 20 years, Pakistan's military told the public that the two mainstream parties, the PPP and PMLN, were corrupt to the core. They planted the seeds of hatred for the existing political class. In Imran Khan, they found a likeable man.*"

Atika Rehman further held that with 115 of the 270 seats up for election-2018, he (Mr Khan) was exactly where the army wanted him: without an overall majority and dependent on their backing. It seemed like the perfect marriage: <u>Khan to all appearances supported army policies, gave retired generals key government positions and consulted serving ones on aspects of governance.</u> Yet four years later, in April 2022, the army's golden boy became the 18th prime minister to be removed from office.

What went wrong? Many say that Khan failed to deliver on his campaign promises and made the country's debt burden worse. *The army, perhaps, had realized that an incompetent leader was as insufferable as a corrupt one.* But 'Imran Khan was beginning to get comfortable as prime minister (Almeida). After three years of working together, he wanted the military to be his junior partner. What happened was inevitable.'

For weeks before Khan's final treat, Islamabad was thick with rumours that his rivals were in talks with senior Generals – and it was the truth. Then the same pro-army parties that were said to have enabled Mr Khan to form a government ditched him; he had to walk alone and without sticks. Instead of accepting defeat, the ex-cricketer began blaming first the US and then senior military Generals for engineering his removal.

Out of office, Khan turned on the army. He called the Generals names and mocked them for their *'neutral stance'*. He bashed the military so relentlessly that the army chief made the usually elusive DG ISI to publicly address Khan's allegations – however, his popularity soared. Atika Rehman, after speaking to some army officer, noted:

> "The officer was alluding to the ISI's ultimate weapon, which it has deployed against many Pakistani politicians: *sex tapes*. Sure enough, explicit clips supposedly of Khan having phone sex appeared online. His party dubbed them fake; the army tactic backfired. **Khan is relaxed about the tapes. He's not losing sleep over them."**

Talking about personal traits of PM Khan, he was always seen reluctant to meet opposition leaders to create unity even on key national security and foreign policy issues; thus, giving way to the agencies including Pak-Army, Rangers and ISI. One example was to get opposition's support for FATF-related legislation. In a similar context, it was not the political leadership that brought together the political forces during the Indian intrusion in February 2019; it was the establishment which did his job. At another occasion; what was the logic and lucidity when the army chief accompanied the prime minister to a meeting with the US president at Washington in 2019; it was neither a fine example of democratic statesmanship nor the diplomatic norm.

At times, the military leadership was requested to sort out problems with other countries arising from some impulsive decisions taken by PM Khan himself or statements made by his cabinet ministers. Gen Bajwa had to go China to control the damage caused by a federal minister's media statement only months into the PTI government.

At another juncture, the Army Chief was found rushing to Saudi Arabia after the foreign minister's statement on the role of the OIC; should one call it a sensible and mature governance. Such irresponsible behaviour [*may be taken as gross mistakes*] on behalf his team members at the global forums caused bigger dents in PM Khan's ruling strategy. The Generals started thinking about alternatives; closer relations between the establishment and the opposition parties developed. PMLN leaders restricted their attacks on PM and the PTI govt because of agencies' flag; misunderstandings amongst the coalition partners about the PM's indispensability started cropping up. Philosophy of *'Brutus – you too'* had started playing in.

LATER: On 5th May 2023; Mr Khan was speaking to media in Islamabad while appearing before the Islamabad High Court (IHC); AND referring to a senior army officer, he alleged:

> *"Dirty Harry had hatched another plan to assassinate him; he and PTI leader Murad Saeed faced life threat from terrorists. Everyone should know that 'Dirty Harry' (Maj Gen Faisal Naseer of the ISI) is responsible if anything happens to us. I have no threats from foreign agencies or terrorists but from Dirty Harry."*

BBC's journalist **M Hanif** once (on 27th May 2023) wrote:

> *"For many years, Pakistan's military establishment believed that in Imran Khan they had found a savior for the country. (But) after only a year out of power he is threatening to become their opponent - and the military is using all its might to save itself from Khan's wrath. As Imran Khan and his party face a country-wide crackdown, Pakistan seems to have come to a standstill."*

The writer added that *'The country didn't quite burn, but Khan's supporters took the fight to military cantonments'*. The army's headquarters, General Headquarters (GHQ), probably the most secure place in Pakistan, was breached and people trampled on the signboards with military logos – a sense of hatred which was allegedly being developed through PTI's social-media campaigns in the cities.

3 OPTIONS FROM THE 'UPPERS' (?)

Ref Imran Khan's meeting with media-men at his Bani Gala residence on 18th April 2022, a week after his departure AND as reported by *Samaa*

TV News, the former PM Khan shared that the establishment had given him three options, of which he had chosen early elections. He had identified resignation and facing the no-confidence motion as the other two options. However, the media-story remained that Khan's assertion was NOT recognized by the military. His story had appeared days after Inter-Services Public Relations (ISPR) Director General (DG) Maj Gen Babar Iftikhar had claimed that *'it was Khan who had approached the military leadership and that no option from the establishment was given'*.

Mr Khan also shared that he had called Chief of Army Staff Gen Qamar Javed Bajwa prior to his two-day trip to Russia in February (2022) during which the army chief had said he should go ahead with the visit, according to the *Samaa TV* report. The former prime minister also reportedly clarified that he had not met anyone besides anchorpersons and party members on his last night in office, thus, putting to rest reports of a meeting with the army leadership the night he was ousted (10th April 2022) from the top office. Khan's comments came days after *the BBC published a story* recounting the events leading up to the ouster of Imran Khan as prime minister.

> {BBC's story had alleged that *'two uninvited guests'* reached PM House, with an extraordinary security detail, via helicopter and held a 45-minute private meeting with Khan. The biggest claim in the story — made by quoting government sources — said that the meeting was less than pleasant. *'Just an hour ago, former prime minister Imran Khan had given orders to remove one of the senior officials present for the meeting,'* the story alleged, without taking any names.}

BBC's story was later rejected by the military's media affairs wing (ISPR) also which termed it to be *'totally baseless and a pack of lies'*; daily **DAWN** dated 10th April 2022 is referred. In a statement, the ISPR had branded the story *'typical propaganda lacking any credible, authentic and relevant source and claiming that it violates basic journalistic ethos'* – further explaining that:

> *"There is no truth in the fake story whatsoever and clearly seems part of an organized disinformation campaign. The matter is being taken up with BBC authorities."*

As per BBC's article, Parliament House was abuzz with activity during the day as the National Assembly was in session. However, it claimed that this activity shifted to the PM House once the session was adjourned for Iftar. Imran Khan had convened an emergency meeting of his cabinet — summoning his legal and political advisers, the NA speaker and deputy speaker and several bureaucrats — where it was decided that the *'CYPHER – the threat letter'* would be shown to a select few officials.

> The biggest claim in BBC's story — made by quoting government sources (?) — was that the meeting was less than pleasant. *"Just an hour ago, former prime minister Imran Khan had given orders to remove one of the senior officials present for the meeting,"* the story alleged, without taking any names. Also, that the sudden arrival of the guests was *unexpected for the former premier*. The story alleged that the necessary notifications for the removal and the new appointment were not issued by the Ministry of Defence. *'Even if the removal was carried out on the prime minister's orders, preparations had been made to declare it null and void.'*

ON CEC's SELECTION: Referring to daily **DAWN** dated 10th April 2022: Mr Khan revealed that the incumbent Chief Election Commissioner (CEC) Sikander Sultan Raja's name was *proposed by the establishment* after a deadlock between the then government and the opposition. In a separate tweet, Mr Khan shared that the PTI would file a reference against the CEC, adding that the Election Commission of Pakistan (ECP) had shown *incompetency* by not completing delimitation of constituencies in time because of which early elections were delayed – BUT till then Imran Khan's political era, and thus assignment of his premiership, had ended.

PETITION FILED IN HIGH COURT:

BBC's News-Report dated **10th April 2022** also talked about how the doors of the Islamabad High Court (IHC) were open late at night to take up a petition asking the court to restrain Imran Khan from possibly de-notifying Chief of Army Staff (COAS) Gen Qamar Bajwa. The urgent petition — which was filed but never fixed for hearing — said that Imran Khan, for political and personal purposes, had misused his powers and recommended the removal of the Chief of Army Staff, urging the court to quash the order in public interest. The report concluded:

> *"It is important to mention that while the petition was prepared, the space for the number of the notification regarding the army chief's dismissal was left blank. The reason for this was that despite the prime minister's request, the notification could not be issued and there was no need for a hearing."*

On that late night, the petition was filed in the Islamabad High Court (IHC), but never fixed for hearing whereas government ministers vehemently denied having any such plans in place. It was filed by Advocate Adnan Iqbal under Article 199 of the Constitution and mentioned the Federation of Pakistan, Government of Pakistan, Prime Minister Imran Khan, President Dr Arif Alvi, Ministry of Law and the Secretary of the Ministry of Defence as respondents. The petitioner held he was filing the petition to *'uphold the enforcement and mandatory constitutional provision with regard to identification of term of the COAS'*.

The petition was a pre-emptive measure to restrain the premier from *'using his arbitrary power to recommend the army chief's approval before the expiry of his term for personal and political motive'*. However, **the fact remains that NO such notification was issued by the prime minister Imran Khan.** Meanwhile, federal Information Minister Fawad Chaudhry had also denied that the government had taken any step to remove the army chief, terming such reports *baseless*. The minister wrote on twitter:

> *"The government fully understands the importance of the army chief and Pakistan Army as an institution. Reports that anyone is even thinking of changing the leadership of Pakistan Army are baseless rumours and lies. This is being done under an agenda. The government condemns these rumours and completely denies them."*

The petition had baselessly raised a number of questions – just on the basis of assumptions: whether the approval of the cabinet was obtained for the issuance of any such supposed notification; whether the prime minister had "unfettered powers" to remove the COAS when he had recommended his appointment and in the "absence of any cogent reason for altering the earlier recommendation"; and lastly whether the premier could remove the army chief for "furtherance of political interests".

The petition framed was manifestly deceptive.

Scenario 261

NO-CONFIDENCE MOVE [NCM] (2022)

[SUMMARY: On 8th March 2022, *most opposition parties in Pakistani parliament submitted a <u>motion of no confidence against Imran Khan</u> to the National Assembly's secretariat. On 27th March 2022, PM Khan waved a diplomatic cypher from US in the public, claiming that it demands to remove Khan's government in a coup. The matter was referred to the court of law because the PDM government held that the diplomatic relations with US had come on stake. On 1st April 2022, Prime Minister Khan announced that in context of the no-confidence motion against him in the National Assembly, the three options were discussed with 'establishment' to choose from viz: <u>"resignation, no-confidence [vote] or elections"</u>. On 3rd April 2022, President Arif Alvi dissolved the National Assembly of Pakistan on Khan's advice, after the Deputy Speaker of the National Assembly rejected and set-aside the motion of no confidence; this move would have required elections to the National Assembly to be held within 90 days. On 10th April 2022, after a Supreme Court ruling (<u>of 7th April 2022</u>) that the no-confidence motion was illegally rejected, a no-confidence vote was conducted and Mr Khan was ousted from office, becoming the first prime minister in Pakistan to be removed from office by a vote of no confidence. Mr Khan claimed the US was behind his removal because he conducted an independent foreign policy and had friendly relations with China and Russia. There was an acute law & order situation on his removal and protests erupted in the whole country.... see the details:]*

NO-CONFIDENCE MOVE [NCM] DEPOSITED:

On 8th March 2022; the joint opposition (labelled as the PDM) comprising PMLN and PPP including Fazlur Rehman's *Jamiat Ulema-e-Islam* [JUIF] and other smaller parties, introduced a no-trust motion in the parliament.

A day earlier, legal minds of opposition parties [PDM] had put forth input on the prospects of the ambitious vote of no-confidence against Prime Minister Imran Khan. A high-level meeting of the opposition leaders in this regard was held in Islamabad; prominent lawyers were also in attendance. The law experts fed the opposition leaders with all legal possible aspects and requirements of the no-confidence motion in the National Assembly. A draft of motion was also prepared in that hi-meeting. At that moment the PDM lacked sufficient votes - 172 in the 342-member National Assembly, to de-seat the prime minister were needed. But PM Khan had two political vulnerabilities that allowed the opposition measure to pick up support.

Firstly, **rifts within Khan's own party [PTI]** had widened; a sizeable number of parliamentarians who had joined the PTI after leaving their original parties intended to join them again. The PMLN, which retained its large base, appeared to have gained ground in its traditional stronghold Punjab, the country's most populous province with the largest number of parliamentary seats AND where PM Khan's handpicked chief minister, Usman Buzdar, had zero acceptance amongst voters and the respective MPAs.

Secondly: **Rising inflation** during the last few months, in fact after-effects of Covid-19 the world over, was made a trap for PM Khan through street protests and Pakistani media made it hype. *Trap in the sense that during subsequent 16-months rule of PMLN with PM Shahbaz Sharif in saddles, the inflation was THREE TIMES multiplied.* But as PM Khan headed a coalition government with a razor-thin majority in the centre, the PTI government needed to keep key partners, the Sindh-based *Muttahida Qaumi Movement-Pakistan* [MQM-P], the Baluchistan-based *Baluchistan Awami Party* [BAP] and the Punjab-based Pakistan Muslim League-Quaid-e-Azam [PMLQ] intact, but it couldn't.

However, PTI leaders and federal ministers vowed to thwart the opposition's attempt to oust Prime Minister Imran Khan through that motion. In a statement, Foreign Minister Shah Mahmood Qureshi said filing the no-trust motion was the opposition parties' constitutional right BUT the PTI along with its coalition partners would defeat the opponents in *political battles.*

On 10th March 2022: Supreme Court Bar Association [SCBA] said that the no-confidence motion filed by the opposition against Prime Minister Imran Khan was in accordance with the Pakistani Constitution. The SCBA body was closely monitoring the rather fragile political situation of the country, and was valid in accordance with *Article 95 – 'which states that the NA was constitutionally bound to summon the meeting of Assembly after the expiry of 3 days and not later than 7 days, after the receipt of any such requisition'*.

Next day, the PTI's federal ministers suggested that the matter should be wrapped up before the *session of the Organisation of Islamic Cooperation* (OIC) in the federal capital. However, most ministers asked National Assembly Speaker Asad Qaiser to convene a session of the lower house of parliament for this purpose within a week; also, suggested that voting should be held a week after three days of debate. The ministers were of the view that the wrapping up of the no-trust motion before the OIC session would be major victory for the PTI government.

Federal Minister for Planning and Development Asad Umar claimed that Pakistan Muslim League-Q (PMLQ) and Mutahida Qaumi Movement-Pakistan (MQM-P) were both supporting the PTI government and leaders of both the parties had given clear statements in this regard; and that coalition partners having issues with PTI leadership were *mere speculations*.

On 11th March 2022; the tensions that had been simmering since the opposition deposited its no-confidence resolution against Prime Minister Imran Khan boiled over within 3 days when a heavy contingent of police raided the Parliament Lodges to expel members of the *Ansarul Islam* — a uniformed force of the JUI-F — who were invited in Islamabad by Maulana Fazlur Rehman to provide security to opposition lawmakers.

> [**On 24th October 2019;** Interior ministry had notified ban on JUI-F's that 'militant wing'; the federal cabinet had approved a summary seeking a ban on Ansar-ul-Islam. The interior ministry on 10th March 2022 issued a notification announcing a ban on the "militant wing" of the JUI-F. The banning of Ansar-ul-Islam, which the ministry referred to as a *"private militia / Razakar Force of the JUI-F"*, came days before the Maulana Fazlur Rehman-led party was slated to lead an anti-government 'Azadi March'.
>
> According to the notification, the federal government had *"reasons to believe that Ansar-ul-Islam was capable of functioning as a military organisation, in violation of the prohibition contained in Article 256 of the Constitution"*. The ban was imposed after approval by the federal government and obtaining the consent from all four provincial governments under Article 146(1) of the Constitution.

Through that notification, the federal government / the Ministry of Interior *"entrusted the provincial governments the power to take appropriate actions under Section 2 of the Private Military Organisations (Abolition and Prohibition) Act 1974, against Ansar-ul-Islam"*.

The authority included, among others, *"the power to abolish / ban the said organisation and take further steps against them on ground"* in order to complete the action, the notice said. The JUI-F had challenged the said ban on *Insar ul Islam* in the Islamabad High Court (IHC) then. However, on 29th October 2019, the IHC Chief Justice Athar Minallah observed that the federal government's notification of a ban on Ansar-ul-Islam — a subsidiary of Jamiat Ulema-e-Islam-Fazl (JUI-F) — was infructuous.]

At least four legislators, along with two dozen *Ansarul Islam* volunteers, were arrested during the operation. A couple of legislators also courted arrest in protest over the police action at the parliamentarians' lodges; all the arrested persons were shifted to the police premises for further action.

Earlier on that day, JUI-F lawmaker Maulana Salahuddin Ayyubi reached the lodges with a few dozen motorcycle-riding volunteers. Some of the volunteers accompanied Maulana Ayyubi, while others gathered outside the main gate. Images of their presence outside the lodges aired on news channels caught the attention of authorities, who asked the Capital Police Chief to remove them from the premises.

In response, a large contingent of Police force, consisting of an anti-riot unit, police commandoes, the Counter Terrorism Department and Anti-Terrorism Force along with prison vans reached the Parliament Lodges under command of the DIG and SSP Operations. All volunteers then moved to MNA Ayyubi's Lodge (A-401) and locked the door. Senior police officers asked them to surrender, but they refused; police cordoned off the premises and blocked all roads leading to the lodges. At around 8pm, the police party broke down the door of the MNA's flat, which led to a physical confrontation between police, legislators and the *Ansarul Islam* volunteers and during the confrontation a number of MNAs and volunteers sustained injuries. Police succeeded in arresting around two dozen volunteers, and four legislators (one Senator and three MNAs), who were dragged and bundled into police vehicles.

In a late-night press conference following the brawl at Parliament Lodges, Interior Minister Sheikh Rashid Ahmed said that all the private militias had been dissolved in 2019. He claimed police did not arrest any MNAs. He claimed that only 19 members of the JUI-F's private militia were in police custody, and he also issued a warning to those who were mobilizing in protest at Maulana Fazlur Rehman's call.

> **Worth noting** was that the interior ministry had, in 2019, 'abolished' the Ansarul Islam after saying that they were 'capable of functioning as a military organisation' – BUT an order of the High Court (IHC) was also there – for media, it was all confusing.

On 14th March 2022: The joint opposition [PDM] held a consultative group to chalk out an effective strategy to make its no-confidence motion successful; the leadership had met over dinner at the residence of the PMLN president Shahbaz Sharif. Pakistan Democratic Movement (PDM) and JUI-F Chief Maulana Fazlur Rehman, PPP Chairman Bilawal Zardari, former president and PPP co-chairman Asif Ali Zardari, Balochistan National Party (BNP) Sardar Akhtar Mengal and other opposition leaders were in attendance. The meeting formulated a strategy to peel off allies of the ruling coalition to muster the required numerical backing to topple the PTI's premier from crest.

A huge dent was seen when **PTI Central Punjab President** Imtiaz Safdar Warraich re-joined the PPP on the same day; the development came ahead of vote on the no-confidence motion moved by the PDM. Next day, on 15th March 2022; PM Imran Khan reviewed his legal and political options in order to foil the opposition's no-confidence motion. Attorney General for Pakistan (AGP) Khalid Javed Khan briefed him on the process of no-confidence vote as well as the available legal options as to how the opposition's move could be handled. One PTI minister held:

> "Even the government functionaries are approaching the *'powerful circles'* to get their assistance for the allied parties' support. When the allies will announce their support for the government then the disgruntled MNAs will reconsider their position. The situation can change in favour of the (PTI) government in the next 48 hours."

PM Imran Khan was holding meetings with the leadership of the coalition partners for their support. Likewise, the premier was also avoiding attacks on the opposition leadership as he used to do in his speeches till couple of days ago. On the other hand, **one section within the government was contacting the opposition leaders for 'reconciliation';** the government was willing to give some concessions to the opposition in case their leadership agreed to withdraw the no-confidence motion.

However, PMLN Punjab President Rana Sanaullah ruled out any dialogue with the PTI govt in the said political situation; suggesting that PM Imran should resign first.

PDM OFFERED POWER SHARING FORMULA:

Meanwhile, the anti-government alliance, PDM, along with major opposition party PPP devised a prospective **'power-sharing formula'** if no-confidence motion succeeded both at Centre and in Punjab. Under the power-sharing model, PMLQ senior leader Pervaiz Elahi could get the portfolio of Punjab chief minister while the size of provincial cabinet would be 'very low' (... *as of then, the Punjab cabinet consisted of 38 ministers, four advisers and four special assistants – headed by CM Buzdar*).

The PMLN lawmaker was to be elected as Punjab Assembly Speaker and PPP's Qamar Zaman Kaira's name was proposed for the slot of province's governor. Most of the ministries in the Punjab cabinet were to go with PMLN MPAs while PPP and PMLQ were to get share under the proposed power-sharing deal. Meanwhile, the ticket of PMLN had become a *"hot cake"* amid fluid political situation. PDM's next move was worked out - that after the no-confidence motion against PM Imran Khan and NA speaker Asad Qaiser, the opposition was seeking to turn its gun towards President Arif Alvi; former president Asif Ali Zardari was being considered to replace Mr Alvi.

A night earlier, four MPAs of the PTI in Punjab Assembly met with the PMLN leadership and assured them of their support and more than 18 MPAs belonging to the three divisions of South Punjab had also agreed to support the PDM. However, the then Speaker Punjab Assembly Ch Pervaiz Elahi, belonging to the PMLQ, announced that a consensus had been reached with the PTI government that the (then) assemblies would complete their terms.

The PMLQ, a party that was being speculated to be an *'at-risk ally'* of the ruling PTI, announced the decision after a two-day consultative meeting on the ongoing political situation developed following the PDM had submitted a no-confidence motion. PTI leadership announced that the party had made its decision and final consultation was underway with other coalition partners as they were working together.

In his interaction with the media after the meeting with PM Khan, Ch Pervaiz Elahi said that the allies of the PTI-govt — PMLQ, MQMP and the BAP — were working together. But, the statement regarding the completion of the assemblies did not win the PMLN and PPP's approval. ***Both the major opposition parties had already thrown their weight behind fresh elections*** whereas, Mr Elahi's statement suggested that the change might only be witnessed in the Centre, in case the no-trust motion was successfully executed. A top legal mind of the PDM had also suggested its leadership to obtain affidavits from the turn-coat PTI MNAs, who were supporting the no confidence move. He informed that other than allies parties MNAs, the opposition had support of 182 MNAs against PM Imran Khan. A PTI leader had also admitted that the biggest dilemma for the incumbent PTI government was that it had *lost support from the media* (also) in that situation; in the media nobody condemned those who were elected on PTI tickets and later planned to vote against their prime minister Khan.

Senate Chairman Sadiq Sanjrani had vowed to support PM Imran Khan in his personal capacity on the issue of no-trust vote; saying that his party – the Balochistan Awami Party (BAP) – had not taken any decision on the no-confidence motion yet. Meanwhile, PMLN Senior Vice President and the former premier Shahid Khaqan Abbasi maintained that some of their lawmakers had received notices from the National Accountability Bureau (NAB) since the opposition had filed a requisition for a no-confidence motion against the government - *"It is not NAB chairman's [Justice (retd) Javed Iqbal] job to interfere in the no-trust move."*

DISSIDENT PTI MNAs AT SINDH HOUSE:

On 16th March 2022; the Pakistan Bar Council – the apex body of the lawyers in the country – convened a meeting of all the lawyers' bodies to discuss the then prevailing political situation. Next day, on 17th March 2022: Several ruling PTI lawmakers announced that they would not follow the party line in the National Assembly ahead of the voting on the no-confidence motion against their Prime Minister Imran Khan; *at least 24 MNAs were staying at the Sindh House in Islamabad* at that moment. Raja Riaz, a member of estranged PTI faction known as the Jahangir Tareen group, claimed that they moved to the Sindh House due to *"security concerns after police stormed parliament lodges and tortured their lawmakers"*.

On 18th March 2022: The ruling PTI lawmakers and workers stormed the Sindh House in Islamabad in protest against the dissident members of the ruling party, who were staying inside the building. The PTI legislatures and workers forcibly entered the building located in the Red Zone of the federal capital ahead of the PDM's no-trust motion against PM Imran Khan. They were seen knocking down the Sindh House gate and shouting slogans while holding Lotas (*spouted globulars*) in their hands to symbolise turncoats.

On the same day, on the request of the opposition leaders, the NA informed the MNAs about the no-confidence motion against PM Imran Khan; it was the requirement under the rules and regulations of the National Assembly; Article 95 of the Constitution was referred. The opposition leaders (PDM) once more urged PM Imran Khan to step down voluntarily as (apparently) he had *lost the majority* in the NA after several ruling party lawmakers announced that they would not follow the party line in the no-trust vote against the premier.

Next day, on 19th March 2022, PTI issued show-cause notices [SCNs] to dissident lawmakers for joining the opposition parties. In the notices, the ruling party reminded the dissidents that they were bound to follow the directions issued by the PTI as its member. It asked the lawmakers to explain within seven days about giving the impression that they were about to leave the party. The SCNs read as:

> "*It is abundantly clear from the provisions of Article 63-A(1) that you are bound to follow the directions issued by PTI as you are a member… and continue to be bound to follow the directions…*"

The opposition parties unanimously said that Speaker NA, Asad Qaiser, had violated the Constitution by not calling the assembly session within the 14-days period; saying the failure to convene the session by 22nd March was an unconstitutional move and warranted punishment under Article 6 of the Constitution (high treason). They accused PTI's Speaker of abrogating the Constitution by summoning the session on 25th March 2022, instead of 22nd instant. The NA Speaker had to take shelter saying that: '… *due to renovations at the Parliament House ahead of the OIC moot, no suitable place was available to hold the session before 24th March*'.

An open show of dissent: Several dissident MNAs, including Raja Riaz, Malik Nawab Sher Waseer, Noor Alam Khan and Basit Bukhari from the ruling PTI came out open and were found staying at the Sindh House in Islamabad; with Raja Riaz and Malik Nawab Sher Waseer saying they would vote on the no-confidence motion tabled against PM Imran Khan in *'accordance with their conscience'* – *was a mockery of consciousness in deed.* That day's media & TV footage also showed another MNA named Wajiha Qamar flying over nowhere — staying at the facility, giving a clear indication which side they would be tilting towards in the upcoming vote that was to decide the fate of Prime Minister Imran Khan.

Raja Riaz, who was a member of the Jahangir Tareen group, spoke to **Geo News** senior anchor Hamid Mir and said there were around 24 PTI lawmakers staying at the Sindh House, citing fears of government action against them similar to the 10th March raid on JUI-F's militia by police on Parliament Lodges. Referring to the media news dated 17th March 2022, he had earlier said that:

> *"If PM Imran Khan gives the guarantee that no police action would be taken against the MNAs irrespective of their decision regarding the vote, he is ready to move to Parliament Lodges from the Sindh House. All media and the nation know that the police attacked the lodges and our opposition MNA was tortured and taken to the police station. After that, we — those who had been dissenting for a long time against inflation, corruption, the SAPMs and the lawlessness, and had been raising our voice in front of Khan sahib — felt that the incident that happened in the Lodges could also happen with us, and this is why we are here."*

When asked by the media persons if he (Raja Riaz) had taken Rs:200 million to switch allegiance, Riaz chuckled and denied. Another PTI MNA, Noor Alam Khan was disappointed to know of allegations being levelled against dissident lawmakers, saying: *"When we came to Imran Khan sahib and had voted for him, were we given Rs:200m then? When we voted for the speaker, did we get 200 million then?"*

Another MNA Dr Ramesh Kumar Vankwani revealed two men from the PTI recently came to the Lodges and accused him of **being a traitor to the party** and even threatened to vandalise his cars. Then he approached Sindh CM Murad Ali Shah through someone and told him that I wanted a room at Sindh House. He added that:

> *"When I came here, I saw a completely different environment. There are around 24 MNAs ... most are joining the PMLN, two to three are joining the PMLQ, and two to three are going elsewhere. Three federal ministers have also left [the PTI]."*

A day earlier, the PTI government had claimed the opposition had detained some ruling party lawmakers at Sindh House ahead of the vote after a statement by Punjab Assembly Speaker Ch Parvez Elahi that around a dozen MNAs belonging to the PTI had *'gone missing'*. Mr Khan said in a public address that opposition leaders were sitting in Sindh House with *'heaps of money to purchase loyalties of treasury lawmakers'* and had asked the Election Commission to take action against the alleged horse-trading.

A video clip had gone viral on notable media TVs and social media showing some of those dissident MNAs counting 'bundles of currency notes' in their hands and lying on the table in front of them. At the same time, PPP leader Faisal Karim Kundi had earlier confirmed the stay of some lawmakers at Sindh House during a press conference with PPP MNA Shazia Marri – saying that '.... *MNAs are being kept there as they feared they could be kidnapped ahead of the no-trust vote.'*

PPP's Bilawal Zardari also claimed that MNAs had been *'threatened with violence, arrests and dire consequences if they participated in the no-confidence vote. Their lives, liberty and family are under threat. MNAs will take any and all means for their own protection against this fascist regime.'*

On 20th March 2022: The opposition (PDM) considered to launch the testing of its **'Plan-B'** in case its **'Plan-A'** - the ouster of the prime minister through no-confidence motion - fell short of achieving the target. As per the planned strategy to make the said no-trust move a success, the opposition also devised a **'Plan-C'** to keep the momentum going had the intended results not attained timely. Federal Minister for Interior Sheikh Rashid said the PTI government would not obstruct anyone from casting their vote on the no-confidence motion tabled in the National Assembly; the ruling PTI would not resort to extra-constitutional measures to sway the results of the motion of no-trust against PM Imran Khan.

Prime Minister Imran Khan maintained that he would rather give up his government than *compromising on his conscience*. Out of sheer frustration, the premier even urged the dissident PTI lawmakers to return to the ruling party's fold, saying that he was ready to forgive them like a compassionate father. An embattled premier said while addressing a public crowd in Dargai:

> *"A decisive moment has arrived in the country's history—whether you [the nation] choose 'bandits' or those striving to end the menace of corruption in the country."*

NA speaker Asad Qaiser, on 23rd March 2022, vowed to fulfil his constitutional obligations through an official Twitter message:

> *"I, as the custodian of the National Assembly of Pakistan, will fulfil my constitutional obligations and will proceed in accordance with Article 95 of the Constitution & rule 37 of the Rules of Procedure and Conduct of Business in the National Assembly 2007."*

National Assembly Speaker Asad Qaiser summoned the session of the National Assembly for 25th March 2022 at 11 am at the request of the opposition parties. The decision to summon the session by the assembly speaker came a day after the joint opposition lashed out at the PTI government for alleged attempts to delay the crucial session under the guise of the Organisation of Islamic Cooperation (OIC) moot in Islamabad on March 22-23, 2022. The opposition leader and PPP Chief Bilawal Zardari had even threatened to disrupt the session by staging a sit-in in front of the assembly.

On 25th March 2022: The session began with the recitation of the Holy Quran and prayers for three deceased members; then the speaker announced that it would be adjourned in light of the parliamentary convention. The NA Speaker Asad Qaiser adjourned the proceedings of the much-anticipated session till 28th March instant without tabling the said PDM's no-confidence motion. This move irked the opposition parties to issue a warning to the speaker that any further delay in tabling the motion would lead to protest.

> *[In Pakistan, it has been the parliamentary convention that the first sitting after the death of an MNA is limited to prayers for the soul of the departed and tributes other lawmakers wish to pay them. According to the tradition, the agenda is deferred to the next day when a member of the lower house had passed away.]*

Next day, on 26th March 2022, the Leader of the Opposition Shahbaz Sharif wrote a letter to National Assembly Speaker Asad Qaiser, expressing reservations on the government's conduct, particularly the delay in convening the NCM session of the lower house. He highlighted that the motion was submitted on 8th March and the requisition was also submitted on the same day, adding that the notices for the motion could have been sent immediately. But that didn't happen, rather some members of the parliament received a copy of the notice on 19th March; he regretted.

Meanwhile, in its ramped-up efforts to salvage the vanishing support to survive the no-confidence-motion, PTI leaders held crucial meetings with

PMLQ and MQM-P; a delegation led by federal ministers Shah Mahmood Qureshi and Pervez Khattak met with PMLQ leader and Speaker Punjab Assembly Ch Pervaiz Elahi to discuss the no-trust move. However, the efforts of the PTI government negotiation committee went in vain because the PMLQ leadership left the decision to vote on the no-confidence motion for the last day.

MR KHAN's 'CYPHER-RALLY' & AFTER:

On 27th March 2022: Thousands of PTI supporters flocked to the federal capital to attend PM Imran Khan's rally in backdrop of the **no confidence motion** (NCM). In his two-hour-long marathon speech at a sparkly, booming show in Islamabad – a cradle of his political movement from the 'container days' – PM Khan's appearance seemed to be a fiery effort to lean into the definitive agenda points of the PTI.

> *[More details of that day's activity are available in* **CYPHER CASE Scenario** *separately]*

PM Imran Khan was in high trouble then. To counteract the threat posed by party dissidents, the PTI government approached the Supreme Court of Pakistan [SC] through a presidential petition, which, among other questions, asked the court if there could be a lifetime disqualification from legislative office for party defectors under Article 63-A of the Constitution, which de-seats a parliamentarian for violating party directives. That step couldn't help Mr Khan either. As both the joint opposition and the government escalated their efforts to woo the PTI's coalition partners, electoral calculations once again came into play. Perceiving the PMLN and PPP as apparently better placed than PTI in the forthcoming general elections, the BAP was the first to join the ranks of the opposition, followed by MQM-P.

On 28th March 2022; the much-anticipated session of the NA to deliberate on the no-confidence motion was held amidst high uproar and noise; after much excitement, the no-confidence motion was finally tabled in the NA against the sitting PM Imran Khan. Before the tabling of the motion, the NA Deputy Speaker Qasim Suri, who was presiding over the session, asked the lawmakers in favour of the motion to rise so that the count could be made. Within minutes, the deputy speaker announced that a total of 161 members of the opposition parties were present in the assembly and, thus, the leave for presenting the motion against the prime minister was granted.

As Mr Shahbaz Sharif stood up to present the motion, the treasury benches resorted to name-calling and continued making noise; some constantly shouted *'cherry blossom'* while other PTI lawmakers kept calling the opposition members *'chor'* (thieves). Nevertheless, the opposition leader presented the motion amid hue and cry made by the PTI lawmakers and desk-thumping from the opposition members.

The day the no-trust vote was scheduled, the opposition was confident it no longer needed PTI dissidents to send Mr Khan home. Imran Khan played his *'trump card'* then. A day before, he addressed a rally in Islamabad that he dubbed *Amr Bil Maroof* (enjoining what is good and forbidding what is wrong – an Islamic order). While continuing to accuse the opposition of buying the loyalty of PTI dissidents, he also warned of a *'foreign conspiracy'* through CYPHER DRAMA behind its efforts to remove him. The general populace immediately picked up that Mr Khan was referring it to the US interference. Khan accused the opposition parties of receiving foreign funds and conspiring at the behest of a foreign power to oust him and the PTI government.

Imran Khan claimed that his visit to Moscow in February 2022, on the day Russia's attack on Ukraine took start – along with his **opposition to the US war in Afghanistan** {ref: **Report no: 320** dated 4th February 2022 available at Crisisgroup.org} – explains US attempts to remove him. Khan also insisted that Pakistan's military leadership agreed the US was trying to oust his government, Mr Khan claimed as evidence a *'threat letter'*; it was a diplomatic cable following his 7th March meeting with the US assistant secretary of state for South and Central Asia. The Biden administration denied any such intention but President Vladimir Putin's government in Moscow backed Khan's allegations.

> *{The said threat letter is separately dealt with as **CYPHER CASE** in the next book}*

No-Trust Motion against CM Buzdar: On the same day of 28th March 2022, PMLN and PPP lawmakers submitted a no-trust motion against Punjab Chief Minister Usman Buzdar, requesting the Punjab Assembly speaker to summon a session on it. The requisition was deposited with the Punjab Assembly Secretariat, and was addressed to Speaker Punjab Assembly Chaudhary Pervez Elahi. A total of 127 lawmakers, including PPP and PMLN MPAs, had signed that no-trust motion against CM Buzdar.

The following day, **CM Buzdar tendered his resignation** to Prime Minister Imran Khan vowing that he would always stand firmly with

Imran Khan to fulfil the promise of *'Naya Pakistan'*. It was alleged by media gurus that CM Buzdar had resigned on the will and instructions of Imran Khan to make a way for Ch Pervaiz Elahi.

Same day, following CM Usman Buzdar's resignation, Premier Imran offered the Punjab chief minister's slot to PMLQ leader Ch Pervaiz Elahi, the incumbent provincial assembly speaker. The official statement from the PMLQ quoted the premier as saying during the meeting: *'I have taken the resignation from Usman Bazdar and I congratulate Ch Pervaiz Elahi for being nominated from my party's side as the chief minister of Punjab.'* In return, Elahi thanked PM Khan for entrusting him with the post of the chief minister, saying he would remain trustworthy.

On 29th March 2022: As the threat of losing his seat of power edged closer, PM Imran Khan formally barred lawmakers from the ruling PTI from attending the National Assembly session on the day of voting—likely to be held in the first week of April then. The premier issued the directives as the leader of the parliamentary party of PTI, a day after the no-confidence motion was tabled in the lower house of parliament against him. *'No member of the Pakistan Tehreek-e-Insaf shall attend or make himself / herself available at the time and day of voting on the resolution of No-Confidence,'* siad a communiqué issued by the PTI.

Surprisingly, following the nomination of Ch Pervaiz Elahi, estranged PMLQ leader Tariq Bashir Cheema, who stepped down as minister for housing AND reiterated that he would support the no-trust motion against PM Imran Khan filed by the joint opposition in National Assembly. The deal reportedly prompted a rift within the party with Cheema revolting against the decision and announcing to vote against PM Imran Khan. Cheema also resigned from the federal cabinet, *giving rise to speculations regarding a rift within the family - Chaudhrys of Gujrat.*

Next day, on 30th March 2022, as the opposition focussed its guns on PM Imran Khan ahead of the no-confidence vote, the political earth of the country shook and seemed to tilt toward the opposition after the ruling party apparently lost its majority in the National Assembly following a pull-out of its key allies. The situation had come about in the wake of the MQMP's seven members crossing over to the opposition's side after burning the midnight oil with the joint opposition and hammering out an agreement in the microscopic hours of the day.

Prime Minister Khan continued with his mantra that the opposition's no-confidence motion against him *'is a huge foreign conspiracy against Pakistan'* but emphasised that he could not name the country which sent the '<u>threatening letter (Cypher)</u>' because its results would not be good for the country. Khan repeated that, as per the letter, Pakistan would face serious consequences if the no-confidence motion failed, adding that the language of the letter was extremely harsh and that the no-trust motion had been mentioned in it several times.

The details about the prime minister's remarks had emerged after he convened an urgent meeting of federal cabinet to discuss the issue of an international conspiracy to topple his government through a secret letter that he waved in his public rally in Islamabad <u>on 27th March 2022</u>. The said letter was sent by former Pakistani ambassador to the United States, Asad Majeed after having talks with the US Assistant Secretary of State for South Asia.

NATIONAL ASSEMBLY DISSOLVED...:

On 3rd April 2022: Pakistan's political turmoil deepened when Prime Minister Imran Khan avoided the said attempt to oust him *and sought fresh elections after dissolving the parliament.* The deputy speaker of parliament, Qasim Suri of the PTI, blocked the said opposition no-confidence motion that Khan had widely been expected to lose, *ruling it was part of a foreign conspiracy and unconstitutional.* Deputy Speaker Suri had said:

> *"No foreign power has the right to topple an elected government under any conspiracy. So, I rule the no-confidence resolution as against the national integrity and sovereignty, and I... disallow the no-confidence resolution."*

That order of the Deputy Speaker (apparently) thwarted the opposition's attempt to come to power, and set up a potential legal showdown over the Constitution in the country. Opposition leader Shahbaz Sharif called the blocking of the vote *'nothing short of high treason'* and posted on Twitter there would be consequences for *'blatant & brazen violation of the Constitution'* and vowed to approach the Supreme Court expecting it to uphold the Constitution. Before, Shahbaz Sharif's petition, the <u>CJP Bandial had announced to take up the issue as suo-moto case</u>.

Meanwhile, the Deputy Attorney General of Pakistan Raja Khalid, the top prosecutor, resigned, calling the government's dissolving of parliament unconstitutional. *'What has happened can only be expected in the rule of a dictator,'* he told local media.

Immediately after, PM Khan lost his majority in parliament when allies quit his coalition government and he suffered a spate of defections within his PTI. The media held that Khan was *as good as gone*, but he urged his supporters to come out in the streets ahead of the planned vote. On the streets of the capital Islamabad, there was a heavy police and paramilitary presence, with shipping containers used to block off roads at every crossing. Police were seen detaining three supporters of Khan's PTI outside the parliament, but the paths and roads were calm otherwise.

Soon after the speaker ended the session, Pakistani President Arif Alvi, acting on the prime minister's advice, dissolved the parliament and called fresh elections in 90 days, citing relevant constitution provisions. Mr Khan also dissolved his Cabinet – a political crisis had taken start. All eyes were set on the outcome of the hearing in Pakistan's highest court. Pakistan's military spokesman, Maj-Gen Babar Iftikhar, told foreign media that the military had nothing to do with the political turmoil, dismissing widespread speculation that a military intervention was imminent.

On 4th April 2022, the Supreme Court of Pakistan [SCP], giving priority to the constitutional crisis in the country, took up the *suo-moto* case of Dy Speaker Qasim Suri's ruling. Immediately *it was declared by the apex court that any directions given by the president and prime minister would be subject to the court's orders.* An urgent hearing started into opposition allegations - the blocking of a no-confidence vote against PM Khan was generally taken as violation of the country's constitution; see the editorial of the DAILY EXPRESS TRIBUNE of 4th April 2022:

> *"This is a good omen. It is good to see, at least, that the executive, the parliament, and the judiciary are all claiming their due constitutional space and asserting their writ. It is a worthy achievement for the people of Pakistan who awe and aspire for representative rule. One hopes this constitutional hiccup too would be a passing reference in our checkered politics, and institutions will triumph over personalized whims and wishes."*

Arif Alvi, largely a ceremonial president in Pakistan, had used his constitutional authority to allow Khan to work as an interim Chief Executive until a caretaker prime minister was appointed to supervise the general election. Also, that President Alvi wrote to both Mr Khan and

Shahbaz Sharif, asking them to put forward names for a caretaker prime minister within three days. For his part, Khan proposed Monday the name of Pakistan's former chief justice, Gulzar Ahmed, to be the caretaker prime minister.

Gareth Price, senior research fellow in *the Asia Pacific program at London*, questioned Mr Khan's claims, that the United States was behind the no-confidence vote against him:

> *"While US criticism of Khan's fence-sitting regarding Ukraine and general anti-Americanism is eminently plausible, a call for regime change, as Khan claimed, seems more far-fetched. A court ruling on whether or not the move (that blocked the no-trust vote) is legal is imminent. Either way, recent events have done little to resolve political polarization. Like many populists, Khan seems happy to conflate himself with Pakistan, describing his opponents as dacoits (bandits) and traitors."*

SUPREME COURT DISCARDED DY SPEAKER'S RULING:

On 7th April 2022: Pakistan's Supreme Court [SCP] set aside the said ruling of Mr Qasim Suri, the Dy Speaker of the national assembly, that had blocked an opposition-led vote of no confidence against Prime Minister Imran Khan. The provocative and controversial ruling of 3rd April 2022 had led to the dissolution of the National Assembly, the lower house of parliament, by President Arif Alvi, acting on Khan's advice. The president had also called for fresh elections in 90 days and appointed Khan as the interim Chief Executive after the prime minister dissolved his Cabinet.

The five-judge panel of the top court led by Chief Justice of Pakistan [CJP] Umar Ata Bandial, however, unanimously declared as unconstitutional all the steps stemming from the deputy speaker's ruling, which had outlawed the no-confidence vote as having been sponsored by a *'foreign power'*, the United States, it was later named openly. The decision on the issue came after four days of hearings by the top court. The short judicial order declared:

> *".... the ruling to be contrary to the Constitution and the law and of no legal effect, and the same are hereby set aside. The advice tendered by the Prime Minister ... to the President to dissolve the Assembly was contrary to the Constitution and of no legal effect.*

> *It is declared that all actions initiated for purposes of holding a general election to elect a new assembly – including but not limited to the appointment of a caretaker prime minister and cabinet – <u>are of no legal effect and are hereby quashed</u>."*

The verdict also restored Mr Khan as the prime minister and his Cabinet as well, ordering the session of the National Assembly to reconvene Saturday morning (<u>the 9th April 2022</u>) to reorganize the vote of no confidence to determine the fate of the embattled prime minister. It added that: *"if the no-confidence resolution is successful then the assembly shall forthwith, and in its present session, proceed to elect a Prime Minister."*

Earlier on that day, <u>the 7th April 2022</u>, the fourth day of hearings, Khan's lawyers defended the controversial move and said <u>the Supreme Court did not have jurisdiction to intervene in parliamentary affairs</u>. The standoff threw the country of 240 million people into a full-blown constitutional crisis, and sent its currency to all-time lows against the dollar on that occasion of judgment. *'As [the] dollar continues to soar, a massive economic meltdown is staring the country in the face,'* Shahbaz Sharif, who was to replace Mr Khan as prime minister, said.

<u>Mr Khan had lost the majority in the 342-member house in the run-up to the said no-confidence vote</u> after lawmakers from his ruling party defected and main coalition partners switched sides and joined the opposition. Khan had repeatedly alleged that the United States conspired with the opposition to topple his government to punish him for his recent visit to Russia and for not supporting the West in condemning President Vladimir Putin's war on Ukraine. Pakistani opposition leaders had ridiculed the charges, and Washington had vehemently rejected them. Mr Khan's attorneys had defended his actions as being in line with the constitution during their arguments before the Supreme Court – but of no avail. Opposition leaders and human rights activists declared the outcome of the legal proceedings as a landmark judgment – *'It is not the political parties or parliament that won or lost. The constitution retained its supremacy'.*

Pakistan's powerful military had distanced itself from the political crisis stemming from 3rd April's controversial proceedings in parliament; in fact they had already done their assignment. *Michael Kugelman*, an expert on South Asia affairs at *the Washington-based Wilson Center*, while commenting on the Supreme Court verdict, said:

> *"After its euphoria subsides, and assuming it wins the no-confidence vote, the current opposition won't have it easy. It'll face an economic mess, and it will be hounded relentlessly by an angry PTI in opposition. Can't rule out the possibility of early elections down the road."*

The united opposition, the PDM, already had announced that Shahbaz Sharif of PMLN, would be their candidate for prime minister. The PMLN, with 83 seats, was the second-biggest party in the assembly, followed by the Pakistani Peoples Party (PPP), with 53 seats. Mr Khan called its cabinet and parliamentary party meetings for next day following the court ruling – saying:

> *"My message to our nation is I have always & will continue to fight for Pakistan till the last ball. The court ruling fulfilled the people's expectations."*

PPP leader Bilawal Zardari hailed the verdict as a ***victory for democracy and the constitution.***

On 10th April 2022: The Pakistani parliament voted no confidence for Prime Minister Imran Khan in the early hours of the day (**during mid-night exactly**). A chaos ended but another was ready to raise tensions in the country's politics. PMLN and the PPP had long insisted that his victory in the 2018 general elections was the result of military interference; a report dated 13th April 2022 at *crisisgroup.org* is referred.

However, beyond that shared belief, the two parties differed over ways to oppose Imran Khan's government; the PPP had been calling for a no-trust vote in the federal parliament while the PMLN hesitated, opting at times to resign from the legislature and at other times to fill the streets in protest. The Khan government brought its two rivals together by consistently targeting their top leadership, Nawaz Sharif & Mr Zardari in particular, through a flawed and defective accountability process overseen by the controversial National Accountability Bureau [NAB]. Meanwhile, public anger at the government was growing because of apparently soaring inflation and governance failures; interference in policing like the earlier governments of PMLN and PPP, deprived citizens of basic services and security. Yet when the opposition agreed on a common goal, ousting Khan through constitutional means – a no-trust vote in the parliament – it posed a far bigger threat to the survival of Imran Khan.

Pakistan has time and again witnessed Pak-Army - America alliance bringing civilian government down unconstitutionally either by soft coup or by boots on ground and by exploiting the corrupt and compromised judiciary and politicians. IK was portrayed as the only leader who tried gallantly to resist that evil nexus, but unfortunately, he was surrounded by legacy-branded and disloyal, incompetent and opportunists type politicians and administration elite, which became a big factor behind his defeat in parliament [on 10th April 2022]. Not to mention the Army top brass who has historically been subservient to US - the battle between Bajwa and IK was won by B+B [Bajwa & Biden] alliance; although a strong public opinion prevailed that *Khan would come back stronger in with 2/3 majority and better prepared.*

However, a section of intelligentsia also kept the opinion that in the backdrop of media analytical notes the world was rapidly turning against the US in a geopolitical scenario, while China, Russia, Iran, Asia pacific countries, Africa and the Muslim world were striving to put a serious dent in US hegemony over the globe. IK had plans to gain a renewed opportunity to steer the country towards an *independent foreign policy*. For Imran Khan and like-minded people, there were ample important lessons from the said defeat.

Also, Mr Khan was bound to rectify the mistakes he made on the domestic front especially in Punjab, the province that mattered the most; and the lack of far-sightedness, judiciousness and know-how he displayed in dealing with Gen Bajwa's sane advice, while ignoring PTI's experienced heads & balanced approach for America. *He could have been firm yet flexible. He chose fighting too many battles at once with no recognised primacies.* Forgetting emotions and rhetoric in the given scenario; the intelligentsia worked out practicalities of whether the parliament could be realistically functional.

> [Going back to 2007-08, by then the two-party political system had been well established for over 20 years in Pakistan, with PPP and PMLN pitched against each other; PPP - legacy of ZA Bhutto and the PMLN - legacy of Gen Zia, who had hanged ZAB. All the political parties combined except PTI making up 174 seats in the National Assembly of the country.]

Truthfully, without the PTI, no one could be the leader of the opposition in the Parliament. Could one imagine a democracy where parliament could move with no opposition party and no leader of the opposition? Nothing could be more dysfunctional and chaotic. In the then prevailing situation on 10th April 2022, with only TWO seats difference between them, the largest political party was out, meaning the combined opposition became the ruling party and no opposition; legislations thus passed were going meaningless in deed.

On another note, and on the same day, the PTI supporters protested against *'regime change'* at Hyde Park, London. They were saying:

> *"No Imran, No remittances; we won't send any remittances until Imran Khan comes back. Overseas Pakistanis were seen withdrawing money from Roshan Digital Account after the ouster of Imran Khan s government, claiming they don't want their hard-earned money to end up in accounts of corrupt looters....<u>Within few hours approximately 1.8 Billion USD were withdrawn.</u>"*

Referring to daily **TheNews** dated <u>11th April 2022</u>: Till two days before, the country was being pulled down by economic meltdown and bankruptcy; the Supreme Court of Pakistan [SCP] arrested the slide. The verdict immediately caused recovery of the rupee, which had hit Rs:191 against the dollar, and a rally in the stock exchange.

During the four-day debate in the SCP's hearing, at one point, signals were given for fresh elections. But the SCP evaluated the interest of the state, economy, and constraints of the Constitution, restored the 3rd April status of the National Assembly - not buying the international conspiracy narrative of the PTI govt. Neither did it show any interest in the in-camera briefing of the PTI govt, nor ordered any inquiry into rhetoric conspiracy plots.

The world media, *including Reuters*, carried stories of international conspiracy and the US money behind the NCM of the opposition. But the popular version also appeared that the interests of America, GCC countries and Pakistan were aligned in many ways, particularly with the exit of Khan's govt which allegedly abandoned Pakistan's foreign policy interests with not only the US and EU but also with the UAE, Saudi Arabia and other Arabian states.

IMRAN KHAN's TERM FINISHED:

The fact remained that the TWO BIGS in the establishment, COAS Gen Bajwa and the sitting ISI DG got angry with the PTI govt due to obvious reasons. As anchor of stability, the establishment held its centre of gravity whether it was Russia-Ukraine crisis or US-induced PTI narrative of conspiracy of balancing relations with domestic political stakeholders; it played a role. However, the new prime minister, new cabinet and the new government of Shahbaz Sharif, had the uphill task to turn around the economy, control inflation, steer Pakistan out of FATF list, attract foreign investment and thwart any Indian designs.

Imran Khan's unbridled term as prime minister of Pakistan ended unceremoniously - following weeks of high political drama and days of constitutional chaos since ending year 2021. The Supreme Court had restored the parliament that Khan had sought to disband and mandated a vote of no confidence that he sought to avoid. Imran Khan was effectively left with a *choice: resign or be voted out of office.*

Imran Khan's political demise was rooted in twin new realities. Inside parliament, Khan's PTI had lost the support of coalition allies, denying him the majority he needed to defeat the vote of no confidence. Outside parliament, Khan appeared to lose the support of Pakistan's powerful military, which had helped him win the 2018 general election, and had recently publicly fallen out with the prime minister over senior military appointments and policy decisions – though both, the PTI and the military, had denied the claims. Within six months, as the major opposition parties, the PPP and the PMLN, ramped up their efforts to dislodge Khan, coalition allies became vocal in their dissatisfaction with him. Senator Anwaarul Haq Kakar of the Baluchistan Awami Party (BAP), a coalition ally that withdrew support for Khan in late March (2022), said:

> "As far as governance was concerned, the (PTI) government had totally failed. There was disgruntlement for the past two years. The party [BAP] was not happy about its share in the federal government and the ministerial portfolio it has been allocated."

Imran Khan became the first Pakistani prime minister to be removed from office after losing a no-confidence vote in parliament.

PTI's MASS RESIGNATIONS FROM PARLIAMENT:

On 11th April 2022: The PTI decided to resign from the National Assembly, minutes before the election for the new prime minister was scheduled to take place. The decision was taken in a party's parliamentary meeting, which was chaired by Chairman Imran Khan, at the Parliament House that afternoon. The PTI's official tweet said: *'The parliamentary party has decided to resign from the assemblies against the imported government.'*

Imran Khan's PTI parliamentary party, once again, faced a split over the *issue of resignations from National Assembly*. While Fawad Chaudhry and Sh Rashid Ahmad said the party parliamentarians would resign en-masse after the election of prime minister (on 11th April 2022). Both they were active in pushing the PTI out of the political scene thus pressurising Imran Khan to resign from the assemblies. Shah Mehmood Qureshi said no final decision had been reached yet while Ali Muhammad Khan said *almost 95 per cent of the party MNAs were against quitting the assemblies.* They believed if the PTI MNAs tender resignations en-masse, the new government under Shahbaz Sharif would get an opportunity to play openly on important appointments and legislation – it was the whole truth.

In the above scenario, Khan's PTI was bound to suffer an irreparable loss. Ch Fawad, briefing the media about the PTI core committee meeting at Bani Gala, said that the PTI MNAs would start resigning from the National Assembly a day after. PTI had nominated Shah Mehmood Qureshi as the candidate for the prime ministerial slot. There were two objectives of contesting the election: one was to challenge the papers of Shahbaz Sharif, as there was Rs:16 billion corruption case against him. Also, the day he would be contesting for the prime ministerial slot, the same day he was to be indicted in that corruption case by the respective court. PTI's Fawad Chaudhry also said:

> *"The resignations of most of the parliamentary party members had been handed over to Imran Khan. The entire nation expected guidance from Imran Khan at this time - if we disappointed the nation, and Imran Khan did not lead a big movement, then it would be betrayal of Pakistan's politics and the Constitution."*

Awami Muslim League's ex-minister Sheikh Rashid declared in categorical terms that he would not sit in the National Assembly with thieves and robbers and he was going to resign from the National Assembly. After the said announcement, Murad Saeed tendered his resignation as member of the NA — the first from the PTI party. He confirmed that he made the decision in line with the party's narrative. He reiterated the former prime minister's claims of a foreign conspiracy, stating that sitting in the NA after these revelations would be akin to be being a part of that plot – *'Should foreign powers have the right to make or break governments in Pakistan?'*

Murad Saeed also highlighted the charges against the opposition's candidate for prime minister, Shahbaz Sharif, while saying: *'They were and are corrupt'*. Former maritime affairs minister Ali Haider Zaidi also followed suit, announcing his resignation on Twitter, while saying: *'No way we should legitimize this foreign-funded regime change in Pakistan. The battle for the sovereignty of Pakistan will now be decided on the streets by the people, not these looters.'*

Former minister for Kashmir Affairs and Gilgit-Baltistan Ali Amin Gandapur also shared a photo of his resignation on the party's letterhead; saying: *'I am proud to be a follower of Imran Khan and will fight till my death for the freedom of Pakistan and parliament'*. PTI leaders Shireen Mazari, Hammad Azhar, and Shafaqt Mahmood shared their resignations on Twitter too.

> [PTI leader Fawad Chaudhry said that the decision to resign was tied to the acceptance of PMLN President Shahbaz Sharif's nomination papers for prime minister's elections, to which the PTI had raised objections. *'It was a great injustice that Shahbaz would be contesting the election for the prime minister on the same day he is to be indicted in a money laundering case. What can be more insulting for Pakistan that a foreign selected and foreign imported government is imposed on it and a person like Shahbaz is made its head'*. [A special court (Central-I) of the Federal Investigation Agency (FIA) was to indict Shahbaz and his son, Hamza, in a Rs:14 billion money laundering case on the same day but the court had to defer the indictment.]

The NA session started shortly for the election of a new prime minister after an unceremonious end of Imran Khan's tenure. Shahbaz Sharif — who was the former joint opposition's candidate for the prime ministerial slot — and PTI's Shah Mahmood Qureshi were in the race to become the country's new prime minister. Both Shahbaz and Qureshi had filed their nomination papers a day before. During the submission, the PTI had raised objections to Shahbaz's nomination and subsequently PTI's Qureshi and Babar Awan had exchanged heated words with PMLN leaders Zahid Hamid and Atta Tarar. *The objections raised against Shahbaz were that the latter was contesting the election on the day of his expected indictment in a money laundering case.* They were of the opinion that Shahbaz didn't deserve to be the new PM due to his *'involvement in corruption cases'*.

Among the two, the possibility of Qureshi going ahead with contesting the election was uncertain as the PTI was deliberating on resignations from the lower house of parliament. Also, that in line with the PTI's decision of mass-resignations, Shahbaz was to be elected as the new prime minister nearly unopposed – and it happened so. The new PDM government continued to urge Imran Khan and the PTI to come and sit on opposition benches in the assembly as an integral part of the democratic process – but the PTI's members kept discarding the invitations and continued to hold the boycott. *A total of 123 PTI MNAs had resigned en-masse.*

Ultimately, **on 17th January 2023;** the speaker of the National Assembly, Raja Pervez Ashraf, accepted the resignations of 34 PTI lawmakers, and one member, Sheikh Rashid, of the Awami League (AML); three days later, 35 more resignations were accepted. Ultimately, on 25th January 2023, the Election Commission of Pakistan (ECP) de-notified 43 PTI lawmakers and two days later announced the by-elections for the vacant constituencies of National Assembly on 16th March 2023. It also announced 31 more by-polls for 19th March 2023 in the same row.

On 1st March 2023; the Islamabad High Court suspended the de-notification of three PTI lawmakers and a day later, the Balochistan High Court suspended the de-notification of PTI leader Qasim Suri and stopped the by-polls on his seat from Quetta. Two days after the Peshawar High Court suspended the notification for by-elections on 24 NA seats from Khyber KP, while the Sindh High Court suspended the ECP's notification for by-polls in nine National Assembly seats till 25th April instant.

The Election Commission of Pakistan (ECP) called off by-elections in 37 National Assembly constituencies in light of the decisions of the high courts concerned. The announcement came as the ECP had kick-started a seven-week election process for the Punjab Assembly with the filing of nomination papers for the 30th April vote. The ECP was also holding by-elections on six National Assembly seats in the province. The ECP issued four separate notifications, calling off the by-polls in 24 constituencies in Khyber-PK, nine in Sindh, three in Islamabad and one in Balochistan, which were scheduled to take place on 16th March 2023 and the 19th. The ECP notifications said that until further orders from the relevant courts, it was suspending the election schedule for the respective constituencies.

Meanwhile, the election process for the Punjab Assembly began as dozens of poll aspirants obtained nomination papers from the ECP regional offices.

PTI's LAST SESSION IN PARLIAMENT:

The opposition's no-trust motion against Prime Minister Imran Khan succeeded an hour past midnight *on Sunday, the 10th April 2022*, with

174 members in the 342-strong house voting in favour of the resolution. PMLN's Ayaz Sadiq, who was chairing the session after Asad Qaiser resigned as speaker, announced the result, after which Imran Khan ceased to hold the office of prime minister, as per Article 95 of the Constitution.

Imran Khan was the first prime minister in Pakistan's history who was removed from office through a no-confidence vote. Before him, Shaukat Aziz in 2006, and Benazir Bhutto in 1989, survived the moves against them. Ayaz Sadiq could not cast his vote as he was chairing the session. *PTI's dissenting members did not cast their votes either.*

Before adjourning the session, Sadiq said the nomination papers for the new prime minister may be submitted by 2pm today (Sunday, the 10<u>th</u> <u>April 2022</u>) and scrutiny would be done by 3pm. He summoned the session on Monday at 11am and said the new premier would be elected then. Later, it was announced that the assembly would meet at 2:00pm instead. Earlier, after announcing the result, Sadiq gave the floor to Shahbaz Sharif, who was the joint opposition's candidate for the post of prime minister. Shahbaz Sharif vowed that:

> *"The new regime would not indulge in politics of revenge. I don't want to go back to bitterness of the past. We want to forget them and move forward. **We will not take revenge or do injustice; we will not send people to jail for no reason, law and justice will take its course.**"*

After Shahbaz, Bilawal took the floor and congratulated the house for passing a no-trust resolution against a premier for the first time in history; saying:

> *"Today is <u>10th April 2022</u>, and the one we had declared selected, the non-democratic burden this country was bearing for the past 3 years, today, **welcome back to purana (old) Pakistan.**"*

Minutes before voting began, National Assembly Speaker Asad Qaiser resigned from his post, saying he could not take part in a foreign conspiracy to oust the prime minister. Qaiser's resignation came almost 15 minutes before midnight, which according to legal experts, was the deadline to implement the Supreme Court's orders to conduct voting on the no-trust motion. By that time, activity was seen at the apex court's premises and official cars were seen entering and going out. Before announcing his resignation, Qaiser said that he had received *important documents from the cabinet*, which he invited the leader of the opposition and the chief justice of Pakistan to see. He said:

> "In line with our laws and the need to stand for our country, I have decided that I can't remain on the position of speaker and thereby resign. Because this is a national duty and it is the Supreme Court's decision, I will ask the panel chairman Ayaz Sadiq to run the session."

After Sadiq took the chair, he paid tribute to Qaiser for remaining with his party and opting for an honourable exit. Further: **'He [Qaiser] had a very good relationship with all of us, a working relationship. He tried to conduct all these proceedings with dignity and together with the opposition.'** Then, Sadiq asked for bells to be rung in the house for five minutes to notify members that the voting process was about to begin, after which the doors of the assembly were closed. Voting on the resolution then began at 11:58pm, and members in favour of the resolution were asked to exit the gate. Sadiq then adjourned the session for four minutes since according to rules, a sitting of the same session couldn't continue through past midnight hours.

The session then resumed at 12:02am, with recitation of the Holy Quran and na'at. Following that, the voting process continued, with lawmakers confirming their votes by writing their names in a register placed near one of the assembly doors. Bells were then rung for another two minutes to signal that voting had ended and members returned to their seats. All government members except Ali Muhammad Khan had walked out of the house and boycotted the session after Qaiser announced his resignation as speaker.

As the lone voice in the house supporting Imran Khan, Ali Muhammad Khan delivered a fiery speech, reminding the former opposition of his leader's achievements, claiming that:

> "Imran Khan sacrificed his government but did not accept slavery. God willing, Imran Khan will be back ... he will be back with a two-thirds majority.
>
> Imran Khan talked about a Muslim bloc, that's his sin. Imran Khan talked about an independent foreign policy, that's his sin ... Russia [visit] is just an excuse, the real target has always been Imran Khan."

Earlier, the session called to decide the fate of Prime Minister Imran Khan through a no-confidence motion, was adjourned multiple times before voting on the resolution could take place. The last adjournment was the fourth of the day as the opposition's clamour for immediate voting throughout the day but had fallen on deaf ears amid lengthy speeches delivered from treasury members on the floor of the house. NA Speaker Asad Qaiser was chairing the session when it began at 10:30am sharp in the morning of 9th April, as per the Supreme Court's directives, and with the recitation of the Holy Quran. It was followed by the national anthem and prayers for the recently deceased mother of MNA Shazia Sobia.

Voting on the no-confidence motion against the prime minister was the fourth item on that day's agenda. PMLN MNA Rana Sanaullah, while talking to reporters, claimed that it had been agreed with the speaker to conduct the vote tonight after Iftar. However, when the opposition enquired about it after Iftar, it was told that the prime minister had not agreed to it.

While the opposition came out in full force for the session this morning, very few members of the treasury benches were in attendance before the session was adjourned for the first time. PM Khan was also not present. A meeting was held between the treasury and opposition benches in the speaker's chamber after the session was adjourned for the first time in the day, where the latter called for holding proceedings according to the Supreme Court's directives. Foreign Minister Shah Mahmood Qureshi and PTI leader Amir Dogar participated from the government's side while Bilawal Zardari, Rana Sanaullah, Ayaz Sadiq, Naveed Qamar and Maulana Asad Mahmood represented the opposition.

Following this, a meeting of the opposition's parliamentary group was called at the opposition leader's chamber. PMLN's Kh Saad Rafique, speaking in the NA after the adjournment, said that the speaker had promised that voting would be held after Iftar. Separately, the government sent a review petition to the apex court against its decision to set aside the deputy speaker's 3rd April 2022 ruling. The petition, however, was yet to be filed since the officers of the court did not process it on receipt. The question also cropped up that instead of placing the said threat letter before lawmakers in parliament, why did PTI use the letter to break the law and dismissed the no-confidence motion? Some claimed that PM Imran was fighting for himself and not the nation; also, that the government was lying about the National Security Council (NSC) meeting's minutes on record.

Meanwhile, amid the crucial NA proceedings, the PTI submitted references against its 20 dissident members to the NA speaker; the references were sent by PM Khan. The references were filed under Article 63-A of the Constitution, which suggests disqualification on grounds of defection for not obeying the parliamentary party's directions in the election of the prime minister, chief minister or vote of confidence or no confidence or money bill etc.

The text of the references said that the dissidents were exposed via *large-scale broadcast and videos* to have left the PTI, joined the opposition for the no-trust motion against the prime minister and no denials or rebuttals were issued to the apparent acts of defection. The references stated that show-cause notices were sent to the dissidents to clarify why declarations to de-seat them from the NA should not be issued against them but the individuals failed to respond to them or clarify their position.

The text said that the members had failed to adhere to their *sacred duty* and had deceived the confidence of the party, the voters and the public by changing their loyalties to another party and caused *irreparable loss to the democratic system ... and blatantly injured the cause and object of the PTI.*

PINCHING & CONCLUSIVE ANALYSIS:

It was a calm night of 10th April 2022; delighted for some and cruel for some others. Moments came when it seemed as if all the pillars of the state were waiting for a catastrophic collision. Calamity seemed ready to strike at the highest levels of the state. Even with his ouster a near certainty, Mr Khan seemed more than willing to turn a simple parliamentary procedure into a farce by forcing the heads of the judiciary and military, along with the entire legislature, to play along to the 'last ball' of his tiresome innings.

> *"Imran Khan was forced to finally let go just as the clock was about to run out on the day, allowing the opposition to finally have its say. And thus, in the early hours of Constitution Day, the PTI government fell not with a bang, but a whimper in the dead of the night"*; an **editorial** of a leading newspaper dated 10th April 2022 is referred.

When it emerged as the single largest party in the 2018 elections, the PTI had promised to be a breath of fresh air. Though political engineering and a faulty results transmission system had tarnished the legitimacy of its victory, the country had been generally willing to give it a chance.

However, the party almost immediately found itself falling short of its lofty ideals.

Due to its failure to secure a simple majority, it shook hands with non-democratic forces to make a claim on the federal government. If the party's leaders had believed that the compromise could be compensated by their achievements in office, they were soon to be let down by their inexperience. Within a year, the prime minister was scrambling to reshuffle his cabinet.

More unfortunate was that instead of introspecting and compensating for its shortcomings, the PTI chose to go after the opposition instead. The strategy put off many who were expecting it to deliver real change. Meanwhile, it became increasingly reliant on the '*establishment for guidance*' in key decision-making areas. This ultimately proved fatal for it when the establishment decided they would no longer be providing any props for the PTI government to stand on.

Though inexperience ultimately became its undoing, the PTI did also record some **commendable achievements**. *Successful handling of the Covid pandemic, the multifaceted Ehsaas programme and a new public health insurance scheme made a positive difference in most citizens' lives.* Many would remember the former prime minister for it. Therefore, even if Mr Khan's time in government was up, it would be unwise to write him off. Imran Khan had always been a ferocious challenger when in the opposition; a fighter who doggedly pursued his goals. His unrelenting zeal and sense of divine mission made him a formidable force in Pakistan's politics. It is important for a true leader to unite the nation, not poison it with divisive narratives and corrosive politics – and Khan knew it well.

A day earlier, on 9th April 2022 – **Fahd Husain** wrote:
It didn't need to end like this…..

The momentous events of that week culminating in the Supreme Court judgement setting aside the constitutional violations by the ruling party's deputy speaker of the National Assembly constituted a defining moment in Pakistan's political and legal history. After nearly being pushed off the rails, the country was back on the constitutional track with greater strength and confidence. Fahd Husain bluntly wrote:

> "But recent weeks have left scars that will not heal easily. The new government is expected to chart a less confrontational course, and

> *it is also expected to build a better working relationship between all institutions, but the toxins of hate and loathing continue to hover in the air we breathe.*
>
> *How does a political party — rooted as it is in the constitutional framework itself — reach such a stage of dysfunctional decision-making? How does it spawn a culture that enables it to override — or at least attempt to — the very foundation of the state?* ***The PTI has been defeated by its own follies and blunders.*** *If it intends to reform and redeem itself in the coming months and years, it will need to first acknowledge the mistakes he has made."*

PTI as a party would therefore stumble and fall; would take a beating, get kicked around and whipped by the contradictions of its own self-righteousness. Hubris invites scorn; but scorn, however, was not the answer to the PTI problem. It allowed its critics the pleasure of venting, and it also enabled the new government to give as good as it got to its arch-rival. There was a vacuum created as PTI receded from people's expectations. There was something fundamentally non-linear about the rise and fall of the party.

Just look at the wide spectrum the IK-cult unleashed: hope, optimism, belief, joy, confidence, expectations, aspirations, anger, vitriol, hate, loathing, disgust, enmity — all laced with a healthy dose of blind support and a denial of reality. How could one leverage and channelise those contradictory and conflicting emotions? The flock that gathered around Imran Khan in the early days was made up of dreamers who genuinely believed they could one day be in a position to make that change – but all pack of failures.

From famous 30th October 2011's *jalsa at Minar-e-Pakistan* onwards, PTI got transformed into one force that thundered its way to victory in 2018, powered as it was by both by the public and establishment. In 2018, it was in power, however, the two elements began to drift apart. The party fumbled and stumbled with the task of governance; the party went too weak to handle the force of the establishment raging inside. Absolute incompetence, unfiltered arrogance and undeserved appointments, all these kept weakening the party even as Prime Minister Imran Khan — the supposed manifestation of the party — blundered his way through the delicate art of governance.

The blatant violation of the Constitution, wild quasi-profane rants, the reckless conspiracy theorising at the expense of national interests and the shocking lack of grace and sportsman's spirit in acknowledging a defeat – all jointly created another set of disappointments for the party itself and its voters.

It didn't need to end like this…. *but was a re-beginning of REFORMED & OPEN HEARTED IMRAN KHAN ahead.*

INAM R SEHRI's other BOOKS (in English)

Judges & Generals in Pakistan VOL-I
[in English] (2012)

Judges & Generals in Pakistan VOL-II
[in English] (2012)

Judges & Generals in Pakistan VOL-III
[in English] (2013)

Judges & Generals in Pakistan VOL-IV
[in English] (2013)

The Living History of Pakistan Vol-I
[in English] (2015)

The Living History of Pakistan Vol-II
[in English] (2016)

The Living History of Pakistan Vol-III
[in English] (2017)

The Living History of Pakistan Vol-IV
[in English] (2017)

The Living History of Pakistan Vol-V
[in English] (2017)

The Living History of Pakistan Vol-VI
[in English] (2018)

The Living History of Pakistan Vol-VII
[in English] (2018)

History of A Disgraceful Surrender [2021]
[in English] (2022)

Grosvenor House
Publishing Limited

Grosvenor House Publishing Ltd
LINK HOUSE, 140 THE BROADWAY, TOLWORTH
SURREY UK   KT6 7HT

www.ingramcontent.com/pod-product-compliance
Lightning Source LLC
Chambersburg PA
CBHW020728160426
43192CB00006B/150